DINO DE LAURENTIIS

DINO

The Life and Films of Dino De Laurentiis

BY

TULLIO KEZICH AND
ALESSANDRA LEVANTESI

Translated from the Italian by
James Marcus

miramax books
HYPERION
NEW YORK

Printed in the United States of America. For information address Hyperion, 77 West 66th Street, New York, NY 10023-6298

ISBN 0-7868-6902-X

First Edition
10 9 8 7 6 5 4 3 2 1

FOREWORD

I'M CONVINCED THAT LIFE MUST BE FACED WITH IRONY. WITHOUT FEAR. I've always thrown myself into everything that I do. I haven't always succeeded. Sometimes you feel as if you're leaving the stadium after your team has lost. But other times, when you least expect it, you feel as if you've won the World Cup. And playing the game—well, it's the great challenge of life. A biography of me? What will we be telling these people? I thought about it a little and said to myself, sure, we'll tell them everything. We'll also give them a few laughs, whenever appropriate. That's how we'll deal with the biography. It will be like life, which is never entirely a bed of roses but which remains the most incredible gift we have received from God. Our primary duty—and the only way we can possibly deserve this gift—is to live it to the very fullest.

—Dino De Laurentiis

PREFACE

UNDER THE SIGN OF THE LION

OSCAR NIGHT, MARCH 25, 2001. THE NEXT AWARD TO BE PRESENTED IS a major one, and a rapid montage of movie clips fills the screen of the Shrine Auditorium. The scenes are taken from two dozen major films spanning a wide range of eras and genres: literary and historical epics (*War and Peace*, *The Bible*, *Waterloo*, *Ragtime*), lavish spectaculars (*King Kong*, *Conan the Barbarian*), groundbreaking artistic work (*Europa '51*, *La Strada*, *Nights of Cabiria*, *The Serpent's Egg*), recent successes (*Breakdown*, *U-571*). The montage ends with scenes from a worldwide box-office smash, released only a few months before. The brilliant psychopath Hannibal Lecter fills the screen, then the star of *Hannibal*, Sir Anthony Hopkins himself, appears. He strides onstage, cradling in his hands the Irving Thalberg Memorial Award, one of the most prestigious honors in film.

Instituted in 1937 in memory of MGM's "boy genius," who'd died the previous year, the Thalberg honors "the most consistent high level of production achievement by an individual producer." From an aesthetic point of view, the actual award—a small bronze bust of Thalberg—is somewhat dubious; upon its debut, *Time* magazine noted the statuette's "effeminate look." Even so, the Thalberg Award is highly coveted, and for good reason. Irving Thalberg remains the very model of a creative producer, with one eye on the balance sheet and the other on artistic quality—exactly as portrayed in F. Scott Fitzgerald's unfinished novel *The Last Tycoon*. Unlike the Oscars, the Thalberg is awarded by the Board of Governors rather than by the 5,722 members of the Academy of Motion Picture Arts and Sciences. And the judging is sufficiently rigorous that, twenty-eight times in the last seventy-three years, the board has declined to award the prize at all.

Hopkins addresses some brief remarks to the audience: "The career of the legendary Irving Thalberg lasted from 1918 to 1936: eighteen years. The career of the living legend we honor tonight has lasted, up to the present moment, sixty years. His name is Dino De Laurentiis. Among the most important of independent producers, he is a dynamic and creative font of film. His passion for the entire moviemaking process has made him one of the most enchanting and enchanted producers of all time."

The octogenarian prizewinner, who has come onstage and embraced his friend, is given a standing ovation. He is the first Italian, and one of the very few non-Americans, to receive the Thalberg. The honor roll begins with Darryl Zanuck and includes such illustrious names as David O. Selznick, Walt Disney, Samuel Goldwyn, Cecil B. DeMille, Jack Warner, Stanley Kramer, William Wyler, Alfred Hitchcock, Ingmar Bergman, Steven Spielberg, Billy Wilder, George Lucas, Clint Eastwood, and Warren Beatty. Clearly De Laurentiis has been admitted to the Hollywood pantheon. And at this point, if we were watching a film, the ceremony marking Dino's triumph would dissolve into a flashback, recounting the extraordinary life that led to this moment.

Born under the sign of the lion immediately after World War I, our hero is the son of a pasta manufacturer from Torre Annunziata, not far from Naples. In 1937 this lazy student, talented salesman, and apprentice actor was drawn to Rome's new film school, Centro Sperimentale di Cinematografia. He watched the action *behind* the cameras, and as clever as he was aimless, he noticed this paradoxical fact: in the cinema, one way to shine is to opt for the shadows, beyond the luminous circle of the spotlight. He began creating opportunities out of thin air, cultivating greater and greater ambitions, making one film after another, until one day he discovered that he had become a legendary figure.

Now he's considered not only a diabolical deal-maker but something more: an artist of a particular type, a card-carrying creator. For more than fifty years, "Dino"—just the one (invented) name—has been enough to evoke art films and B-movies; studios created from nothing and occasionally ending up as nothing; investors, writers, and directors joined like beams, bricks, and mortar to build the very edifice of success; triumphs and pratfalls and endless resurrections. The director of *Local Hero*, Bill Forsythe, recalled that as a boy he used to joke with his friends, "De Laurentiis is on the phone, and he's calling *us*." Even to these Scottish slackers, Dino's name was one worth dropping. At a certain point in that half-century career, De Laurentiis became The Producer: the title and the name were synonymous. There are thousands of producers; fewer, but still quite a few, first-rate producers. But only a very few producers have inspired a myth.

The myth does benefit from the occasional bit of exaggeration. For example, Dino is credited with some six hundred films, a figure that is true only if one includes the titles he simply acquired or distributed. But even the shorter list of films he truly produced is astonishingly eclectic. At roughly the same time, he produced two works by Fellini—*La Strada* and *Nights of Cabiria*—and the historical epic *War and Peace*. This was his characteristic pattern: putting a big-ticket spectacle into production at the same time as an art film. How could one man succeed in such different genres? That question leads to another: Who is the author of a film?

The French auteur theory is now dominant, and most critics and film historians alike consider the director the true creator of a movie. But what about the producer, who can influence the conception, the realization, and the ultimate structure of a film? Dino has often said that he has encountered only a handful of directors whose vision and creative control truly compare to those shown by the author of a great book: Rossellini, Fellini, De Sica, Bergman, Altman, Pollack, Forman, Lynch, and Ridley Scott. The others, he says, are intermittently excellent craftsmen who must be monitored, guided, and often challenged.

A film, after all, can be created in two different ways. Either it's invented frame by frame, sequence by sequence, which is how the masters do it, or it's stitched together following the script's pattern, which is how most directors do it. This second group needs a producer to participate in the creative process, and even the masters may benefit from somebody peering over their shoulders and prodding them to do their best work. This is no small claim on Dino's part. For De Laurentiis, control over the final cut marks the line between professional filmmakers and dilettantes. Over the course of his long career, Dino has worked with many of both, and though his age entitles him to become a producer emeritus, he intends to work with many more.

Our conversations for the preparation of this book began in January 1999 at Cinecittà, in his office at Theater 5, where he was overseeing the progress of the submarine battle movie *U-571*. Immediately, we were caught up in his hyperactive frenzy, taking in the spectacle of Dino simultaneously answering incessant telephone calls, consulting with his treasured assistant, Elvira, shuffling cards, examining scripts, issuing orders, exchanging sly signals with his wife, Martha, as she busies herself with his production commitments, and incessantly jotting down appointments and projects on tiny slips of yellow paper stuck in a mosaic on his desk. Then he'd make a dinner reservation, hug his toddlers, who'd been brought by to say hello, ask if we wanted coffee or needed to use the bathroom, and call his daughters in America to see how they were doing—again, all in a nonstop blur.

Over the course of two years, our conversations with Dino took place in a villa on Via Appia, at the Palace Hotel, on the island of Capri, and again in Rome, several times in a suite at the Hotel d'Inghilterra. Naturally we met at several shrines to moviemaking: Cannes, the Venice Film Festival, and the Berlin FilmFest. There were also many telephone calls between Rome and Los Angeles to exchange information, verify facts, or simply to maintain the friendship. Dino responded to our questions graciously and willingly; his openness faltered on only two topics: the tragic death of his son, Federico, killed in an airplane crash, and the reasons why his marriage to Silvana Mangano was much less happy than it seemed in the press.

Dino seems free of animosity, describing almost everyone as "friendly" or even "very friendly." This attitude reminded us of the promenade that concluded *8½*. But if you're patient and continue the conversation, something emerges from behind the smoke screen of serenity: a glint in his eye, a significant pause, a pointed adjective. After so many automatic absolutions, he's still capable of overruling himself and issuing a condemnation on appeal.

From the beginning, the three of us agreed that we had no interest in creating a cinematic history; instead, we wanted to reconstruct the romance of a particular life. However, within the limits of possibility, we have carefully checked Dino's references to names, titles, and dates in available documents, newspapers, and books. And when his version of the facts diverges from other testimony, we've attempted to compare the stories, despite the impossibility of establishing the exact truth of things. Ultimately, some uncertainty is inevitable.

There are events, even recent ones, that are recounted in four or five different versions, and it's impossible to supply a definite answer to certain questions. (Who, for example, discovered Silvana Mangano, the star of *Bitter Rice*?) At this point, we can only note the various versions of events, one after another, as testimony to the elusive nature of human existence. This very bewilderment, in fact, is what gives birth to myth and legend, the fictions that are often "truer," more emotionally significant, than the official story. As much as any other figure, Dino De Laurentiis justifies the classic motto attributed by the director John Ford to a Wild West journalist: "When you're torn between reality and fantasy, *print the legend!*"

CHAPTER 1

BORN LUCKY

THE YEAR 1919 WAS A FATEFUL ONE IN ITALIAN HISTORY. THE NATION WAS in mourning: the First World War, which killed six hundred thousand Italians, had ended only months before, in November 1918, and already a new and turbulent chapter was beginning. On March 19, the future dictator Benito Mussolini founded the *fasci di combattimento,* the units of the Fascist organization, in Milan. But the tragic consequences of that event were years in the future, and the times were relatively tranquil when, on August 8, at five in the morning, the protagonist of our story first saw the light. In a traditional family like the De Laurentiis clan of Torre Annunziata, names are transmitted from one generation to the next, and so the newborn received the name of his maternal grandfather, Agostino.

At the time, Torre Annunziata boasted fewer than forty thousand inhabitants. Located about seventeen miles from Naples, the town was famous for pasta, with nearly a hundred businesses connected to making or selling it. In *Francesca and Nunziata* (1995), the novelist Maria Orsini Natale offers a vivid picture of Torre Annunziata in 1919:

> A carriage passed through the busy, rustic animation of the street, grazing the procession of wagons pulled up in front of the *pastifici*. Lined up one after another, these establishments had little resemblance to factories. . . . With their main doors thrown open, however, they were clearly not ordinary dwellings: inside you saw vast corridors crammed with sacks, and the pasta itself, with bits of it dancing around on the floor. . . . In the open gaps between the buildings, and along the steep terrazzo staircases climbing up from

> the port, the sea made intermittent appearances. It was so limpid, its blue color so thoroughly saturated, that each glimpse had the effect of an electric shock. Capri seemed close enough to touch. To the north, on the flank of Mount Vesuvius, only a handful of *palazzi* had been built, so there was an unobstructed view of the volcano against the sky, with white patches of snow and an erect, pearly puff of smoke.

Into this picturesque landscape came Agostino, surrounded by pasta factories, with the sea in front of him and Vesuvius at his back.

Agostino's father, Rosario Aurelio De Laurentiis, was a lawyer's son from Torella dei Lombardi, a village in the Avellino province, in the same region as Naples and Torre Annunziata. There were seven children in the family, and Aurelio's three brothers attained positions of some prestige: two were priests, the third a criminal lawyer in Rome. Aurelio too was slated for the priesthood, but he fled the seminary. He became a civil servant, posted to Torre Annunziata, where he kept a tolerant eye on the poachers, men he knew were trying to keep their families fed. Perhaps he could benefit too. ("Do whatever you want," went his classic formulation, "and drop off the fish at my house.")

One of Annunziata's residents was Aurelio's future wife, Giuseppina Salvatore. A born businesswoman, she ran the wholesale flour, bran, and grain warehouse that her father had left her mother. After marrying Giuseppina, and gaining a foothold in the pasta business in a town devoted to pasta, Aurelio decided to open a factory. However, he couldn't afford the capital investment, so he sold pasta from a third party, packaged and labeled with the De Laurentiis name. He began distributing the product throughout the entire province of Naples, including the islands: Ischia, Capri, Procida. Once the former *brigadiere* had scraped together enough money for a factory of his own, he opened Pastificio Moderno.

Giuseppina soon became the animating spirit of the establishment, despite the demands of a brood of seven children, all of them born at home at Via Mazzini 27. First there was Celeste (1915), then Luigi (1917), then Agostino (1919), followed by Rosa (1922), Alfredo (1924), Raffaella (1928), and Anna (1932).

Agostino was "born with the shirt"—that is, wrapped in the placenta—which local folklore considered an omen of prosperity. The labor was quick and uncomplicated, and the baby was as healthy as an ox.

There was, however, one thing about the young Agostino that worried his family: he wouldn't speak. He cried, laughed, and screeched but declined to utter a single syllable. This concerned everyone but Giuseppina, who urged her husband to be calm: "Look at it this way: when he begins to talk, nobody will be able to make him stop." In fact, at the age of five, Agostino finally said the word *mamma*, followed by a torrent of speech. Here was the rich vocabulary he had stockpiled during his years of disquieting silence. Even as a grown man, he would recall how his weeping mother took him in her arms, carried him to his father, and said, "Do you hear him speaking?"

Why the long silence? Perhaps it was the fact that, in typical Neapolitan fashion, everybody at home spoke much more than was necessary. Surrounded by other people's words, Agostino may have preferred to keep his thoughts to himself, to observe, ponder, and dream. "Ever since I was a little boy, I got into the habit of concentrating on my dreams. I've always dreamed, and the dreams in my life have been extremely important—especially once I discovered that they could come true. Yes, a dream can become reality: all it takes to make it concrete is will, imagination, and at least a minimal spirit of sacrifice."

When it came to sheer will, Agostino had a fine example right under his nose: his mother, the center of the De Laurentiis family universe. Combining force with sweetness, always knowing exactly what she wanted before she took a single step, Giuseppina controlled every situation. Her influence over her children was enormous. When they had problems, they ran straight to her, and they would continue to do so even as adults—Dino included. She is described in the fine memoir by Enzo De Bernart as "one of those marvelous Italian mothers who magnificently raise seven children in the midst of hardship, joy, sorrow, and lamentation of every kind, and who give the impression of having done so as a lark, a game (albeit a completely natural one)."

As for Aurelio, he was certainly a great provider. True, he liked to linger at the *caffè* with his friends, and true, there were a number of minor dalliances with other women. Giuseppina tolerated these amorous adventures in the context of his basic fidelity—as long as the adventures were kept out of her sight.

To be quite honest, my father was an uncontrollable womanizer, and I have a few stories to recount on that subject. For example, one day in Rome (and he was already getting pretty old) he visited an ice cream store on the Corso with a young woman. At a certain moment, purely by chance, my mother and one of my sisters strolled in. As soon as he saw them, he hid behind a newspaper and pretended to read, but the paper was upside down. My mother noticed and swooped down on him, ripping the paper out of his hands. You can imagine the rest.

The boy who didn't speak until he was five became something of a live wire, with his father's exuberance and his mother's will and intelligence, though he devoted little effort to his studies. Giuseppina often spoiled him, egged on by *her* mother, Raffaella, who lived with the family. So when Dino finished grade school, his father decided to send the little rebel to a boarding school not far from Torre Annunziata run by the Salesian religious order. The young boy never adjusted to the discipline of the place.

Every morning you wake at dawn, make the sign of the cross, and pray. Then you clean yourself up and have breakfast, preceded by the sign of the cross and a prayer. After breakfast everybody goes to mass; after mass there's a half hour of recreation; then you go to class, commencing the lesson with the sign of the cross and a prayer. I had gotten a religious education at home, without a grain of bigotry to it. But at the Collegio they made you hate prayers: enough is enough!

After a little while I couldn't take it anymore, and I bombarded my mother and father with desperate appeals: "I can't handle it here, I don't want to continue." Then one day, taking advantage of the recreation period, I slipped through the open gate in the garden and escaped on foot toward home, where I arrived a couple of hours later, breathless. At the sight of me my mother began to weep, fearing my father's reaction. But the consequences of the incident were less grave than she had foreseen. Papa let me talk, somehow understood me, and decided to transfer me to the Convitto Nazionale Vittorio Emanuele in Naples. It was still a religious school, with Sunday mass and catechism, but that was as far as it went. The rest of the time it was, thank God, a normal school.

He remained at the Convitto for two years. In part, his persistence was due to Corrado Del Vecchio, a cousin of his father. A pilot who'd lost both legs during the First World War, Del Vecchio taught mathematics at a Naples high school. Agostino spent every weekend with Uncle Corrado, who told enthralling stories that swept from one subject to another, embracing the entire range of knowledge.

These conversations left their stamp on Agostino's evolving personality, encouraging the boy's curiosity. Still, he hated the rigidity of the classroom. He resisted it as long as he could, then escaped a second time. He ran to the Del Vecchio household and begged for help. Uncle Corrado telephoned his cousin Aurelio. "Come retrieve your son," he told his cousin, "and find a different solution for him." Agostino knew exactly what to ask his father. "Enroll me in the Istituto Commercial," he proposed. "Get me a train pass, and I'll go to school in Naples each morning and return home in the afternoon."

Aurelio, no doubt recalling his own flight from the seminary, agreed to his son's proposal. The arrangement worked for almost a year. True, Agostino didn't become any more devoted to his studies. On the other hand, he spent every afternoon at the pasta factory, where he pitched in and had a great time. Eventually he had a new proposition for his father: "Instead of sending me to school, why don't you let me work with you?"

Aurelio accepted the fact that his son, like him, would never earn a diploma—that mark of achievement so treasured by middle-class Italians of the South. He agreed. The boy quit school at once.

By now Pastificio Moderno was a thriving business, employing about one hundred workers and manufacturing 220,000 pounds of pasta each day. Aurelio had created a network of salesmen, each assigned to a particular territory—Naples and the provinces, Rome and Lazio, Calabria, Sicily, and so forth. Soon after Agostino joined the company full-time, Aurelio had an argument with one of his representatives and decided to put his son to the test. He showed him the special features and secrets of the *campionario*, a sample case of different types of pasta: ziti, spaghetti, linguine, bucatini, macaroni, cannolicchi. Aurelio also carried cheaper pasta made without semolina, and even sold the *munuzzaglia*, the bits and pieces left from making various types of pasta.

Agostino left for his territory in the islands, proud of his new job.

Besides selling his father's products, he also was responsible for collecting late payments from the customers—a task that worried the fifteen-year-old. On the boat to Capri, he developed a strategy. Since he wore glasses for myopia, he decided that he'd use the borrowed authority they provided and pretend that he was at least a year or two older. In short, he invented a character. This was his first audition, and he easily got the part.

As he called on one customer after another, the new salesman's excellent manners made a good impression. Mentioning that he happened to be the owner's son helped too. Agostino's greatest asset—which he'd use to straighten out a million different messes, for decades to come—was his overwhelming skill as a communicator. He knew exactly how to charm, how to dazzle, and he managed to sell much more pasta than anyone had expected. After a couple of months, the gratified Aurelio recognized that his son was a born salesman. He enlarged Agostino's territory and bought him a second-class commuter ticket on the Rome–Reggio Calabria line. Agostino hit the road nonstop.

At home there was little talk of politics, although the De Laurentiis children sensed among the adults a fairly lukewarm enthusiasm for the Fascist regime. Agostino managed to avoid Mussolini's youth organizations—not from any conscious spirit of opposition but from a combination of indifference and absence. As he crisscrossed the miserable terrain of southern Italy, however, the apolitical adolescent saw the disparity between the triumphalist bluster in the newspapers and the tragic reality of the country.

In a Reggio Calabria hotel, he watched through the keyhole as an old prostitute taught the erotic tricks of the trade to a young peasant girl—a moment Agostino recognized as a single scene in a panorama of appalling moral misery. Living conditions were often primitive. One night in Crotone, seized by an attack of dysentery, Agostino was forced to thrust his buttocks out the window; the pensione had no plumbing. Southern Italy seemed to be an undeveloped country, repressed and depressed, or perhaps forgotten. No wonder the retailers ordered the shoddiest grade of pasta: their customers had little but the shirts on their backs. Yet what saddened the young salesman the most was the passivity of the people. Nobody protested; everybody submitted to misery and indignity as if there were no future, no prospect of change. For a young boy who had decided for himself when to quit school, when and where to go to work—indeed, when to utter his first words—this attitude was difficult to understand.

Of course, Agostino realized that he was lucky. He kept one percent of his sales and collections revenue, which was a tenth of the other salesmen's commissions. Still, it was enough to pay for his first innocent luxuries, such as the stylish clothing he loved. He devoted himself to horseback riding: he particularly relished the way the girls paid attention as he and his mount traversed the streets of Torre Annunziata ("like a knight from the olden days," his sisters recall). He also enjoyed fishing and the sea, passions he'd savor for the rest of his life. And for the moment, anyway, his family was on solid economic ground.

"My father bought a brand-new automobile, and the moment I saw it, I immediately wanted to try driving. All I could manage was a short trip, though: at the first curve I failed to turn the wheel and smashed into a wall, wrecking the vehicle." Despite this mishap, Agostino continued to drive his father's car without a license, often tackling the trip from Torre Annunziata to Naples.

Dashing off to Naples to go dancing in fashionable nightspots, he noticed attractive women—a great many women—and thus began another of his passions. "He would hardly finish with one before beginning with another," his sister Rosa remembers. The customs of the era kept things on a fairly innocent level: for actual sex, a young man had to avail himself of the so-called *pezzentelle*, impoverished prostitutes who brought clients back to their homes.

Everything was going well for Agostino—very well, in fact. Yet the restless adolescent wasn't satisfied. He sensed that there must be something more to life, something better; he didn't know exactly what he was looking for, but he was absolutely determined to find it.

The answer arrived by chance. One day while at the train station, he spotted a poster promoting a film school—something he hadn't known existed. Rome's Centro Sperimentale had opened its doors in October 1935, using a temporary space in a basement at Via Foligno 40. Presided over by noted film theorist Luigi Chiarini, the new school offered courses for actors, directors, cameramen, and film technicians of all kinds.

Suddenly Agostino knew what he wanted to do. In September 1936 he sent off a request for information on beginning "an artistic career in filmmaking." There was no response, so he repeated his query the next year.

> If you lived in a provincial town like Torre Annunziata, where there was nothing to do in the evening but go to the movies with your friends, the cinema was a world of fantasy. I had always been in love with it. I was always collecting photos of the stars, especially the American ones, but also Italians like Vittorio De Sica and Assia Noris, cutting them out of magazines and pasting them in notebooks. For me, the actors *were* the cinema. I didn't have the faintest idea of how a film was made, of what went on behind the cameras. Still, to work in the cinema was one of my dreams.

On this second attempt, Agostino made a shrewd move: he enclosed a series of portraits taken by a fashionable Roman photographer. The reply, dated September 8, 1937, soon arrived: "In regard to your query, please be advised that your first test, based on the photographs you mailed, has been successfully passed. At your convenience you are invited to present yourself in Rome (at your own expense) to take an additional and definitive test in person."

> When I got that summons, I was shaking from head to foot. But I said nothing to my family. Instead I invented a story for my father: I claimed that I needed to make a quick trip to the capital in order to visit a customer interested in an enormous quantity of pasta. Then I left.
>
> I presented myself on Via Foligno, where Chiarini—still young, but already with that perfectly shaved cranium of his—welcomed me in person. He gave me the third degree, surrounded by a committee of teachers I would come to know well. There was the critic Umberto Barbaro, the veteran actress Teresa Franchini, and several others. Each of them asked me a few questions: where do you come from, what have you studied, and so on.
>
> Then the director cut to the chase: "Do you realize that an actor must have the capacity for fantasy? Let's check it out: take the chair and bring it to the center of the room. Now imagine that it's a small boat, imagine that you're in the middle of the Gulf of Naples. In front of you there's a beautiful girl. Think of a real girl, there must be one you like, no? The moon is shining up in the sky. Use your imagination and let me see how you would behave in such a situation. *Imagine* what you would say to the young girl in

the boat, because if I give you a few lines to recite, you'll end up floundering. Stay calm, and say whatever comes to mind." I was certainly never silent with the girls, so I narrowed my eyes and began to concoct the usual whoppers: "What a marvelous moon, see how the stars are shining, may I kiss you?" Junk like that. After a little bit I noticed that Chiarini was exchanging amused glances with the other examiners. Then he interrupted me and said, "Enough, you can go; we'll let you know."

I waited and hoped, and after a few weeks some incredible news reached Torre Annunizata: I'd been admitted to the first-year acting course. I leaped into the air with joy and immediately ran off to tell my mother. And she said in alarm, "Who will tell your father?" That evening we were all together at the table—parents, maternal grandmother, brothers, and sisters. They had already heard the news from my mother, who told them to keep their mouths shut.

"Papa, I need to tell you something."

"What do you want, Agostino?" he said, attacking his plate of spaghetti.

I told him the story from the beginning: the poster, the exam, the admission. I concluded by saying that I would like to begin the acting course next week, if he would give me permission.

Silence followed. We all looked at our plates. My father finished his spaghetti without answering, then put down his fork and looked at me: "I've always known that I had a slightly crazy son, but until now . . . Still, when I'm dead, I don't want any of you children to scold me for having denied your deepest ambitions. You want to be an actor? It seems like a waste of time to me, but if you insist, I'll make a deal with you. I'll support you in Rome for a year, during which you'll receive an allowance sufficient to pay for a furnished room and your meals. If nothing has worked out after a year, I won't send you a single *soldo* more, and you come back to your job at the pasta factory." I accepted, embraced him, and got ready to go.

His departure wasn't painless. Agostino had an affectionate circle of friends and sweethearts; there was one girl in particular, who lived across the street, who'd signal him to come upstairs the moment she was alone in the house. He had a supportive, doting family. Yet his desire to escape the sadness of the provinces was urgent, and his career as a spaghetti salesman promised little but years of the same routine, along with perpetual dependence on his father. In the end, then, friends, lovers, and even family took second place.

CHAPTER 2

AT CINEMA SCHOOL

IN ROME AGOSTINO ESTABLISHED HIMSELF IN AN EXCELLENT FURNISHED room at Via Sanremo 1, in the San Giovanni quarter, right near the school. (Silvana Mangano lived just four steps away, but they wouldn't meet for a decade.) Money from home paid for his lodgings, two meals a day, and cigarettes. He was hardly rolling in cash, yet he did sometimes share his supper with a classmate he liked: the skittish and taciturn Pietro Germi. The future director of *Divorce Italian Style* had arrived from Genoa with an abundance of grit and a marked lack of cash. A friendship developed between the two young men. Agostino did his best to soothe the anxieties of his friend, who was always in love and always unhappy. When Pietro was abandoned for the hundredth time, by a girl who decamped for Naples without leaving a forwarding address, Agostino sent an appeal to his friends down south. Though they managed to locate her, Germi never won the fugitive's heart.

At the Centro the acting classes were run by Pietro Sharoff. Between brilliant lectures on Diderot and Stanislavsky, this Russo-Italian hybrid urged his pupils to concentrate before uttering a single line. Also on the faculty were Alessandro Blasetti, a genial and generous director, and Francesco Pasinetti, a Venetian gentleman on the verge of publishing his pioneering history of the cinema. There was the impetuous and highly cultivated Umberto Barbaro, who was always against something, beginning with the government, and who had secretly enrolled in the Communist Party. (Chiarini, who protected him, pretended not to know.) But some of Agostino's liveliest encounters were with the venerable Teresa Franchini. After a life on the stage, the fifty-six-year-old actress maintained a cult of diction, refusing to allow the slightest hint of vernacular inflection. "Signora," implored her unlucky pupil, "I'm Neapolitan! If you force me to speak perfect Italian, with those open and closed vowels, my spontaneity goes out the window." Her response: "Do it your way, then, but you'll always be a dialect actor."

A few of Agostino's papers are preserved in the Centro's archive, including some of the film reviews that Pasinetti asked his pupils to write. Regarding E. A. Dupont's *Varieté*, the young student emphasized the strength of the camera work and montage, and he praised Louis Jouvert's acting in Julien Duvivier's *Carnet di ballo*. While the essays betray a certain lack of cultural polish, it's clear that Agostino was passionate about the school: he liked the curriculum, admired his professors, and had harmonious relations with his classmates.

There was almost no discussion of politics. Nor were political matters imposed on the curriculum, not even by the ultra-Fascist Chiarini, who often appeared in full uniform. Agostino did have one encounter with Il Duce. One morning he and his classmates found themselves on Via Appia, learning how to act in the open air. Mussolini galloped by on his white horse, then wheeled and halted. The professor gave a Roman salute and clicked his heels, and Mussolini asked him who these young people were and what they were doing. Hearing the explanation, the dictator nodded, exclaimed, "Bravo! You are the future of the Italian cinema!" and rode off. This prophecy of Mussolini's would be perhaps his only one to come true: along with Agostino, the group included such future luminaries as the actor Massimo Serato and the actress Alida Valli.

Toward the end of the year the students were asked to respond in writing to the question, "Why do I want to be an actor, and which roles would I prefer?" Agostino wrote in reply:

> It's not very easy to say why one wishes to be a movie actor. . . . I'm certain that today, after a year of theoretical and practical experience, my reasons for choosing this career are quite different from those that led me to enter the Centro in the first place. Back then, I thought I could be an actor because I possessed a decent physique and a certain sensibility. Now I realize that isn't enough, that it's essential to have some very different qualities: a willingness to master one's physical resources, for example, and

> a capacity for fantasy in the creation of movement. . . . Once I've gotten a grip on those things, I want to probe a little deeper into my personality, in order to get a better idea of my own possibilities and inclinations.
>
> What I need to keep in mind above all is my land of origin: Naples. As a Neapolitan, I have a personality that is anything but melancholic. Instead I'm fairly jovial and open to life. Which isn't to say that the Neapolitan spirit is empty: no, all the highest sentiments of men can be found there. That's why I believe I'm best suited to "comic-sentimental" roles, which conceal within their depths a dramatic element. . . . For the moment, and in light of my physique and age, those are the roles for me. Certainly time and experience will bring to light possibilities that I'm unaware of today.

This self-analysis sounds sincere though slightly reductive. In reality, Agostino had serious doubts about the path he was taking. When he gazed in the mirror and studied his face and profile, he concluded, "I can't become an actor. It's not only that I lack the physical stature; I'm also missing the kind of presence that bores right through the screen, the presence you need to become a star."

He did, however, take to heart the Centro's most important lesson, which is that the cinema consisted of much more than actors. Gradually he realized that he belonged behind the camera rather than in front of it. What about being a director? The job seemed to require a wider cultural background than the boy from Torre Annunziata possessed. Thumbing through a magazine, the young man spotted an article informing readers that a minimal level of cultural literacy required knowledge of at least one hundred books; an actual list followed. Agostino tore out the page and began gathering the prescribed books, a canon of world literature: Tolstoy, Dostoevsky, Balzac, Manzoni, and so on. Then he forced himself to read them cover to cover, one after another.

This much reading was a new experience. Little by little he developed a taste for books. He realized that, besides giving pleasure, literature could offer more significant benefits as well. Soon he noticed that he was able to express himself better and that his vocabulary had expanded. He produced more ideas, more easily, and a great many things that had never crossed his mind before now stimulated and intrigued him. Reading became a habit and would eventually become almost a vice.

After embarking on the book binge prompted by his desire to become a director, Agostino decided he could be a producer instead. Rather than shooting films, he could conjure up their very existence and market them to the public.

Agostino was certain of one thing: he would not become an actor. He hated the idea of standing around the set, waiting for his cues or, even worse, hanging around at home hoping for a callback. He wanted to be the person *making* the calls, not the one sitting by the phone. He wanted a seat at the table where the decisions were made.

In the meantime, though, he accepted a flattering offer to play the protagonist in *Long Pants (Pantaloni lunghi)*, the first directorial effort by his friend Germi. (The prints, alas, would be destroyed during the Nazi occupation of Rome.) Pietro had already discarded an earlier title, *Puppy Love (Primo amore)*, as too obvious. Both titles expressed the gist of the short film, which revolved around a simple dilemma: a fifteen-year-old boy must obtain a pair of long pants in order to court a young girl. Shot before a live audience, *Pantaloni lunghi* was an apprentice effort and had no commercial release. Agostino's work earned the praise of Chiarini himself, who was hardly an effusive type: "Your Neapolitan spontaneity is astonishing." Still, this encouragement didn't alter Agostino's secret resolve:

> When Germi made this film, it was the first one he ever directed: too bad there's not a single copy left. Anyway, he kept telling me, "What a great job you're doing! You're going to have a great career!" And when the film was finished and Pietro screened it for the professors, Chiarini said, "Excellent work! You're going to be a great actor." I accepted all these compliments, but I didn't change my mind. I no longer wanted to become an actor. My character just wasn't right for it.

The end of his first year in Rome approached, which meant the end of his allowance from home. Agostino sent his father a letter, thanking Aurelio for his help and assuring him that the future looked bright. The young man also said, quite definitely, that he would not be returning to the pasta factory. Agostino asked his father to think of him, from now on, as an autonomous and independent creature.

And so it was. There was no more money from home, and the difficulties began. Agostino had put aside a small nest egg during the final weeks of his allowance: eating his meals in the modest trattoria on Via Foligno, he limited himself to a bowl of soup and a miserable hunk of French bread. Yet he needed to find work, and the obvious place to start was Cinecittà, the prestigious citadel of the cinema inaugurated by Mussolini in 1937.

Agostino had already strolled through its gates many times, and he'd worked as an extra in a handful of films. Now, wandering the streets of the studio, he ran into the producer Peppino Amato, a former star of the silent screen and a notorious womanizer. Amato—who had spent some time in America, where he had supposedly tap-danced down the sidewalks of Broadway—happened to come from Naples, and their common origin gave the young man the courage to stop him: "Don Peppino, I'm a student at the Centro and I'm a Neapolitan like you. I know you're putting together a film, *Batticuore*. Could there be a small part for me?"

"Come along," the producer replied. "Let's see if I can give you a hand."

Amato introduced the young man to the director Mario Camerini, a true professional who would later work for many years with De Laurentiis. Wasting no time, the producer made his pitch: "Why don't we let this young tough play the boy who brings the flowers to Assia Noris?" Camerini looked him over, ordered him to walk back and forth, and agreed.

> I emerged with a job—two weeks of work at a good salary!—but before we said good-bye, Amato had a word of advice for me. "Hey, young tough," he said, "don't make me look bad. Get here on time tomorrow morning." And then the wardrobe person chimed in: "And wear a pair of black shoes." Which created a problem: as a classic provincial from the South, I had nothing but brown shoes.

This is the opening of a story De Laurentiis would offer up to friends, journalists, and TV interviewers for the next five decades. His daughters, who've heard it countless times, call it The Tale of the Shoes. For the protagonist, the story represents something important, something more than a good story. He considers it the first significant test of his philosophy of life, one founded on loyalty, honesty, and triumphant confrontation with any and all obstacles.

I climb down from the Tuscolana tram and meanwhile I'm thinking: "Black shoes? I realize you need them to play a groom, but where the devil will I find any? This gig is manna from heaven, I can't let it slip away. I have to resolve this problem."

I pass by the window of a shoe store and what do I see? A pair of beautiful black shoes, just right for the occasion. Something induces me to enter, a kind of higher force. The only person there is the owner, a man of about seventy. I ask to try on the shoes. Addressing me with the familiar *tu*, he brings the shoes from the window and I slip them on. I rise, take a few steps. "Perfect, they'll do just fine. I'll take them."

I let him wrap them up for me. Then I do my song and dance: "Listen, there's a problem: I don't have any money to pay you. Let me explain. I'm an actor, and I've been offered a small part in a film with Assia Noris, and they told me to show up tomorrow morning with black shoes. If you'll let me buy them on credit, I'll be set for the next three or four months of my life."

"What would you do if you were me?" he replies, with a perplexed expression.

"Look me in the face and trust me," I tell him. "The first thing I'll do tomorrow evening, after I collect my salary, is come here and pay you."

A long, hesitant pause, then a sudden decision: "Take the shoes and get out of here!" Incredible: I convinced him!

At the end of the next work day, I present myself to the cashier, but my explanation doesn't produce a single lira: "You're signed up for several days of work. If I pay you today and you don't show up tomorrow, they have to reshoot the scenes. You'll get paid when the entire job is done."

What could I do? I give the shoe store a wide berth until I have the money in my hand. Then I hurry over to the store, only to find it closed. Luckily there's a sign attached high on the wall, with the name and address of the proprietor. He lives right nearby, so I go over there and he opens the door. For a moment he doesn't even recognize me, then he says in surprise, "Ah, it's you?" I give him the money in an envelope and he says, "I didn't think I would see you again."

Fifteen years pass, I'm in my office at the Vasca Navale, and my secretary Liliana announces, "*Dottore*, there's an elderly gentleman here who wishes to speak with you. He won't settle for anybody else." In general I try to see everybody, I'm not the type to send people packing, so I say, "Send him in."

> A little old man appears: "*Dottore*, do you remember the black shoes for that film with Assia Noris? I'm the one who gave them to you. Now my store has gone out of business and I need work." I gave him a job as a custodian, and that took care of things for the rest of his life.

The young man from Torre Annunziata had finally gotten his (newly shod) foot in the door of the cinema. Assia Noris was no longer a photo to cut out of a newspaper and paste in a scrapbook. Now she was the beautiful, flesh-and-blood woman in a nightgown who was sitting next to him on the bed. And when the young man presented her with a bouquet, she favored him with a smile. The cameras rolled, Camerini cried, "Excellent! Print it!" and De Laurentiis's career in the cinema was officially under way. He would never look back.

CHAPTER 3

A YOUTH SPEAKS

It was now September 1938, and omens of war were gathering throughout Europe. Agostino paid little attention. This pattern would persist his whole life: he always experienced his personal problems—particularly work-related problems—with an overpowering intensity. He'd relegate the rest of the world to the background, only occasionally casting a distracted glance in that direction.

What counted for Agostino right now was gaining ground on the professional road he'd just started down. There was, however, one hitch. Because he was so young, the Centro asked him to repeat the initial course of study. Our hero was willing to oblige, but he needed a scholarship and the earliest he could obtain one would be February 1939. He wrote to the director, explaining his financial fix and requesting a special dispensation. But on his request, which survives in the archive, we find an emphatic *No* scrawled in Chiarini's handwriting: the rules would not be bent.

Agostino searched for another way to get by. He couldn't turn to his family; even if his father had been willing to subsidize him for a second year, he was no longer capable of doing so. Aurelio was now in grave financial difficulties himself.

> At Torre Annunziata there were many pasta factories, one next to another, and my father was very friendly with a proprietor who was named, I believe, Coniglio. His factory was right across the street and bigger than my father's. They all relied on bank loans to do business. One day this Coniglio asked a favor of my father. What

did he want? He asked my father to sign some promissory notes for tens of millions of lire, which were dependent on Coniglio obtaining certain supplies of farina, pasta, semolina, and who knows what else. Although there was no guarantee that these supplies would materialize, my father signed the notes as a courtesy. Every time a note came due, Coniglio hurried over to the bank to pay it, until, one day, he didn't. Then, to avoid the notes' going into default, my father decided to pay them out of his own pocket. "To avoid soiling my good name," he said. He was forced to sell the pasta factory: he didn't go bankrupt, but he lost almost everything.

What would happen now? My father, from whom I inherited certain qualities, didn't give up. He said, "We failed, but we kept our name intact. Now we need to start over." He had saved just a small nest egg with which to start another business elsewhere, since he didn't want to stay in Torre Annunziata. He moved the entire family to Naples, to a house on the Vomero, and opened a bakery. He made bread for the bakeshops. This was a more modest activity than the previous one, yet my father found it no less noble.

He had landed on his feet, and for many years he dedicated himself to this work. Until finally I said to my mother, "Tell Papa to give up the bakery and come to Rome."

"And what will we do in Rome?"

"I don't know, we'll see, but in the meantime, just come."

They came. Papa bought an apartment on Viale Eritrea, and since he considered it essential to be involved in a business, I suggested that he open a photographic studio. He did an excellent job, I must say, and kept at it until his death. He was still running the place in his eighties and earning some pretty good money too.

Within Rosario Aurelio's multiple incarnations—civil servant, pasta maker, baker, photographer—we can recognize some of the characteristic De Laurentiis traits, especially the willingness to start over from scratch. The Foto Lif studio, opened by De Laurentiis the elder at Via Antonio Gallonio 9 in Rome, became one of the most successful photographic enterprises in the city.

As it turns out, the surrender of the Pastificio Moderno factory coincided with the beginning of a crisis that would destroy Torre Annunziata's pasta industry. Maria Orsini Natale's novel *Francesca and Nunziata* describes the Milan Trade Fair of 1937, where a company owned by Mario and Giuseppe Braibanti presented "the first automated device for the manufacture of edible pasta." At first, the proud pastamakers of Torre Annunziata insisted that they would beat the competition. Even if they had water and farina up north, the thinking went, they "lacked the sun and the skill." Natale writes, "They didn't yet recognize the calamity that would befall them. . . . Of the numerous mills, the dozens and dozens of pasta factories, large and small, only a few would survive—a small enough number that you could count them on the fingers of one hand. It wasn't the war that destroyed them, nor the insane world, but the machines, those eternal enemies."

Those were the difficulties faced by the people of Torre Annunziata. In Rome, Agostino too was struggling to put food on the table, but at least he wasn't trapped in a dying industry. He accepted whatever employment came his way. He worked as a stagehand, electrician, extra, and director's assistant; he even took a turn with the clapperboard. He landed a bit part in *L'orologio a cucù* (*The Cuckoo Clock*), announcing Vittorio De Sica's arrival by boat in one of the initial scenes.

> I scratched along with the courage of desperation and never looked back. I did everything, and I'm not ashamed to admit it. Indeed, I repeat it often, and gladly, to remind young people that it takes a good dose of humility to learn the cinematic trade. While I was knocking myself out, though, I felt like I couldn't go on this way. I needed to get moving, and the only thing I lacked was an idea.

The idea finally took shape when he read about the crisis at the FERT studios in Turin. (The acronym stood for "Fiori Enrico Roma Torino," commemorating the man who founded the place in 1919.) Agostino recognized an excellent opportunity. But how could he present himself, with neither a career nor capital to speak of—with, in short, nothing?

First he scraped together enough money for a train ticket and his initial expenses. Arriving in Turin, he checked into the Sitea, a good hotel he couldn't actually afford. The essential thing was to look his very best, and our hero decided that the moment had come to change his name. *De Laurentiis*, with that double *i* evoking some remote nobility, was fine, but *Agostino* was too long. Better to use a modern, abbreviated form: *Tino.* Or rather, *Dino.*

As the new Dino saw it, there was no point going around on foot like everybody else. The new role he'd invented for himself required an automobile, preferably a fancy one. And so he telephoned Luigi Pestelli, head of the publicity office at Fiat. "I'm from Rome," he said. "I'm the producer Dino De Laurentiis."

The producer explained to Pestelli that he was in town to scout locations for a new movie, and it would be convenient to have a car at his disposal. In exchange, he promised publicity for Fiat in the (as yet nonexistent) movie. Pestelli warmed to this charming southerner, who must have seemed exotic in hyperaustere Turin, and he agreed to Dino's request. Our hero had played his cards perfectly. When he showed up at the FERT gates in a beautiful Fiat, with a chauffeur, nobody could guess that he didn't have a single lira in his pocket.

At the time, the man in charge of FERT was the director Carlo Borghesio, who would later make a small name for himself by directing several films for the comedian Macario. Since he was eager to find clients for his moribund studio, Borghesio welcomed this dynamic young man from Rome. He gave him a tour of the two soundstages, the dubbing and synchronization equipment, the Moviolas, and other facilities. Dino took note of everything, and when he revealed his ambition to resurrect the establishment, he got an enthusiastic response from his host.

Turin, as Dino well knew, was considered impregnable to outsiders. Yet it was overflowing with industry and economic resources: why shouldn't the Italian cinema, which had in fact been founded here, enjoy a local resurgence? Dino set out to find a local mogul who would be willing to invest in a new and improved FERT. Borghesio suggested that he contact Mario Steffenino, a wealthy designer and manufacturer of ultramodern furniture. Introductions were made; Steffenino invited the visitor from Rome to supper, where Dino sketched out his entire plan. Borghesio had already agreed to put the studios at Dino's disposal for a certain quota of productions. All they needed to do was to arrange financing for the new company: Real Cine. The regal sound of the name—made up on the spot by Dino—was too much for Steffenino to resist. He promptly agreed to become the company's managing director and raise the capital.

So much for the conquest of Turin, as recounted by Dino sixty years after the fact. He happily adds that life was good to him up north:

they gave him a suite at the Sitea, and during his off hours he enjoyed a busy bachelor's existence. When we sift through the documents, however, a prologue emerges.

In fact, Dino did not approach Steffenino with nothing but a business plan. Before Real Cine got off the ground, our hero worked on a pair of short films for FERT. The first, a comedy titled *Troppo tardi t'ho conosciuta* (*I Met You Too Late*), was shot in July 1939. The project was a fiasco, and all prints of the film have vanished. There are, however, a few surviving stills of De Laurentiis costumed as a sailor, in a striped T-shirt and tattoos, playing a character named Dino. In this case, he did double duty as inspector of production—a job he probably owed to his friendship with the director, Emanuele Caracciolo, whom he'd met at the Centro.

He had better luck with the second project. *L'ultimo combattimento* (*The Last Fight*) was a semiautobiographical film written by the ex-middleweight champion Enzo Fiermonte, who also starred. Fiermonte had just returned from the United States, where both the boxing underworld and his American wife had caused him major problems. Dino went to meet Fiermonte in Naples after his transatlantic crossing and immediately signed him to an exclusive contract. His success with the pugilist's film neatly balanced out his failure with the comedy. Indeed, these two projects represented a great leap forward in his career. Certainly they made it much easier for Dino to position himself as the savior of FERT.

By now it was early 1941, and Europe had been at war for the past eighteen months. As usual, Dino's mind was elsewhere. Having gotten Real Cine off the ground, he realized that one piece was still missing from the puzzle: he had no films to make. If he didn't hustle, somebody would call his bluff. Rushing back to Rome, he gathered a pile of screenplays and feverishly read through them without finding anything he could unequivocally commit to. He was twenty years old, he'd produced only two short films, one of which was a flop, and he didn't yet feel capable of separating the cinematic wheat from the chaff.

He reached out for help to Roberto Dandi, managing director of Industrie Cinematografiche Italiane (ICI) and the man to whom Dino planned to entrust the distribution of his future (still imaginary) films. While meeting with him, Dino accompanied Dandi to the screening of a Swedish movie, *Swing It Magistern.* Dandi decided against acquiring the little musical for ICI, but Dino saw a certain appeal to the story, which followed a musician and a model who were in love with each other but shared a weakness for deception, which led to all sorts of shenanigans. Why not make an Italian version? An exultant Dino telephoned Steffenino and announced, "I've found a film that's been a success all over Europe. We'll remake it and risk nothing."

As the producer recalls, "I wouldn't want to take credit for anything I didn't do, but I just may have invented the remake, which was then, at least in Italy, a real novelty. This is a question for historians of the cinema, though."

To rough out the screenplay, Dino called Pietro Germi, who was always looking for work. For the dialogue, however, he aimed higher, approaching the celebrated writer Salvator Gotta. Acquiring the rights (or unashamedly stealing them—we'll never know), the fledgling producer then pulled off what would become a typical De Laurentiis coup: he managed to hire the universally esteemed Ferdinando Maria Poggioli to direct. At the same time, he signed up the actress Maria Denis, whom Poggioli had just directed in a current hit, *Addio giovinezza*. The team was in place.

Retitled *L'amore canta* (*Love Sings*), Dino's remake was shot at FERT during the spring of 1941 and released in September. This initial Real Cine production didn't get much of a welcome from the critics, and both the director and the star were less than enthusiastic. (As Denis would later note, "It wasn't worthy of Poggioli or me. A simpering piece of work. Made for the unwashed public.") The public, unwashed or not, was more receptive, which encouraged Dino to repeat his formula.

This time, he fastened onto a German film by Willy Forst, which he rechristened *Margherita fra i tre* (*Margherita and Her Three Uncles*). Like its predecessor, this was something of a screwball comedy. To marry the man she loves, the female protagonist must obtain the consent of her three uncles, pretending to be a different person with each one. Dino called screenwriter Ivo Perilli, who in 1934 had directed *Ragazzo*, the only Italian film ever prohibited by the Fascist censors. After showing Perilli the German original, he said, "We're going to do a quick-and-dirty remake. Would you like to direct it?" Since the film was slated to be shot in the record time of three months, Dino may have had problems hiring a more experienced director. Yet he probably had another motive as well. Perilli, after all, served as intellectual right-hand man to the director Mario Camerini, which put him in close touch with the director's wife, Assia Noris, who was eventually persuaded to star in *Margherita fra i tre*.

The shoot took place during the final months of 1941, and Perilli would later recall only the aerial bombardments that pummeled Turin. Dino's biggest worry about the bombing was that it might put the production behind schedule. And what about the notoriously tempermental Assia Noris? The young producer had already decided on an approach that would pay off for the next six decades. De Laurentiis showered his actors with tenderness, praise, respect, and encouragement: "I pamper them when they're nervous, I bring them a sweet, I send them flowers, I invite them to supper." When the film came out in July 1942, it did well enough to break even. But the very fact that Dino had pulled it off further solidified his beachhead in the world of production.

One token of his new legitimacy was an interview that appeared in the December 6, 1941, issue of the weekly magazine *Film*, entitled "A Young Man Speaks: Dino De Laurentiis." The subject began with a declaration that he'd repeat throughout his career: "If a film is no good, it's the producer's fault!" The author, identified only as *V. C.*, speculated about Dino's age: "As young as he is, De Laurentiis refused to confess his age to me. Twenty-four? Twenty-eight? Thirty? . . . To see him on the job, with his air of an amused observer, you would never suspect that he carries the entire organization of the film on his shoulders."

Dino, who was in fact twenty-two, explained his on-set lack of concern:

> By then I've already done everything that was necessary. My task, aside from a few minor details, is done the day the filming begins. . . . The producer's job is organizational. It only makes sense, then, that his job ends the moment the film is actually being realized. If that's not the case, everybody is in trouble. . . . And if a film is deficient for any reason, ninety times out of a hundred the fault is that of the producer, who didn't select the right collaborators, who didn't organize the production, who doesn't (to be blunt) know how to practice his trade. And if, on the contrary, a film is released and becomes a big hit, the credit should go to—well, I'll say no more.

After recapping Dino's rather short career as an actor and producer, the article concluded with an important announcement: "Meanwhile, in just the last few days, this young man has made a great leap forward: one of the biggest Italian production houses has offered him a one-year contract. And Dino De Laurentiis has accepted with a certain legitimate pride."

The offer, which surprised Dino as much as anyone else, came from the founder of the Lux studios, Riccardo Gualino. This extraordinary man, who is not as widely known as he deserves, was among the orginators of the modern Italian cinema. A creative and energetic industrialist, a pioneer in the use of artificial fibers, a great collector and patron of the arts, Gualino never hid his distaste for the Fascist regime. In 1931 Mussolini used a minor financial scandal to slap him with a five-year internal exile in Lipari. Drawing on the experience, Gualino wrote *Solitudine* (*Solitude*), a book that only enhanced his prestige. After a short period of expatriation in France, he returned to Italy with the idea of dedicating himself to the cinema, and in 1934 he founded Lux. By the time he summoned De Laurentiis in 1941, Gualino headed the most prestigious and important production house in Italy.

Lux had important projects lined up, and Dino was impatiently eager to participate. He immediately was named director of production on *Malombra*, an adaptation of an Antonio Fogazzaro novel. The film is a lush Gothic melodrama, prefiguring *Rebecca* in its obsession with love beyond death. The director, Mario Soldati, had already successfully adapted another Fogazzaro novel, *Piccolo mondo antico* (*Old-Fashioned World*), and the hope was that he would create yet another satisfying period piece.

Dino immediately left for Rome. There he took a suite on the top floor of the Hotel Flora on Via Veneto. Every morning he was the first to arrive at the office on Via Po, at precisely 7 A.M. This earned him the silent admiration of Gualino, who was just as much of an early bird. An austere and solemn figure, this new employer fascinated De Laurentiis. After his rapid rise through the world of low-budget cinema, Dino knew that there would be plenty to learn at Lux.

The preparations for *Malombra* moved forward but not without a few hitches. For starters, the fiery, perennially agitated Soldati—with whom Dino immediately formed a profound friendship—had fallen in love with Alida Valli during the filming of *Piccolo mondo antico* and insisted on using her again. Gualino, on the other hand, wanted to offer the actress Isa Miranda an opportunity for a comeback after an unlucky sojourn in Hollywood. Soldati refused to consider Miranda and then, in a typical about-face, he granted her a screen test. Her performance was enough to convince everybody, including the director himself.

The bulk of the film was shot in the Renaissance-era Villa Pliniana, near Lake Como, owned by a marquis with a sonorous name: Cesare Valperga di Masino e Caluso. The shooting schedule called for several night scenes, which was something of a problem, since the area was subject to an antiaircraft blackout. For Dino, the solution to such a problem was to ignore it. Indeed, the war might as well not have been taking place: often Massimo Terzano's lights illuminated half the lake, prompting terrified protests from the residents.

Meanwhile, though nobody on the production discussed it openly, Fogazzaro's novel was reputed to carry a curse. Several accidents—most notably, the death of a child, who was watching the shoot when a terrace collapsed beneath him—seemed to confirm this fear. As a Neapolitan, Dino might easily have been preoccupied with the evil eye. Yet he paid little mind, intent only on sticking to the schedule.

His task was further complicated by his star, who had just participated in a séance for the first time. Rattled by her communications with the beyond, the diva called in sick and the film ground to a halt for several days. In fact, it wasn't only the spirit world that troubled Miranda. She was also tired of both the challenges of her disagreeable role—she played a beautiful, raving lunatic—and the obvious, offensive unhappiness of the director, who was still pining for Alida Valli.

During her long nights of isolation and loneliess, Isa chose the director of production as her confidant. Dino may have comforted her a bit too enthusiastically. Her husband, Alfredo Guarini, chivalrously confronted his supposed rival and declared himself ready to cede the field. Unwilling to transform a fling into a grand passion, Dino swore that his interest was entirely professional: he wanted only to shield the star from her director's hysterical behavior. This was enough to calm Guarini. He thanked Dino warmly while the actress, in the presence of her husband, embraced her young *consolatore* for the last time. In the wake of this episode, De Laurentiis made a vow that he would keep forever after: "To avoid interfering with discipline on the job, never sleep with an actress while the film is being shot. Only afterwards."

Despite its modest box-office performance (and a few carping reviews), *Malombra* was counted a great success at Lux. Once the dust settled, Soldati would characterize the film as "the most beautiful I ever shot." And De Laurentiis discovered that he felt quite at home in an intellectual circle like the director's. In fact, he emerged from the experience with a real taste for cinematic art.

Satisfied with Dino's work on *Malombra*, his bosses now entrusted him with a film by Renato Castellani, a fussier and more demanding director than Soldati. This was *Zazà*. Again the leading lady was Isa Miranda, who had narrowly lost the part to Claudette Colbert when George Cukor made his American version of this French comedy.

Castellani would later deliver a glowing tribute to Dino's gifts: "I never shot a film with such tranquility, such serenity, nor was I ever given the sort of support I got when making *Zazà*. . . . Everything was arranged like a musical score, courtesy of that De Laurentiis boy. Because in those days he *was* a boy. He was a genius. An Italian-style genius, multiform, extroverted, who occasionally made a mistake, paid for what he had broken, stumbled, fell again, and had a laugh over the whole thing. He was like Napoleon, on the throne or in the dumps, with an irresistible charm."

No wonder Castellani wanted this peerless director of production on hand for his next film, *La donna della montagna* (*The Mountain Woman*). This time, however, the war finally got in the way, and the movie was issued in a botched version. Despite Dino's efforts to ignore it, the European conflagration was finally catching up with him, and even greater sorrows would soon be looming over the young producer.

CHAPTER 4

ON THE RUN IN ITALY

Over the past two years, Dino had escaped being shipped off to the North African front. In fact, he'd managed to avoid any military service whatsoever—thanks to the good graces of a colonel he met on the set of *Malombra*. At the first call-up, before the start of *Malombra*, this guardian angel had allowed Dino to take shelter in the military hospital at Como and issued him a six-month leave. But now the leave was up and he was informed that his dossier had been transferred to Naples, his home district, where he was obliged to present himself in order to obtain an additional deferment.

Hard at work on *La donna della montagna*, our hero alerted his mother and asked her to pull together the necessary documents. Giuseppina assured him that everything would be ready. The day before his appointment, Dino arrived in Naples with his uniform in a suitcase and spent the night at his family's house. The following morning he showed up at the military hospital, escorted by the string-pulling colonel, who pointed him toward a door down the corridor: "Knock, enter, and introduce yourself: 'De Laurentiis, Agostino, driver.' Hand over the request for the deferment. They'll have a pro forma discussion with you, then they'll stamp your papers and you'll be fine for another six months."

Dino entered calmly and clicked his heels in a military salute. He noticed, however, that there were two German officials present along with the Italian lieutenant. There was no discussion, just a quick stamp on his papers and a dry comment: "You can go." To the young producer, it appeared that he had gotten off lightly indeed. But the moment he left the room, he glanced at the top page. The stamp read "Croatia."

The colonel, as bewildered as Dino if less worried, examined the document and told his young charge that there was no use complaining: he would have to report without delay to the Tenth Artillery Regiment, Border Patrol, based in Trieste. The Germans, suspicious of the excessive number of leaves issued by the Italian Army, were now insisting that every soldier not actually on his deathbed had to join the ranks.

Hurrying back to Rome, Dino informed his boss that he had been posted to Croatia and would need to quit work on *La donna della montagna*. With the authoritative swagger of a man of power, Gualino found out exactly who commanded the Territorial Defense Force in Trieste. He telephoned General Giovanni Esposito and got an additional sixty days of leave for "driver De Laurentiis." Two months later, the day of departure finally arrived. Reaching Trieste, Dino descended from the sleeper car still wearing his civilian clothes.

> I took a room at the Hotel Savoia, changed into my uniform, presented myself at the Belleno barracks at the foot of Via Rossetti, and asked to speak with General Esposito. This high-ranking officer seemed like a decent man. I screwed up my courage and threw my cards on the table: "Signor General, may I speak with you frankly? You must know that I've muddled along for the past two years with a convalescent deferment, meaning that I've never held a revolver or a rifle in my hand, I don't know how to shoot, and I would never be able to get myself out of a jam. So if you post me to the Croatian interior, you're sending me off to die: I'm in no shape to defend either my country or myself. But meanwhile, I have other qualities that could be useful to you."
>
> "Like what?"
>
> "I could organize shows at the front."
>
> "Really?" said the general, sounding interested. "I was just telling my officers that we must arrange some entertainment for our boys on the front line. What sort of shows did you have in mind?"
>
> "I can find some projectors and show films; I can pull together a little orchestra, bring in some actresses and singers."
>
> "The job is yours. What do you need?"

> "I could use a truck for the equipment, an automobile, and a dozen soldiers to give me a hand."
>
> Now that I'd gotten carte blanche, I ran to the phone and lined up a few films. I also threw together a kind of variety show, procuring four little starlets. For those poor guys on the Yugoslavian front, going head to head with Tito's partisans, it was a relief just to catch a glimpse of ass and hear somebody sing a song. The organization of those shows for the troops remains one of the great successes of my career. Sure, all that coming and going from Trieste to the Croatian or Slovenian interior was a little dangerous. But we never had any trouble moving the show from one outpost to another. We gave an afternoon and an evening performance, returned to the city, and my helpers went to sleep in the barracks, while I slept in my comfortable room at the Savoia.
>
> It went on this way until one day, returning from the front where we had given a show with some Neapolitan singers, we found the streets of Trieste invaded by a mob. They were tearing all the Fascist regalia and portraits of Mussolini off the walls and throwing them out the windows. It was July 26, 1943.

Italy had finally turned against its dictator. In the forty-five days that followed, with Mussolini under arrest and Marshal Pietro Badoglio in charge, the situation grew more and more chaotic. Suddenly, on September 8, an armistice was declared.

This left the Italian military in utter disarray. With no orders, the commander of the Twenty-third Army Corps in Trieste, General Alberto Ferrero, tried to stall. He ignored the pleas of the partisans eager to enlist his forces in the Resistance and, at the same time, avoided the demands of the Germans to surrender and hand over all military equipment. Within hours, Ferrero ordered a strategic retreat. At dawn, columns of the Royal Army departed from Trieste in the direction of Cervignano. Among the troops was that impresario in uniform, Dino De Laurentiis.

By now the soldiers in Dino's service had become his faithful retainers, addressing him as "Doctor De Laurentiis." They promptly accepted his suggestion that they stick together and travel in a supply truck, stocked with flour, bread, and even a cook. This truck was perhaps the fiftieth in a line of vehicles that stretched as far as the eye could see. Nobody knew where they were going, how long the retreat would last, or what would happen to the disintegrating columns. Dino's men comforted themselves with the thought that at least they were unlikely to die of hunger.

> We were on one of those roads in Friulia, the kind that run right through the flat countryside, when there suddenly appeared a Tiger, the biggest of the German tanks. There were also about a hundred soldiers, all of them armed to the teeth. The commander ordered us to halt, and the entire column stopped. Back in the rear we couldn't make out what the Germans were saying or what our own officers were saying in reply. It was clear enough, however, that the Germans were demanding that we surrender unconditionally and turn over our weapons. And it was just as clear that the Italians were refusing. At a certain point the Germans began shooting. And what took place then was straight out of a silent comedy: without receiving any orders, the vehicles began fleeing in every direction, to the left and to the right, slipping down the narrow paths and bouncing through the meadows.

Dino and his companions in the supply truck anxiously veered down one country lane after another, traveling dozens of miles before allowing themselves to halt at a respectful distance from the German fire. Then he gave a little speech: "Listen, if the Germans catch us now, they'll line us up against the wall, because as far as they're concerned, we're traitors. We've got to stop in a village or at some isolated farmhouse and offer the people everything we have: the pasta, salami, even the truck itself, in exchange for some civilian clothes. We put them on and we beat it." Passing from farmhouse to farmhouse, distributing bread or grain or flour, the little band scraped together an assortment of civilian clothing. As each man assembled a complete outfit, he prepared to leave by exchanging rapid salutes, embraces, and wishes for an eventual reunion. On his own, hiding in ditches and stables, bumming rides, and locking himself in the bathroom on trains, Dino made his way to Rome.

Reclaiming his room at the Hotel Flora, he immediately telephoned Mario Soldati, who was even more agitated than he had been on the set of *Malombra*: "Agostino, thank goodness you called! The Germans are hunting down all the anti-Fascists. We're in terrible trouble." Dino insisted that he had nothing to do with politics in Trieste;

all he had done was organize variety shows, unlike Soldati, who had recently vented his frustrations in the newspapers after years of silence. But the director cut him off: "You don't seem to realize that you're a deserter and that you must escape with me. We'll meet at the station and jump on the first train heading south." Where could they go? Dino proposed that they take refuge with his family, which had fled to their ancestral village of Torella dei Lombardi. "My father had some property there," Dino recalls, "and they raised grain, chickens, and pigs. In short, it was a place where we could hide, eat, and sleep while we waited for the Americans to arrive."

At 6:27 A.M. on Wednesday, September 14, Dino and Soldati scrambled aboard a train bound for Avezzano. Each eight-person compartment was crammed with at least thirty passengers, including numerous stragglers from the army, hastily and often ridiculously disguised as civilians. Dino realized that this was a dangerous epic indeed, but he never imagined at the time that he'd be transformed into a character in a story. A couple of years after their tragicomic journey, Soldati published a memoir called *Fuga in Italia (The Flight into Italy)*, in which he referred to Dino by his original name, Agostino.

In this "fugue for two voices," it's difficult to decide which of the two is Don Quixote and which is Sancho Panza, especially when we compare Soldati's version with Dino's own recollections. The producer amiably disputes his old friend's account: "Mario took some liberties, but when it comes to recalling the past, so do I." In *Fuga in Italia*, Agostino is presented as a faithful shadow, comically indifferent to discomfort. The mice, suspicious sounds, and other annoyances that drive Soldati crazy during a night in a farmhouse fail to disturb his companion's slumber. Not even the thunder of a nighttime bombardment awakens him, nor is he bothered by the bedbugs in a Rio Nero fleabag. Still, Soldati's narrative does present a faithful portrait of Dino: with his clear-eyed pragmatism, he's almost always the one to take the initiative for their survival. He locates the shortcuts, steers clear of dangerous encounters, finds them food to eat and places to sleep.

> The railroad line to Avellino was full of tunnels—perhaps it still is today—and since the steam locomotive was pulling more cars than it was designed for, it was chugging painfully throughout the entire uphill journey. Every time the train entered a tunnel, the smoke filled

> the compartments and threatened to suffocate the passengers. Poor Soldati was dying of asphyxiation. I took a handkerchief, dipped it in water (we were carrying some in a canteen), and held it to his face, but he still felt ill. So I said, "Mario, there's only one way to save ourselves. As soon as we're out of this tunnel, we'll jump off the train. It's going so slowly that we won't get hurt. Otherwise you're going to die in here."

Their flight continued on foot, then on two broken-down bicycles, rented from a woman for an exorbitant fee. They found almost nothing to eat but bread and water. One bizarre encounter followed another. At one point the fugitives were mistaken for American paratroopers, and then a band of deserters decided that Soldati was a defecting officer. If Dino was consumed by the problems of day-to-day survival, his companion, saddened by the Italian tragedy, abandoned himself to bitter ruminations: "I wish we had never seen this day; I wish we had been born at any other moment in our history." On September 16 they stumbled upon a column of German soldiers and hid in a ditch; later they would learn that they had crossed paths with Rommel and Kesselring on their way to Salerno. At Castel di Sangro they ran into an actress they knew and finally ate a solid meal.

> Near Benevento one of the bicycles got a flat tire and we couldn't fix it. We asked a passing *contadino* [farmer] for help. He didn't have any rubber cement, but he did explain how to make a *pupatella*—that is, how to isolate the punctured area by folding over the inner tube and knotting it beneath the hole. At once we figured out that this *contadino* was a homosexual, and as usual, Soldati couldn't resist the opportunity for a little buffoonery. He pretended that he was a homosexual as well, in hopes of wheedling a little cash out of the guy.
>
> When we reached the outskirts of Benevento, though, we didn't feel like laughing anymore. Allied planes were bombing the place. We took cover and waited, and when things calmed down, we ventured back onto the street. Our route took us straight across the city, and I witnessed the most horrifying spectacle of my entire life. I'll never forget it: wrecked houses, and corpses scattered all over the rubble—men, old people, children, women, dogs.
>
> It was impossible to ride the bicycles, so we wheeled them along. The street signs were all uprooted, bent, illegible. If we took

the wrong road, we were fucked. Still, there was nothing to do but rely on instinct: we pointed ourselves south and entered a narrow lane. On one side, a few meters away, there was a German jeep. It seemed to be abandoned, there was nobody in it, but at precisely that moment five German devils popped out of a ruined palazzo, having stolen everything they could get their hands on. That explained the jeep! They looked at us, we looked at them, and in the silence, staring straight ahead, I whispered to Mario, "Don't turn around, keep walking, don't turn around." Behind us we heard the characteristic sound of a magazine being snapped in: *click*. "Don't turn around, Mario," I insisted. Meanwhile we reached the beginning of a downhill, and the German must have thought, "Why bother killing those two wretches?" So we mounted the bikes and rode off at a breakneck pace.

After ten minutes, which felt like an eternity, we halted, exhausted and thirsty. Nearby there was a pool of water, but when we approached to take a drink, we discovered that it was full of corpses. By now evening was falling. We halted at a farmhouse and curled up around our bicycles to prevent anybody from stealing them.

The next morning we hit the road once more. But the Allies started bombing again, and we decided to take shelter in some woods. Then we stopped ourselves, because there was an entire German army hiding in there underneath their tents. "From the frying pan into the fire," I said. "Mario, it's better to risk the bombs, because if the Germans catch us, they'll shoot us on the spot and that will be that!"

The two resumed their voyage on bicycle, but the tires kept going flat and the trip was a torment. The aerial bombardments continued on all sides; the Germans kept darting in and out of their path. Finally, on Sunday, September 19, they rode from Fontanarosa to Gesualdo, Villa Maina to Torella dei Lombardi, where the De Laurentiis house appeared at the top of a rise.

One of my sisters stepped out onto the balcony and, seeing us in the distance, began to shout: "Mama, Agostino has arrived!" There were embraces, kisses, and tears. We cleaned ourselves up. But we needed to be careful; it was better for us to stay hidden, because there was still a sinister Panzer guarding the piazza on behalf of our German comrades.

> On the evening of September 25 the town was deprived of electricity because the departing Germans had blown up the power station. On September 27, a regiment of Oklahoma Indians appeared. The family woke us in the middle of the night: "The Americans have arrived!" Soldati had been sleeping in one of my mother's nightgowns, which was white and hung down to his feet. Immediately we ran out into the street. With his gold eyeglasses and snow-white gown, Mario was a strange figure. Upon seeing him, one soldier grew excited and began to shout: "*The pope, the pope!*" Curiosity, exclamations, applause—they had mistaken him for Pope Pius XII, whom he slightly resembled. And what did the son of a bitch do? He began to give them all his benediction. That's all it took: immediately the Indians showered us with cigarettes, chocolate, and tins of Spam.

Pure legend? In *Fuga in Italia*, Soldati describes the arrival of the Americans in a less comical (and less ecclesiastical) vein: "They have enormous helmets and leggings—American leggings from the Civil War. As they walk, they glance around sadly, shyly, indifferent to the applause. They are dusty and sweaty. They look exhausted, as after a long march. . . . They seem profoundly tired: tired of fighting the war, tired of being shipped to Italy, tired of liberating the population, tired of our enthusiasm and our welcoming cries. Agostino, at my side, notices none of this, and screams like a banshee and claps his hands and insists that I push my way to the front and address them in English."

At this point Mario and Dino diverge even further in their recollections. In Soldati's book we read that Leo Longanesi (the eventual publisher of *Fuga in Italia*), the humorist Stefano Vanzina, and the director Riccardo Freda arrive in Torella on September 28. De Laurentiis, on the other hand, insists that they crossed paths with the three friends near Sorrento. According to Soldati, the group departed Torella on October 3 with a safe-conduct pass issued by a certain Major Hausen, a baritone from Omaha.

In any case, they traveled in a jeep. Driving through the ruins of Eboli, they learned that the Americans had entered Naples a few days earlier, but it was still impossible to get into the city. A more accessible location, perhaps, was Capri, liberated by a U.S. destroyer on September 12 and currently serving as an R and R facility for American aviators. The changing of the guard from the Germans to the Allies was accomplished without a single shot's being fired—in accordance with the attitude traditionally held by the local populace. Tranquility continued on the island, under the enlightened rule of the military governor, Colonel Carl E. Woodward.

Dino convinced his friends that under the circumstances, the wisest solution was to try to reach Capri. Renting a boat, they made the crossing from Sorrento in less than two hours, their hearts in their throats the entire time. To accommodate the wave of refugees, a reception camp had been set up at the Carthusian monastery, with room for five hundred ex-military men. Dino, however, had a better idea. From his days as a traveling salesman he knew the lawyer Peppino Brindisi, whom the Allies had named regional administrator. When De Laurentiis appeared before him, accompanied by the two literary celebrities, Soldati and Longanesi, Brindisi bent over backwards to arrange something: "Money I can't give you, and food is even more of a challenge, because Capri has been under siege. I can, however, assign you a house. It belongs to a Fascist who fled, so I'll requisition it and set you up there."

The little band installed itself in the Villa Mazzarella on Via Caselle, near Anacapri. Yet the basic problem of survival remained. As Vanzina would later write, "That October, for thirty days, Capri was like an aging but still beautiful woman, to whom Italy, in a state of emergency, had entrusted its suitcase full of valuables. . . . In the famous piazzetta we saw Senator Croce—who had decamped from Sorrento with his family in one of the fire brigade's motorboats—sipping his aperitif."

Soon it was possible to buy just about everything on the island. But the new currency introduced by the Allies—the Am-lira—was a disaster, and between the five unlucky residents of the villa there was scarcely enough money to pay for a hunk of bread, a coffee, and a cigarette. To combat hunger, the persistent Brindisi obtained from the governor an emergency distribution of plain pasta, 250 grams per person. Yet the people still rioted beneath his window: they didn't want the tube-shaped pasta, they demanded the longer varieties. Again, it was time for Dino to come up with an idea.

> One day we were hanging around the piazzetta, sitting on a low wall because we didn't have enough money to buy anything in the bar, and I noticed that after the American flyers consumed their

ginger ale, they threw the bottles on the ground. I watched a bottle fly, I watched another, then three, then four, and an idea popped into my brain. "Mario, Leo, Steno," I said, "I have one thing to tell you: if you want to eat tomorrow, gather up as many bottles as you can." When we were done, we'd collected between fifty and a hundred bottles. "Which of us has the most beautiful handwriting?" I asked. Longanesi, a famous graphic artist, was the obvious choice. "Great. We'll get some slips of paper, and you can write 'Souvenir of the Blue Grotto' on each one, along with the date. Tomorrow we'll go to the grotto with the bottles, fill them with water, put a cap on them, and I guarantee that we'll sell at least fifteen or so. At a dollar apiece."

The next morning we rowed a boat all the way to the Blue Grotto, which is at some distance: a real drag. We filled up the bottles, returned to the piazzetta, and started shouting: "Get your souvenir of the Blue Grotto!" Soldati, who spoke perfect American, chatted up the soldiers, singing the praises of our product. To make a long story short, we sold every single bottle and had more than enough in our pockets to feed ourselves. The next day we gathered more bottles, but we wised up, and instead of going to the grotto, we filled them with water from a drinking fountain and got down to business. And meanwhile we were eating, smoking, laughing, and seeing a future for ourselves. Nobody can understand what it means, when you're hungry and finally manage to eat and can say, "We'll eat tomorrow too." The future becomes tinged with pink: it's another life, and nobody who hasn't experienced it can really appreciate it.

Another time, while our heroes were lolling around the piazzetta, they watched Brindisi arrive, his face dark.

"My friends," he told them, "the island is dying of hunger. And to think that I have permission from the air force and the military police to go pick up five hundred tons of provisions in Sicily: fagioli, dried chestnuts, peas, stuff like that. Unfortunately I can't find anybody willing to make the trip. They're all terrified because the sea between Naples and Sicily is full of mines."

Dino said, "What if I go?" At once he approached a group of sailors and asked, "Why don't you want to make this trip?"

"Because the pay is bad and it's very dangerous."

"Let me make you a proposal. I'll tell the lawyer Brindisi that we'll go down to Sicily to pick up the goods and risk hitting a mine. Is the pay lousy? Fine. But in exchange, he'll authorize us to stop in Naples before we return and sell one hundred fifty tons of provisions on the black market, so we can get something out of the deal as well. Then we'll bring the remaining three hundred fifty tons back to Capri."

Brindisi agreed immediately. But Longanesi, Soldati, Vanzina, and Freda, who until this point had wanted to join the expedition, were forced to remain on dry land. There was no point in risking the entire group.

> It might have been luck, it might have been chance, it might have been the Madonna of Montevergine, but the fact is that we left with the binoculars glued to our eyes in order to spot mines, and we never came across a single one. The crossing lasted a week because we proceeded at a crawl. At Messina we loaded up the provisions and returned slowly to Naples, where we unloaded one hundred fifty tons. The black market at the port was an incredible organization, outside of every jurisdiction. There were certain docks where there wasn't a member of the Camorra [a local mafia] in sight, yet they could make entire shiploads disappear. The stuff the Neapolitans pulled off during the war was insane. Anyway, when I returned with three hundred fifty tons of provisions, I became the hero of Capri, and the old people on the island remember it to this day.

At last the moment came to leave the idleness of Capri and return to the fray. After obtaining permission, our heroes reached the mainland on a U.S. Navy PT boat, trusting that the liberation of Rome would take place within a few weeks. It was a hope shared by General Mark Clark, commander of the American Fifth Army, who was eagerly anticipating Operation Overlord—the D-Day landing in Normandy—when he would enter the Italian capital as victor. However, Hitler had ordered his generals to fortify the zone around the Valle del Liri in central Italy and to fight to the bitter end along the so-called Gustav Line, which the Allies hadn't yet breached. And aside from the enemy's stubborn resistance, the American advance was seriously hampered by the rough terrain and bad weather.

Meanwhile, the landing at Anzio, on January 22, 1944, was a nightmare, with heavy losses of men and equipment. (Many years later, in 1968, Dino would dedicate a film to this episode: Edward Dmytryk's

Anzio.) Instead of penetrating inland, the Allies were stalled. For months, most of the action took place at the foot of Monte Cassino, a monastery that the Germans had turned into a fortress. The bloody, nerve-wracking battle for Hill 593 (as Monte Cassino was denoted on the military maps) lasted 119 days. Meanwhile, Dino and his group were stuck in Naples.

According to a diary that Longanesi later published, their sojourn in Naples—a city one contemporary observer described as a "giant, drifting raft"—began in the early days of November. Dino, Soldati, Vanzina, and Longanesi arranged to share an apartment in the infamous Monte di Dio quarter, and there they would remain for nearly eight months.

A vivid description of that difficult time emerges from the pages of Longanesi's book. The city was overrun by Allied military men, often drunk and dangerous, surrounded by black marketeers, prostitutes, and shoeshine boys. Artillery rumbled in the distance, gunfire and explosions echoed across the bay, and one night a tethered blimp burst into flame above Sorrento. Longanesi, without even an overcoat, wrapped a blanket around himself when he went outside. There was very little to eat: bread and vegetables were rare, and meat was completely unobtainable. They subsisted on polenta, potatoes, and some boiled greens. "We pass the days shut inside," wrote Longanesi, "asking ourselves: 'What should we do?'" They listened to Mozart and Chopin, read, talked—by candlelight in the evening, due to the shortage of electricity. Quarrels broke out between Longanesi and Soldati, partly because Mario, eternally hungry, tended to help himself to other people's provisions. But there was an additional tension between Soldati's virulent anti-Fascism and Longanesi's more tolerant view of Italy's civic follies—an ironic foretaste of the nation's volatile postwar democracy.

True, the political panorama was hardly inspiring. The difficulties of choosing between a monarchy and a republic were already becoming clear. Freda and Longanesi approached various aristocrats, bearing a final proposal to save the monarchy: first, the unpalatable King Victor Emmanuel would be eliminated by hired killers, then his son Umberto parachuted into the country to restore his good name among the partisans of the North. Paradoxically, it was Longanesi, frantic with worry about his family back in Rome, who suffered most from the royalist government's belligerent radio broadcasts.

With his usual lack of interest in political discussions, Dino endured perhaps the only period of true inertia in his entire life. Mostly he worried about survival: he was still able to help his friends by dipping into the proceeds from his Sicilian expedition, but his reserves kept dwindling. Luckily, some of the soldiers who had joined Dino on the retreat from Trieste showed up in Naples: "Half of them were involved with the Camorra, and the minute they saw me our troubles were over, because they were convinced that by leading them during the retreat, I had saved their lives. At once they assured me, 'You and your friends don't have to worry about food. We'll take care of it.' And in fact we did eat well for a while."

Still, they just barely managed to hang on, coping with joblessness, cold, hunger, and tensions between the military government and the populace. To add to their misery, there was a massive Luftwaffe bombardment on March 13 and 14, causing more than three hundred civilian deaths near the port. And if that weren't enough, on May 19 Mount Vesuvius awakened with its last eruption of the twentieth century. The cinders, ash, and lava mounted with each passing day, engulfing nearby towns and finally threatening Dino's hometown of Torre Annunziata.

Through it all, Dino had never stopped thinking about the cinema. Anticipating the moment he'd be able to return to work, he persuaded his friends to write stories and treatments, promising to compensate them handsomely once he was back in business. He obtained a few scattered scripts, and while he never did actually pay for them, he saved them for years in the hope that something might be done with them—and in memory of that period of enforced bohemianism.

On May 18, 1944, the Allies conquered the summit of Monte Cassino, and the German troops on the Anzio front were on the verge of surrender. The road to Rome was finally open. Dino and his companions learned, to their enormous relief, that on the evening of June 4 units of the Eighty-eighth Division had liberated the capital. A few days later, thanks to Soldati—who, at Dino's insistence, had asserted his status as the husband of an American woman—our stragglers obtained a passage to Rome in a jeep driven by a black soldier.

They loaned us a kind of uniform, without shoulder patches, which made us look like military men. And so, after having left disguised as civilians, we finally reentered Rome disguised as American soldiers. We found an absolute void: there was no film, there was nothing. The Italian cinema had died in the war.

CHAPTER 5

BIANCA AND THE BANDIT

WHEN DINO RETURNED TO ROME IN THE SUMMER OF 1944, AFTER TEN months of involuntary exile, what was the city like? His first impression was that things were much the same as before.

> I have a very precise memory of my arrival in the city, because there are certain images that you can never get out of your mind. We walked into Libotte, a restaurant on Via Francesco Crispi, where I always used to go to eat: when I had no money, they gave me credit. I can see it again like a scene in a film: we enter the restaurant and who do we run across? Alida Valli and Mario Camerini, tranquilly seated at a table as if nothing had happened.

It was obviously a very happy encounter. By the end of dinner, however, ugly reality had returned. For starters, there was the bill for the meal, a ruinous sum, and they were lucky to be eating in the first place, since the kitchen was short of almost everything.

In fact, nothing was as it had been before. Between new arrivals from the country and stragglers from the military, the city's population was growing at an incredible rate, and the authorities couldn't ensure an adequate food supply. The trams and buses were still out of commission (jeeps were the main form of transportation), electric power was irregular, the owners of the few functioning telephones were allowed to make only four calls per day. With the black market roaring, stores and houses were looted daily, often on the pretext of political retaliation. Ruthless men shifted seamlessly from the Resistance to criminal activities. The regional administrator of the military government, Colonel Charles Poletti, ordered a curfew from 11 P.M. to 5 A.M. Once a week, Poletti delivered a reassuring radio address to the populace, but clearly the initial enthusiasm for the liberators was on the wane. And the movie theaters? At first they screened leftovers, including an assortment of old American films. Then came the arrival of *Sergeant York* with Gary Cooper, which sold out every night.

Dino had one goal: to start producing movies again.

Under Poletti's orders, Cinecittà had been converted into a shelter for the homeless, who numbered in the tens of thousands throughout the city. The technical equipment had already been plundered—first by the Fascists, who carted off whatever they could to furnish yet another of Mussolini's cinematic follies in Venice, and then by the Nazis. The studio was a wreck. The newspapers ran articles talking up the resurrection of Italian cinema, but nothing happened. Meanwhile Dino was itching to return to work.

He joined forces with Marcello d'Amico, the amiable older son of the famous film critic Silvio d'Amico. Marcello was a fledgling attorney with little enthusiasm for a legal career; he too would eventually become a producer, sacrificing a good part of his family fortune in the process. While they waited for the cinema to show some signs of life, the two decided to try their hand at theatrical comedy, which was currently in vogue.

The script for *Il suo cavallo* (*His Horse*) was a merry, pungent satire on the defunct regime. Dino and Marcello produced it together, borrowing a million lire from Riccardo Gualino of Lux and enlisting the usual suspects as collaborators. Soldati, Longanesi, and Vanzina knocked out the script, while Renato Castellani stepped in to direct. Yet Dino also pulled in top-drawer talent of every kind. The music, for example, was supplied by Nino Rota. The soliloquizing Paolo Stoppa played Mussolini's white horse, and Carlo Campanini spared nothing in his mocking caricature of the dictator (who was then still alive, courtesy of the Nazi-sponsored Salò Republic). In addition, the production included twenty changes of scenery and innumerable costumes.

His Horse, which made its debut on September 4 at the Valle, turned out to be that theater's biggest fiasco since the opening night of Pirandello's *Six Characters in Search of an Author*. Critics deplored the play's intellectual excess, and Dino found himself in complete agreement. At once he summoned a pair of hacks to make the script more acceptable. Vanzina took offense at several ostentatiously vulgar additions, including a scene (acclaimed by his colleagues) in which Stoppa, Campanini, and the austere Sergio Tofano, a grand old man of the theater, sang "Lili Marlene" dressed as whores. The public, in any case, wasn't buying: although northern Italy remained in the hands of Mussolini's puppet government, the traditionally cynical Romans were already tired of anti-Fascist humor, preferring to laugh at the Americans instead.

In October the partners dissolved their production company. Dino made a last attempt to salvage the remnants of the show, moving it to a theater in Naples. But *His Horse* remained a financial catastrophe, which created numerous headaches for the producer and led him to make a private vow regarding the theater: *never again*. It was a promise he would keep.

Now De Laurentiis holed up in the little apartment he'd rented at Via Gregoriana 48. Some days he lacked enough money to eat and the porter, Oliviero, who had figured out the situation, would respectfully bring him a modest meal, explaining that he wanted him to taste his wife's delicious cooking. Once his fortunes changed, Dino wouldn't forget Oliviero: he put him to work as head electrician on numerous films.

After his brilliant early career, the disaster of *His Horse* must have been something of a shock. But Dino never wasted time licking his wounds; his economic anxieties required solutions, not blame. While he surveyed the situation and waited for opportunity to knock, there was little to do but go to the cinema to watch the new arrivals from overseas and try to keep tabs on the latest tastes and techniques. It was in front of a cinema—the Quirinetta, much frequented by film people and intellectuals because it showed the movies in their original versions—that he met Bianca Maria Da Paolis, his future wife.

It must have been an afternoon in October 1944. We can imagine Bianca, twenty at the most, dismounting her bicycle, dark-haired and radiant and draped in one of those flowered dresses so familiar from photographs of the era. Enchanted by this apparition, Dino asked Marcello d'Amico to introduce him. His friend obliged, saying: "Here is a person who finds you very beautiful."

Accustomed to arousing masculine interest, Bianca didn't blink an eye. As far as she was concerned, the casual encounter might have ended right there, with a gallant compliment and fleeting glance of admiration. But Dino couldn't get this woman out of his head. He embarked on an intense courtship, complete with flowers and love notes. Bianca was already engaged—to an older doctor and friend of the family, whom she didn't love—and so she was initially reluctant. But the two began to see each other and the sparks flew, to such an extent that Dino asked her to move into his apartment, a single room with a bath and tiny kitchen and rudimentary furnishings. This became the scene of their impassioned affair, not to mention their first quarrels.

Because she didn't live with her family but lodged with an English cousin, Bianca enjoyed unusual freedom to come and go as she pleased. She was a "nice girl," the well-brought-up daughter of a bank director, yet she had a tormented history. Her mother, Maria Antonietta, beautiful and high-strung, had died when she was very young, and her father had remarried a woman with a prickly temperament. Bianca had never developed a warm relationship with her stepmother and frequently relied on the peacemaking efforts of Uncle Nino Papa, her late mother's brother. To complicate matters further, there were also two stepsisters—a detail right out of a fairy tale—and though they weren't evil, they were showered with all the affection and privilege denied to Bianca. Her well-meaning father proved too weak to stand up for his first-born daughter. Given this atmosphere, it's no wonder that Bianca was little disposed to accept orders and limitations from anybody.

In the beginning, of course, Dino knew nothing of these childhood traumas. When he first learned of them, this child of a serene and reassuring family may have felt a certain fascination with Bianca's difficulties. Certainly Dino's attraction to temperamental women, which would persist for many years, seems to clash sharply with his own sunny, pragmatic character: it's like a hairline crack in his customary rationalism. But in that early phase of his relationship with Bianca, passion conquered all.

All, that is, except for Dino's professional woes. These too, however, began to improve. Lux finally reopened its doors and Dino, along with Marcello d'Amico, returned to producing with *Le miserie del signor Travet* (*His Young Wife*). The script had been caught in the nets of the Fascist censors; its author, playwright Tullio Pinelli, would later become a collaborator of Fellini's. The story recounted the multiple frustrations of a modest worker, played by Carlo Campanini (after his turn as Mussolini in *Il suo cavallo*). Soldati directed, enthusiastic about this opportunity to re-create a Roman version of his native Turin, which was then still occupied by the Germans. Between the artificial fog and phony snow of the exteriors, which had been reconstructed at the Farnesina studios, and a handful of venerable palaces in the Prati quarter, the illusion was perfect.

Early 1945 was a difficult time to make a film in Rome. Like Roberto Rossellini, who was shooting *Roma, Città Aperta* (Open City) at the very same time, Dino had to cope with dicey electrical power, expired film stock, and dwindling funds. Yet our hero, having jumped through innumerable hoops, was rewarded for the first time with his name in the opening titles: *Produced by Dino De Laurentiis.* When the film came out in December, it won praise and prizes. Gino Cervi, marvelously enjoyable as the haughty, paternalistic department head, received one of the very first Silver Ribbons, an award presented by the National Syndicate of Italian Film Journalists.

Travet also marked Dino's first encounter with Alberto Sordi. The actor, who would work with him for many years, already had a grip on what would become his classic character, frantic and meddlesome. It seems Sordi modeled his behavior on Soldati's, spoofing the director's mercurial moods and frenzies.

Meanwhile, although Dino and Bianca fought fiercely, their relationship moved forward. The young woman was always with De Laurentiis: she sought him out on the set, and in the evenings they ate out with his friends, who were (and would always be) his colleagues. The two seemed very much in love. Their affair seemed to satisfy other needs as well: Bianca was looking for an escape hatch from her oppressive family situation, and Dino was "carnally attracted" (his own phrase) to a degree he had never before experienced. The attraction, which would take some time to exhaust itself, kept him from even glancing at another woman.

To general jubilation, the war in Europe ended on May 8, 1945. It was now possible to think in terms of a reunited Italy—and to do business in the northern half of the peninsula. Hoping to recover a little of his lost funds, Dino decided to bring *Il suo cavallo* to Milan, and he asked Bianca to come with him.

This created a problem. Bianca may have been used to doing whatever she pleased, but in that era, it was still a major transgression to run off with a man. How could she justify the trip in her father's eyes and keep him calm? "Find an excuse," suggested Dino.

"The only possible excuse," she replied, "is that we're going to get married."

"Tell him whatever you want, as long as you can come to Milan with me." (Or so Dino recalls. Bianca insists that they had actually discussed getting married. From this point on, in any case, the contrasting accounts by the two protagonists differ so dramatically as to assume a Pirandellian flavor.)

> Our arrival in Milan was a disaster. What we found there was wind, snow, nasty weather. I became seriously ill with bronchial pneumonia. I was forced to drop our booking at the theater; I gave up the entire enterprise and entrusted somebody (I don't remember who) with the task of mopping up the mess. Do whatever you like, I told him, send everybody home. The doctors admitted me to the hospital, where they began the treatment, which at that time was a long one: it took weeks.

While Dino's condition grew worse and worse, the director Alberto Lattuada arrived from Rome with a film project, *Il reduce* (*The Survivor*). The producer Carlo Ponti—who would later form a partnership with Dino—had already passed on the idea. De Laurentiis, however, liked the story: returning home to Turin during the war, a soldier finds his house destroyed by bombs and his sister reduced to prostitution. When she is killed, he reacts by transforming himself into a bandit, living out a typical postwar tragedy of the kind that filled the Italian newspapers of the day.

Lattuada later recalled their unconventional meeting: "De Laurentiis was in the hospital in Milan. I called him and a nun summoned him to the phone. . . . 'Are you sick?' I said. 'I'll come right over.' 'Sure, I'm sick,' he said, 'but don't worry about it, I'll produce the film, it's fine.' He was practically speaking in a whisper! I went to find him in one of those disastrous hospitals of the era. He was wearing a little gown. 'Listen,' he immediately said to me, 'we have to make the film with Magnani.'" Clearly Dino's recovery was not yet complete, but soon after, Bianca insinuated herself into Allied circles and managed to wangle some penicillin, which proved to be an effective cure.

> The story of *The Bandit* (I changed the title) appealed to me at once, because it conformed to my vision of the cinema at that time: a vanquished Italy, emerging from both the German and American occupations, would provide one of those human stories that turn out to be universal. Meanwhile, there were other problems to deal with. When I was finally able to get out of bed, I was still very weak. I told Bianca that in order to make the film, we needed to move on to Turin—to the Hotel Sitea, where they would give me credit. There I would be able to recover my strength with the aid of a trustworthy doctor and to begin looking around for a way to set things up. At that moment I had no idea where to find financial backing. When you're sick, you can't get much done, and those treatments had depressed me.

However debilitated, Dino was back on the job. He soon found a partner in the person of Luigi Rovere, a self-made man who wanted to get into film production, despite his wife's fierce opposition. Dino took an instant liking to him. After all, Rovere was cut from a similar cloth: born to a working-class family, he had already become a seasoned craftsman by age twenty, when he constructed a small factory for the production of liquor cabinets with built-in radios. The two formed a company, RDL (for Rovere–De Laurentiis), and immediately got under way with *The Bandit.* Playing on Lattuada's eagerness to return to work, Dino offered him a modest five hundred thousand lire to write and direct the film, and he additionally insisted that Lattuada enlist his wife, the actress Carla Del Poggio, in the project. Then, taking further advantage of his friend's presence in Turin, Dino asked him to be a witness at his wedding. He had decided to marry Bianca.

The simple, private ceremony took place at 10 A.M. on December 16, 1945, at the Beata Vergine degli Angeli church on Via Carlo Alberto, right next to the Sitea. The bride wore a child's overcoat with a fur collar, while the groom recalls that he could hardly stay on his feet.

> When I was still in the hospital in Milan, Bianca told me that she was pregnant: "How am I going to tell my father?" I really liked the girl and the idea of a son was very tempting. Until that moment the idea of marrying her hadn't even occurred to me, nor the idea of getting married in general, because I didn't have the economic means to support a family. But when I heard that she was expecting

a child, like a good Neapolitan I decided that we would get married as soon as we arrived in Turin.

We got married, and the moment approached when I would have to go back to Rome and cast the film. At this point Bianca told me that there was no longer a baby on the way. What did that mean? That there never was one? Or that something had happened? Whatever it was, our relationship moved onto slippery ground at that precise instant—at least for me.

Bianca has a different story: "I was never pregnant, and I never told Dino anything of the kind. He married me because he was crazy in love with me; when we left for Milan, we had already planned the whole thing, to the extent that he even made promises to my father. It's true, though, that I never had any intention of having children and that I wasn't mature enough for marriage."

Feeling like a dupe, Dino returned to Rome to cast *The Bandit*. The relationship was still involving on a sexual level, at least, and his work continued to absorb all his attention. Reclaiming his office at Lux and extracting an advance of 2 million lire from Gualino, he immediately signed up Italy's most popular actress, Anna Magnani. He went to her with a check in his hand, one she couldn't refuse: a million lire, which was all the spare cash he had. Then the debate over the male protagonist began.

Lattuada wanted Andrea Checchi, and I didn't agree. I said, "He was fine in *Malombra*, there's no doubt about his acting, but nobody knows who he is. We can't make the first great postwar film with a name that means nothing to the public." Then I proposed an experiment to Alberto: "Let's go down to the street, to the market, wherever you like, and take a survey. Let's see who knows Checchi and who knows Amedeo Nazzari (an Italian leading man)." It was easy to predict the outcome. I always try to convince the director without imposing my own will; that's not my style. I try to make them see my point of view, and I indicate that I'm willing to be convinced otherwise. The moral of the story: Nazzari won the ballot. We made the film with him and Anna Magnani, in Turin, on the streets and in live locations, with very limited technical means. And since we often ran out of film stock, we had to print from negatives, because the positives didn't exist.

The shooting began in May, on a series of almost arbitrary locations, without any sound equipment. The dialogue was then deciphered from the script girl's notes and dubbed in at the Moviola, via a sort of reverse lip-reading.

Various anecdotes have been passed down in regard to this eventful production. One involves the gifted cameraman Aldo Tonti, whose commitment to another film in Milan delayed his arrival: Dino, on the strength of a signed contract, sent two gun-toting *carabinieri* from Turin to fetch him. (Some witnesses insist that they were actually extras in costumes.) Meanwhile, the movie camera that De Laurentiis had borrowed from the Ministry of Defense ran on batteries, and on any given day, the production lacked enough funds to buy additional supplies. This meant that Tonti was often forced to crank the camera by hand, as he had in his apprentice days. He knew from long experience that to obtain the requisite twenty-four frames per second, the cranking tempo should approximate that of the Fascist hymn "Giovinezza." So when it came time to film the death of the protagonist's sister—the most tragic scene in the movie—Tonti hummed the defunct regime's anthem throughout the entire take.

There were other snags too, none of which rattled the producer, who was determined to show everybody what he was made of. Confronted by a strike, he filled in as head electrician and didn't lose an hour of production. To speed things up, he also offered his services as an extra: he can be seen toward the beginning of the film, leaving a bar. Nor was he intimidated by Magnani's wild explosions. His star was more tired and nervous than usual, because she was appearing in a theatrical review at the same time as she shot the movie. Still, Dino didn't even flinch when Magnani, having had three or four glasses of fake vodka thrown in her face by her leading man, hurled herself at Nazzari and accused him of trying to blind her. All that interested him was getting to the end: making a successful film. Well aware that his entire future might hinge on the outcome, he was ready for anything.

> One day I was at Lux and I said to Gatti, "We need to come up with some way to promote this film." I've always been of the opinion that you can make the most beautiful movie in the world, but if you don't have the right promotion and don't release it at the

> right moment, it will vanish after a week. Back then the only form of publicity was the poster. My idea was this: there were bandits on the Italian streets and they were robbing people. There was one in particular—his name doesn't come to mind—who was working the highway between Rome and Naples, kidnapping prominent figures and demanding a ransom. Being a lunatic (and quite young!), I thought, "I'll get in my car and drive from Rome to Naples at night, and this guy will kidnap me, and the headlines will read, 'Producer of "The Bandit" Is Kidnapped by Bandit So-and-So.' Then, with my typical savoir-faire, I'll convince him to let me go, maybe even tell him the whole story." But my plan didn't work. No matter how many times I drove back and forth between Rome and Naples, nobody kidnapped me.

Released in October 1946, the film was a great success. It also showcased Amedeo Nazzari in a completely new role, bitter and problematical, which won him a Silver Ribbon and kicked off a further stage in his career. Italy's leading star until the fall of Mussolini, the actor had been worried that he would never regain his supremacy. His gratitude to Dino was lasting: he made several more films with him, including *Nights of Cabiria*, in which he took Fellini's self-ironic style to heart and risked making fun of himself.

> Nazzari had some mysterious difficulties with women. All he could do with them was get drunk and quarrel, in exactly the way Fellini depicted him. The fact is that Nazzari was well aware of being a temperamental leading man: he was the only Italian actor you could describe that way. He had a little problem with booze, but he drank in the evening, after work. On the set he was sober, serious, friendly. But I couldn't say that we knew one another well, that we really shared anything. I'm not even sure we ever went out to dinner together.

CHAPTER 6

THE END OF A MARRIAGE

AFTER SHOOTING *THE BANDIT*, DINO AND BIANCA RETURNED TO ROME. It was already summer, and they had been away nearly a year. While his work would no doubt demand many future road trips, it was time to stop living like gypsies. First the couple moved from the Via Gregoriana apartment, which was too small, to Bianca's grandmother's house at Via Olana 7. From there they would soon relocate to the Parioli neighborhood, to a lovely apartment owned by Bianca's uncle, who was in Lisbon. Business continued to pick up, and soon Dino was able to permit himself the luxury of a maid and a cook.

The couple often went out to a Tuscan restaurant in Piazza Poli, mostly in the company of Lattuada and Carla Del Poggio; Mario Camerini and his irresistible wife, Tully Hruska; Soldati and *his* wife, Jucci; and Sergio Amidei, who vainly paid court to Bianca. (He wasn't the only one: they all liked her.) There were also regular visits with their respective clans. At Dino's affectionate urging, most of his family now lived in Rome, and his brothers, Luigi and Alfredo, had already begun to work at his side.

> This has truly been one of the luckiest things in my life: to work side by side with my brothers. Among the seven of us siblings, Luigi has always been the best. An excellent student, he got degrees in law and foreign languages in Naples: he specialized in Bulgarian and won a scholarship to go study the language in Sofia. There he had great success as the editor of a magazine of cinema and culture, which unified the country's intellectuals, and met his future wife, Maria Rendina, who worked at the Italian embassy. But as the war

went on and the bombardments took their toll, he was forced to flee, sacrificing everything he had accomplished in Bulgaria.

Returning to Italy, he met up again with Maria, married her, and immediately began to work with me. He was an extraordinary advisor. I asked him to oversee the construction of the Dinocittà studios, and I must say that without his help, I might not have been able to get the job done. He followed me everywhere, giving me valuable advice, until I left for the United States. At that point Luigi began to produce on his own, flanked by his son Aurelio—who, continuing the family tradition, has steadily established himself as one of the most important Italian producers.

As for Alfredo, the younger, I have some vague and distant memories of him as a boy. He was eighteen years old, if even that, when he fell in love with a Neapolitan girl, the daughter of a colonel in the customs department who was a cousin of my father's. In their wrath, both my papa and the colonel tried to convince him to break things off. Alfredo fled Naples and came to Rome, and from that time on he remained with me. I introduced him to the cinema, and at once he intuitively understood the organizational problems, and in short, he became my right-hand man. I can say without fear of error that he came to be the best director of production in all of Italy. He had a single vice: he was a compulsive gambler. He wagered everything, like De Sica. All his earnings went to gambling, until he lost all the money he had and some that he didn't have. I scolded him all the time, but there was nothing you could do. And yet I would pay anything to have him here still, with all his debts, and I would pay anything to have Luigi here too.

Bianca's family welcomed her husband with affection and respect. All of them, from her father to her grandmother (who already doted on her extraordinary grandson-in-law), were convinced that he had a great career ahead of him. Dino was very fond of Uncle Nino Papa and was always delighted to visit his villa on Via Appia.

The young couple seemed to share a happy life, but Dino felt that their quarrels were beginning to outweigh their moments of passion.

At home we had two sabers hanging on the wall. One morning after a night of love, we were fighting for some reason, and Bianca took one of them down. Then I grabbed the other. I didn't have the courage to start slashing, but she did; in fact I still have the scar. It was a crazy thing: she could have taken my eye out. At that point I realized that even though everything was still marvelous in bed, if we kept going on this way, she would kill me, or I would kill her.

What's more, Dino had a growing conviction, shared by various friends of the time, that Bianca had married him in part because she had ambitions to become an actress. Bianca insists that the exact opposite is true. According to her, she lacked even the slightest interest in such a career, and it was Dino who pushed her into it, going so far as to set up an audition when the director Gianni Franciolini was casting *Notte di tempesta*. Soldati attended the audition, which took place on the island of Ischia, and dispensed plenty of advice. Nothing panned out: evidently Bianca's jaw-dropping beauty failed to translate into much of a screen presence.

In the meantime, the couple did some traveling together. Italy had been devastated by the war: many roads were impassable and bridges destroyed. Nonetheless, Dino loved to travel by car, and as soon as he could afford it, he bought a big American convertible, in which he and Bianca roamed the length and breadth of the peninsula. There were trips to visit his sisters, who still lived in Torre Annunziata. Sometimes Dino took Bianca along to various locations where his films were being shot.

And in September 1946, there was the Venice Film Festival along with its brand-new French counterpart in Cannes. Despite his youth, Dino appeared at the latter as an official representative of the Italian film industry, as well as the producer of two movies in competition: *Travet* and *Il bandito*.

That year, however, *Open City* triumphed. In Bianca's recollection, Rossellini lacked the nerve to attend the screening and remained outside, seated at a café with a friend. He got fidgety, though, and toward the end he sent his companion inside on a reconnaissance mission, which resulted in the news of his victory: inside, the entire audience was weeping and cheering. Dino was nowhere to be seen. Perhaps he was at the casino: to his wife's regret, he had discovered a passion for roulette.

In any case, *Il bandito* still made an excellent impression. The French poet Paul Eluard sang its praises, and the Communist critic Georges Sadoul was prompted to speak of a "new style" in *L'humanité*. Given this wave of recognition, De Laurentiis and Rovere found

Lux more than willing to bump the ultimate production costs up to 18 million lire. Since they had spent only 12 million on the actual film, the two partners rubbed their hands in glee at having made such a killing. But the real winner turned out to be Gualino: *Il bandito* grossed 184 million lire nationwide and was the fourth-biggest box-office performer of the year.

What's more, this success came in the face of opposition from neo-Fascists and conservative elements in the government. There was a mounting campaign, supported both openly and in secret by the censor's office, against the emergent neorealist cinema; these warts-and-all stylists had committed the ultimate sin of revealing Italy's miseries to the world. Characteristically, Dino steered clear of these polemics as much as possible. What concerned him was defending his rights as a producer.

> They called us hacks. The government, at least some of the time, put up with us, despite the fact that they disliked the cinema and the people involved in it. Why did they dislike us? Because we gave the impression of making antigovernment films. And because up until then, nobody understood the power of a successful movie.
>
> But during the postwar years, when the Italian film industry had been killed off by the German and American occupations, there suddenly appeared a new group of filmmakers: ourselves. We looked around and discovered these extraordinary stories of real life. We managed to film them in the most makeshift way, in that dimension of absolute poverty that the critics then christened neorealism. Look, we shot on the streets because we didn't have a single penny. We had nothing: only ideas and enthusiasm. And in this way we made films that found audiences everywhere and became part of cinematic history. It was by means of this calling card that we regained most of the world's sympathy. I would argue that the cinema was the first great ambassador of Italy in defeat. As I see it, the cinema also touched off Italy's postwar economic boom: foreigners saw one of our movies and it made them want to know us better, to visit our country and buy our products.

Between October 1946 and April 1948, as Italian life rapidly returned to normal, Dino wrote regular letters to his partner on Via Barbaroux in Turin. These allow us to reconstruct what was going on at RDL, and they give a real sense of the period. Here, for example, is the opening of a letter dated October 10, 1946: "Dear Luigi: This is the first letter I'm writing on the portable Olivetti I bought in Rome, at list price, just like in Turin: 27,000 lire. I'm billing that amount to RDL, although I plan to resell the typewriter in Buenos Aires for cash."

Dino was about to leave for South America to prepare for the film *Anita Garibaldi*, whose story had been roughed out by his brother Luigi and the writer Carlo Alianello. His successive letters give a good picture of the relationship between his production company and Lux, which shouldered 70 percent of Dino's costs. On October 19 he informed Rovere that he was departing "with high hopes and best wishes." He added, "In case my wife should need anything, I told her to contact you. Regarding anything else, I've left instructions with my brother Luigi." Dino would have liked to travel with Bianca, who'd been preparing for the trip with Spanish lessons, but at the last minute he left alone, because the tickets were too expensive. In any case, it would have been difficult for his wife to leave Rome; her father was suffering from a serious illness, which would claim his life within a matter of weeks.

Dino reached Rio de Janeiro after twenty-two hours of travel. Immediately he told Rovere that he would like to establish a company to import and export films between Italy and South America. This was his first voyage overseas, after all, and he grew inebriated by the thousand and one marketing possibilities a new continent seemed to offer him. As he wrote his partner on October 23 from Buenos Aires, "Here there's a great deal to do in many areas, including your furniture business."

Dino also tried to find a South American buyer for *Quattro passi tra le nuvole* and several other Italian films to which he had acquired the rights. He asked the price of everything, seemed dazzled by a hundred different prospects, and in a letter dated November 9, told Rovere to expect a very important contract "that will make us a heap of money." In the same letter, meanwhile, he lamented the fact that they had sold Lux the rights to *Il bandito*: "Here they're anticipating box-office receipts of 500,000 Argentinean pesos, which is to say 50 million lire. I'll never stop feeling like a moron over this. We'll just have to deal with it. Patience!" Dino made no headway with *Anita Garibaldi*. The Mexican diva Maria Felix, upon whom the coproduction depended, turned out to be unavailable when they would need her: the film was postponed and ultimately canceled.

Dino returned to Turin on December 11 and then continued to Rome. In a letter of January 2, 1947, he proposed a backup project, *La figlia del capitano* (*The Captain's Daughter*), to Rovere:

> If, as it seems, we're forced to put *Anita* on hold, then let's make this film immediately. Read Pushkin's novella, because at the moment I can't send you the screenplay. Right now we're discussing the budget, which is pretty high—more than 50 million lire. . . . If the Lawyer [Gualino] accepts the budget, we'll go ahead, otherwise we'll think of something else. In any case, I fixed RDL's share of the costs at thirty percent, like I did on *Anita*, because the expenses are really too great: the film will run at least 40 million lire. I've convinced Camerini and Gatti [Gualino's second-in-command] to shoot it in Turin, and as soon as we have a solid screenplay and budget, we'll come up there to scout locations. Think about how we can reconstruct an entire Russian village in the snow.

Dino and Camerini arrived in Turin at the end of January to review the available actors and inspect locations for the exteriors, but in the end they decided to shoot the film elsewhere. The Russian village of Belogorsk was meticulously reconstructed forty miles southwest of Rome, near Nettuno, and the work moved forward steadily, sometimes without regard to cost. It was the first "literary" film that Dino produced, and he drew on everything he had learned while working on *Malombra*. He urged everybody to read the Pushkin novella and tried to stick faithfully to his source. On August 12 De Laurentiis wrote a triumphant letter to his partner:

> *La figlia del capitano* is a knockout. I can assure you that the result is better than anything I had foreseen, and aside from its artistic qualities, it's undoubtedly a film destined to earn a big wad of cash. Tonti, who is here now, has a sly smile beneath his mustache. I'm very happy. Gualino called me yesterday to discuss a few things regarding the film's presentation at Cannes and rather cleverly asked if we were willing to sell our share of the gross. I replied that although we were hoodwinked once, it wasn't so easy to hoodwink us a second time.

In September 1947 *La figlia del capitano* followed in the footsteps of *Il bandito* at Cannes: that is, it won no jury prize but was widely acclaimed by the public. The weekly magazine *L'Écran Français* crowned the protagonist, Irasema Dilian, "queen of the day," and before descending into obscurity, she did enjoy a fleeting moment of fame.

As her husband proceeded from one triumph to the next, Bianca both followed in his wake and attempted to carve out her own space. She was ultimately drawn to the idea of being an actress (perhaps in the theater, since her movie audition hadn't worked out), so she took elocution lessons. Her big chance seemed to arrive in the summer of 1947, when she was invited to participate as a guest in the Sharoff Academy's annual production. Bianca was cast in the role of Elsa in Frank Wedekind's *Spring Awakening*. In a review of the opening night on July 27, one newspaper noted that the public had mobbed the Eliseo Theater mostly out of curiosity "to see De Laurentiis's wife act." The comment deflated all of the aspiring actress's hopes (and demonstrated the prominent place the young producer had achieved in the Italian theater world). At the same time, the romance between Dino and Bianca was approaching its rancorous and predictable conclusion:

> Things weren't working out, and I even had a vague suspicion that Bianca was cheating on me. I decided that the moment had come to put an end to our relationship. I said nothing to her, though, because otherwise we would have had some ugly fights, and at that point I just wanted to get it over with. I thought, "If I tell her we're breaking up, she could have two reactions. Either she'll agree, or we'll end up killing each other." The memory of that saber duel was still vivid.
>
> So I put together a plan. Taking advantage of the fact that she really loved to ski, I suggested that she spend a week up at Sestriere. "I'll reserve a nice sleeping compartment for you and arrange things at the hotel," I said. "You spend some time up there, relax, and when you come back, we'll talk a little more calmly about our problems." She gave me a big hug, and at the station I said goodbye as though nothing were going on. "*Ciao, buon viaggio*, call me tomorrow!" I returned home, packed my bags, and gave the maid her instructions (she was a redhead, and I can never trust myself around redheads): "Tomorrow when the signora calls, tell her that I've left and that she needs to get in touch with this lawyer."
>
> I named Bianca's lawyer, not mine: it was easier to inform *her* legal advisor that I was trashing the marriage. I told him bluntly, "We don't get along any more. When we fight, it's at risk of life and

> limb, and after everything that's happened, I feel nothing for her. She probably feels nothing for me either, and perhaps she never did. I'm still young, it's too early for me to ruin my life. I want a separation. I want out."
>
> Working through the lawyers, and without ever crossing paths with my wife, I quickly got what I wanted. Despite all the misery, I was lucky to have been married in Turin, because I had no problem obtaining a divorce in Switzerland, at Mendrisio: Turin is the only Italian city that allows you to divorce under Swiss jurisdiction.

At first, Bianca made no objection. But when it came to the annulment before an ecclesiastical court, she dug in her heels and refused to cooperate. According to protocol, she would be obliged to declare that before the marriage, she and Dino agreed not to have children. She insisted this was a falsehood and she refused to lie to a religious tribunal. Instead, the annulment would take place nearly twenty years later, in 1966. By then, according to Bianca's version, she agreed to the necessary declaration only "at the cost of great sacrifice." Dino sees it differently: "That was when she understood that the annulment would be to her advantage as well."

After he packed his bags and left, Dino would encounter Bianca only twice, both times by accident. On the first occasion, recalls Dino's daughter Raffaella, Bianca wasn't even aware of his presence. This was during the late 1960s, in a fashionable restaurant on the Côte d'Azur. The producer's companion, Silvana Mangano, suddenly pointed her finger with an imperious gesture and said, "Look, your wife!" Raffaella, then quite young, glanced up to see an enchanting woman at some distance from their table, wearing a black sequined dress.

The second time was in Switzerland, in the company of Kurt Hruska, the brother of Camerini's wife, Tully, and dentist to Mussolini, not to mention three different popes.

> I had gone to Geneva for a hernia operation; this would have been in 1975 or 1976. While I was convalescing, I had a visit from Kurt Hruska, who not only looks after my teeth but is a great friend. By now it was a custom: whenever I needed Kurt, he would join me wherever I was, because I trusted nobody else. That day we had gone out for a coffee, since I was now able to walk, however slowly. At the bar we ran into Bianca and Kurt began to say,

> "May I introduce—" And I said, "You want to introduce me to my ex-wife?"

An epilogue: while she was in Rome for the production of *Daylight* in 1996, Raffaella got the idea of seeking out the first Signora De Laurentiis, whom she had never met. Although Bianca seemed invariably to be in transit between London, Geneva, and Miami, Raffaella managed to track her down. The two met, took a liking to each other, and exchanged confidences. When she returned to Los Angeles, Raffaella showed Dino a photo of her and Bianca together, and asked him, "Do you know who this is?" At first, after so much time, Dino was stumped. Then he recognized his ex-wife and demanded an update. As it turned out, Bianca had had a second marriage—again brief—to an American film producer named Jack Levien, who was later confined to a wheelchair. A third marriage, to the Swiss multimillionaire Gualtiero Giori, lasted ten years: they had two sons, who in turn made Bianca the adoring grandmother of six grandchildren. Then came a fourth marriage, to an Englishman of ancient lineage, Lord Shaftsbury. Much younger than his exotic wife, and famous for having scaled the summit of the Himalayas, he introduced her to Britain's crowned heads. This marriage too ultimately ended in divorce. Upon hearing that Bianca had taken tea at Buckingham Palace, Dino commented, "I knew she would never get lost in the shuffle, because she was a hell of a girl." Bianca adds, "Tell Dino that of all my husbands, he's undoubtedly the biggest success."

CHAPTER 7

SILVANA

DINO NOW FACED NOT ONE BUT TWO SEPARATIONS. HIS MARRIAGE TO Bianca had ended painfully and now his partnership with Rovere was also coming to an end, albeit on a more friendly note. In November 1947 he founded Dino De Laurentiis Studios, with its offices at Via Tevere 1.

The former furniture manufacturer, bitten by the cinematic bug, struck out on his own. Rovere would make a couple of important movies with Germi, nudge Fellini into his directorial debut with *Lo sceicco bianco (The White Sheik)*, and win recognition and prizes. All went well for him until the mid-1950s, when a string of ill-fated films and some exorbitant sums borrowed from film producer Angelo Rizzoli put him out of business. Like Marcello d'Amico, Rovere discovered that the path of cinematic production was full of pitfalls. All it took was a step or two in the wrong direction to bring about disaster. Dino, it seems, was the exception: he would prove himself capable, when confronted by mishaps, of making extraordinary efforts to get himself out of a hole.

At this point, destiny steered Dino toward two fateful encounters. First, Lux entrusted him with the film that would spread his name around the world. And on the set of that very film, *Riso amaro* (*Bitter Rice*), our hero would encounter Silvana Mangano.

At the dawn of 1948, Silvana was essentially an illustrious unknown. Just shy of eighteen, she worked as a model for a fashion house run by the Mascetti sisters in Via Veneto. Professionally speaking, all she had to her credit was an appearance in the 1946 Miss Rome contest and a few bit parts on the screen.

Her father, Amedeo, a handsome man of Sicilian extraction, was a railroad conductor, while Ivy Webb, her equally attractive mother, hailed from a modest English family in Sussex. The Mangano clan, which lived on Via Mirandola in the working-class Tuscolana neighborhood, was perpetually short of cash. There were four growing children—Silvana; her older brother, Roy; and her younger sisters, Patrizia and Natascia—and the war only increased the financial pinch. Shy and reserved since adolescence, Silvana always insisted that she made her initial, fleeting appearances on the screen solely to earn a little money.

When the opportunity arose to make *Bitter Rice*, dreams of stardom were the last thing on her mind. Instead she was consumed by her unhappy love for a well-to-do young man, who reciprocated her feelings—but not enough to rebel against his family and marry a girl from an inferior social class. On the heels of that romantic disaster (or possibly concurrent with it), there was a relationship with the twenty-two-year-old Marcello Mastroianni, who lived in Silvana's neighborhood and was infatuated with her. The two future movie stars dated only for a short period.

In any case, Mangano was cast in *Bitter Rice*. How that happened is a matter of some dispute, with many people eager to take credit for discovering her. To begin with, there was the director Giuseppe De Santis, who came up with the initial idea for the film. Returning from a trip to Paris in September 1947, De Santis found himself in the Milan train station, where he came across flocks of female workers traveling from the rice paddies near Vercelli. The sight aroused his curiosity. Drawn to this multitude of freewheeling women, who were constantly bursting into song, the young director had to question them, hear their stories. Back in Rome, he talked about the experience with his friend Carlo Lizzani, and together they wrote a treatment entitled *Bitter Rice*, which they brought to Lux.

Dino's account, needless to say, is a little different:

> One day Gatti called me and said, "I want to make a film about the rice pickers. It seems to me there's enough material for an excellent story, plus a little bit of sex—within the accepted limits of

> the situation, of course." I agreed that such a film could be very popular with the Italian public, although we never dreamed it would create such an international sensation. "Who would you like to make it?" I asked Gatti. And he said, "I have in mind a Communist director, a fine one, who I think would do a good job: Giuseppe De Santis. Check him out." I gave De Santis a call. The Communists had a vision all their own, but Peppe understood the potential of the entire spectacle: the rice pickers, the paddies, the Piedmont. . . . We had him write the screenplay.

As it happened, De Santis delivered the script on April 18, 1948, the very day on which the left-wing People's Coalition suffered a crushing electoral defeat. Suddenly the crowd at the Lux office balked at the idea of making a proletarian movie, with a Communist director to boot. The project remained on track only because De Laurentiis threw his weight behind it:

> I was never interested in party politics. Basically I'm a socialist, but I've never labeled myself as such. During the postwar era I felt sympathetic toward various figures in the Christian Democratic Party, and I certainly never shared the Communist position. With De Santis, though, there were no political conflicts. Gualino and I approved the screenplay for *Bitter Rice* because it seemed like a pure and simple story of love and death: if there was an ideological element in there, we never noticed.

The initial candidates for the role of the *mondina*, or rice picker, included Carla Del Poggio, Gina Lollobrigida, Martine Carol, and Lucia Bosè. De Santis has often insisted that somebody had already spoken to him about "this Mangano" and that he had completely forgotten about her until one day he ran into the young woman on Via Veneto. He adds, "The idea of Mangano playing the role was fervently protested by the people at Lux—especially by De Laurentiis, whose opposition was absolute. He kept arguing that this unknown would be real trouble." Dino's response?

> Pure invention! At an earlier point we had lined up Lucia Bosè, who was already a known quantity: she had won the title of Miss

Italy. But I was concerned. I told Peppe, "We'd better be careful here. If we screw up the character of the *mondina*, we screw up the entire movie."

"But what do you have against Bosè?"

"I've got nothing against Bosè; as a woman she's just fine, but I'm worried that she's not plebian enough—that she won't look credible when she starts picking the rice. She's a city type. She doesn't have the air of somebody who can do hard labor in the countryside." We were having this conversation while we strolled along Via Veneto, and as we reached Caffè Rosati we saw posters from the election. On one of these posters there was a photo of a busty, beautiful girl.

"That's her!" I said.

"Who is she?" Peppe asked.

"I don't have the faintest idea," I said, "but this is our *mondina*. She's plebian, she's beautiful, she's likeable, she's fresh, she's young. She's everything we need." I made inquiries; I discovered her name. Her father seemed quite pleased at the idea of some cash coming into the household but predicted that his daughter wouldn't be interested. I asked to speak with her personally, and when her father introduced me, I managed to convince her.

"Look," I said, "this film could be a turning point in your life. You'll earn a nice piece of change, and your family isn't rich. I'm not asking for an immediate answer. Just come to the audition, then you can decide."

"I can't do it," she said.

"Try, and then decide," I said. To make a long story short, we did the audition: it was a stunner, a real stunner. We showed the audition to Gualino, who loved it. In fact, he wanted to sign Silvana to an exclusive contract. Then we completed the cast with Vittorio Gassman and Raf Vallone, who was a former soccer player turned journalist, now appearing in his first film.

To those who recall the pale, diaphanous, and elegant Mangano of more recent years, it may seem strange that she was chosen to portray an earthy country girl. But one glance at the electoral poster that Dino mentions, emblazoned with a curvy and slightly impudent Silvana displaying spread fingers in a V-for-victory sign, and Dino's instinct is confirmed.

The *Bitter Rice* shoot got under way in the summer of 1948. Dino was frustrated because he didn't yet enjoy absolute power over the production and was forced to defer to Guido Gatti.

> I was on a salary at Lux, like Ponti and the others. I wasn't a producer in the complete sense of the word: the real producer-financier of the film was Gualino. What's more, at that point I was obliged to examine and judge screenplays solely on the basis of their budgets. The creative and artistic piece of the equation was Gatti's. It's true that I participated in various meetings and gave my opinion, but I certainly didn't have the last word. The last word was Gatti's; he represented Gualino.

Still, it was Dino who gave the orders out in the field, if we're to trust a telegram from De Santis to Gualino, in which the director threatened to quit the project if the producer kept second-guessing his decisions. Eventually, Gualino had to come up to the location to resolve their quarrels.

Three months of shooting in the summer heat turned out to be long and exhausting. The production was housed near Vercelli in the barracks of a model farm owned by Fiat. From dawn until dusk, the cast and crew stood in the rice paddies, soaking wet, while the local mosquito population feasted. During the off hours, some ventured down the dusty road to Vercelli, but once they arrived, there was nothing to do. Even current events seemed to conspire against the shoot. On July 14 a gunman attempted to murder the Communist official Palmiro Togliatti as he left the parliament in Rome. The entire country teetered on the brink of an explosion, and when the news reached the set, which was dominated by leftists, work shut down for the day.

Nonetheless, there were some pleasant interludes. Dino and his brother Luigi brought in their sister Lina, a gifted cook, to feed the cast and crew, and there were no complaints about the food. Their landlord, Fiat boss Gianni Agnelli, made frequent visits to the set. He was notoriously susceptible to the charms of beautiful women—which in this case meant both the American Doris Dowling and Silvana, the possessor of what one journalist called "the most majestic bosom in Western Europe."

Even Mastroianni, in the hopes of reigniting his relationship with

Silvana, came to visit her on the set. She welcomed him a bit evasively, pleading overwork, and managed to avoid a one-on-one encounter all day. When night fell, Marcello was alone, desolate, and hungry. Finally the actress Anna Maestri came to his rescue, offering him a container of fried fish.

Throughout the entire shoot, Dino made constant trips back to Rome, to confer with Gatti and also to tend to a new project. In his typical, tireless style, he had rented and restored the existing studios on the Farnesina hill, founding a new company called Teatri della Farnesina. At once he put two new films into production; they would come out in rapid succession in the fall. First there was Mario Camerini's *Molti sogni per le strade* (*The Street Has Many Dreams*), a neo-realist comedy starring Magnani and Massimo Girotti. Dino was forced to mediate in the usual daily clashes between the director and the diva. What's more, Magnani was embittered by her failed romance with Roberto Rossellini; she slept very little and arrived on the set with bags under her eyes, a fact that worried Aldo Tonti as he looked through the camera's lens.

Nor was the other work in progress a model of serenity. *Il cavaliere misterioso* (*The Mysterious Rider*) featured Vittorio Gassman as the famous Giacomo Casanova, a role that required not only a great many erotic exploits but athletic ones as well. The director was Riccardo Freda, one of Dino's companions during his wartime rambles. Unfortunately, their relationship was no longer a harmonious one. Freda's behavior was consistently nasty, and De Laurentiis refused to deal with him: it fell to his brother Luigi to run interference and keep the film from collapsing.

Dino was juggling numerous projects while the *Bitter Rice* shoot progressed near Vercelli. But clearly he wasn't too distracted to respond to the charms of the curvaceous *mondina* at the center of the film; as the weeks went by, his bright red Buick came chugging across the rice paddies with increasing frequency.

> During the work on *Bitter Rice*, they were all over Silvana—from Gassman to Vallone to De Santis—and she behaved very well, I must say. I watched her, I liked her, I told myself, "Look what a great piece of ass she is!" While the shoot was going on, however, I

maintained a completely professional attitude. It was only on the last day of work, after the farewell toasts and the champagne, that I said to her, "What are you doing now?"

"I'm going to Turin," she said.

"If you like," I told her, "I'll drive you there and we can continue on to Rome together. How's that?"

She accepted, and during the drive I convinced her to spend a couple of days in Turin with me. She said, "In that case I'll have to pick up a few things." We checked in at the Principi dei Piemonte, I accompanied her with great joy while she made her purchases, and we spent our first night together. It was the beginning, but a beginning that could have been an end too. I returned to Rome thinking that perhaps we wouldn't see each other again. For me it had been one of those lovely adventures that you can have with a beautiful woman.

Bitter Rice was soon ready for release. The preview audience at Lux liked what they saw. Yet the film wasn't released until September 1949—almost a year later. Why the delay? Gualino may have acted to oblige a Christian Democrat politician in exchange for some earlier favor. Now such intrigues seem incredible, but in postwar Italy, the intensifying Cold War made even the earthy and independent *mondina* an object of fear. When the film finally came out, the left-wing press panned it, condemning the director's melodramatic take on rural labor. (Indulging in some melodrama of his own, the editor of *L'unità* would write, "It's as if De Santis had slapped me.")

However, the delay surrounding *Bitter Rice* didn't prevent the management at Lux from launching Mangano's next film; indeed, they had high hopes for their new star. Her second project was *Il lupo della Sila* (*The Lure of the Sila*), another rural melodrama, this one set in the Calabrian mountains. Gatti insisted that Dino oversee this film and the later ones with Mangano, since he had discovered her and knew how to handle her. Meanwhile, his fleeting adventure with Silvana had gradually become something more:

One evening when I was having dinner with the director Duilio Coletti, Silvana, and two screenwriters, Perilli and Mario Monicelli, I announced that we'd be leaving the next morning to scout locations in Calabria. She said, "I'll come too." And then all of us chimed in: "Great! Come along, you can keep us company."

We took off in a single car and without a driver: they sat in back, Silvana and I sat in front. As I recall, our automobile attracted everybody's attention. Watching us pass by, the peasants stood there with their mouths open. "*Vogghiu viaggiare!*" one of them shouted, meaning: "Take me along!" I also remember that at a certain point, Silvana tried to beat the heat by unbuttoning her blouse and going bare-chested. "Silvana," I told her, "we're passing right by these people, it's dangerous." But she was doing it without malice, because she didn't have a grain of it. During that epoch she was completely naive. . . .

When we reached the tiny hamlet of San Giovanni in Fiore, there were no hotels, only a single inn. Given that the car wasn't working perfectly, we didn't feel like going on to Cosenza and decided to pass the night there. At the inn they told us that they had only one room, in which they could rearrange the beds in such a way that we could sleep in them together. The bathroom was downstairs and outside, and we're talking about a stable, not an actual bathroom! That's how the South was, back then. Still, despite the logistical snags and the slogging away on foot, they were enjoyable days. We were young and eager to laugh, and the petrified forest in the Sila is an unforgettable place. My relationship with Silvana grew stronger during the trip.

The work on *Il lupo della Sila* threw the couple together, and their love matured rapidly. In the red Buick, the young producer and the actress traveled back and forth between Rome and the Calabrian set. On one occasion they stopped at a beautiful hotel on the coast near Sorrento. On another they pulled over by the side of the road at night, with the radio on, and began to dance in front of the headlights. Everything was so romantic, so perfect! Dino realized that he was deeply in love: perhaps it had been true from the beginning, when he had minimized the whole thing, dismissing it as no more than an amorous adventure. One day while they waited at a stoplight, he looked over at Silvana and was struck by an idea, as if he were seeing her for the first time. He blurted out: "What lovely children you could give me!"

She laughed, but then in the spring of 1949, she became pregnant.

Here was the replay of a familiar situation for Dino, with Silvana in the role previously played by Bianca. She fretted: how would her family react to the news? And again Dino uttered the calming words, "I'm telling you, we're getting married." This time, however, things were moving in the right direction, during the first and happiest phase of what would prove to be a long, tormented union.

CHAPTER 8

A FAMILY IS BORN

In Rome, on July 17, 1949, Dino and Silvana were married. Elegant in a dark suit with a snow-white flower in his buttonhole, the groom appeared happy and very moved. The bride, in a high-necked white dress with a generously flared skirt, smiled from beneath an enormous, awkward hat. Some time later, discussing her wedding dress—which had been made for her by the very same Roman atelier where she had once worked as a model—she would add an amused footnote: "As for the hat, I have to point out that it wasn't my fault. I was relying on the good taste of a friend. And at the last minute, she surprised me with a kind of broad-brimmed lampshade, which hid my face and forced me to walk like a blind woman."

Since the annulment of the groom's previous marriage was turning out to be a lengthy business, the couple had a civil ceremony. One newspaper reported that on the day of the wedding, Silvana made a vow to attend mass one evening a week and would pray for a religious ceremony as well.

Immediately after the reception, the couple departed in the Buick for a long trip throughout Europe, which took them from Switzerland to Belgium, France to England. On reaching this last destination, Dino was summoned home for an urgent piece of business. The direct ferry to Calais had no room for his car, so the producer solved the problem by renting a military cargo plane to carry the Buick—thereby demonstrating to his wife his absolute refusal to be hindered by any obstacles.

Dino had married the woman he loved and he was ecstatic. Meanwhile, his career had really started to take off. In April he had his first big hit as a producer with *The Firemen of Viggiù (I pompieri di Viggiù)*, a little film with no artistic ambitions, made in great haste. Dino, a born gambler, had staked everything on it, and his wager paid off.

At the time there was just a handful of variety shows in the Roman theaters: one with Totò, one with Magnani, and one with Carlo Dapporto. In short, the greatest comics were having successful runs in the capital, but it was tough for them to tour the rest of the country, because the war had left the roads and the transportation system in such a mess.

One night I saw all three shows, one after another, and a thought struck me. If I could get a director to shoot a piece of this show, then a piece of that show, and concocted some little story to tie the whole film together, we would have a surefire product. I call up Mario Mattoli, who liked the idea, and he suggested a gimmick to hold the pieces together. He told me to acquire the rights to the popular song "*I pompieri di Viggiù*" and insert the *pompieri*, or firemen, between the scenes. I made up an estimated budget, which must have been around 2 billion lire in today's money—that is, half the cost of a normal movie, something we could shoot in three weeks.

I went to Lux to discuss the project and Gatti told me he wasn't interested. I called Rovere and got the same answer. The only remaining option was the film credit division at the Banca Nazionale di Lavoro. I introduced myself to the sales manager and explained the project. He inquired as to what sort of security I could offer. At that point I had no property to my name, so I told him, "*Dottore*, look at me, I'm penniless. If your bank finances the movie, there's only one thing I can offer as security." And what would that be? "My face." Those were my exact words: "If you think I have a trustworthy face . . ."

It was a reprise of that earlier situation with the shoes. The manager looked embarrassed for an instant. Then he suggested that I make my request in writing and call him the following week. I did what he asked. And although I was sure that he would tell me to drop dead, I called his office just the same. To my astonishment, his secretary immediately set up an appointment for me.

At our meeting, the manager said, "Listen, I'm sixty-five years old and I'm about to retire. I've done this job my entire life, and

I've been offered all sorts of things as security, but nobody has ever offered me his own face. But you know what? I like your face, and I'm going to give you the funds." I almost fainted. He gave me a fixed-term loan, meaning that I needed to pay back the money with interest within a certain number of months.

I saw the finished film and thought we had done a good job, although I doubted it would do much business in Rome, where everybody had already seen the shows. I proposed a distribution deal to Gatti, but after he screened the film, he turned it down. The same scene transpired with the other distributors.

Now what? If I didn't pay off this loan, my career was finished. The only thing left to do was find a couple of theaters and release it directly myself. At that time in Italy there were first-run, second-run, and third-run theaters. I couldn't find any first-run locations, but I did manage to line up the Quirinale on Via Nazionale and the Bernini, which no longer exists, near the Corso. In April 1949 we booked both theaters. I was now the distributor of my own film, with a one hundred percent stake. Well, thank the Lord: when the box office opened at two in the afternoon on Friday, there was already a line forming outside.

On Monday Gatti called. Having seen the receipts, he now wanted the film. I asked for twice the amount I had mentioned the first time around, Gatti accepted, and he handed over the cash. The first thing I did was run to the bank and settle my debt in advance. The manager told me, "For a change I behaved like a banker instead of a clerk, and you didn't make me regret it."

What did this incident teach me? That in your relationships with banks—and I've had quite a few of them—you always need to tell the truth. In good times and bad, the banks understand, and they can help you. But if you tell lies or fudge the balance sheet, sooner or later the scam will come out, and all confidence in the relationship is destroyed. The banks always trusted me, because they knew I was telling the truth.

I pompieri di Viggiù was a popular blockbuster rather than a critical success, but for Dino it marked a fundamental shift in his position in the movie industry. Now that he had rolled the dice and won, he could dictate the rules of the game. Soon other gratifications followed: important ones, even presitigious ones. In September 1950, at Cannes, *Bitter Rice* finally debuted on the international stage. The skittish proprietors of the festival snipped out one upsetting scene, in which a corpse was hung from a butcher's meat hook. But immediately after the festival, the film opened in the Italian theaters, to great public acclaim, and raked in an impressive pile of money.

Nor was *Bitter Rice* a strictly Italian phenomenon. The film arrived in the United States in December; thanks largely to Silvana's magnetic beauty, it was booked for long runs in the big cities and earned an Oscar nomination for Best Picture. It did stir up its share of controversy. In February 1951, for example, the chief of police in Albany, New York, interrupted a show in a local theater, declaring the film "improper and reprehensible." Meanwhile, a Catholic organization had already invited its flock to launch a boycott. But these protests didn't stop the film's triumphal march across America, which gave the name Dino De Laurentiis its first worldwide exposure. Mangano too was a hit with this new audience; her popularity rocketed to a new high, and the press dubbed her "the atomic Italian."

The newlyweds took up residence in Rome, in a villa on Via Appia rented from a Roman aristocrat. It was a luxurious and tranquil place, surrounded by a lawn with a swimming pool, all securely protected by high myrtle hedges. Silvana spent many hours at home, personally tailoring the layette for the expected infant. Yet even in her advanced stage of pregnancy, the couple continued to entertain. On New Year's Eve, they threw the first of many, many parties, which would increasingly bring together personalities from the worlds of show business, industry, and politics.

Barely two weeks later, on January 13, 1950, their daughter Veronica was born. The newspapers talked of nothing else, as though this were the offspring of a royal couple. But in the ramshackle kingdom of Italian postwar cinema, what better aspirants to the throne could there have been than the irresistibly ascendant producer, barely in his thirties, and his splendid diva? Soon the photographers were admitted to the Quisisana clinic, and the first photo of the little family grouping ran widely: Dino, with a tender smile, bends over Silvana's bed, while his wife, in a chaste white nightgown, sweetly returns his gaze and hugs the newborn to her breast.

The mother herself declared, "This year, I'd rather produce a second child than a third film." Indeed, she'd earlier confided to a French reporter, "When I began to make films, I always felt like weeping. I'm only nineteen, but I'm happy to note that my life as an actress already belongs to the past. . . . Fame and glory? I couldn't care less about it. What I want is to be a good mother to my family."

To celebrate the happy event, Dino gave Silvana a ring:

> I went to Bulgari, where I'd never been before, and I asked them to show me a few things. He—meaning Papa Bulgari—brought out a magnificent white diamond ring. I've always loved simple jewelry, and I admired the ring very much. "How much does it cost?" I asked. A million lire, an enormous sum at the time. I said, "Bulgari, my friend, it's beautiful, but I don't have the million lire." He replied, "I trust you. You'll give me the money when you have it." So I bought it. I must say that it always worked that way with Bulgari, because I often liked things that I couldn't pay for at the time. Ever since then I've remained their most loyal customer.

Meanwhile the gifts kept flowing in, from friends, family, even strangers. A fan from Vercelli sent a packet of rice with a brief note addressed to "the new papa," expressing hopes that the enclosed would be less bitter than it had been for Silvana. The screenwriters for Dino's next project, *Botta e risposta*, sent a bouquet of roses, along with a new script and the following note addressed to the baby: "From now on we'll need not only the approval of your father and mother but authorization from you as well."

Botta e risposta (I'm in the Revue), which was released in February 1950, recycled the formula from *The Firemen of Viggiù* in a more elegant and costly guise. It was a selection of sketches, dance numbers, and songs, with cameos by such international stars as Louis Armstrong and Fernandel, all assembled by Mario Soldati.

The film did hit one unfortunate snag. Intentionally or not, the director shot a brief comic episode at the railroad station, directly in front of a poster announcing the Vatican's declaration of the Jubilee Year. This supposed irreverence prompted the Ministry of Culture to exclude the film from all state-sponsored subsidies or awards. For Dino, who had been counting on his 50 percent of the take, this was a major blow. Still, his motto remained *Andare sempre avanti*: Ever onward. And in any case, the public gave the movie a warm welcome. In fact, a whimsical imaginary dialogue appeared in the March 31 issue of *Spettacolo*, which featured a despairing Dino on the brink of tears because he couldn't produce a failure, not even to gratify the critics who had been flailing away at his recent triumphs.

Within a few months Dino would strike out on his own, with fellow producer Carlo Ponti. Yet he had one more movie to make under the Lux banner: *Napoli milionaria (Side Street Story)*. Eduardo De Filippo's original play, first performed in 1945, was one of the comedic summits of postwar Italian theater, recounting a survior's return to a devastated city. Dino took the play to heart, recalling, as it did, wartime Naples, in which he had passed so many desperate months. Yet the author brought such magisterial power to his tale that it struck Dino as a classic, an eternal narrative that could speak to everyone. He was eager to strike a deal with De Filippo but hedged his bets by forcing the author to hire Antonio De Curtis, the consummate slapstick comedian universally known as Totò.

> I asked Eduardo to sell me the rights to the comedy, and he refused. But he did agree to make the film with me on a fifty-fifty basis: his contribution would be the text, direction, and some money—very little money. We started to put together a budget, which assumed that we would shoot the exteriors in Naples, and the numbers were much too big.
>
> Then I proposed that we reconstruct a Neapolitan alleyway at my own Farnesina studios. He agreed, as long as he could bring in a few real Neapolitans to populate it. It was a good idea: it would have cost twice as much to shoot in a real alley in Naples. And the best thing was that these Neapolitan families decorated the set themselves. All it took were a few comments from Eduardo—"This is your home, those are your props, arrange them any way you like"—and they got right down to business.
>
> Like so many other films, *Napoli milionaria* was a flop when I made the rounds of the distributors. Nobody wanted it. They said it was too theatrical, that it wouldn't interest the public. The real trick, though, was convincing Eduardo to cast Totò, whom he hated. Maybe he was a little jealous of the guy's popularity. Totò, on the other hand, envied neither Eduardo nor anybody else: he was a simple creature.
>
> I told De Filippo, "You have a 50 percent stake in this, but we're

> the ones taking the risk. For just a moment, then, put yourself in the producer's shoes rather than the author's. If Totò's in the film, we're guaranteed a certain amount of success no matter how things go. So for the love of art—and for the good of the film—you're going to have to kneel at Totò's feet and convince him to do his whole shtick: you know, playing dead with the *prosciutto* under the bed, and so forth."
>
> There was a meeting between the two, which I unfortunately missed. Then Eduardo came to me, sighing, "Hey, Dino, I really did have to kneel, but I convinced him." And I should add that although Eduardo made a beautiful film, its initial success was due to Totò.

Although *I pompieri di Viggiù* had included a sketch by the comedian, *Napoli milionaria* marked the beginning of the affectionate rapport between Dino and Totò. Their relationship was to last until Totò's death in 1967, shortly after he appeared in two episodes of De Laurentiis's *Caprice Italian Style (Capriccio all'italiana)*. Including not only Dino's solo productions but the films made in tandem with Carlo Ponti, the grand total amounts to nearly thirty collaborations. In the entire history of world cinema, it would be hard to find such a long-lasting pact between a producer and an actor.

> One day, which I'll never forget, Totò came to visit me and began to weep, because he had discovered that his wife was cheating on him. It was this grief that led to the creation of "*Malafemmena*," one of the most beautiful Neapolitan songs ever written. And after this painful personal experience, he changed. Although he tried to act like the same old Totò, he was different. His good friends, like me, could tell; all it took was a single glance. Totò was not only a very great actor, on a par with Chaplin: he was, unlike Chaplin, a man of great humanity. He represented the true Neapolitan animal, which is to say he was a good man, always ready to give and forgive.

Napoli milionaria came out on September 21, 1950, to even more acclaim than Dino had expected. But in the meantime—on June 3, to be precise—another thought had occurred to him: why not form a partnership with Carlo Ponti? The new company represented a union of two extraordinary personalities. De Laurentiis and Ponti were the most seasoned and ambitious producers in the Lux stable; indeed, they seemed destined to compete rather than form a fellowship. But perhaps the two rivals had sized each other up and decided to take the path of least resistance: sometimes it's better to neutralize one's adversary than to waste time fighting him.

CHAPTER 9

HE AND THE OTHER

LUX STUDIOS PLAYED A LARGE ROLE NOT ONLY IN DINO'S EARLY CAREER but in the history of Italian entertainment. When Gualino reopened for business after the war, he established himself at Via Po 36, in a *palazzetto* that no longer exists. This headquarters consisted of four floors plus a basement with two screening rooms, of which the more elegant of the two was quickly dubbed the *bomboniera*, or candy dish.

The fourth floor, forbidden to filmmakers, was reserved for Lux's "serious" activities. That is, the corridors were lined with the offices of the various companies that formed the connective tissue and banking arm of Gualino's industrial and commercial empire. The boss himself, an aloof figure, occupied the entire third floor. He arrived at the office early each morning at the wheel of his compact car—a spartan vehicle in contrast to the sumptuous machines driven by his producers. Eyeing Ponti's Packard and De Laurentiis's Buick from the balcony, Gualino would speculate, "Could it be that those guys are earning too much money?"

Stuffier and more sharp-tongued than his boss, Guido Gatti occupied an office on the second floor. This former musicologist was the managing director (and de facto chief executive) of Lux. Customarily he turned up on Gualino's floor around noon, when his boss, having busied himself with money matters all morning, took a break to check out the films in progress. A few of the elect—usually famous filmmakers or actors—were admitted into the sanctum sanctorum of the screening room, almost always under Gatti's vigilant eye. Gualino addressed them with courteous, encouraging comments or made enticing offers, none of which featured a very high level of compensation.

The second floor, where Gatti held court, also housed the publicity office entrusted to Vittorio Calvino. Here too were the administrative offices, a favorite destination for all those employees awaiting an advance or the latest payment on their contract.

And then there was the first floor, a hotbed of bustling confusion with an atmosphere, as Fellini described it, somewhere "between a train station, a stock exchange, and the waiting room at a whorehouse." Around the clock, the place was crawling with directors, screenwriters, technicians, and actors, all of them knocking on the doors of the independent producers. These included Marcello d'Amico, Antonio Mambretti, Luigi Rovere, Baccio Bandini—and the two thoroughbreds in the pack, De Laurentiis and Ponti. Lux never produced a film directly. The company always worked through these independents, who built nests for their own enterprises in the headquarters on Via Po. Though called "independent," the producers were in reality quite dependent on Valentino Brosio, Lux's organizational kingpin, who always kept on his desk, like a badge of nobility, a volume of Proust.

And what of Carlo Ponti? An attorney, a wizard at contracts and calculations, he had been born in 1910 in Magenta, about sixteen miles from Milan. (Like Dino, who grew up at about the same distance from Naples, he came from a suburban rather than a rural background.) Ponti's father, Leone, was the legal guardian of Antonio Mambretti, a young landowner, and the trustee of his substantial fortune. In 1940 Mambretti founded a film company called Artisti Tecnici Associati. At once he offered Carlo a job. Not yet thirty, Ponti assumed the reins as director of production on a highly successful film, Soldati's *Piccolo mondo antico*. He then made *Sissignora* with Ferdinando Maria Poggioli, persuaded Lattuada to direct his first film, *Giacomo l'idealista*, and after a number of additional jobs, landed at Lux. There he continued his string of successes, making movies with Lattuada as well as Pietro Germi and Luigi Zampa.

By 1948 De Laurentiis and Ponti were Gualino's most visible producers, which made them natural rivals. Fellini often told an anecdote about their initial animosity. Occupying offices on opposite sides of the same corridor, Carlo and Dino conducted their battles according to a fixed ritual. First one would open his door, shout an insult at the other, and slam the door shut again. After an instant, the other one would fling open *his* door, shout an insult in return, and retreat, only to await another salvo from across the corridor. And so it went, to the amusement of various bystanders. (Without restraining his laughter, Dino now denies the whole thing, attributing the scene to Fellini's famously fervid imagination: "Rather than insults, there was always a certain sympathy between Ponti and me. And above all, mutual respect.")

Despite their picturesque spats, in fact, the Neapolitan and the Lombard got along just fine. Both were brimming with enthusiasm and competitive spirit, which didn't prevent them from airing their differences or finding each other unbearable at times. Carlo was almost ten years older than Dino, and he had a degree: he spoke like a lawyer and a cultivated person. When Gualino attacked his favorite painters, or when Gatti pulled out Stravinsky or Schoenberg, Carlo could easily sustain a conversation. Dino had no such refinement. Yet he was proud that he had made his own way, with neither a hallowed name nor a patron to help him, gambling on his own imagination and initiative, displaying an icy determination when needed. What's more, Ponti's demeanor tended toward a certain superiority, as if he'd happened upon the world of film by pure chance, almost against his will. Dino *chose* the cinema and loved it passionately. One could say that aside from his family, he thought of nothing else.

> Ponti produced for Lux with the same contract I had. We both had a salary, plus we got a percentage on each film that we made, which varied from twenty to thirty percent of the profits, on the basis of a fixed cost. Sometimes Gualino would supply one hundred percent of the financing for a film. Then we producers would promise to deliver it within a certain amount of time and for a certain price, meanwhile assuming all risk for overruns. If, on the other hand, a finished film appealed to him, Gualino would offer to buy out our share. That way he could take advantage of our continuous need for cash to pay our suppliers, cast, and crew.
>
> Ponti and I were the best at Lux: in fact we were the most successful independent producers in Italy. So one fine day we asked ourselves, "Why not go out on our own?" There was also the fact that Gualino wasn't faring so well. One day when I was in his office, he fainted and banged his head. They carried him away, and his son Renato begged me to keep the incident to myself, adding that this had already happened several times. After a couple of days, however, Gualino was at his desk again, and he plugged along for a while, looking more and more exhausted.

In reality, Dino had more profound reasons for leaving behind the protection of Lux. Gualino and Gatti represented the somewhat enlightened summit of a conservative, traditionalist Italian society, with its careful distinctions between the social classes and rigid (at least theoretically) moral principles: a society that the war had swept away and destroyed.

Dino's extraordinary, youthful self-assurance had helped him to survive the war years. By age thirty he had already seen a great deal: his comfortable, familial world plunged into economic crisis; flight, hunger, and the massacred dead; his own seesawing between professional success and disaster. At least twice already he'd started over from scratch, and during the course of a single five-year period he'd married, divorced, remarried, and become a father.

Dino represented the new Italian man, reborn from the ruins amid many, many contradictions. Lux seemed ensconced in the dusty shadow of the past. Under Gualino's tutelage Dino had learned all the essentials, and he would always treasure these lessons, regarding the maestro with grateful admiration for the rest of his life. Still, he could no longer endure that rigid mentality, that lack of daring. Above all, he felt that the moment had arrived when he could make it on his own. He was ready to stand alone, without depending on anybody else's judgment.

He did not, however, leap into the void. Despite his abundant exuberance, Dino retained the coolness necessary to weigh the pros and cons. One element in his favor was Silvana, the diva of the moment: since she was still under contract with Lux, a certain continuity in the relationship between De Laurentiis and Gualino's company was guaranteed.

But Dino was most encouraged by the financial factor. Recent events had proven that he could earn decent profits as a producer without having deep pockets himself. What's more, he was convinced that he could always find money for a good idea; indeed, this would become one of his guiding principles. Take *The Bandit*, which he had made with precious little cash and considerable logistical acrobatics. Didn't that film bring him not only economic but also artistic gratification? Not to mention the colossal success of *I pompieri di Viggiù*, which outpaced even *Bitter Rice* at the box office. Gualino and Gatti had no affection for that kind of small comic film, which was becoming the building block of the Italian cinema. At the same time, they regarded neorealism with great suspicion: compared to Rossellini, in fact, Totò was almost tolerable.

Ponti, however, seemed to be on the same wavelength as Dino. What better reason to join forces?

> We formed Ponti–De Laurentiis, with little or no capital. When the moment came to choose a name, there was a brief debate: whose name do we put first? And since he was a few years older than me, I made the following suggestion. "Let's call it Ponti–De Laurentiis," I said, "but when the credits in the movie come up, the card can read, "Produced by Dino De Laurentiis and Carlo Ponti." This wasn't mere etiquette but a substantial issue, because I considered myself more of a filmmaker, more of a showman. Ponti was mostly a gifted lawyer with a nose for business, for deals.
>
> We put no money of our own into our first films. But we were always short of cash—partly because of production costs, partly because our profits were slow to materialize, and partly because our general expenses were high. I'm talking about an era when we stayed afloat thanks to four-month promissory notes. Every morning Ponti and I got in the car and we made the rounds of what I used to call *i sepolcri*: that's the word Italians use for those Easter pilgrimages from one church to the next. We went from bank to bank with our payment notices and begged them to give us however many millions of lire we needed to honor the notes that were coming due. If we defaulted on any of those, we would piss away our credibility and that would be the end of our company. And ultimately we had to be sure to repay the principal itself, because that was the only way we could count on one bank or another to bail us out as the notes came due.

In the atmosphere of Lux, the oddball alliance between Ponti and De Laurentiis resembled the nonaggression pact signed by Ribbentrop and Molotov in 1939: a union, provisional and purely utilitarian, of two natural adversaries. More simply, it was a marriage of interests, entered into with one eye cocked toward the inevitable divorce. In any case, Gualino did nothing to hold back his two crown princes. Considering their declaration of independence to be a physiological need, he bore them no grudge and continued to fund and coproduce their most ambitious efforts.

The new company established itself in a series of warehouses on Via della Vasca Navale, in the San Paolo neighborhood, near the dog track and directly behind the basilica. At this point Dino abandoned the makeshift studios he had outfitted on the Farnesina hill, and it was he who insisted that company have its own production facilities.

> I've always started with the principle that the studio is an essential working tool. Without a cinematographic facility, you can never schedule this production or that one. And it's also cost effective, because if you own a studio, as big or small as it may be, you're able to install your own technical equipment and build your own sets. It's a way of containing costs, especially if you manage to keep general expenses down. The problem I had later on, in connection with Dinocittà, is that the facility was enormous and the general expenses were sky-high.
>
> As for the Vasca Navale complex, I don't recall precisely, but I have the impression that I brought it into Ponti–De Laurentiis as a kind of dowry. I use that word in the abstract sense: in reality we rented the premises, because the owner didn't want to sell them. But those warehouses were in a state of complete abandonment. I was the one who whipped them into shape again.

The partnership between Ponti and De Laurentiis rose and fell during the first half of the 1950s, an epoch of exceptional growth in Italian society, which was already entering the early phase of an economic boom. It seemed that every business brimmed with enthusiasm, a great desire for notable accomplishments, and an ambition to expand onto the international stage—none more so than Ponti–De Laurentiis. The partners produced more than twenty films during the period, covering a wide range of subjects and styles, and that figure doesn't even include the collaborations with Totò. Always attentive to popular taste, the producers threw their weight behind such familiar names as Vittorio De Sica, Mario Camerini, and Alberto Lattuada. Yet they also offered numerous opportunities to such younger directors as Federico Fellini, Luigi Comencini, and Mario Monicelli.

Obviously too there was the Mangano phenomenon, which both partners were happy to encourage. The only difficulties here came from Signora De Laurentiis herself, who was less and less interested in burnishing her own glamorous image. Still, Silvana starred in the very first film made by the partnership, *Il brigante Musolino* (*Musolino the Bandit*). Replicating the winning formula of *Il lupo della Sila*, this popular 1950 production once again teamed the diva with the rugged Amedeo Nazzari.

It was followed by *Anna* (1951), a deluxe Hollywood-style romance that raked in more than a billion lire at the box office. Under Lattuada's expert supervision, Silvana played a nightclub dancer with a guilty conscience, who longs to become a nun. She next appeared in *Mambo* (1954). For this production, the partners went so far as to enlist a Hollywood director, Robert Rossen, along with the great choreographer Katherine Dunham, who taught Caribbean-style dances to Silvana. Again Vittorio Gassman played the indefatigable heavy, and again he was defeated by the protagonist's righteous behavior.

What's more, Silvana appeared in two additional PDL productions that same year. In *Ulysses*, she played both Penelope and Circe to Kirk Douglas's errant, torso-baring hero. And finally, she appeared as a prostitute in *L'oro di Napoli* (*The Gold of Naples*), a role that proved to be an important affirmation of her abilities as an actress.

Silvana was not, however, the only glamorous name to be associated with the partnership. From time to time Roberto Rossellini streaked like a comet across the PDL production schedule, and Dino continued to hold him in high regard. He directed *Europa '51* with Ingrid Bergman, whom he would soon marry, as well as an unusual Totò feature, *Dov'è la libertà?* The Totò film emerged from conditions of maximum confusion. According to legend, near the end of shooting, Totò arrived on the set one day at 2 P.M., which was precisely the hour at which Rossellini customarily departed. So a number of key scenes were shot by Fellini instead—a comradely gesture that enabled the film to be wrapped.

> I always had the sensation that Rossellini was head and shoulders above anybody else in the cinema. He downplayed everything, he made do with next to no cash, but he had an extraordinary vision and a unique ability to carry it out. When I count off the most important directors in the world on the fingers of one hand, I tend to forget De Sica and Rossellini, but he's absolutely the best!
>
> Starting with *Open City*, he tended to direct films that were subject to constant interruption, because there was no money, no film stock, no nothing. The fact is that Rossellini often produced

his own movies, even if that meant selling his own car to keep going. To create films under those conditions is the mark of a genius. When it's Saturday and you don't have any money to pay the cast, and meanwhile you have to figure out what to shoot on Monday—well, how can you make the masterpieces he made without being a genius?

The truth is that Rossellini did plenty of things for money. Fellini had an attitude of total intransigence: he made the films his way or not at all. But Rossellini, always weighed down with debts and plagued by a thousand domestic problems, took whatever he was offered. When I produced *Anima nera*, for example, it's not that I thought, "This is the perfect film for Roberto." Instead I said, "Roberto, do you need some cash?"

"Do I ever!" In such cases he had no artistic or moral qualms: he made sure that the script was appropriate, adjusted his style, and accepted the job. Yet even in *Anima nera* you find notable sequences, with his fingerprints all over them. That's how Rossellini worked. He put himself at the service of the film: "You want a Totò movie? Fine, I'm a professional, I'll make you a Totò movie." But if you begin to analyze *Dov'è la libertà?*, you find beautiful things that don't exist in any other Totò film. Here and there it's a little bit inconsistent, but who expects consistency from Rossellini?

Surveying PDL's productions, it's hard to assign credit to and assess the strengths and weaknesses of each partner. In his book, *Fin de race*, Antonio Altoviti, although a longtime colleague of Ponti's, seems to favor De Laurentiis, whom he describes as a font of "imaginative resources and imperious decisions." He adds, "Much of the time it was simpler to work for Dino than for Carlo. The former, with his cool professionalism, often seemed like the real Milanese, while the latter, messy and imprecise and prone to restlessness, seemed like the Neapolitan." Dino himself has a slightly different interpretation of their relative strengths:

Ponti was always the one with his feet on the ground. He would go off in the morning to inspect a piece of land for a possible investment, while I passed the time looking for a new actor, a new script. The fundamental difference between us—and I can say this without any fear of his contradicting me—is that I love my work. I've always believed that you can't make movies if you don't

> passionately love the cinema. But Ponti viewed the whole thing in a more detached manner, as if it were just one more business activity. As far as I could tell, the cinema didn't interest him all that much. Whether he was buying a piece of land or making a film, it was all the same to him. I don't say this to diminish him in the least, only to explain how we were different.

Despite persistent rumors, at least one point of friction between the two partners was imaginary: the rumored rivalry between their consorts, Mangano and Sophia Loren. The two stars hardly knew each other and never spent time together. There was neither the time nor the opportunity for them to form a friendship, but they never considered themselves antagonists. They overlapped on the screen only once, in the nightclub sequence from *Anna*, when Sofia Lazzaro (as she was then called) appeared as an uncredited extra.

> There was no problem between our *prime donne*. When we founded the company, Silvana was already an undeniable star and every producer, including Ponti, was quite happy to have her services. As for Sophia, there were some difficulties getting her established, and I must say it's to Carlo's credit that he believed in her possibilities from the beginning.
>
> I remember the first few times she came to the office and waited—for as long as an hour!—to have supper with him. In the beginning, Loren was not as enticing as she would be several years later: as she matured, she began to overflow with beauty and sexuality. Eventually Carlo lost his head and married her, prompting the accusation of bigamy and all the problems that resulted from that. By then Sophia had turned out to be an extraordinary actress. After Anna Magnani, in fact, I would say that she's the best Italian actress, with that powerful Neapolitan quality of hers.
>
> When I bought the rights to *The Gold of Naples* from Giuseppe Marotta, there was a part for Silvana, but Sophia was the obvious candidate for the pizza cook. And that was the film that got the ball rolling for her; until that moment she hadn't done anything significant. Ponti stuck close to the set, naturally, because every time Sophia was involved, he showed up. I also followed the work closely, as usual. But I should tell you the truth: when you have a screenplay of that quality and a director like De Sica, you trust him, you give him absolute freedom, and there's little or nothing to say.

The Gold of Naples was perhaps the last successful film produced in perfect agreement between the partners. Afterwards, they diverged ever more sharply.

When we realized that we were disagreeing about a great many things, we separated and each went our own way. It was a friendly separation, by mutual consent, but it took a long time. The Ponti–De Laurentiis company was actually experiencing a period of financial difficulty, which was complicated by Carlo's emotional problems. Madly in love with Sophia, he had decided to marry her no matter what the cost, and Milanese or not, he behaved like the most hot-blooded Neapolitan. He ran off to America and married Sophia in Mexico without having concluded the legal separation from his former wife.

Carlo had insisted in good faith that our laws had no jurisdiction over a wedding that took place abroad, but he was wrong. This meant that he couldn't return to Italy, not just then. So for as long as he was stuck in the U.S.A., I communicated with him via phone, or wrote letters, or sent our American representative, Luigi Tedeschi, to Los Angeles. That was how I kept him up to date on the situation of our company, which was in debt to the tune of several hundred million lire. "What are we going to do?" I kept asking him.

It was this state of affairs that eventually led me to negotiate with Carlo to buy out his share of the company. We concluded our partnership in complete agreement. And in perfect harmony we split up our bundle of films, according to how much work we had done on each title. In this way the company became all mine. I had a tough life for a couple of years while I straightened out the debt situation.

I have to say that I always found it very romantic that a man of Carlo's prestige would risk everything for love. And let me add that despite our differences in temperament and outlook, if our partnership had continued, Ponti–De Laurentiis could have become one of the biggest production companies in the European market—perhaps even one of the biggest in the world.

CHAPTER 10

WIFE AND DIVA

ON THE THRESHOLD OF HIS THIRTIES, DINO HAD QUITE CONSCIOUSLY SET out to recast the very foundations of his existence: there was a new company with Ponti and a new marriage with Silvana. Now, however, came an unforeseen development. When he married her, his new wife was a beautiful unknown. Her indelible image had allowed her to conquer an unexpectedly substantial role, but at the time of their wedding, *Bitter Rice* had not yet been released, nor had the phrase "atomic Italian" entered the language.

But after the film began its triumphal march through the European markets, Dino discovered that he had married not only the woman of his dreams but a movie star—which, for a producer, made for an excellent resource. Already a major success in his field, De Laurentiis found his popularity surging in the tabloid press, simply because his wife happened to be the first real postwar sensation.

Silvana, meanwhile, behaved like an anti-diva, which imbued the family portrait with a certain schizophrenia. On one hand, Dino—being, in his own words, a "good Neapolitan"—was happy to indulge that desire Silvana had expressed from the very beginning: to cut short her cinematic career in order to be a wife and mother. On the other hand, his spouse's success was too enormous to be casually shelved. (In its American release, for example, *Bitter Rice* took in what were then the biggest foreign receipts of all time.) What's more, the actress was under contract with Lux. And contracts, of course, must be respected.

Perhaps Silvana thought otherwise. After the birth of Veronica, she put on about twenty pounds and began dressing like a middle-class matron rather than a movie star. She wore extremely high-necked clothing, as if she were much older than twenty, and seemed absolutely intent on erasing the sensual image of the *mondina*.

The diva spent July 1950 on the island of Ischia, with the baby and her in-laws, enjoying a period of rest. But now it was time for her to undertake a crash diet in anticipation of *Il brigante Musolino*, even as Dino dashed back and forth preparing for the shoot. Luckily the extra weight hadn't put a dent in Silvana's fame, and the newspapers were all on her side. They spoke approvingly of the fact that she dressed like a housewife and praised her habit of spending every afternoon with her little daughter.

At this point, Mangano was still accessible to the press and gave the impression of a nice, tranquil young woman. Soon, however, reporters noted her chain-smoking, her nervous fingers continually twisting and tugging at her hair. Then the familiar seesawing of the couple's pronouncements began. Silvana would repeat in interview after interview her decision to stop acting, while an equally determined Dino used all his powers of persuasion to get her in front of the camera again. Each time, he left her with the impression that this would be her last appearance. Meanwhile, one successful vehicle followed on the heels of another.

While all this was going on, the family first moved from the rented villa on Via Appia to an apartment in the Parioli neighborhood, and then rapidly back to Via Appia, since Dino needed green grass around him to breathe. Completely gratified by her role as mother, Silvana no longer had any use for celebrity. She stopped hiding her peculiar indolence, which would ultimately reveal itself as the mask of a secret anxiety.

Dino, on the other hand, was totally immersed in his work, pursuing professional dreams both for himself and Silvana. Nor did he mind assuming, from time to time, the temporary role of prince consort: doesn't the sun set every night in order to let the moon shine, almost as if it had its own light? Well, Dino knew exactly how to make Silvana shine. Without his efforts, in fact, she might have been lost, dreamy and obscure, a faint glimmer in the vast firmament of the Italian cinema—a cinema which, within the span of just a few years, had become the second-biggest box-office champion, right behind Hollywood. The moment was extremely favorable, and De Laurentiis refused to let it slip away.

He adored his wife and often indulged her, even if he didn't always understand her and didn't feel she understood him. They were utterly different. He was active (or hyperactive); he always had something up his sleeve; he was an extrovert, full of life, a bizarre combination of lucid pragmatism and loose-cannon imagination.

Silvana, on the other hand, was passive, reserved, sometimes grumpy, often impenetrable. She never got out of bed before noon. She liked to stay up late and seemed to forget that her husband, on his feet since six in the morning, happily went to bed at a decent hour. When finances got tight, she didn't even consider moderating her sartorial expenses, as if the problem didn't affect her. In her daily routine she appeared apathetic: aside from knitting and embroidery, she hated all household chores and would much sooner listen to classical music, regretting her lost career as a ballerina. She became animated only when she spent time with or talked about her daughter or when she was playing with the dogs—especially her favorite, the German shepherd Ador.

Dino admired Silvana, as if she were a natural phenomenon that grew ever more mysterious and fascinating. Yet he never lost sight of his own strategies or of the rules of the game. Silvana was able to do what she wished, she was the absolute mistress of her own time, but only until the moment arrived for a new film or promotional tour or honorary banquet. Then Dino became an authoritarian, dictating schedules and timetables, and his wife, however grudgingly, was obliged to obey his orders like any other contract player.

On February 16, 1951, the producer departed with Silvana and Ponti for an international film festival in Punta del Este, Uruguay. The Americans, who had an assertive presence in the South American market, showed up in force, armed with such films as *Sunset Boulevard*, *Harvey*, and *All About Eve*. There was also an assortment of box-office titans on hand, including Gary Cooper, Linda Darnell, and John Wayne. It was the Italian cinema, however, that made the biggest splash, astonishing everybody with its freshness and snapping up most of the prizes.

Meanwhile, Mangano herself got a boost when *Bitter Rice* opened in Brazil and Mexico. The film received a clamorous welcome, and the diva was the recipient of "the oddest expressions of admiration and the noisiest songs of praise." The reporters dwelled on her sense of restraint: she never appeared in scanty outfits or in the pool, and her elegant simplicity struck them as a pleasant change from the typical Hollywood vampishness. Dino, as outgoing as she was shy, seldom left her side. He also took advantage of the moment to sign a contract with the biggest Brazilian film company, committing himself to make several color films with Brazilian stories, one of which would feature his wife.

De Laurentiis had attained a certain level of personal luxury: he could allow himself a fabulous house, servants, and expensive cars, like his custom-built 1951 Hudson and Pininfarina's first Model 1900 convertible. Silvana too behaved as if she were born to riches. She proved to have quite a taste for furniture, which only became more pronounced once she became friendly with the Tuscan art director Piero Gherardi.

But contrary to appearances Dino's finances weren't all that solid; maintaining this level of splendor required a constant balancing act on his part. Still, Dino believed it was worth the trouble. Given his grandiose and generous nature, how could he resist offering the very best to Silvana and his family? In the black-and-white Italy of the fifties, De Laurentiis was already thinking in Technicolor. If his wife was a star and he a great producer, their residence needed to be spectacular: splendid, spacious, equipped with gardens and a pool. The villa on Via Appia, to which they returned at the end of 1951, fit the bill perfectly.

Again they rang in the New Year with a marvelous party, attended by everybody in the film world. In a black lace dress, with a few extra pounds due to her second pregnancy, the lady of the house happily let herself be photographed wearing a pointed party hat and a tacky pair of glasses. The guests included the ever-faithful Tonti, Totò, Lollobrigida, Soldati, Gassman, and Camerini, plus Roberto Rossellini and Ingrid Bergman.

What followed was a year of almost nonstop travel. In April, Silvana and Dino attended the Cannes Film Festival, which had been permanently shifted to the spring. Observers noted that the Italian diva had the air of a dutiful wife accompanying her husband on a business trip. Silvana took a break from the road to give birth to Raffaella on

June 28, and she spent most of the summer in Cortina with her sister Patrizia and the children. Come September, though, there was a quick, obligatory trip to the Venice Film Festival, and toward the end of that month the couple departed on a long journey, accompanied by Silvana's mother, father, and sisters.

Their first stop was in Paris, for the premiere of *Anna*. Unfortunately, the French had soured on the atomic Italian. There was endless nitpicking about her appearance: she looked pale, her lips were bloodless, she wore no makeup, and her clothes displayed an almost masculine severity. Silvana didn't help her public image much: during interviews she responded in monosyllables, and she drifted off to sleep while her film was being screened.

Their next stop was London, a friendlier place. The English were delighted to discover that Ivy Mangano, Silvana's mother, was a daughter of Albion, and Silvana and her two sisters struck everybody with their charm. Dino announced his plans for *Mambo*, in which Silvana would finally be able to indulge her appetite for dance. He seemed to be making a case that the Italian film industry was now capable of competing with its American counterpart.

While the rest of the family returned to Rome, Dino and Silvana continued on to New York, where an Italian Film Week was kicking off on October 6. A few days later they flew out to Hollywood at the invitation of Paramount Studios. Emerging from this cinematic lion's den, the producer had nothing dramatic to announce, but two months later, in Rome, the Ponti–De Laurentiis company signed a contract to coproduce and distribute various films with the venerable studio, marking the first step in Dino's gradual conquest of America.

And what of 1953? A scandal and a controversy marked the beginning of the year. In January the newspapers announced that somebody was selling a photo of Silvana in the nude. The whole business was a fake: her head had in fact been pasted on the naked body of an unknown model. According to rumor, the scam artists had tried to blackmail Dino, who promptly went to the police. The producer denied it. He did, however, express his hope that the culprits would be thrown in jail as promptly as possible.

In that bygone era, nobody would publish the incriminating image. The newspapers limited themselves to reproducing the original photo, in which Silvana was wearing a bathing suit. It would take four decades, Mangano's death, and the deteriorating taste of the popular press to resurrect the manipulated photo: at that point it appeared on the cover of a supposedly serious weekly, where it was promoted as a major scoop.

The controversy, meanwhile, originated in London. Speaking with the English press, Vittoria De Sica offered a few unflattering appraisals of various Italian actresses. Mangano, Silvana Pampanini, and Gina Lollobrigida, he said, "are merely breasts and legs, and their artistic abilities can't possibly compete with their physical gifts." Lollobrigida's response was scorching, Pampanini's was resentful, and Mangano, on vacation in the mountains, delivered her seraphic comeback via the telephone: "It could be that he's right." And Dino? The consummate diplomat, he declared himself "surprised that one of our most representative men of the cinema would take aim at these actresses, who certainly contribute to the great success of Italian cinema around the world."

In fact, De Sica's diatribe, which had doubtless been inflated by the press, didn't interest the producer at all. His eye was already trained on much wider horizons. For even as De Laurentiis made himself known in Hollywood, taking shrewd advantage of Silvana's fame, Hollywood was reaching out to Italy. In part it was the war that had narrowed the distance between Rome and California. In part it was the impact of neorealism, which had made it more desirable to shoot films in authentic settings. Nor should we overlook the fact that the Hollywood studios preferred to reinvest their European earnings abroad—and that production costs and salaries were notably cheaper in the Old World. All of these elements led to an extraordinary fusion, which would be dubbed "Hollywood on the Tiber." (Dino is almost certain that he coined the phrase, which quickly became common usage.)

In this sense 1953 was a seminal year: William Wyler came to Italy to shoot *Roman Holiday*, featuring Gregory Peck and the newly discovered Audrey Hepburn. At the same time, Dino was preparing to launch the first great international project in the history of Italian cinema.

CHAPTER 11

THINKING BIG

INSPIRED BY GUALINO'S LESSONS AT LUX, ANIMATED BY HIS DREAM OF CREATING an international cinema, Dino undoubtedly was thinking big. He envisioned films shot in English (which he didn't understand), with appearances by the great stars of Hollywood (with whom he couldn't exchange a single word), the whole thing underwritten by large reserves of capital (which he didn't possess). By the early 1950s, however, the producer couldn't deny that the real action was taking place in Los Angeles. He refused to be cut out of it, despite the obstacles. In fact, the challenge attracted him, as if it were an immense blackjack table.

This attitude put him in opposition to Ponti, who preferred a less risky policy. Carlo wanted to stick with the Totò films, which cost little to make and earned plenty, and with those tales of romance and tragedy enjoyed by the vast legion of Sunday moviegoers, whose ranks hadn't yet been decimated by television. Carlo's reasoning was simple enough. Why should they risk their necks to make a spectacular that could sink them financially, when they could earn equal (or even bigger) profits with the usual junk?

> With Ponti, we never had a financial structure that would allow us a complete production-distribution cycle: we were living day to day. We worked with minimal guarantees from the distributors, selling the completed films to Lux, Titanus, and other companies. And the film division of the Banca Nazionale del Lavoro took its cut from these contracts, having already advanced us low-

interest loans. So we scraped along until each film was released, but if the film didn't rake in any cash, we were in trouble, and meanwhile we had to keep covering our general expenses and our interest payments.

These were serious problems. The general expenses had to be tallied on a film-by-film basis, but sometimes the budget was too modest to absorb the appropriate items. Sometimes we exceeded our estimates, and in those days, if you went over by even a little, it was already too much, because we were always on the ropes: a bounced check would be enough to put us out of business. I realized that we had to free ourselves from this nightmare of promissory notes. And in order to do that, we needed to think on a bigger scale, with a single financial point of reference.

Ponti, who had his doubts, tried to rein in his partner. But Dino refused to give up his dreams, which were perhaps tinged with megalomania. The first widescreen epic that De Laurentiis tackled, dragging Carlo along behind him, was *Ulysses*.

His memories regarding the early phase of this project are foggy. It's certain, however, that the initial impulse came from the director Georg Wilhelm Pabst, an underemployed German cinematic master. Pabst had come to Italy at the invitation of a Milanese production company to film *The Odyssey*, and while he was scouting locations on Ischia he met Silvana, to whom he offered a role. Consulting an ancient press clipping that recounts these confused events, Dino can't hide his perplexity: "I certainly don't recall that it was Pabst who got *Ulysses* under way."

It's a strange thing to forget, because in 1954, right on the heels of Dino's first international adventure, the eminent novelist Alberto Moravia published *Contempt*, the tale of a German director summoned to Italy to make a film of *The Odyssey*. (It was later brought to the screen by Jean-Luc Godard in *Le mépris [Contempt]*, produced by none other than Carlo Ponti.)

The title means nothing to Dino: he hasn't read the book or seen the film. In other words, he was unaware that years after his appearance in Soldati's *Fuga in Italia*, he had fed the imagination of yet another great Italian writer. For Moravia's novel includes a portrait of a producer, Battista, with more than a passing resemblance to Dino.

Battista, we read, "always kept his feet on the ground and said mostly interesting things, even if they were uttered to feed his masculine vanity. Toward the end of dinner, for example, he told us about his recent trip to America and a visit to the Hollywood studios, recounting the whole thing with vivacity but also with considered judgment."

The ambiguous portrait that emerges from *Contempt* is quite unusual, especially if we recall that in that era, the producer—even the type who wrapped himself in an aura of omnipotence—was often treated by critics as a despicable oddball. Witness the pronouncements that the director Michelangelo Antonioni put in the mouth of the pompous producer Ercolino in *La signora senza camelie* (*The Lady without Camellias*): "For me the new formula is sex, politics, and religion, preferably all at once." In the pages of his novel, however, Moravia analyzes Battista's attitudes, ideas, and entrepreneurial insights with an open mind. There's none of the haughtiness that characterizes the usual confrontation between eggheads and filmmakers. Was the author of *Contempt* around while *Ulysses* was being filmed? Did he even make an uncredited contribution to the screenplay?

> No. Moravia worked with me on several occasions. I made *La romana*, *io e lui*, and perhaps a few other films based on his books. I knew him well, and we had an excellent relationship, but he had nothing to do with *Ulysses*. As I recall, Gatti and I were discussing some possible projects for Silvana, who was still under an exclusive contract with Lux, and I said, "We could have her play Penelope." That's how the idea for the film came about. In the end Silvana played two roles, Penelope and Circe. At first there were going to be three, but to make the film shorter, we cut the character of Calypso out of the script.
>
> Once our decision to adapt *The Odyssey* became final, the first problem was to find somebody to play Ulysses. I immediately thought of Kirk Douglas. To my mind, there were no other choices. Douglas was already a star, and this would allow us to sell the film all over the world—which was essential, because the production was going to cost plenty.

In the Hollywood of 1953—where you were only as good as your last film—Douglas's ascent to star status had been hobbled by the failure of *The Juggler*. Still, the negotiations with his agent proved to be sufficiently complex.

I showed up in Los Angeles with my rotten English and contacted Kirk's agent, Ray Stark. He would later become co-owner of Columbia, an important producer, and somebody I constantly dealt with for twenty years. Back then, though, he was merely Kirk Douglas's agent.

When I proposed *Ulysses* to him, he said, "What is this crap?" He didn't even know who Homer was, he knew nothing about him. I had a first draft of the screenplay with me, already translated into English. And after he read the script it was even worse: "All these gods, these divinities—how are you going to film them?"

But since what counts in America is the Almighty Dollar, I cut right to the chase and said, "Ray, how much are you asking for Douglas these days?"

He said, "For a film like this, two hundred fifty thousand." Today that sum would be equivalent to tens of millions of dollars, I think. Plus we'd have to transport him, put him up in a villa, and so forth.

I suggested that I have a chat with the actor and see if the film would interest him. Kirk read the script and found it fascinating, because he's an intelligent man and maybe he knew something about Homer. He told me that he was willing to do it, as long as I would have Irwin Shaw rewrite the screenplay. I said that was no problem. Later, of course, we had to keep Shaw on a short leash, because he was trying to Americanize Homer a little too much. I brought him to Italy to work with Camerini, and it took a long time: it was a lengthy and exhausting gestation. The fact is that in Italy, in Europe, we always have a certain respect for authors like Homer and Tolstoy.

At first it wasn't easy working with Kirk Douglas. He's a perfectionist, and if he happened to stumble over a line—well, you know how actors are. Later on everything went fine, thanks in part to his Belgian friend Anne Buydens, whom I had appointed head of our publicity office. In fact, Anne eventually became Kirk's wife: perhaps I was something of a matchmaker too. In the cinema you have to do it all!

I chose Camerini to direct because I had known him since *Batticuore* and had tried him out on *La figlia del capitano* and a few

> other things. He was a real professional. The only problem was that Mario didn't speak any English, and we had to keep a translator on call. He was such an expert director, and such a gentleman, that you couldn't help but like him. When it was necessary, though, he could be very stubborn about getting what he wanted.

To judge from the account in Kirk Douglas's autobiography, *The Ragman's Son*, the work on *Ulysses* suggested nothing so much as one of Hemingway's "moveable feasts." The first encounter between Silvana and Kirk, who was then growing a beard for his role, took place at Cannes in April. Upon her arrival, she found a bunch of yellow roses in her hotel room, along with a note that said, "Welcome. Kirk." Immediately after, the star and his companion Anne were Ponti's guests at Amalfi, making side trips to Positano and Capri. The shoot finally got under way at Porto Ercole on May 18, but the vacationlike atmosphere continued: the star was able to alternate maritime scenes and spectacular dives with plenty of off-camera swimming. When the production moved to Rome, Kirk happily settled in at Villa Gioia, a stupendous residence that had been rented for him on Via Appia.

This gesture was typical of Dino, who had earned a reputation for giving his top actors and screenwriters a princely welcome. During breaks in the shoot, the producer often invited Kirk and Anthony Quinn (who played Antinoo) to take a dip in the pool with him. One occasion was Raffaella's first birthday; another, the producer's fourth wedding anniversary. Douglas was gratified to be treated as one of the family. He also enjoyed working on an Italian film set—a kind of bedlam, with people yammering in every conceivable language.

Of course there were moments of friction throughout the project, but almost all of them ended in laughter. During an August break, the De Laurentiis clan took refuge in the cool air at Arcinazzo, and there was another break in September, to allow Silvana and Kirk to make a promotional appearance together at the Venice Film Festival: they arrived in a gondola for the sumptuous ball at Palazzo Volpi, and the resulting photos appeared in every newspaper.

There was only one exception to this atmostphere of affection; relations between the star and the director remained tense. When De

Laurentiis threw a wrap party at the Apuleius de Ostia Antica restaurant, with all the waiters in ancient Roman garb, Camerini barricaded himself in his house and swore that he wouldn't attend. Dino himself went to lure him out. When the director finally entered the restaurant, Kirk, more antic than ever, welcomed his adversary by falling to his knees and serenading him with an extemporaneous Italian number called "Papà." Embraces, toasts, and high spirits soon ensued: this was the atmosphere of the cinema during Rome's tenure as Hollywood on the Tiber.

> Kirk Douglas was the driving force behind the success of *Ulysses*. I recall that in Italy, the film broke box-office records in every single city and region. They had never seen receipts like that! And there was no technology like we have today. We shot the film in a small studio at Vasca Navale, slapping together a contraption, which would now seem prehistoric, to rock the ships back and forth as though they were on the waves. For its time, *Ulysses* was an excellent film: I saw it again a few years ago, on American television, and I must say that it holds up pretty well. Of course we'd do it completely differently now, starting with the script! In any case, it's a film that triumphed all over the world.

Later Dino produced a second version of the Homeric epic for Franco Rossi's *Odyssey* miniseries: eight episodes broadcast by Radio Televisione Italiana (RAI) in 1968, with an average audience of 16 million people. Relying on a version of the poem by the Nobel laureate Giuseppe Ungaretti, which became extremely popular, the series turned out to be much more sophisticated than Camerini's film, and it still retains much of its charm. (It was also the first large-scale European coproduction for television, shot in Yugoslavia with Italian, French, and German participants.)

Camerini's *Ulysses* had a less inspiring run in the American market. In Hollywood circles, however, it was a subject of admiration and curiosity, and one of its fruits, certainly, was the friendship that arose between Dino and Charles Bludhorn, the president of Gulf + Western. This relationship in turn laid the groundwork for a long collaboration between the producer and Paramount, which would result in nearly thirty films over the course of four decades.

In the meantime, the moment had come for Dino to begin his next project. During the shoot, the *Ulysses* set had drawn innumerable visitors. One was Mike Todd, the famous producer of *Around the World in 80 Days*, who was about to become Dino's antagonist. The bone of contention was an undertaking that, until that moment, the entire world of international cinema had considered impossible: a film version of Leo Tolstoy's *War and Peace*.

CHAPTER 12

HOLLYWOOD ON THE TIBER

The first news items appeared in the press toward the end of 1952, when it seemed that Silvana Mangano would star in the new epic. At once a joke began circulating among the *caffès* on Via Veneto: "Ponti and De Laurentiis are producing *War and Peace*, but Ponti read only the first volume, and De Laurentiis only the second."

If Ponti read *War and Peace*, I didn't know about it. But in any case, I did the work for him, reading both volumes twice. The idea originated one day when I was in a bookstore. I was looking for something that would stimulate me, because I'm a ravenous reader. I happened to pick up the Tolstoy, I bought it and took it home, but at that point I didn't open it, because I had too much to do. When I finally began to read it, though, I was entranced. I kept repeating to myself: "It would be a dream to film this. But if the greatest producers in the world haven't made it yet, there must be a reason."

There was a reason: *War and Peace* was simply too vast a narrative. That was my impression after reading the book once. But when I read it a second time, I began to realize that fifty percent of the episodes could easily be eliminated, reshuffled, or forgotten. And like a flash of lightning it occurred to me that the film needed to be built around Natasha, Andrei, and Pierre—around their love affairs. I said to myself, "If I take this tack, I've got a popular story on my hands: you can never go wrong with a romance. And with this love triangle in the foreground, I can fill in the background with the main parts of the plot, as many as I can fit into a two- or three-hour spectacular."

The task of reducing the text to a treatment was entrusted to the faithful Ivo Perilli, along with Camerini, perhaps in anticipation of repeating his experience with *Ulysses*. These two were also joined by other screenwriters, among them Soldati, who was named second-unit director after Germi withdrew.

When I had the treatment in hand, I went to Gatti. He told me, "I'm extremely interested, but only in the Italian rights, because the project is too expensive." As I recall, he offered 20 percent of the costs. How could I find the rest? At that point I decided that I'd better take a trip to America and see what they thought of the idea. In the wake of *Ulysses* and *Mambo*, I had established a good relationship with Paramount. At the New York office they said, "It's an interesting project, but you'll have to talk to the heads of the studio in Los Angeles." I flew straight there and was told, "It depends on the director." I proposed William Wyler and extracted a promise that if he would agree to make the film, they would finance it.

I contacted Wyler, whom I had met when he was shooting *Roman Holiday* in Rome. He said that he needed two or three days to refresh his memory of the novel. Then we had a lengthy reunion, which commenced with the director saying, "I want to do it, but only under certain conditions. I need this, I need that, I need this as well . . ." And while Wyler went on about the film, as if it were already in front of his eyes, I realized that doing it his way would push the price up to 10 or 15 million dollars. Sick at heart, I was forced to give up on Wyler. I couldn't manage those kinds of costs, and Paramount had set its own limits.

Then came another twist. While I was at Paramount for a meeting, King Vidor showed up by surprise. "Dino," he said, "is it true that you want to make *War and Peace*? That's *my* film." It's not that somebody suggested him to me: he suggested himself. There had been a little resentment toward him in Hollywood, inspired by some harsh comments about the industry he made in his autobiography, *A Tree Is a Tree*. But the success of *Duel in the Sun* still had a resounding effect.

At Paramount they told me, "Be careful. Vidor is getting old and there are plenty of crowd scenes in the film."

"Not a problem," I said. "We'll have the second-unit director shoot all of those." And at once I told Vidor, "Look, for reasons of time, and to save you some labor, you'll shoot all the scenes involving the principal actors. But as for the battles, or the episode at the

Beresina bridge—scenes that we'll mostly shoot up in the Piedmont—well, you can discuss those with the second-unit director. He'll take care of them for you." In the end, Soldati directed almost all of Napoleon's scenes. And I pitched in too, personally directing a cavalry charge with the help of the art director, Mario Chiari.

In sum, *War and Peace* was a typical example of cinematic stitching. While Vidor was at Cinecittà, for example, shooting Pierre's duel in the fake snow on Stage 5, Soldati was in the Piedmont, in *real* snow, shooting the Beresina. And I was the guy commuting between one kind of snow and the other.

But how did the clash unfold between Mike Todd and De Laurentiis? How did the Italians win?

For this film I always had Audrey Hepburn in mind, ever since I saw her in *Roman Holiday*. Natasha could be played by nobody else. The book describes her as a young girl of fifteen or sixteen, and no star of that age existed. So I had to find an actress who had that fresh, light quality of youth. And that actress had to be Audrey.

But just as I was wading into the preparations for the film—and I was in good shape, because Paramount and Lux had both come aboard, and all I needed to do was find a bank to finance the inevitable cost overruns—the news came that Mike Todd had decided to make *War and Peace* with none other than Hepburn. The game would be won or lost, I realized, on the strength of whoever signed her up. But where could I catch up with her? She was in Europe on a vacation, because she was about to marry or had just married the actor Mel Ferrer.

I made an appointment with Hepburn. I talked to her about Tolstoy, I talked to her about Natasha, and then, on the spur of the moment, I told her, "I've been thinking of Ferrer for the part of Prince Andrei." That did it. She said yes on the spot, and the moment I announced that Hepburn was under contract, Todd gave up.

Before giving up, in fact, Todd offered the actress twice the salary she had negotiated with Dino, which she loyally refused. He also made a futile suggestion that he and his rival produce the film together. But no, this was to be Dino's project alone, despite the endless finagling it entailed.

> I signed up Ferrer for strategic reasons. It's true that he turned out to be an excellent choice for Andrei, but frankly, I had other names in mind at the time. Still, if I had said to Hepburn, "Come shoot *War and Peace* in Rome, where you'll be separated from your new husband for several months," it could have been a problem. With both of them, the film got made.

In *Audrey: A Biography of Audrey Hepburn*, Charles Higham makes the opposite argument. Mel had been chosen several months before Audrey, the author insists, and the idea that he was attached to the project as a kind of prince consort was nasty industry gossip. This discrepancy aside, Higham shows a great deal of enthusiasm for the relationship between Audrey and her Italian producer: "She was very fond of the mercurial, tiny, and extravagant Dino, with his endless stream of Italian anecdotes, and of his wife, the ravishing Silvana Mangano. . . . [Silvana] was now the mother of a gorgeous brood of little Italian children with enormous dark eyes and curly black hair, who would fling their arms around Audrey in a manner that made her heart almost stop beating and tears of happiness well in her eyes. Evenings at the De Laurentiis home were wonderful, and Audrey felt a strong empathy for the Italians, with their warmth, their outgoing, slightly crazy sense of humor and energy, their fits of sulking, laughter, and tears. Like so many people raised with extreme discipline under conditions of hunger and privation, Audrey was captivated by people who lived at the center of life, free of anxiety."

Audrey's affection for Dino deepened with his response to some bad news: she was pregnant. Unstoppable as ever, he refused to bat an eyelash, even though this meant that the first half of the shoot needed to be shifted to follow the portion planned for July. It was no small matter, reorganizing a schedule that included set construction, studio time, and military assistance for the battle scenes. Higham chronicles all these misfortunes in admirable detail, emphasizing Dino's good-natured willingness to roll with the punches.

Finally, a sad and unforeseeable event resolved the whole mess: in March Audrey had a miscarriage. Dino and Silvana remained at hand and did whatever they could to help her through this terrible moment. A conscientious professional, Audrey agreed to begin the shoot according to the original schedule. When the moment came to start, however, she was unable to pull herself together, and the production stopped once more. Installed in a villa that Ferrer had discovered in Frascati, which was full of the flowers and animals that she liked, Audrey remained fragile and anxious.

Higham records yet another problem. Once she was on the set, the star complained about each of her twenty-two costumes and raised the hackles of the wardrobe designer, Marie De Matteis, by insisting on a Givenchy gown from Paris, despite the fact that it would clash with Russian styles of the period. Nor was Hepburn satisfied with the script: she kept adding more and more material from the novel. Since Vidor was unable to shoot the scenes in chronological order, the cast kept zigzagging from one sequence to the next, which impaired Audrey's concentration. Day after day, she retired to her Frascati villa in a state of misery, and only Dino was capable of wheedling a smile out of her.

And what about Henry Fonda, who played Pierre? In *Fonda: My Life*, the actor recounts the whole adventure from his point of view. Five minutes after an apparently casual handshake with De Laurentiis, whom he'd just met, in the lobby of the Beverly Hills Hotel, Fonda got a telephone call in his room. Dino had enjoyed their meeting, he was told, and wondered if the actor would be willing to read a copy of *War and Peace*. He agreed. The book showed up, Fonda read it, and he found it excellent. His first thought was that they would cast him as Pierre—despite the fact that at age fifty, he was too old: "I thought De Laurentiis was out of his mind to want me, but I wasn't going to tell him that because it was one juicy part."

As for Dino's recollections:

> I was well aware that he wasn't an obvious choice for the role and that he was the wrong age. Pierre is described as being in his twenties, or a little younger, and he's a corpulent type: altogether the opposite of Fonda. In fact I already had found an unknown who was perfect. But Paramount wanted a big name at all costs, so I said, "You want Henry Fonda? I'll get Henry Fonda." The only unknown in the film was Anita Ekberg. I had picked her out of a group of starlets in New York, immediately thinking, "If we can get her to act just a little bit, she'll do the trick."

The entire Fonda clan, including Susan Blanchard, Henry's then wife; his adolescent children, Jane and Peter; and his adopted daughter, Amy, were welcomed by Dino with customarily marvelous accommodations on Via Appia. In their respective memoirs, Jane and Peter both describe that unforgettable Roman holiday. Jane, in particular, remembers having entertained herself for hours by spying on their celebrated neighbor, Gina Lollobrigida, through a pair of binoculars.

Still, Fonda's stay in Rome was anything but serene. At once he found himself clashing with Vidor and Dino, who considered Pierre a romantic character; he himself saw Pierre as a bumbler and tried to give this impression by wearing a pair of glasses whenever he could. The moment Dino arrived on the set, he would summon the actor and force him to remove them. Fonda returned home each evening with his nerves on edge, and his marriage suffered. After a month Susan and the children departed for New York. It was a sad situation for Fonda, alone in the large empty villa with a maid, a cook, and a driver who spoke no English. To distract himself he wandered around the ancient quarters of Rome, and in an antique store on Via del Babuino, he met his future consort, the Italian Baroness Afdera Franchetti. From that moment on his work went more peacefully and with more positive results. As one critic later observed, "Fonda appears to be the only cast member who read the book."

The history of a cinematic monument like *War and Peace* has numerous chapters, each one different from the last. One might describe the deployment of multiple studios or the construction of the sets, including a faux Moscow along the avenues of Cinecittà. Others might detail the thousands of costumes or the staging of the three battles, which were shot at various Italian locations after a scouting expedition to Finland and a round of negotiations with the Yugoslavs failed to pan out. Austerlitz was fought near Pinerolo, Borodino on the outskirts of Montelibretti, and for the Beresina, Dino chose a site on the Po River near Valenza.

In the Italian Parliament, meanwhile, a bloc of right-wing deputies questioned the propriety of using the military in a film production. Dino just shook his head and pressed forward. The level of worldwide curiosity about the project was mind-boggling: by the end of May 1956, more than twenty-seven thousand press clippings had poured into the publicity office. Clearly De Laurentiis had to deliver something extraordinary.

The first cut, at more than four hours, was extraordinarily long. Dino pressured Vidor to trim things down, and after sacrificing many costly, beautiful scenes, the director got the film down to three hours and twenty-five minutes.

The world premiere of *War and Peace* took place at the Capitol Theater in New York on August 23, 1956. For Dino, it represented a personal triumph. Perhaps drunk on his own success, this peerless manipulator of public opinion immediately made a daring announcement: his next project would be an adaptation of *The Divine Comedy*. He dropped this bombshell during a press conference at the Hotel Pierre, standing in front of a giant poster of Dante Alighieri. The movie would require four years of work, he explained, fifteen principal actors and actresses, and two directors, one American and one Italian. At once the announcement touched off a fierce competition among the newspapers to assign actors and actresses to the classic roles; obviously they expected Mangano to play Beatrice. Yet the project, assuming it was ever under serious consideration, would soon be abandoned for more feasible initiatives.

In the meantime, Dino and his Beatrice, now considered the royal couple of the Italian cinema, commenced a triumphal tour of the United States. They ended up in Hollywood, where they were feted by a legendary rival. David O. Selznick had once dreamed of producing his own version of Tolstoy's novel. Now he gallantly organized a reception for his guests, with various stars and local personalities, at Tower Grove—a historic Beverly Hills mansion once owned by John Barrymore, then Greta Garbo, and now inhabited by Selznick and his wife, Jennifer Jones. It was as if a defeated general had invited his victorious opponent over for dinner, after the battle was over.

War and Peace opened in Italy with a gala at the Teatro dell'-Opera in Rome on October 26, 1956. Again it won applause not only from the public but from the critics, who were unusually respectful and in some cases effusive. Many argued that *War and Peace* marked the dawn of a new, truly post-DeMille era in the history of the big-budget spectacular, revealing a level of seriousness and commitment not recently found in Hollywood films. It didn't manage to earn an Oscar, yet *War and Peace* got three important nominations—for Best Director, Best Cinematography, and Best Costume Design—which further confirmed its value. And although the opening titles still read *De Laurentiis–Ponti*, this new formula for the thinking man's blockbuster was clearly stamped with Dino's personality, taste, and characteristic foresight and perseverance.

CHAPTER 13

THE MAGIC PAIR

THE PRESS CLIPPING FROM A PROVINCIAL NEWSPAPER IS DATED 1964, when De Laurentiis and Federico Fellini, after breaking with each other some years before over *La Dolce Vita*, proposed working together once again. The headline reads, "The Magic Pair." What better way to define the bond of work and friendship that existed between the two? Throughout his life, the topic of Dino has caused Fellini to run through the entire gamut of feelings: affection and anger, esteem and resentment, joy and incompatibility—everything except indifference. And when Fellini's name surfaces in conversation with Dino, especially since the director's death, one senses a similar cascade of feelings.

As a producer-director team, the pair achieved an unsurpassed record: two consecutive Oscars for Best Foreign Language Film (for *La Strada* and *Nights of Cabiria*). But in the late 1960s, they kept pulling the rug out from underneath each other. First Dino refused to produce *La Dolce Vita*. Then Fellini shrugged off his directorial duties on *Il viaggio di G. Mastorna (The Voyage of G. Mastorna)*, even as the massive sets were being built at Dinocittà. There were recriminations, arguments in the press, lawyers, official documents. Yet veterans of Fellini's circle insist that despite the most bitter rages, nothing ever lessened the director's admiration for his old accomplice. And the same is true of Dino. Often Fellini called him Dinone ("big Dino"), and Dino responded by calling him Fefè.

How long had they known one another? Fellini's usual answer was "forever." Dino, though with some uncertainty, comes up with a more precise date: "I would say that we met on the set of Rossellini's

Open City, in a makeshift studio on Via Degli Avignonesi. I seem to recall that it was a scene with Fabrizi in it." The two filmmakers developed a cordial understanding and crossed paths often in the convivial madhouse that was the postwar Lux headquarters. What's more, it was De Laurentiis who offered the brand-new screenwriting duo of Fellini and Tullio Pinelli its first assignment in 1946: the revision of *Il passatore*, an RDL script about a famous nineteenth-century bandit.

Soon enough, however, Fefè moved into the director's chair. This development sometimes led to friction. In 1953, for example, Fellini approached De Laurentiis with the script for *La Strada*. According to the director's autobiography, Dino proposed that Silvana star in the film along with Burt Lancaster. As Fellini recalls, he tore up the contract in response. Dino disagrees, bristling at the very idea.

> None of that is true. The real story of *La Strada* went like this. One day Fellini called me and said, "Dino, nobody wants this film of mine. I'm sending over the screenplay for you to read, and we'll see if you're interested."
>
> I read the script, called him back, and said, "Formidable. But what actress did you have in mind? Who plays Gelsomina?"
>
> He came over on the double, escorted me to the screening room, and who did I see on the screen? Giulietta Masina dressed as a clown. "It's perfect," I told him. It's not true that I ever suggested Silvana for this role, nor did I do that on other occasions. Because, first of all, she didn't want to be forced on anybody. And second, she didn't like being an actress, and the less she worked, the happier she was. And third, when we really wanted to make a film with Silvana, like *Anna* or *Il brigante Musolino*, we built it around her role.
>
> As for Giulietta, there wasn't even a minimal discussion. I was so convinced by this figure leaping off the screen that I told Federico: "We're going to make the film, all we're missing is the male lead." In a flash it occurred to me that the gypsy Zampanò could be played by Anthony Quinn. I didn't mention him right there on the spot, though. At that moment Quinn happened to be making *Attila* for us, and I got an inspiration. I convinced the director, Pietro Francisci, to pretend he was sick. Then I asked Fellini if he would shoot a couple of scenes as a favor to me.

The trick worked: Francisci absented himself from the set, and Fellini anonymously assumed the direction of *Attila* for two or three days. In this way he got to know and like Quinn. So when Dino tossed out the actor's name as a possible Zampanò, his suggestion was accepted at once. The task of casting Matto was more laborious. Before selecting the American actor Richard Basehart, Dino insisted on auditioning his old friend Alberto Sordi, who turned out to be wrong for the part. It was an awkward verdict to deliver, and Sordi was flabbergasted, which opened a serious rift in his relationship with Fellini.

The shoot began in late October, and less than a year later, a print was screened at the 1954 Venice Film Festival. As it happened, *La Strada* went head-to-head with Luchino Visconti's *Senso*, kicking off a long, bitter feud between the two directorial camps. Dino was glad to see his own production win the Silver Lion. He was less happy to see various critics attack the film, unable to accept a cinematic fable from a director they had considered a neorealist.

Hoping to give *La Strada* a fresh start, De Laurentiis relaunched the film in Paris, organizing a gala at the Salle Pleyel in March 1955. It worked. The film was a smash all over the world and brought home fifty international prizes—including, of course, the Oscar, which a beaming Dino accepted on the stage of the RKO Pantages Theater in March 1957, with Masina, Fellini, and Pinelli in the audience.

> On the two films I made with Federico, we had only a single conflict, and that didn't concern *La Strada* but *Nights of Cabiria*. What happened was that he wanted to insert a fairly long sequence: the "man with the sack" episode. It revolved around an encounter between Cabiria and a mysterious nocturnal benefactor, who brought food and clothing to the homeless on the edge of town, pulling these gifts out of a sack. The character was played by Leo Catozzo, Fellini's customary editor. I said to Federico, "Cut it out, it doesn't work." And he didn't want to.
>
> Although I always gave myself the right to determine the final cut, I had never used this provision. I always talked with the director and tried to convince him. But Fellini didn't want to listen to me, and I was perfectly confident about my judgment, so I arranged for that part of the negative to disappear from the developing lab. When he couldn't find it, Federico went crazy. But he was well aware that I had spirited it away and was willing to accept that. Even he understood that the episode didn't really work.

> Many years later, when I was already in America, he called me on the phone and said, "Dino, will you give me that piece of film now?" I think he wanted it for a cultural event of some sort.

In reality, Fellini wanted the clip for a special film called *Fellini's Wastebasket*, made of up various sequences cut from his work as a director. But he also had a different tale to tell about the "man with a sack" episode. As he recalled it, the cut was made in response to an off-the-record request by the film ministry—which was effectively a condition for getting it past the censors. The figure of the benefactor supposedly would have offended the Catholic charity organizations. Dino denies this absolutely: "No, no, nobody else ever saw that piece of film: only me, Federico, Catozzo, and a few other technicians. It couldn't have offended anybody, because nobody saw it."

Fellini, of course, had his own methods for outwitting the censors. At one point he took the bold step of showing *Cabiria* to Cardinal Giuseppe Siri in a Genova screening room and extracting from him an official stamp of approval. With this green light from the ecclesiastical corner, *Cabiria* made its way to Cannes, where Giulietta was unanimously awarded the prize for Best Actress, "*avec hommage à Fellini*."

The film went on to replicate the triumphs of *La Strada*. And on March 26, 1958, a second miracle took place at the Pantages Theater: Fred Astaire and Dana Wynter handed Masina yet another Academy Award for Best Foreign Film. This time Dino had remained in Rome, because neither he nor anybody else even considered the possibility of winning two years in a row. When the news arrived the next morning, he could hardly believe it.

Obviously this second Oscar left Federico and Dino with a strong desire to work together again, but although they seemed destined for a lengthy partnership, they would paradoxically fail to complete even a single additional project. Not for want of trying. On the heels of *Cabiria*, De Laurentiis immediately put another Fellini project in the pipeline: an excellent script called *Viaggio con Anita (Travels with Anita)*. It was the story of an intellectual who hurries home to his native Adriatic village in order to be at his dying father's bedside—and who secretly brings along his beautiful lover. To some degree, the story was autobiographical: Urbano Fellini, the director's father, had died not long before in Rimini.

The script thrilled Dino. This was not only a classic Fellini vehicle but a film with a strong emotional impact, and both Sophia Loren and Gregory Peck had expressed interest in starring. Soon, however, difficulties arose in connection with Loren's contract: Carlo Ponti made demands that Dino considered nonsensical, and no doubt this contractual tug-of-war had some connection to certain small or great resentments that had accumulated during the five years of their partnership. Even these problems became moot when Ponti was accused of bigamy. At that point Sophia, feeling that she should share the exile of the man she loved, reluctantly withdrew from the project.

Irritated and disappointed, Fellini declared that without Loren, *Viaggio con Anita* was dead in the water. Dino proposed that they change gears: he offered up various titles to replace the aborted project, including a version of *Casanova*, until they settled on an abandoned script, *Moraldo in città*, which had originally been conceived as a sequel to Fellini's 1953 film *I vitelloni (The Young and the Passionate)*. Then Fellini decided to update the screenplay, setting it amid the tumultuous world of Via Veneto in 1958. After a certain amount of fiddling, he came up with that astonishing slice of contemporary life, *La Dolce Vita*.

The fact that he didn't produce *La Dolce Vita* still infuriates Dino. He speaks of the whole business reluctantly and attributes the decision to the negative opinions floated by his experts, Chiarini, Perilli, and Gino Visentini. He also alludes to a regionalistic prejudice: "I turned down the project because, being Neapolitan, I couldn't accept a situation in which a father kills his two babies before killing himself."

Perhaps this version of events is too simple. No doubt other considerations entered into Dino's decision. For one thing, the film lacked an American star, an element that would guarantee a certain performance at the box office. And Fellini's project seemed to be (and in fact was) dangerously vast in conception. According to Arturo Tofanelli, a producer who proposed taking the film off Dino's hands, De Laurentiis incensed Fellini by wanting "to stick his nose into the script and pare down expenses." This, of course, is the cinema's eternal battle.

Dino asked for 50 million lire to give up his rights to the film. Tofanelli hoped to get the money from Lux, but Gatti turned him down flat, and once De Laurentiis had thrown in the towel, almost all the major Italian producers and distributors followed suit. Finally, Peppino Amato took Fellini's case to the all-powerful Angelo Rizzoli, and a deal was struck. Over time Dino has given various versions of the events that deprived him of a third great success with the director. Perhaps it simply came down to those great stumbling blocks, money and morals. "I was worried about the extravagant cost of the film," he told one interviewer, "and about its vulnerability in regard to the censors. Back then the censors really gave you a beating. I was uncertain for quite a while. Then I ceded *La Dolce Vita* to Amato and moved on to *The Great War*."

Did the dispute wreck the friendship between the director and producer? Apparently not. On the afternoon of March 15, 1959, just before he began shooting *La Dolce Vita*, Fellini slipped away from the set. He showed up unannounced at Dino's villa on Via Appia and burst inside shouting, "Where is he? Where is the great man?" De Laurentiis, who was watching television with his brother Luigi and his children, hurried over to the visitor. Fellini hugged him tightly and repeated over and over, "Dinone, embrace me, wish me good luck." They embraced, they kissed, and Silvana, on a couch in the living room, smiled as she observed the scene. There was still a vague possibility that the actress would play Maddalena in the film: half joking and half not, she immediately asked Fellini, "When do I start?" But nothing would come of it; the role of the sickly rich woman was ultimately played by Anouk Aimée.

Years passed. Then, in January 1964, as Fellini was preparing to shoot *Juliet of the Spirits*, Dino learned that his old friend was squabbling with his erstwhile patron, producer Angelo Rizzoli. Could it be time for a rapprochement? After some amiable discussions, Dino and Fellini signed an unusual contract, dated February 13. According to this document, they would make *Juliet of the Spirits* together if Rizzoli declined it, or as an alternative, a film "of a modern kind, *i.e.*, without any costumes." There was also an option for a second film. Alerted to the situation, Rizzoli grew alarmed and accused Federico of wanting to betray him "with that Neapolitan down there."

In the end, *Juliet* was the last project Fellini would direct for the elderly Angelo. That left the second film. The contract between the old friends had specified an appropriate title, *What Mad Universe*, a science-fiction novel Fellini had asked Dino to option. By now, however, the director had something quite different in mind, which he didn't initially share with his partner. This was a short novel by Dino

Buzzati called *Lo strano viaggio (The Strange Voyage)*, which he'd read in a magazine eighteen years before: the story of a young man who mysteriously finds himself in the afterworld.

Traveling up to Milan, Federico invited Buzzati to knock out the screenplay with him. And so *Il viaggio di G. Mastorna (The Voyage of G. Mastorna)* came into being—amidst many doubts on Dino's part. The producer was less than enthusiastic about filming the otherworldly travels of a dead man. Throughout 1965, while Buzzati moved forward with the script, Fellini and Dino's brothers, Luigi and Alfredo, scouted locations in Naples, Milan, and Cologne. In the new studios at Dinocittà—where the director felt uncomfortable from the very first day, calling it "a space station, an inaccessible outpost"—various sets began to take shape. These included a scale model of the Cologne cathedral and the airplane in which the cellist Giuseppe Mastorna believes himself to be landing safely. (Instead, the plane crashes, and the protagonist crosses over to the kingdom of the dead.)

Other pieces of scenery were hammered together, among them a Neapolitan set at Vasca Navale, and Dino procured hundreds of costumes. But now Fellini revealed an alarming listlessness. The maestro was in fact experiencing the crisis that he'd depicted earlier in *8½*: he was a director about to embark on a film he no longer wanted to make. He had come to believe that *Mastorna* was bringing him bad luck—that messing around with the afterlife was not a smart thing to do. On September 14, 1966, Fellini had the following message delivered to his producer: "I must tell you that I've been debating within myself for some time, and that I've finally come to a conclusion. . . . I can't begin the film because, despite everything that's happened, I wouldn't be able to complete it. . . . I'm so sorry, *caro* Dino, to have arrived at this decision, but it's the only thing I can do."

A war between the two friends exploded, with the newspapers fanning the flames. Dino filed a claim for 1 billion lire in damages; the court granted him 350 million and a bailiff showed up at the villa Federico shared with Giulietta Masina to begin the seizure of property. Since the attached goods added up to a smaller sum than that granted by the court, Dino also asked for the seizure of any funds still owed to Fellini by Rizzoli.

The skirmish was interrupted by the official premiere of *The Bible* at San Carlo di Napoli. Meanwhile Luigi and Alfredo De Laurentiis did everything they could to broker a truce between the director and producer. Fellini had made the situation worse by declaring that he was ready to make the film for a different producer. In fact, he may already have been in the midst of secret negotiations, but the intermediaries kept trying to cobble something together.

Finally Dino and Federico agreed to meet one evening in January 1967, in the park surrounding the Villa Borghese in Rome. When the appointed time arrived, the producer joined the director and his lawyer in their car. The trio circled the park slowly, over and over, with Dino's car and driver following. After an hour the first car came to a halt, the occupants climbed out, and the two enemies exchanged a peacemaking embrace. All around them, meanwhile, retainers from both sides, who had been squatting on the grass, leaped forward in jubilation.

Since Fellini no longer wanted to work at Dinocittà, preparations for the film recommenced in the old studios at Vasca Navale. There was some thought of signing up Mastroianni for the lead role, but he was unavailable in April or May, when the shoot was scheduled to begin. It was also too late to hire an American star, so Fellini settled on Ugo Tognazzi. On March 13 he sent Dino a cheerleading note: "I've decided to use Tognazzi. Godspeed and good luck to us all!" The actor, who hadn't yet made his break into real stardom, was overjoyed at the news and ran off to telephone his father. But on the evening of April 10, at a decisively unfavorable juncture, the director was rushed to the hospital with severe chest pains.

Dino couldn't believe it. Suspecting Fellini of faking illness to get out of making the film, he sent his own team of doctors to the Salvator Mundi Clinic. But when the physicians returned with a catastrophic diagnosis—possible cancer—De Laurentiis was unable to hold back his tears. Luckily the next few examinations put these fears to rest. Federico was suffering from pleurisy, an inflammation of the membrane separating the lungs from the abdomen, with complications from anaphylactic shock. The doctors prescribed a long convalescence, which had just begun when Dino himself had to be rushed to the hospital after an attack of appendicitis.

Did all this put *Mastorna* on hold? Of course not. The recuperating director soon received a visit from Paul Newman. He'd been sent by Dino, who hoped that the maestro would cast him as Mastorna in place of Tognazzi—who, unjustly dropped from the project, ended up suing everybody.

In May the convalescent Fellini told one interviewer regarding Dino, "There's no longer any acrimony between us. On the contrary, I believe that Dino has a great deal of regard for me." It wasn't clear, however, whether the director still wanted to make the film or if he intended to make it with somebody else. As pragmatic as ever—and perhaps equally disenchanted by a project that had brought him such grief—Dino ended the suspense by relieving the director of his obligations. In return, on August 21, Fellini signed a contract to make three films with De Laurentiis over the next five years. He would never make a single one.

By now, the *padrone* of Dinocittà had lost all hope of breaking even on the project. Another Neapolitan producer, Alberto Grimaldi, nonetheless expressed interest in acquiring the rights to *Mastorna* and reimbursing all of Dino's expenses. On September 25 Grimaldi presented Dino with a check and brought the entire dispute to an end. Fellini recounts the grand finale in this way: "Dino fell to his knees, shouting, 'San Gennaro exists, he's right here in front of me, his name is Alberto Grimaldi!'" Today Dino dismisses this little scene as more fruit of the director's imagination, but he does say, "Not even this new San Gennaro could pull off what would have been a real miracle: convincing Fellini to make the film."

Oddly enough, the long controversy didn't destroy Dino's wish to work with Federico again. Shortly after, De Laurentiis telephoned him to ask if he'd like to direct *Waterloo*. Recalling the offer, Fellini commented, "At that point I realized that between the two of us, the lunatic wasn't me, it was him. Compared to Dino, I have the good sense, the practicality, and the mental rigor of a civil servant."

Then, while Federico was shooting *Fellini's Roma* in 1972, Dino tried again. He sent over Lee Falk, the creator of a popular comic-book series called *Mandrake the Magician*, to persuade Fellini to direct a film adaptation. The answer was no. A year later, while Federico was making *Amarcord*, the producer put a more concrete project on the table: *Casanova*.

The two discussed the idea, off and on, for a year, but the project collapsed in the face of several obstacles not even Dino could overcome. Fellini didn't want an American star (although he would eventually accept Donald Sutherland when he made the film for Grimaldi), and he refused to shoot *Casanova* in English. In addition, he was mulling over some ideas of his own for telling the story. Seeing that the project was going nowhere, Dino turned it over to another production house, Cineriz, which would in turn hand it off to Grimaldi, who soldiered on in the face of operational difficulties, personal clashes, snags, and interruptions. De Laurentiis noted the tribulations of the film with a weary air, as if to say, "I knew it." But he didn't stop wooing Fellini with an eye to future collaborations.

Their surviving correspondence certainly confirms that their relationship remained as sunny as ever. On July 18, 1977, Federico wrote, "The warm friendship that unites us is reciprocal. It's beyond discussion. At least until the next quarrel. How are you doing? I'm going through a period of stagnation and stifling immobility (aside from the sexual sphere, which still leaves me astonished and disbelieving)." And on December 17 of the same year, De Laurentiis wrote, "I'll take this opportunity to repeat how absurd it seems to me that an artist like you, who still has so much to say, has resigned himself to withering away in the limbo of contemporary Italy. Come to America, Federico, and like me, you'll find new enthusiasms and a new life. I promise you that nobody but me will have the privilege of producing your first American movie."

Of course, Fellini stayed put. On April 25, 1977, he alluded to a film version of the Greek myths, to be written by Anthony Burgess: "It could be a fantastic film, much more so than all the *Superman* and *Flash Gordon* pictures." And on October 6, 1980: "Do you know that the public here no longer goes to the cinema? The public is gone, and I don't know where it went. Did they all move to your part of the world? If that's the case, tell them to go home and start going to the cinema again." Dino responded from London on October 14: "Ah, *caro* Federico, the public doesn't go to the cinema when there aren't any interesting films there." In the same letter, meanwhile, he returned to the proposition he had made two years earlier: "If you would direct *Mandrake* with Jack Nicholson, you would see the public dragging its butt to the cinema once again, all over the world. Just think about it: the wizardry of Fellini the director combined with the wizardry of Mandrake the magician. The film could be shot anywhere, and it would be extremely entertaining. At least consider it. If you're interested, I'm ready to make it immediately."

Year after year, Dino kept up the pressure. In an interview with *La Stampa* in December 1980, he confessed, "I never stop cultivating the dream of a Fellini film. Sooner or later I'll convince him. And I think it will be to his advantage. Fellini needs somebody to force him out of his shell." He struck a similar note in a January 1982 interview with *La Repubblica*: "How is it possible that Signor Fellini, our greatest living filmmaker, makes no films? The television people can find 35 billion lire to make *Marco Polo*. At Signor Craxi's behest, they can even round up 6 billion to make *Garibaldi*, but nobody can find 3 billion to make a Fellini film? It's shameful."

> When I decided to produce *King Kong* in 1975, I made the announcement at a press conference. I hadn't yet hired a director, and when I spoke with Fellini, he said, "Don't you realize that I would be happy to make *King Kong*?"
>
> I said, "Fefè, there's plenty of things you want to make, but at the last moment you always change your mind."
>
> He said, "I could seriously consider making *King Kong* with you." That's as far as it went. But if you ask me, Federico was giving the idea some real thought.

From Los Angeles, Dino kept trying to bring Fellini back into the fold, proposing odder and odder projects. At one point he recalled his dormant *Divine Comedy* project and told the director, "Let's make it!" Then he grew irritated at the news that Fellini was negotiating a Dante adaptation with CBS, and he burst out, "If you sign up with another American firm, I'll shoot you in the knees." That wouldn't be necessary: Fellini returned from his mysterious trip to the United States without having signed anything, which led to Dino's insinuation that the director had never set foot outside of Rome. This prompted a resentful reply from Fellini, a further reply from Dino, and their millionth argument was under way.

The two did speak on the phone and even sought each other out. Fellini always had some entertaining tidbit to report to his friends about Dino's Californian adventures. In his imagination, he had transformed his old colleague into the protagonist of a comic strip: a Neapolitan in the cinematic Mecca. As Dino emphasizes, "my relationship with Federico became much, much better from the moment I left for America. We never lost sight of each other. We stayed in touch from a distance, and when I came to Rome, he hurried over to the Grand Hotel and jumped all over me like an eager puppy. Being at a distance brought us closer together."

Dino and Federico's volatile yet enduring relationship makes sense in terms of their equal and opposite drives. All his jokes aside, Federico considered Dino a true member of the creative tribe and never gave up the hope of reclaiming him for art. The producer's ambition, on the other hand, was to bring the poet back down to earth: for his own good, for his old age. No doubt if they had remained together, Fellini and De Laurentiis could have conquered the world (at least the world of the cinema), but each would have needed to turn over to the other some essential part of himself. Each of them was convinced that he knew exactly what the other needed, and each suffered from the fact that his opposite number never figured it out. Fellini repeated his opinion often: "Dino's strategy for liberating me is to have me make *Mandrake*." Despite his dismissive tone, however, he always seemed to leave open the possibility that he might make the film after all. Did he? No. But to lessen our disappointment at so many fizzled encounters, we still have *La Strada* and *Nights of Cabiria*—the two masterpieces that the "magic pair" left to the history of the cinema.

CHAPTER 14

AN IDEAL COUPLE?

In 1955 Dino began work on *War and Peace*. That year also saw a real turning point in the De Laurentiis family life. On January 29, at four in the morning, Federico Aurelio Francesco, the first male heir, was born in the Quisisana Clinic. Now the dynastic succession seemed assured. Silvana smiled and confessed, "I feel suffocated with joy."

The producer, in the United States for *War and Peace*, immediately returned to Italy in time to decide the baby's name. A photo of Dino, Veronica, and Raffaella standing at Silvana's bedside, with the mother cradling the newborn in her arms, was reprinted in papers around the world. A Roman astrologer (with a decided lack of visionary ability) declared that thanks to some favorable astral alignment, the boy had three paths open to him: politics, art, or emotional contentment. Instead he would be cursed with an unlucky destiny—a destiny that was, happily, beyond anybody's imagination in the early days of 1955.

Meanwhile, even as Dino was negotiating with Hepburn, he continued to take for granted that Silvana would be the protagonist of *War and Peace*. This idea presented some problems. It so happened that Silvana was a year younger than Audrey, yet she no longer had the freshness needed for the part of Natasha. Driven by perhaps unconscious motivations, she had transformed herself into a demure, middle-class *signora*, very much in keeping with the sober style of the 1950s. She spoke as if her youth belonged to the distant past.

By now Silvana was beginning to pay for her ostentatious indifference toward her career and her popularity. In July 1955 a Sicilian newspaper published a ranking of the six divas preferred by the local populace. Silvana brought up the rear, behind Sophia Loren, Gina Lollobrigida, Yvonne Sanson, Antonella Lualdi, and Rossana Podestà, and the article took a slightly scolding attitude toward her finish in last place: "Finally, there is the *sophisticated lady* of the Italian cinema. . . . La Mangano has dropped a few rungs. Her seclusion, however intertwined with her serious nature, no longer serves her well."

Silvana lost no opportunity to point out that her favorite film was the one she didn't have to make and that she would stop working immediately if she weren't married to a producer. But was her career truly in trouble? Her appearances on the screen continued at a brisk clip and always with excellent results at the box office. This suggests that Dino, who didn't take his consort's conspicuous hatred for the cinema too seriously, was shaping Silvana's career with great skill and attentiveness. Thanks to his efforts, her salary hit some truly fabulous heights for the period. For example, when Titanus produced De Santis's *Uomini e lupi* in 1956, the male protagonist Yves Montand received 35 million lire out of total budget of 400 million. But Mangano, on loan from Lux, was paid 80 million, and soon her price would top the 100 million mark.

There's some question as to whether the issue of work was a real source of contention between husband and wife or simply an arena for harmless skirmishing. A certain tension is revealed in an article written in July 1955 by Camilla Cederna. At first the journalist noted that "Silvana's face is transformed into a little girl's when her husband speaks, and that she is in continuous, open, and affectionate disagreement with him."

Then Cederna recorded the following little scene: "'My wife is the anti-diva *par excellence*,' proclaims De Laurentiis in a loud, shrill voice. ('Hear ye, hear ye!' Silvana seems to interject, winking in his direction, and meanwhile she forms an amusing, crescent-shaped crease beneath her nose.) He continues: 'Maybe this is a source of power for her, but it's also a big mistake.' ('Ouch!' is what we read in his wife's eyes, anxious eyes that are immediately squeezed shut in a vise of helplessness and endurance, while she pretends to cover her ears.)" Then Cederna records Dino's diagnosis: "'Silvana has a complex about not being an actress, she has a complex that she's conquered the public only because she showed off her legs, she has a complex that she becomes ugly when she's made up for the cameras!' (Silvana counts her complexes on her fingers and imitates her husband's vexed and indignant expression.) 'And let's keep in mind that she has enormous abilities as an actress: all she needs is the slightest willingness to show what she can do.'"

The facts do seem to support Dino's point of view. In 1954 alone, *Mambo* was released in September, *Ulysses* in October, and *The Gold of Naples* in December, and all of them were major hits. Silvana was then anointed at the Silver Ribbon ceremonies on July 16, 1955, with a decidedly triumphant Dino at her side.

The so-called Italian Oscars were then in their tenth year. The 1955 ceremony was a tremendous moment for the nation's filmmakers—Italy was now second only to the United States in movie production—and accounts of the evening, which was broadcast on television for the first time, provide a small panorama of the era. In the verdant setting of the Belvedere delle Rose on Via Cassia, the atmosphere was intimate and elegant. After the heavy mugginess of the day, the coolness of the location felt delicious, and the women threw "light summer stoles of white ermine or pale mink over their bare shoulders." The Silver Ribbon for Best Actor went to Marcello Mastroianni. De Laurentiis, Ponti, and Fellini all won awards for *La Strada*, once again beating out Visconti's *Senso*. And then Mangano received the Silver Ribbon for her work in *The Gold of Naples*. Wearing a flowered silk ensemble with wide, stiff skirt, Silvana stepped up to the podium and quickly declared that she suffered from "microphone anxiety." Speaking rapidly, she thanked her director, De Sica, and disappointed the audience by returning at once to her seat.

"She was very beautiful and extraordinarily pale," one guest recalled. "She asked a journalist for a cigarette. He offered her a Nazionale. She puffed on it absently and coughed, bending over double, then smiled as if to excuse herself and asked her husband for an American cigarette. (She allowed the journalist, however, to kiss her hand.) Pulling out his ribbon, Mastroianni approached her: 'How's it going, Silvana?' 'You saw the whole thing: giving me a prize is like playing a trick on me.'"

After so much time, here were the ex-lovers from the Tuscolano neighborhood, side by side once more. If their fleeting encounter aroused a spurt of retrospective jealousy in Dino, nothing could truly spoil this special evening, so richly endowed with satisfaction. He had triumphed over his partner Ponti (who hadn't wanted to make *La Strada*), he had beaten Lux (the producer of *Senso*), and he had seen his wife win an award for a prestigious picture which he himself had produced. And finally, the guests of honor were his own illustrious collaborators: King Vidor, Audrey Hepburn, Mel Ferrer, and Henry Fonda, all of them in Rome for *War and Peace*.

A few days later the president of the Republic, Giovanni Gronchi, received the prize winners. This time, along with the "noted and internationally famed producers" Ponti and De Laurentiis, Fellini and Visconti put in an appearance. Silvana's dark outfit was elegantly simple, but on her feet, as a tiny token of anarchy, she wore a pair of old sandals and no socks.

Hollywood on the Tiber indeed. That same year, De Laurentiis realized another dream. He had long desired a seaside villa and would have happily gone back to Capri, but Silvana needed tranquility, which was in short supply on that glamorous island and celebrity watering hole. Instead, soon after Federico's birth, Dino acquired Casa del Mare from the heirs of the industrial titan Guido Donegani. This imposing, two-story edifice stood on the promontory of Cap Martin, Monte Carlo, where it had been erected in 1905 by an English lord. The purchase represented one more grandiose move on the producer's part. It also confirmed his natural instinct to combine his personal needs with his public image: the villa was at once a gift for his wife and his adored children, a response to his own appetite for the sea (and for a high-style habitation), and a finishing touch added to the picture of the Italian cinema's "royal family." Facing the bay, surrounded by nearly eight acres of gardens shaded by century-old olive trees, giant banana palms, cedars, and eucalyptus, Casa del Mare contained twenty rooms and seven baths. The bedrooms were on the top floor, and below these were various sitting rooms, plus an enormous living room with a magnificent mosaic floor and marble walls.

As its new owner had foreseen, Casa del Mare proved to be an ideal shield from outside attention, and a perfect location for entertaining friends. The entire clan traveled there regularly for summer and winter vacations, and the residence would become the backdrop for many memorable episodes in the family's history.

The splendor of the house and the fame of its inhabitants did arouse the curiosity of the press, Italian and otherwise. In the July 1956 issue of *Nice matin*, a reporter described the scene: "Elegant pieces of garden furniture are scattered among one shady oasis and the next. . . . A double staircase of marble descends from the grand terrace toward the flowering pathways, with some tarps discreetly hidden in the greenery." The grounds opened onto a private beach, but Silvana (whose principal enemies were "nerves, heat, and noise") preferred the pool with its sky-blue tiles. Staffed by seven Italian servants, Casa del Mare was the most orderly, tranquil villa on the French Riviera—until the weekend, that is, when there arrived by plane from Rome or London a "person who makes the place lively and animated: Silvana's husband, Dino De Laurentiis." The newspaper noted that the producer's temperament was the opposite of his wife's: "He's a businessman who's always effervescent, always in a hurry, always gabbing on the telephone. As far as he goes, the Mangano Enigma doesn't exist. De Laurentiis doesn't want his wife to turn her back on the screen. . . . In a few weeks, work will begin on his version of Tolstoy's *Resurrection*, and then he'll go to Indochina to shoot *La diga sul Pacifico* with René Clément."

In fact the production of *Resurrection*, which was supposed to star Montgomery Clift, seemed imminent. In August, at the New York premiere of *War and Peace*, Silvana's hair was gathered in a chignon, with a part in the middle and two sleek bands drawn back to cover her ears. When someone asked if this "Russian-style" coiffure was a new style or a publicity stunt, the astonished Mangano explained that she was merely getting used to the hairdo for her next role: Katyusha in *Resurrection*.

When the project was canceled, the diva hardly seemed disappointed. In an earlier interview she confessed, "When I first read *Resurrection*, the character of Katyusha moved me profoundly. But now that I'm about to be immersed in the role, it fills me with horror." She felt less and less enthusiasm for the film industry generally. During her sojourn in New York, while her husband was celebrated as a globe-trotting producer, the diva went around without makeup, in a plain skirt, blouse, and flats. To one inquiring journalist, she declared, "I'm a mature woman with children. . . . I'm no longer what I was eight years ago, I'm no longer sexy. And I make films only for the money."

Over time the conflicts between Silvana and Dino had grown bigger rather than smaller, and not only in regard to her attitude about work. The two played differing roles in the home, as well. It was Dino who organized the household, who worried about bills and even small expenses, from Federico's toy automobile to shoes for the children. He was the one who made sure that they ate well, who occasionally cooked for their friends, who maintained his reputation as a model host who looked after every last detail. Silvana hated to cook and removed herself from household matters. She contributed to the domestic atmosphere by acquiring costly antique furniture and original artworks and dedicated herself to the small things.

He was constantly on the move, while she could hardly wait to shut herself in, to read, to listen to music. He devoured novels, always on the lookout for new film ideas; she read inaccessible essays to improve her mind. When it came to soccer, Dino rooted for Lazio and Silvana rooted for Rome. The producer's friends were all in the movie business. Silvana always insisted that the world of the cinema was a sham, composed of boring people: "None of them know how to keep quiet, they all talk through their hats and pretend to be what they're not, and everything remains so superficial." But she was actually the one who stayed up late with her friends in the evening, while Dino, who had been at work since dawn, fell asleep on his feet. Yet the marriage held together, and during those years, Silvana and Dino were considered the indestructible couple of the Italian cinema.

What kept them united? Who knows if Silvana understood (perhaps she would understand later) that this brusque and affectionate man attended to her deepest needs, protecting her from the external world and possibly from herself? Without being forced to struggle or compromise, Mangano had become an internationally famous star—thanks to Dino, who made so many decisions for her. As a woman she was adored, as a mother she was contented, and her whole existence unfolded in a setting of luxurious ease that could hardly be displeasing. However unambitious she might be, Silvana loved the beautiful clothing, the precious furnishings and objects: animated, perhaps, by a proud sense of vindication, she was eager to forget her modest origins and to have other people forget them too. After her marriage, she did her dogged best to erase her image as a *mondina*—the role that had made her famous—and transformed herself into an irreproachable mother and a reluctant actress.

But this was merely a phase, a period of transition. As Dino's prestige (and their standard of living) became more and more elevated, Silvana aimed higher still, reinventing herself as a charismatic, high-society figure. Her perennial project was to refine not only her appearance—an easy task, given her natural elegance—but her spiritual life. "Despite her children, her career, and her husband," wrote the journalist Maria Livia Serini, "she still has a problem to resolve. For some time, she has forced herself to read difficult books, which she understands only in part and conscientiously annotates like a student preparing for an exam: Greek or Indian philosophers, medieval poetry. But she speaks only reluctantly about her reading. It's part of her secret personality, which she appears to jealously defend." The first person Silvana meant to defend herself from was Dino, whose explosive personality often seemed to occupy all the available space.

There was no doubt about Dino's love and dedication. De Laurentiis (as his wife habitually called him, as if to establish some sense of distance) seemed to exist to satisfy, gratify, and pamper Silvana. But he did it in his own way. The producer's personality was not a malleable one: impatient, used to conquering every obstacle no matter what the cost, he didn't pause to analyze his wife's troubled sensibility. Instead, the familial routine worked on the strength of his decisive pragmatism. It was only within the limits set by Dino that Silvana could carve out her own space.

Perhaps, then, Mangano was taking revenge when she spoke contemptuously of the cinema, which represented everything to her husband, or when she belittled him in front of others. Dino, meanwhile, was attracted not only to Silvana's beauty but to the very elusiveness of the woman he had married. He was accustomed to running roughshod over things and situations, yet his wife secretly escaped his grasp.

Still, in this marriage of polar opposites, there remained several points in common, which kept the partnership on its feet for the first few years. There was mutual affection and respect; Silvana appreciated Dino's responsible attitude, and he loved her retiring nature. Both had a strong sense of family. At their home on Via Appia or in Monte Carlo, Silvana's sister Natascia was essentially a permanent guest, and often at least one grandmother was around as well. In *Annabella* magazine, Giuseppina De Laurentiis gladly recounted how much she adored her daughter-in-law: "At first, Silvana seems like a cool, distant woman. Partly it's because of her character, which is extremely reserved. . . . When she's at home, though, she's a different person. Most of the time when we're together at the villa on the Côte d'Azur, she and I stay up late chatting and gossiping. Both of us completely lack the ability to go to bed early. Often it turns out that we're the only two people awake in the entire household. Silvana works at her knitting, I read or simply chat with her. We talk about the children, cooking, any old thing."

And, naturally, there were the children. When a journalist asked De Laurentiis if he would like to take a second honeymoon with his wife, the producer replied, "I'd like it, and how! But it's not possible. Where would we leave our kids? Once you've brought children into the world, you live only for them. Neither Silvana nor I would find it hard to give up even our favorite things in order to stick close by our kids."

By now, in fact, Dino had become a full-fledged paterfamilias. The era of nursing and diapers was over, and the three tots were turning into real conversationalists, each with a distinct personality. This change too was causing some new problems for the hyperactive producer. Could he work in a frenzied manner and still find time to be with his children, to follow their exploits as they grew up, to enjoy them? The answer was no. For Dino, at least, the cinema was an all-encompassing passion, and to realize his own projects—which were always risky, always inspired by grandiose aims—he had to cope with all manner of economic, contractual, and logistical squabbles on a daily basis. That left little time for his children.

He would be a loving father, ready to step in during their moments of need, but he wouldn't be around much. All he could do was entrust matters to his wife. When she wasn't employed on the set, she had much more free time than he did. (When she was working, a battalion of aunts and uncles, plus a well-drilled domestic staff, including a British nanny, were hurled into the breach.)

Luckily husband and wife were in agreement on basic issues of discipline. In the De Laurentiis household there were only two timetables that the children were obliged to heed—those regulating when to get up and when to go to bed—and only two prohibitions: no dangerous games and no offending the neighbors. Otherwise, there was a great deal of freedom. From time to time, of course, punishment was in order. Then Dino staged an unvarying ritual: he primly marched the culprit into his study and delivered an emphatic scolding.

Of course, there were a good many differences in their parenting styles. From the time her first child was born, Silvana made an elaborate effort to appear self-assured; she didn't want her kids to grow up clinging fearfully to their mother's apron strings. Even so, she admitted being apprehensive. Dino's approach was more decisive. During a cruise on a friend's yacht, he resolved to teach the three-year-old Federico to swim. Fastening a rope around the boy's waist and slipping a lifejacket over his shoulders, he tossed him overboard without any further instruction. All this transpired without his wife's knowledge, since she would have lost control. "I would have screamed or fainted."

And what of the children themselves? In an article she dictated to a journalist in January 1959, Silvana recorded the following exchange with her son:

"Federico. Do you enjoy life?"

"Yes."

"And how does it feel?"

"Hard."

If the family's youngest member and "little despot" expressed himself in this way at scarcely four years of age, there was a reason. Of all the children, Federico was the most nervous, the most stubborn, the most capricious. He would start shouting at the merest trifle, and when contradicted, the normally kind, pleasant child promptly became furious and mean-spirited. Sooner or later everybody capitulated in the face of his screaming, except for Raffaella, who exasperated him by remaining calm.

According to Silvana, Federico considered the women of the house to be of only secondary importance: he obeyed them in order to get what he wanted. The only authority he recognized was Dino, for whom he had, in Silvana's words, "a pathological adoration. It's enough to recall that at six months, when he began to say the word *mamma*, he used it exclusively to summon his father. . . . Only this year, listening to his sisters, did he resign himself to calling me by that name, and he began calling his father *daddy*, just like the British nanny taught him to."

If Federico was the most overbearing of the children, Raffaella was the one who most resembled her father. Vivacious, independent, she was the only one who knew how to take care of herself. Veronica, meanwhile, took after her mother, who described the sensitive oldest child as "gloomy, jealous, attentive to how we behave. If she sees me being more affectionate with the others, she's capable of turning white, as if she's gotten some terrible news." Veronica was drawn to the fine arts, to painting and studying music. Raffaella loved sports and became a good swimmer, with a fierce devotion to staying underwater: at home or in the car, she often pinched her nose shut and held her breath to see how long she could stand it.

For the most part, Dino agreed with his wife's assessment of their children's temperaments. Meanwhile, the girls observed their mother and came up with some provocative evaluations of their own. Veronica was convinced that Silvana smoked several thousand cigarettes per day, and she told one journalist that she preferred to spend evenings with her mother because that was when "she's the most awake." Raffaella, at age six, heard her mother exclaim, "I want to die," and asked her, "Why are you saying you want to die? You should say you want to live. You always seem so tired of life that living is like dying for you."

Dino listened to such things in astonishment, unsure as to whether these observations denoted a lively intelligence or whether they were the symptoms of some deep malaise. Yet he seldom brooded over the whole business. The facts were what mattered, and at the moment the facts seemed reassuring enough. The children were growing up healthy; they were animated; they had toys and clothing; they attended such exclusive schools as the American-run Marymount. True, the kids saw him only at dinner or on Sundays, and even his summer vacations at Cap Martin were fairly brief. Aside from that, their contacts were fleeting. Yet each of his appearances represented a celebration for the children, a significant event, a break in the monotonous grind of daily life. Could most fathers say the same?

CHAPTER 15

BETWEEN BANGKOK AND MONTE CARLO

THE TRIUMPH OF *WAR AND PEACE* BEGAN A RELATIVELY TRANQUIL PERIOD for Dino. In the second half of the 1950s, his frenetic activities settled into a kind of routine; he finished one film and began another, attended one festival and moved on to the next.

In January 1957 he and Silvana traveled to Pechbury, a Thai village on the Indian Ocean, for *La diga sul Pacifico*, an adaptation of the Marguerite Duras novel, directed by René Clément. Originally the cast was to have included James Dean, who'd signed an option just a few days before his fatal car accident. In his place, Dino hired Anthony Perkins, an emerging star working outside the United States for the first time. In *Anthony Perkins: A Haunted Life*, Ronald Bergan recounts Perkins's bewilderment at finding himself on a set where the director spoke only French and where everything needed to be explained via a translator.

Perkins and Mangano played a brother and sister with a faint suggestion of incest hovering over them, suffering under the heel of their domineering mother, Jo Van Fleet. Keeping all the bases covered, the two protagonists also got to strut their stuff in a modern-dance number called the crawl. In the United States, where the film would first be released as *This Angry Age*, then as *The Sea Wall*, one critic summed it up as "*The Glass Menagerie* goes to the Orient."

To generate publicity—and to counter the (accurate) rumors that he was gay—Perkins allowed the press office to spread the story that he was flirting with Natascia Mangano. Silvana, meanwhile, spent her evenings shut up in her room reading or writing letters, as she always did when she was away from home. According to rumor, the ever-solicitous Dino had arranged for the purchase of several dozen yards of black fabric, used to block out all the ambient light from Silvana's bedroom. Still, the diva never pulled rank on the set. She showed up punctually each morning like a bit player on her first job and faced the workday with infinite patience.

Alas, *La diga sul Pacifico* turned out to be an accident-prone production. On one occasion, while they were shooting exteriors, a tremendous typhoon blew in, forcing the cast and crew to run for cover. On another, Mangano and Van Fleet nearly lost their lives when their car skidded off the road and plunged over the bank of a river. Although the water was fairly shallow, the riverbed was made of shifting sand, and the car rapidly began to sink. Luckily a group of bystanders threw ropes to the two actresses and towed them back to shore.

On March 27 De Laurentiis was in Los Angeles, picking up his Oscar for *La Strada*. In May he was at Cannes, where he and Silvana organized a memorable reception for *Nights of Cabiria* at the Cap Martin villa, chartering a private train for their guests. In September, husband and wife made their customary appearance at the Venice Film Festival, chatting for photographers and journalists on the roof of the Excelsior Hotel. Then Dino was busy planning *La tempesta* (in the U.S.A. released as *Tempest*), a remake of the 1947 Mario Camerini film *La figlia del capitano*. The production would elicit an unusual degree of cooperation from the Yugoslavs; not only did they provide hundreds of foot soldiers and cavalry, they even built a new fort on the outskirts of Belgrade. And so it went. Another production, another trip, another press conference, and then it was time for the royal couple to move on.

Meanwhile, vacations on the Côte d'Azur succeeded one another in a regular rhythm: Easter, summer, Christmas, winter. Sometimes the couple went out for New Year's Eve. Other times they continued their old custom of celebrating at home. Relatives and friends visited in shifts, and the group almost always included Mario Camerini and Tully Hruska, Alberto Sordi, the administrator Fausto Saraceni and his wife, the actress Teresa Pellati, and the costume designer Bruna Parmesan. One glamorous occasion followed another, and the newspapers provided the appropriate coverage.

Most years Dino and Silvana attended the traditional Monte Carlo Gala, sponsored by Princess Grace and Prince Rainier. Organized as a charity benefit, this annual reception welcomed the beautiful people of the moment to the Sporting Club's terrace. There you would find Aristotle Onassis and his wife Tina (who was eventually succeeded by mistress Maria Callas, then second wife Jackie Kennedy), Aga Khan, and the former monarchs of Yugoslavia. There were American producers such as Darryl Zanuck and Jack Warner, writers like Noel Coward and Jean Cocteau, and movie stars like Greta Garbo (who stayed strictly out of the public eye) and Kirk Douglas.

The ritual of these evenings was always the same. The guests ate, they listened to music (the Platters and Harry Belafonte were all the rage), they danced, and then they lined up at the gambling tables. For Dino, this was the moment he'd been waiting for. Unlike his first wife, Bianca, Silvana was perfectly in sync with him here: she too liked to gamble. Frequently the two stayed up into the small hours losing large sums at chemin or baccarat, always without batting an eyelash.

In the April 12, 1959, issue of *Lo Specchio*, for example, there was a boxed feature dedicated to "A Night with Dino De Laurentiis." There we read that Dino, having reserved a table at the Sporting Club for the annual gala, arrived quite late with a group of friends. At the end of supper, "during which the champagne flowed like water," the guests danced, then moved on to the casino, located next to the banquet rooms. Dino, who lost heavily all evening, was photographed at the wheel of his Cadillac with a gloomy expression. On the other hand, he had his lucky evenings too, and from time to time the newspaper would deliver a tidbit like this one: "The bigwigs took their places at the gambling tables, and whatever Jack Warner lost, Dino De Laurentiis won."

> Sure, I was a gambler. I won plenty, I lost plenty. Never at poker, though. I played at the casino, mostly at chemin de fer. I spent some unforgettable nights with Gianni Agnelli. At the time Fiat was still being overseen by the managing director, Vittorio Valletta, so Gianni was free to pass a few evenings at the casino with his friends. Then the business began to take up all of his time and he stopped gambling. And I stopped too.
>
> It's funny: these days I don't feel the slightest attraction to the casino. Yet I spent entire evenings at the table with De Sica, with Peppino Amato—who once really exploded at a guy in Cannes

who was cheating him, shouting out in that peculiar French of his, "*Je fais un quarantotto!*" We also ran into Angelo Rizzoli many times, but he was never a true gambler: you never saw him at the chemin tables. He liked to circulate with chips in his hand, piling them up on a table in order to distribute them to his friends.

Darryl Zanuck, on the other hand, was a real chemin man. I recall that during the early 1950s, the casino at Monte Carlo was always full of Americans. There was Jack Warner, and there was Darryl, who always said, "I'm leaving tomorrow," and never left. Finally I asked him, "All you do is say you're leaving and then never leave. What's that all about?" And he, who had a beautiful woman with him, told me, "Dino, I've discovered some amazing innovations here in Europe." He explained that Americans restricted their lovemaking to the normal, canonical act. In Europe he was just discovering that there were many other ways to do it.

I began to gamble when I was young: I drove to Cannes with some friends and lost practically everything. Then, as I was driving back, I hit Monte Carlo before entering Italy, and since I still had a few soldi in my pocket, I decided to try my luck again. I have my own numbers for the roulette wheel, which I always use: 8, 11, 17, and 23. This time I put my chips on 17, won, put everything on 17 again, won, put everything on 17, won, and then repeated the trick one last time. From that moment on I became crazy about gambling. Then, at the Casinò di Venezia, I discovered chemin de fer. Until then I had never played chemin. But on that occasion I won, won, won, and from then on I was bitten by the bug.

I stopped about fifteen years ago. Why? One fine day I told myself, "If I gamble and lose 200 or 300 million lire, it really bothers me. But if I win 200 or 300 million lire, that doesn't change my life. What's more, it makes me tired. I stand there for hours and I don't enjoy myself." I realized that the passion was gone. Maybe it was because films had begun to cost so much that I was gambling millions of dollars with each production. Or maybe the impulse simply died. I wouldn't know how to find a logical explanation.

In part, though, I think it can be chalked up to two trips I took to Las Vegas. The casinos there are so squalid, with those slot machines that I hate, and when you play chemin, you're not even pitted against another human being, the way you are in France or Monte Carlo. I came back from Las Vegas thinking, "No more gambling."

Now I limit myself to an occasional hand of *scopone* with my friends, but never for money. The last time I went to Cannes—I don't even remember for which film—I accompanied my nephew Aurelio to the casino, but I stopped at the bar for a drink and never even touched a chip. Gambling, if I'm not mistaken, is like a woman: for as long as she entices you, you think only of possessing her. Then, when the moment of grace passes, you move on. Gambling is the same: when it's over, it's over.

CHAPTER 16

DINO GOES TO WAR

ON AUGUST 8, 1959, DINO TURNED FORTY. NO DOUBT HE SPENT PART OF the day in his office at Vasca Navale, with his feet propped up on his enormous desk and a cigarette in his mouth: that's how he's invariably pictured in the newspapers of the era. If he found a moment that day to take stock of his life, he had every reason to be satisfied.

He'd been a producer for two decades. He'd come out of the war without a scratch, founded and broken up at least four substantial companies, and opened or reopened three movie studios, along the way creating artistic triumphs and commercial blockbusters. He had faced down crisis after crisis, crossed the oceans a hundred times, risked and struggled, shouted and cajoled, gambled and mediated. He owned two beautiful homes and a fleet of expensive automobiles. As far as his family went—yes, his relationship with Silvana remained a little tense, but Dino was still deeply in love with his wife. He certainly didn't anticipate any of the tempestuous events to come.

Born under the sign of the lion, De Laurentiis had lived up to his astrological pedigree. In "Beneath the Lights of Cinecittà," in the November 1958 issue of *L'Europeo*, the uncompromising author and journalist Oriana Fallaci dubbed him the greatest of all Italian producers. Fallaci, who intended to conduct "an uninhibited investigation into the secret world of the Italian cinema," brought her customary tartness to the proceedings. She began, "If I hadn't already seen the man they call the Cecil B. DeMille of the Italian cinema with an apron on, preparing to cook spaghetti in a New York hotel, and if I hadn't happened to see him walking around barefoot and in a bathing suit at his beautiful house in Rome—circumstances that would demythologize even the most ferocious of dictators—I would have been extremely worried about meeting him at his office at Vasca Navale, where his glance is the equivalent of an order and his shouting makes the ceiling tremble. . . . At times he's slightly nervous, due to a lack of sleep. He rises at six in the morning, goes to bed at two A.M., and sleeps with one hand resting on the telephone, waiting for a call from Los Angeles or Mexico City."

That morning, Fallaci tells us, the atmosphere was particularly tense, because De Laurentiis had just read in *Variety* that the *real* Cecil B. DeMille intended to make a blockbuster based on the life of Simón Bolívar. Dino had been planning this project for two years. He was furious, and nobody dared remind him that he had an appointment with a journalist. Yet his anger cooled the moment he decided to mount a counterattack.

The result: "The door opens and De Laurentiis, in shirtsleeves and a loosened tie, waves me inside. . . . He's already reserved three seats on the next nonstop flight to Los Angeles: one for him, one for his secretary, and one for the business agent. And at this hour, the real Cecil B. DeMille must be praying to Moses, imploring him to intervene with San Gennaro and keep Dino on his good side. But San Gennaro's not listening to Moses. He's only listening to Dino, who, pointing his index finger at me, declares: 'We'll fix the whole business. I'm used to these little pranks. The same thing happened with the late lamented Mike Todd, God rest his soul.'"

During the interview, Dino gnawed on a cigarette, answered a long-distance call with the phone tucked under his right ear, and made another, simultaneous call to San Paolo with a different phone tucked beneath his left ear. He examined some publicity materials, signed a letter, greeted an aspiring starlet, fired her, and dictated a telegram to his secretary. And meanwhile he explained his philosophy to Fallaci. "A low- or medium-budget film is good for nothing," he insisted. "The competition from TV is too strong for us to fight it with mediocre movies. My theory of production goes like this: make either films of absolute artistic value, like *La Strada* or *Nights of Cabiria*, or big spectaculars like *War and Peace*. . . . The public, no matter how lazy or demanding it may be, will always go to see a film with an interesting subject, fancy production values, rich colors, and a cast of internationally famous actors. The more you spend, the more you earn: that's my argument. And this is one of the issues that Carlo Ponti and I couldn't agree on."

Despite his fire-breathing behavior, the essential fact that emerged from Fallaci's article was Dino's absolute identification with his work. In contrast to many of his colleagues, "producing a film is not, for him, a hobby, or one more form of financial speculation to fatten up the portfolio. It's a job that excludes every other activity." Dino agreed: "It's a profession that I love in the same way I love my wife." And his wife added, "I believe that he would rather commit suicide than change his profession."

Dino would not make *Bolívar*; for that matter, neither would DeMille. By March 1959 Dino was engaged in several very different battles. On the corporate front, he crossed lances with his colleague and rival Goffredo Lombardo, considered by many the most powerful man in the Italian cinema. From his father, Gustavo, this seemingly omnipotent figure had inherited Titanus, which not only encompassed film production, distribution, and financing, but owned two of the biggest studios in Rome and controlled a third. How did Lombardo get Dino's goat? During this period De Laurentiis was facing a possible eviction by the owners of the Vasca Navale complex. To foil this threat, he put in a bid to acquire the place for 220 million lire and declared himself ready to sweeten the pot. Meanwhile, though, an unknown company called Feltria outbid him with an offer of 255 million lire. Dino then discovered that Feltria was merely a front for Lombardo. At a meeting of the National Union of Producers, he demanded that his rival be dismissed from his post as president of the organization. By the time he concluded his fiery speech, the entire assembly was on his side. Lombardo, unprepared for such an attack, stepped down, and the next day the whole matter ended up in court.

The dispute ended in June with a complete reconciliation. Indeed, De Laurentiis, who says that he's always been friendly with Lombardo, doesn't even remember the clash. Yet the coverage this spat received in the newspapers for three straight months was one more confirmation of the position our hero had staked out for himself. As one magazine put it, "Dino is a force of nature, and he can't be stopped."

It must have been gratifying for Dino to read such things about himself, if he took the time, but at that moment he was hunkered down at the Vasca Navale complex, shooting interiors for his next project, *The Great War*. This film had plunged him into tougher battles than the one with Lombardo.

The screenwriter Luciano Vincenzoni has recounted his own version of how *The Great War* came into existence. As everybody knows, the act of writing an autobiography is seldom conducive to gospel truth, and this problem is only multiplied when the autobiographer is a writer, for whom fantasy is second nature. Often, however, the embellishments of memory prove more suggestive than the naked truth. Doubters need only consult Fellini's clamorous oeuvre—or the case of Vincenzoni, a Treviso native enticed by Rome and the cinema during the late 1950s.

Down on his luck, semi-starving, and encumbered by humiliating debts, Vincenzoni (then in his early thirties) found himself contemplating his last 1,000-lire banknote. With courage born of desperation, he decided to take a taxi to the De Laurentiis studio and confront the legendary Dino in his den. As he arrived at Vasca Navale, his situation became even worse, because the taxi meter now read 1,500 lire. All Vincenzoni could do was plead with the driver to wait.

He slipped through the gates and, unannounced, found his way to the producer's sanctum sanctorum, where Dino was meeting with Carlo Lizzani. Annoyed, De Laurentiis prepared to slam the door on the intruder. Then Lizzani, who knew and liked Vincenzoni, interceded: why not hear him out, just to see if he had any good ideas? Behind his imposing desk, Dino granted the petitioner fifteen minutes, no more, to make his pitch.

The conversation lasted a couple of hours, and Dino optioned all of the intruder's ideas on the spot. Vincenzoni would receive a million lire per project, plus an additional million as a monthly salary—plus some cash to pay the cab driver. Dino couldn't restrain his laughter. And soon enough, one of Vincenzoni's ideas would hit the production pipeline: *The Great War*.

Alas, the screenwriter's account of his desperate mission to Vasca Navale must be modified. As it turns out, this particular treatment, inspired by Stanley Kubrick's *Paths of Glory* and de Maupassant's short story "Deux amis," had already made the rounds from one producer to another. Monicelli expressed some interest in directing the film, so the project was acquired by Amato. It would have been the director, then, who discussed the script with Dino. And it was the enthusiastic producer who immediately cut a deal: he would cede *La Dolce Vita* to Amato and get the rights to Vincenzoni's treatment in return.

Dino let the opportunity to produce Fellini's great film slip through his fingers. Still, he revealed an instinctive grasp of the social shifts to come in the 1960s. European society was about to shrug off the strictures of the postwar years, dismantling one social and moral taboo after another, experiencing a paradoxical passage from economic boom to revolutionary utopianism. In 1959—as Fellini shot his epochal panorama, Jean-Luc Godard delivered a provocative New Wave manifesto in the form of *Breathless*, and Michelangelo Antonioni reflected on the identity crisis of the middle class in *L'Avventura*—Dino envisioned a comedy on a previously untouchable topic: the Great War. He felt an instinctive affinity for this tale of two slobs in uniform, soldiers who avoid combat any way they can, and then die like heroes when they're captured by the Austrians.

Dino was drawn to the story's emotional elements. His short stint of military service in Yugoslavia had been more than enough to convince him of the absurdity of war. Further, as a product of the impoverished and neglected South—whose inhabitants were sometimes reluctant to consider themselves Italians—he had little use for a culture founded on monuments to the fallen. What counted for De Laurentiis was the essential misery of the situation: it was natural to be afraid; it was natural to want to survive.

It's also true that most Italians, for better or worse, lack any sense of nationalism. They're complete individualists. Everyone has the right to his own dignity, no matter what the cost: that was the heart of Vincenzoni's story. Dino's instincts told him that the audience was mature enough to face the subject without any hypocritical softening. Many, in fact, would recognize themselves in the film. All he needed to do was serve it up in as scathing and spirited a manner as possible, relying upon the skilled collaboration of Monicelli and the two screenwriters, Agenore Incrocci and Furio Scarpelli.

Plus, of course, he needed to find the right actors. He immediately signed up Vittorio Gassman, who had just turned in an electrifying performance in Monicelli's *I soliti ignoti (Persons Unknown)*. He paired him with Alberto Sordi, an actor who had come to personify the Italian character itself, with its multiple vices and malleable virtues.

> I had offered Sordi one of his first significant roles in 1945, in *Le miserie del signor Travet*, and we had crossed paths innumerable times since then. Our friendship only grew stronger when I lobbied for him during our discussions of *The Great War*. Luckily I managed to convince everybody that Sordi and Gassman would be the ideal actors.
>
> There was also a certain resistance to the title, until I put my foot down: "This film will be called *The Great War*, and that's that." In the end Monicelli was smart enough to approve the two protagonists, and we rewrote a few scenes to adapt them to their typical characters. Without Sordi and Gassman the film still would have been excellent, but it never would have had the success it did. What distinguished it was the mingling of the sacred and profane, the humorous aspect with the underlying drama: a very rare thing at the time.

Dino's decisions were shockingly bold in the context of late-1950s Italy, still ruled by an antiquated mentality. The polemics burst forth immediately. At the press conference to announce the project in January 1959, several journalists leaped to the defense of the Italian soldier, whose honor was being impugned by the film's "sensibly frightened heroes" (to quote Dino's antirhetorical description). De Laurentiis fired back at once. In a letter addressed to the editor of *Il Mattino*, Giovanni Ansaldo—whose stature as a prince among journalists didn't intimidate the producer in the least—Dino refused to give an inch.

> Before talking about antipatriotism and waving around the idea of preemptive censorship (a privilege that nobody has in this day and age), you should have done your homework. . . . In the course of my career as a producer, I don't believe I've ever done a disservice to the Italian cinema or to its good name in the world. . . . My

> ambitions are not merely commercial: I view the cinema as a combination of art and industry and do my best to ensure that my films operate on a dignified, elevated level. These are the conditions under which I am currently preparing to produce a film about the First World War.

In another letter to the Italian papers, he supplied a kind of lucidly pragmatic manifesto:

> Only a crazy producer would consider working on a film that offends his audience's most cherished feelings. And I have no intention of throwing a half-billion lire out the window. I will make the film with or without the approval of these pseudopatriotic demagogues, these defenders of an empty and mediocre cinema. I have no intention of kneeling before those who want the film industry to limit itself to shallow comedies.

While the argument raged, the neo-Fascists in the parliament tried to prevent the Ministry of Defense from loaning any equipment to the production. To clarify his intentions, Dino sent the film treatment to Giulio Andreotti, the new head of the defense ministry. On the evening of April 3, Dino got a phone call: the minister had prepared a letter with his personal response. Dino wanted to send a messenger at once, but the offices were closed. He spent a sleepless night, almost certain that Andreotti's reluctance to make the call himself meant that he wouldn't support the production. In fact, the minister praised the project and authorized the army's participation.

Here, then, was an official stamp of approval, but when Monicelli traveled to Udine to scout locations, the local prefect warned him that the armed services organizations might stir up some trouble. Again Dino refused to be boxed in. He announced that if any difficulties arose, he would move the entire production to Yugoslavia, where he had already shot *La tempesta*. This ploy led to a sudden spurt of patriotism among the generals, who hurriedly negotiated with the producer to keep the shoot on Italian soil.

Assured of the military's participation—in exchange, of course, for a mutually agreeable fee—Monicelli began shooting in Friuli on May 25. The director was delighted with Sordi's and Gassman's work. In a pair of bravura performances, the two egged each other on without ever descending into sterile rivalry: they simply wanted to squeeze every drop of emotion out of their onscreen duet. To direct some of the crowd scenes, Dino called in Alessandro Blasetti, who got the troops revved up by peppering them with patriotic outbursts.

The film was shot and edited in record time, to make sure it could be shown at the twentieth Venice Film Festival on September 5. There it received the Golden Lion in a tie with Rossellini's *General Della Rovere*. (Curiously enough, Dino had come within a hair's breadth of winning two Lions: it was he who first acquired the rights to Indro Montanelli's book, which was the basis of Rossellini's film, but when the author found another producer, De Laurentiis relinquished the option.) The moment the trophy was delivered into Dino's hands, he ordered seven identical copies, which he distributed to his collaborators: Sordi, Gassman, Monicelli, Vincenzoni, Incrocci, Scarpelli, and Silvana (who had a minor part in the film).

Still the controversy wasn't dead. When *The Great War* began previews in Turin on October 27, the protests flared up again: 2,350 former military chaplains, among them 42 bishops and 4 cardinals, gathered to denounce this "deplorable film," which insulted "the generous sacrifices made on behalf of Italy's honor and its salvation." They demanded that the movie be banned "to protect our youth, who will be poisoned by its depraved images." These were the death rattles of an Italy that was changing even faster than the bigots and reactionaries feared. The public gave *The Great War* an extraordinary welcome: almost a billion and a half lire in receipts. Even the critics—including a few who had initially opposed the project—were now unanimously favorable. And Sordi, winner of the Silver Ribbon and other prizes, was so delighted by the whole business that he signed an exclusive contract with De Laurentiis.

Even while working on *The Great War*, Dino was producing another war-related film. *Jovanka e le altre (Five Branded Women)* presented almost as many obstacles as *The Great War*. Set in Yugoslavia, it followed the story of five women who'd had love affairs with the occupying Germans and had their heads shaved by the partisans as a badge of shame. When he first heard the plot, Dino had one of his inspirations: "In a flash I saw an enormous poster with the shaved heads of the five girls, and underneath, the names of five famous actresses." Reading through the screenplay, he decided that Gina Lollobrigida should play the protagonist. Meanwhile, he signed up the director Martin Ritt, whom he admired more than ever after having seen *No Down Payment.*

The troubles began at once. First, there was the inconvenient fact that the Yugoslav partisans in Ugo Pirro's original novel were fighting Italy's army of occupation. The villains were transformed into Nazis. Today, Dino denies that the decision was made under pressure from the government: "The fact is that the Italians conducted a war in which the human factor really counted, while the Germans everywhere exceeded them in sheer cruelty." More serious difficulties arose when the Yugoslav government refused to collaborate on the film or even to authorize the shoot. Dino realized that in this region, the partisan war was considered a quasi-mystical event, a story that couldn't possibly be told by a foreigner. No problem, thought Dino: he'd shoot the film near Klagenfurt, Austria, where the terrain was quite similar. But there too, historical sensibilities got in the way; the Austrian extras were reluctant to don Nazi uniforms.

Meanwhile, on the eve of shooting, Lollobrigida withdrew from the project. The official reason was that she was unwilling to have her head shaved, and in fact, she had worn a kind of skullcap for the screen test. According to some, however, the star didn't want to risk being just another face in the crowd, especially when the crowd included four top-drawer actresses: Vera Miles, Barbara Bel Geddes, Jeanne Moreau, and the young Carla Gravina. Of these, only Gravina agreed to have her hair cut off in front of the press. Miles also went along with the tonsorial program, although she had her scalp shaved in private. But both Bel Geddes and Moreau opted for the skullcap, creating real headaches for the makeup artist.

When Gina defected, the producer didn't blink an eye. Instead, he pulled the customary ace from his sleeve: Silvana. She was more than willing to step in and utterly indifferent to the idea of sacrificing her locks. Asked about the issue, she responded at unusual length: "I must say that my first impression of my shaved head was pretty terrible. . . . I was worried about the reaction of a person who's very important to me: my son Federico. He's not even five, and he adores women with long hair, at least to judge from the way he stares at them. What saved me, though, was another of his great passions: war. I explained to him that I needed to be a partisan, to shoot with a submachine gun, to fight like a man. Wouldn't a man with long hair be ridiculous? I managed to convince him. And then Raffaella and Veronica got into the game: all three of them wanted to get their heads shaved as well."

The production challenged Martin Ritt. His background was in the theater, so he was unaccustomed to shooting exteriors, and the Italian-style chaos on the set was distracting. What's more, the project entailed transporting 114 cast and crew members up the Grossgluckner, to an altitude of nine thousand feet. With his Hollywood maestro in crisis, Dino turned to his old companion from the Centro, Pietro Germi, who had been hired to play a minor role as an actor. Germi agreed to help the struggling director. In a typical act of generosity, he demanded neither money nor a title credit in exchange for having saved the movie.

By March 1960 *Jovanka e le altre* was ready for release. Enzo De Bernart in the publicity department came up with a real brainstorm. Anticipating the feminist revolution to come, he organized a preview in Milan for women only. As he later recounted, "I set the whole thing up with the fire department and the police, in order to make sure that on this particular evening, not a single man would cross the threshold of that theater. Only women. A small army of twelve uniformed girls at the door prevented any men from entering, in an energetic and categorical fashion. In the glare of the floodlights you saw fathers, husbands, and boyfriends waving good-bye, having already arranged to pick up their women afterwards. Dino arrived with Silvana on his arm and attempted to go inside. My girls were unrelenting. 'But I'm the producer of the film,' he said. 'You're still a man,' they replied."

Recalling this project and other Dino events, De Bernart reflected on his boss's strength as a producer: "Dino knows the craziness of the masses; he shares their passions and their deepest impulses. So when he's sitting at the Moviola, he's able to cut a film, discarding the superfluous bits in order to make the whole thing work. Sometimes, in the midst of that superfluity, you'll find noble images or flashes of thought. The artist always runs the risk of indulging himself by leaving that stuff in. But unless somebody gets in the way of Dino's instincts, that's the stuff he always cuts out." Here was a summary of the producer's modus operandi. Despite the logistical juggling, the vast sets, unruly crews, and astonishing budgets, filmmaking often came down to a fairly simple process: subtraction.

CHAPTER 17

TROUBLE IN PARADISE

IN THE SUMMER OF 1960, SILVANA DEDICATED HERSELF TO A TASK SHE loved: home decorating. She replaced the wallpaper in the living room of the Via Appia house, planted roses, redecorated the nursery, had several windows enlarged, and had a porch built for rainy days. But as she confided to the journalist Maria Livia Serini in *L'Espresso*, she felt a gnawing sense of unhappiness: "The years pass and I always remain the same. When your thoughts and your problems never change, you grow bored. . . . I'd like to have another baby. But I'd also like to make a good film with a good director, a good story, good dialogue—and a role, for once, that's congenial to me."

Despite the routine of the last few years, Silvana *was* changing. She had recently spent a good deal of time with Jeanne Moreau in Rome and was intrigued by how differently the French actress thought about her work. For Jeanne, who was always curious and eager to meet new people, acting was a way of communicating. For Silvana, it was little more than an obligation. If she hadn't married a producer, perhaps everything would have been different: she might have found the courage to assert herself more often. But Dino didn't seem to understand her feelings, mistaking dissatisfaction for indifference.

In August the family traveled to Cap Martin for their vacation. A familiar existence awaited them: the annual gala at the Sporting Club (where Maria Callas was in attendance), suppers at Le Pirate, quick trips to the roulette tables, and quiet times with the children and a handful of friends, including Gassman and his mother.

A change of pace occurred, however, with the arrival of Piero Gherardi, accompanied by the photographer Tazio Secchiaroli, the makeup artist Otello Fava, and the costume designer Cleo Paggi. Silvana was about to take on a glamorous and gritty role in *Gli assassini*—she would play a prostitute allied with a gang of thieves, who were pulling off a big job in a casino on the Côte d'Azur—and Dino had entrusted her transformation to Gherardi and his crew. The art director elongated Silvana's eyes, with a tilt up toward her temples, enlarged her mouth, fitted her with a blond wig, wrapped her head in an assortment of lilac-colored scarves, and slipped a long cigarette holder between her fingers. Silvana then patiently submitted to a succession of necklaces, dresses, jewels, hats, and furs.

She liked the idea of a masquerade, of turning herself into a kind of icon, which was one reason why she had agreed so promptly to have her head shaved for *Jovanka*. As her hair grew back, she had dyed it a reddish yellow and adopted a style of makeup (chalky foundation, brick-red lipstick, harsh eyeliner) that the newspapers called her "horror movie look." Gherardi's effects were less extreme. Still, they went a long way toward defining the diaphanous, aristocratic image that Silvana would project in the coming years, and the art director himself would become one of her most intimate friends.

Charmed as always by the genial Piero—whose manipulation of facial planes caused hidden aspects of the subject's personality to emerge—Dino watched him transform his severe, enigmatic wife into a kind of platinum vamp. After eleven years of marriage, Silvana still baffled and eluded him. And while the rest of his family regarded him as a patriarchal dictator, to be venerated and pampered, his wife still maintained a certain distance, as if to shield herself from his steely resolve.

In mid-September Silvana announced that she was expecting a fourth child. Federico, who often felt overwhelmed by his two older sisters, hoped for a younger brother to even the score. To some degree, Silvana shared his feelings: perhaps another boy would thwart the supremacy of the current alpha males, her husband and the domineering Federico. The little boy was spoiled by his father, she felt. Dino gave him the lion's share of his attention, and when his daughters grew jealous, his only response was, "This is man-to-man stuff."

For his part, the producer hoped that the new arrival would smooth out his crisis-ridden relationship with Silvana. While he still loved his wife and did everything possible to please her, she remained distant, often scornful, and always unhappy. He had tried over and over to figure out the cause of Silvana's problems. Sometimes it seemed to him that she didn't love herself; this sad self-loathing made him love her more, but how long could he endure her surly behavior?

There was also the question of her erratic maternal role. Clearly Silvana adored the children, yet often she hardly seemed to be present for them. She tended to stay in her room and let other people handle child care. If one of the children were ill, she would sit next to the bed and embroider for a few hours, but she would never tuck in the covers or administer the medicine or take a temperature. There were a dozen or more people to handle these tasks: the governess, the nurse, the cook, the driver, and a clutch of maids. To Dino, raised in a climate of familial warmth, this behavior was incomprehensible, and in fact the governess's function as a barrier separating the mother from her offspring on a daily basis had a profound impact on the De Laurentiis children. Veronica and Raffaella recall how they awaited the little bonus vacation at the end of each school year as if it were a miracle. Just imagine: an entire week at Lido di Venezia with their mother, her three sisters—and no maids or tutors to spoil the fun!

The family remained at Cap Martin through October, while Dino shot the exteriors for *Gli assassini*. (The film had been rechristened *Crimen* and was released in the United States as *. . . And Suddenly It's Murder!*) The children were happy to have their summer break prolonged. Their father often came up from Rome to keep an eye on the set, and from time to time, taking advantage of the mild autumn, he bundled them up in warm sweaters and treated them to a ride in the speedboat. The off-season atmosphere softened disagreements, and Dino felt unusually relaxed throughout the entire shoot.

In the constant company of her dachshund Filomena, who had a small role in the film, Silvana gave a number of interviews during the same period. Over and over she explained that there had been a misunderstanding: it was not true that she detested the cinema. If she did, she would have already quit the business. Instead she now had artistic ambitions of her own, and these had made her selective about what she took on. Although she was not yet entirely secure about her own abilities, the actress, on the threshold of her glorious thirties, did aspire to greater autonomy. She would like to choose her own projects, she suggested, and perhaps work with other producers.

Clearly itching for at least a modicum of independence, Silvana began to act out in uncharacteristic ways. In early January 1961, Dino and Silvana were having supper with a group of friends at Le Pirate. The small orchestra struck up "The Children of Piraeus," the theme song from Jules Dassin's *Never on Sunday*. To amuse herself, the actress started imitating the star of the film, Melina Mercouri. She would sing a passage, then throw her glass in the air so that it smashed on the floor. She did it again, then again. The other guests followed her example, eventually shattering more than a hundred glasses to the strains of the Greek melody. At the end of the party, which lasted until the small hours, Dino paid for the glassware along with the check.

Nor were these tensions hidden from the public. On January 28 Bernardo Valli interviewed the producer for *Il Giorno*, speaking to him at the Vasca Navale offices. "When people discuss De Laurentiis and wife," the journalist wrote, "they insist that their relationship can't be understood without a thorough immersion in Freud. This is the unanimous opinion throughout the cinematic world." According to Valli, nobody in Rome was able to overlook the scornful phrases that Silvana directed at Dino. She derided him in the presence of friends or even strangers—who were then eager to share the dirt with everybody on Via Veneto. De Laurentiis, pretending to ignore his wife's temperamental wisecracks, never gave the impression of being hurt. The journalist continued, "He's a man who's very enthusiastic about his profession. He discusses it in a loud, excitable voice. Yet the moment the conversation turns to his family, he shows an unexpected modesty. In a sense, his professional secrets are everybody's business, but his private emotions are sacred and enveloped in a typically Neapolitan solemnity."

It was in this climate that Silvana brought forth a baby daughter, Francesca, on May 10, 1961. The birth was immortalized by yet another family photo in the newspapers. A few days later Ted Kennedy, who was visiting the set of *Barabbas*, presented the baby with a gold plaque, which included a calendar for the year 2061 and the following inscription, "Wishing Francesca De Laurentiis a century of peace and happiness."

Meanwhile, Francesca's father seemed to be cramming a century's worth of work into a single year. Along with his commitment to the enormous undertaking of *Barabbas* (for which the shoot would last 157 days), not to mention his postproduction duties on *The Last Judgment*, De Laurentiis was pressing forward with several ambitious projects. In April he had purchased a large plot of land in Rome from a government agency. On this 125-acre property—which, due to its location, was eligible for grants from an economic development fund—he planned to build the most technologically advanced film studio in Europe, if not in the world. In the same grandiose spirit, the producer had decided to throw himself body and soul into the realization of that ultimate blockbuster, *The Bible*. And on October 31, as if his plate weren't already full enough, he announced the creation of an overseas subsidiary, the Dino De Laurentiis Corporation of America.

In late June Dino's frenzied activity was interrupted when Amedeo Mangano died in Paris after a long illness. It was the first major death the family had faced. At the airport Silvana looked tired and drawn, and Dino, standing protectively at her side, defended her from the paparazzi by hurling an overnight bag at a TV cameraman (an act for which he later apologized). No wonder Silvana declined to appear at the Venice Film Festival later that summer, where Vittoria De Sica's *The Last Judgment* was making its debut. In this case, Dino had misjudged his audience. The film, which he'd embraced with great enthusiasm, was a flop: the critics panned it, the jury ignored it, and the public deserted it in droves.

Fortunately, both *A Difficult Life* and *Barabbas* met with great success when they were released in December. In a feature entitled "Italy's Vibrant Directors," the January 1962 issue of *Life* correctly identified Dino as the most important Italian producer. Meanwhile, Silvana had an important professional breakthrough of her own. As the producer of Carlo Lizzani's *The Verona Trial*, Dino offered her one of the key roles of her career: her impassioned incarnation of Edda Ciano Mussolini, the dictator's daughter.

Edda, who was still a popular figure in Roman high society, had never crossed paths with Silvana. She refused to even glance at the script, which recounted the most tragic episode of her life: the trial that took place in Verona in January 1944. At that point her father, whom the Nazis had installed as the puppet ruler of the Salò Republic, was forced to deliver her husband, Galeazzo Ciano, to the firing squad. (His son-in-law had apparently voted against him in the reconvened Grand Council of Fascism.) Understandably, Edda seemed unenthusiastic about revisiting this portion of her past or seeing it enacted on the big screen.

In her statements to the press, the widow articulated "a bitter and ironic resignation." As she put it, "My private life—especially certain ancient pages of it—is no longer private but the property of the state." Other members of the Mussolini family tried to block the production, but Edda, having conferred with her lawyers, was skeptical about these efforts. Silvana showed her usual restraint. On various occasions she expressed her profound sympathy for Edda's ordeal, along with her own eagerness to portray the widow in a worthy manner. Dino, on the other hand, lashed out against those who would hamstring the film, declaring his right—as he did during the dispute over *The Great War*—to follow his own instincts as a producer.

The press covered the story on a day-by-day basis. Meanwhile, director Carlo Lizzani found a middle road between documentary and melodrama, creating a memorable, highly successful film. With the help of Gherardi, who provided her with a period wardrobe, Silvana came up with a incisive, realistic portrait. In his memoir, *Through the Twentieth Century*, Lizzani added a bizarre footnote: "Edda Ciano lamented the fact that Silvana Mangano wore a *tailleur* that was evidently not to her taste. Yet the costume designer for *The Verona Trial* was the great Gherardi, the winner, during his long and prestigious career, of several Oscars! I should acknowledge, though, that several years later, in an interview on French television, Countess Ciano confirmed the trustworthiness of my film and said that she had appreciated Silvana's superb characterization."

In July 1963 Mangano was awarded the Donatello Prize. She didn't go to Taormina to collect it, but shortly after, paralyzed by emotion as she always was in these situations, she did mount the podium to accept the Grolla d'Oro for Best Actress. To celebrate, the entire De Laurentiis family spent a few days at a resort in the Val d'Aosta. This region of northern Italy happened to be a trout-fishing mecca, so Dino was able to involve the children in his outdoor pursuits, spending hours with them amidst the greenery and the open air.

It was an interlude of true happiness. Even Silvana, feeling fulfilled as both an actress and a woman, was relaxed and calm. At least temporarily, trouble seemed to have been banished from paradise. But changes were on the way, bringing genuine turbulence in their wake.

CHAPTER 18

DINOCITTÀ

By the beginning of 1962 De Laurentiis was ready to start constructing an immense studio complex on the land he had purchased in Rome. With disarming pride, he planned to name the place after himself: it would be called Dinocittà, or Dino City.

With his typical impulse to push ahead, Dino began shooting on the property before he had actually built the studio. In the summer of 1961 the sets for *Barabbas*—distillations of Jerusalem and ancient Rome, designed by the architect Mario Chiari—began to rise on Via Pontina. With a budget of ten million dollars, *Barabbas*—depicting the inner torments and misadventures of the thief pardoned in Christ's place—was definitely a big-budget spectacular. To direct the film, the producer enlisted a highly skilled American, Richard Fleischer, who was best known for *The Vikings*.

The *Barabbas* shoot left its mark in the anecdotal history of the cinema. For starters, there was its grandiose reputation as "the film that stopped the sun," due to an inspiration of Dino's: on February 15, 1961, he had the acrobatic Aldo Tonti haul his cameras up a steep hill to shoot the crucifixion scene during a solar eclipse. A crowd of thousands of extras was assembled for the scenes in Verona's ancient amphitheater. Last but not least, there was the romantic passion between Anthony Quinn and Iolanda Addolori, who would become the actor's second wife and bear him two children. At first Dino balked at Quinn's whimsical demand that the beautiful Venetian, an assistant fashion designer, be reassigned as his personal tailor. But following his custom of keeping his stars happy—within the limits of possibility, or slightly beyond them—the producer convinced Iolanda to go along with the plan, promising her a handsome bonus. (She was, in any case, hardly repelled by Quinn.) This was neither the first nor the last time that De Laurentiis exercised his skills as a cinematic matchmaker.

> In a certain sense *Barabbas* was the first film shot at Dinocittà, when the studio didn't yet exist. Fellini had discussed the novel with me while he was making *La Strada*, pointing out that it offered a character especially suited to Anthony Quinn, who was then playing Zampanò. At the time, in fact, Federico promised to direct the movie—just imagine that! But he really liked the book, and he was right.
>
> And in any case, *Barabbas* proves my point that when you have a great story, you can produce an excellent piece of work even with a skilled professional like Richard Fleischer. Of course, if I had chosen a more heavyweight director, perhaps the film would have snagged another nine Oscar nominations. Instead, it was merely an enormous commercial success throughout the world.

On January 15, 1962, workers laid the first stone for Dino's celluloid city, an event celebrated with festive solemnity. Amintore Fanfani, the president of Italy's Council of State, was on hand, along with a gaggle of political and industrial figures, plus half of the Italian cinema, from Fellini to Goffredo Lombardo, from Sordi to Camerini, Castellani to Nazzari to Lizzani. Vittorio de Sica gravely read from a parchment proclamation, which would then be slipped into a silver container and buried within the first stone by Fanfani. "This parchment," intoned De Sica, "which will momentarily be enclosed inside the first stone in the construction of the Dino De Laurentiis Center for Cinematic Production, embodies Dino De Laurentiis's ongoing wish to give a solid, lasting foundation—industrial, social, moral, and artistic—to the work he has already undertaken in the cinematographic field. This vast complex, whose construction commences with this very stone, will benefit the entire Italian film industry, which, since the beginning of the twentieth century and particularly during the last fifteen years, has contributed so much to Italy's image and prestige throughout the world."

Once begun, construction proceeded at a brisk pace. The supervision of the site—which employed five thousand workers and technicians—was entrusted to Luigi, who had just returned from an exploratory trip to the most technically advanced Hollywood facilities. The plans called for four soundstages, three of which could be joined together, and 250 offices for production and administration, carpentry, props, and wardrobe, plus film processing and printing facilities. There would also be studios for dubbing and musical recording, dressing rooms for the actors, and two penthouse apartments: one for Dino and another for the star of the moment. Every studio would be outfitted with tanks and pools for aquatic scenes. De Laurentiis also planned to outfit the entire establishment with central air-conditioning so that filming could continue comfortably both in the cold of winter and the heat of summer.

Particular care was lavished upon the acoustical systems, which the Torinese technicians designed to reduce any external noise by sixty decibels. (At that time, the most high-tech systems in other international studios masked only thirty-five decibels.) What did this mean? If a jet flew over Dinocittà during a shoot, generating a racket of one hundred decibels, only forty decibels would be audible within the studio. This feature would reduce the amount of reshooting that had to be done, which saved both time and money.

The lighting too took advantage of some innovative and cost-cutting arrangements. Incandescent bulbs were abandoned in favor of quartz lamps, which were smaller, more manageable, and capable of producing a more intense illumination with less electricity. In addition, the lights were mounted on a kind of monorail system, eliminating the dangerous and unwieldy snarl of cables on the studio floor.

Reports of this $30 million initiative appeared in every newspaper around the world. It was widely considered an act of faith in the very future of the movie business, since the Hollywood studios were just then being snapped up by manufacturing cartels or television networks. Dino was called "Italy's master impresario" or even "this Italian Horatio Alger." No wonder Eric Johnston of the Motion Picture Association of America showed up for a visit in March, intrigued and perhaps a little worried by the growing European competition.

In interviews, the producer didn't hide his hopes that other industrial enterprises would join him in what was then a largely vacant area of the city. Dino foresaw an American-style schedule for the workers, from 9 A.M. to 6 P.M., and he made plans for a cafeteria capable of serving two hundred at a time. However, not all of the employees-to-be were convinced. Some objected that the studio's location on the industrial outskirts made it almost impossible to reach via public transportation.

While the feverish planning continued for *The Bible*, which Dino envisioned as a sensational calling card for his new venture, an American paper leaked the news of a major indiscretion on his part. According to the story, which appeared in December 1963, De Laurentiis had entered into a secret agreement with the ruling Christian Democrats to move the obsolete Cinecittà into his own cutting-edge studio complex. The topic would generate arguments for quite some time. For the moment, Dino issued a hurried denial, acutely aware that the construction was still in progress and that he couldn't afford to have it halted. By January 1964 he and his general staff had officially installed themselves at the complex. By the end of March the daily *Il Giorno* carried what must have been a very reassuring headline for De Laurentiis: "The Future of the Cinema Has Already Begun at Dinocittà." His dream was finally open for business.

Among the first clients was Carol Reed, whose version of *The Agony and the Ecstasy* appealed to Dino's taste for the grand undertaking. The project required a meticulous copy of the Sistine Chapel and its vaulted ceiling, from which Charlton Heston would dangle for week after week as he pretended to paint Michelangelo's vast fresco. In his autobiography, the actor recalled the set with astonishment: "Our Sistine Chapel was the crux of the film, the reason we were making it. After a great deal of debate, Fox had erected on the largest soundstage in Europe (De Laurentiis Studios outside Rome), a full-size replica of the interior of the Sistine Chapel, which was roughly the size of a tennis court. It was an incredible achievement, certainly one of the most effective sets I've ever worked on . . . or seen." The shoot lasted all summer, and Heston found his acrobatic efforts to be something of a trial: "I'm good with horses, wild animals, fire and flood, shot and shell, not so good with high places or spiders."

Dinocittà was also the backdrop for one of Dino's oddest (and least successful) undertakings: his attempt to make a movie star out of Princess Soraya Esfandiari Bakhtiari. This beauty had married Shah Mohammad Reza Pahlavi on February 12, 1951, in an ultrasumptuous ceremony; in 1958 she had been discarded because of her inability to produce a male heir.

> Soraya was in Italy and she was all you read about in the newspapers. Everywhere you saw photos of this beautiful woman who had been repudiated by the Shah of Iran. Given her notoriety, I thought we could try to make her into a movie star. Let's see if I can convince her, I told myself, and I went to chat with her. After putting up a brief resistance, Soraya caved in. "But first," she said, "I need to make sure I can act." Great, I thought, let's set up a screen test.
>
> When the word got around, we were literally besieged by journalists and paparazzi at Dinocittà. One evening after supper I told the princess to stick close to home: "The photographers will assume that you're going to bed. Around 1:30 in the morning I'll send somebody to check out the situation—and if the coast is clear, which is what I'm hoping, I'll come and take you to the studio myself."
>
> That worked out fine. When the last photographer had finally scrammed, I picked her up and brought her back to the studio so we could hold a nighttime screen test. I had to improvise the whole business. I thought, "I don't have a partner for her, I don't have a script, what am I going to do?" Then I remembered Anna Magnani's monologue in *Una voce umana*, so I stuck a telephone in Soraya's hand and said, "Let's see what you can do." We made the scene up as we went along, and it was an excellent audition, which convinced her to give the cinema a try.
>
> I had her sign a contract with an option for two additional titles. But we never exercised the option, because the film didn't come out the way I had hoped. At first Soraya was supposed to have her cinematic baptism with Lattuada, but we couldn't find a subject that would do the trick. Since we couldn't come up with an appropriate story, and we didn't think that Soraya was capable of portraying a real person, I got the idea of wrapping her in this three-episode structure.

The "three-episode structure" was a novel trilogy of short films with the collective title of *The Three Faces of a Woman*. Dino lined up a trio of superb directors for the project: Michelangelo Antonioni, Franco Indovina, and Mauro Bolognini. Even Alberto Sordi, in a temporary huff with Dino over contractual matters, was eager to participate in this ambitious operation. He appeared in the final segment, "Latin Lovers," delivering a grotesque incarnation of a gigolo.

Unfortunately, none of the episodes truly caught fire. Antonioni's

"The Audition" (which included a restaging of Soraya's screen test) was perhaps too coy for its own good. The middle segment, Bolognini's "Legendary Lover," was also something of a washout. In it Soraya was paired in a neurotic duet with Richard Harris, and the English actor turned out to be as crazed and erratic on the screen as he was in real life.

That left "Latin Lovers." Alberto Sordi's scathing caricature had its fans, and there was praise too for the director's skillful composition. Indovina, a Sicilian intellectual making his debut behind the camera, reserved most of his charm for the female protagonist, which ultimately led to a passionate affair on the set.

> It was quite clear that the so-called melancholy princess had only a single problem: the absence of star-level charisma. She was a beautiful woman, of course, elegant and classy, everything that we were looking for. But there are people who literally leap off the screen, and others who instead remain only images: beautiful things to look at.

Meanwhile, the announcement of her contract and the rumors from the set had generated enormous curiosity both in Italy and abroad. The buzz reached its peak on February 11, 1965, when the film had its sensational preview at Milan's Teatro Nuovo. The proceedings were broadcast live on television, a rare event at the time. The princess wore a couture ensemble and lavish amounts of jewelry (insured for 60 million lire) on loan from Bulgari. But at the end of the evening, as she fled the crowds for the safety of her Rolls-Royce, she may have already understood that her first starring role in film would also be her last.

It was immediately obvious that this splendid creature was no star. Over the next few days the reviews appeared, respectful and perplexed. One defined *The Three Faces of a Woman* as "a 3,000-meter trial run." In Germany and France the comments were less tactful. To make matters worse, Dino sent two envoys to London to organize a private screening for the shah, who hadn't seen his ex-wife since the day he repudiated her. Backed into a corner, the shah delivered his own disenchanted verdict: "It's a truly horrible film, but her acting isn't so bad."

Soraya's failed attempt at celluloid stardom undoubtedly was one of Dino's defeats, even though the film itself did decent business. As for Soraya, she resumed her globetrotting lifestyle and enrolled in the Actors Studio in New York, with the short-lived intention of taking classes there. De Laurentiis maintained an eloquent silence about his future plans for her. Eventually, the only thing remaining from her adventure in the cinema was an ongoing relationship with Indovina. Alas, the forty-year-old director died in a crash at the Palermo airport in 1972.

> "Operation Soraya" was one of my numerous attempts to discover a new star. (Another one, even unluckier, was when I hired Ira Furstenberg for Lattuada's *Matchless*.) But in reality, I gave many actors and actresses their first shot at the big time. Some made it, others didn't. The central element is always that charisma—an invisible, almost ectoplasmic thing—determines whether the audience will remember a certain face.

Over time, *The Three Faces* has acquired a certain documentary value. Particularly in "The Audition," which was set in the studio itself, the film captures the dawn of Dino's glory days in his new palace on Via Pontina. In fact, the producer briefly played himself in Antonioni's segment, surrounded by his brother Alfredo, the office manager Bruno Todini, the cameramen Otello Martelli and Arthur Zavattini, the makeup artist Alberto De Rossi, and an additional flock of collaborators. In a playful move, Dino's face is never made visible. This striking omission caused one critic to insist that by maintaining such a respectful distance from his subject, the director was surely enveloping him in his own myth, but De Laurentiis, of course, never needed any help in that department.

Over the next few years Dinocittà would host dozens of films, including Franco Zeffirelli's *The Taming of the Shrew*, with its enormous sets by Renzo Mongiardino. (Recalling Dino as a "tremendously helpful" presence, the director would later call on his production services for another Shakespearean adaptation, *Romeo and Juliet*.) The stars of *The Taming of the Shrew* were, of course, the royal couple of the moment: Elizabeth Taylor and Richard Burton. Both declared their satisfaction with the atmosphere on the set and the professionalism of the crew. Burton, in fact, soon returned to Dinocittà to shoot his own version of *Doctor Faustus*. Taylor followed suit in 1967, when John Huston chose the Via Pontina facility for *Reflections in a Golden Eye*, which featured not only Marlon Brando but some superb camera work by Aldo Tonti. Huston, who by now felt at home in the studio, returned again two years later for *The Kremlin Letter*.

De Laurentiis himself used the facility for *Barbarella*, based on a comic-book series by Jean-Claude Forest. Dino once again crossed paths with Jane Fonda, whom he'd met as a girl during the making of *War and Peace,* starring her father. By now the young star was married to Roger Vadim, the director of the film and the discoverer of Brigitte Bardot, and Fonda titillated audiences with a scantily clad performance in what came to be called "a sexual version of *Alice in Wonderland*."

One film followed another at Dinocittà, many directed by the most important names in the cinema, from Maurice Pialat to Sergio Leone, from Yves Boisset to Jean-Luc Godard. It's true that toward the end of the 1960s, the American superproductions for which the facilities had been built were made less frequently. Certainly none of the later productions could top the one that took place in Dinocittà's inaugural year. In May 1964, with the intrepid John Huston behind the cameras, shooting was about to commence on Dino's most ambitious project to date, *The Bible: In the Beginning*.

CHAPTER 19

NOAH'S ARK

ON JULY 14, 1961, DINO MADE AN APPEARANCE ON A POPULAR ITALIAN television show, Gianni Granzotto's *Incontri*. He shared the stage with three journalists, Paolo Monelli, Carlo Laurenzi, and Maria Livia Serini:

> *De Laurentiis:* If you don't mind, Granzotto, I'd like to ask a question.
>
> *Granzotto:* Go ahead, please.
>
> *De Laurentiis:* You, Paolo Monelli, have you read the entire Bible?
>
> *Monelli:* For sure!
>
> *De Laurentiis:* Excuse me, Laurenzi, what about you?
>
> *Laurenzi:* Not entirely.
>
> *De Laurentiis:* Not entirely. Okay. And what about you, signora?
>
> *Serini:* No, not all of it.
>
> *De Laurentiis:* Have you read it, Granzotto?
>
> *Granzotto:* Not in its entirety.
>
> *De Laurentiis:* I see! But hold on. Here we are—no, let me subtract myself for a moment. Here *you* are, there are four of you, and three haven't read the entire Bible. . . . That alone would be sufficient justification for the fact that I'm thinking of making it into a film.

As the debate continued, Monelli put a question of his own to Dino: "Would you be considering a big-screen version of the Bible if you weren't interested in conquering the American public, with its notorious appetite for the colossal?" The producer fired back that because the Bible, despite its massive cultural clout, was in fact not widely read, there was urgent need for a film adaptation.

It was in the course of preparing for *Barabbas* that De Laurentiis, an omnivorous reader, found himself flipping through the Holy Book. The stories he found there tempted him to embark upon a biblical production that would surpass Cecil B. DeMille's model in both faithfulness and quality. Dino envisioned a mighty spectacle, yet he wanted it to be scrupulously accurate in its cultural, philological, and religious aspects. To that end, he planned to assemble an international commission of clergymen drawn from Catholicism, Protestantism, and Judaism. Like most such high-minded proposals in the cinematic world, this one came to nothing. Dino pressed on; he decided to mobilize fourteen directors for a three-part work that would last twelve hours. Then, as he moved forward, Dino scaled the project down.

> The idea for *The Bible* came to me while I was tossing and turning in bed in a New York hotel room, unable to sleep. I opened the drawer in the night table and found the Bible: it was in English, which meant that I was limited to flipping through the pages. But that inspired me to buy an Italian version, because I had never read it. The next day I went to the Rizzoli bookstore and picked up a copy. I was enthralled. "*Madonna mia*," I told myself, "there's enough material here for a hundred films. This is one of those dreams that I want to transform into reality."
>
> I returned to Italy and began to think of a film with multiple directors. After long reflection, I called Visconti and Fellini. Vittorio Bonicelli suggested Robert Bresson for Genesis, so I brought him in from Paris. The idea was to entrust Visconti with the story of Joseph and his brothers, partly because of the overlap with *Rocco and His Brothers*. Fellini would make Noah's Ark, and Bresson would make Adam and Eve. There was also Orson Welles, who knocked out a few pages for Abraham and Isaac.
>
> We wasted a year wrestling with this suggestive, highly collaborative formula. Then, at a certain point, I realized that I had surrounded myself with these great masters, each of whom demanded the maximum time and space to translate his bit of the Bible to the big screen. An example: Visconti, having been handed a fragment that should have lasted about forty minutes, planned on expanding his segment to three hours.
>
> In a sense, I had a product on hand that was better suited for

> television. Still, I wanted to make a film for theatrical release: the key was to compress and concentrate the material. With that in mind I called Christopher Fry, who had already written *Barabbas*, and commissioned a script.

In the introduction to a collection of his screenplays, Fry recounted that when he was first asked to write a script for *The Bible*, he assumed the request was a joke. Then, immediately after, he felt like a kind of Hercules, completely inadequate to the task and suffering a crushing sense of fatigue. "*The Bible* takes us from poetry to the beginnings of history," said Fry. Clearly the task of hammering out a workable screenplay—one subject both to practical demands and to Dino's criticisms—was long and complicated. But the producer pressed on, assembling the financing for his scriptural spectacular.

> As we were revising the screenplay, the papers gave the story more and more coverage. Meanwhile, I still wasn't sure exactly what the film would *be*—which episodes it could include, or even how many. At times I doubted whether we would be able to move much beyond the Garden of Eden.
>
> Then I got a call from Abe Schneider at Columbia, whom I already knew. He said to me, "We've read that you're going to do the Bible. Is that true? Because we're very interested in the project. Where can we meet?" I told him that I was too busy to fly to America, and we arranged to meet in London, where he was about to go on business.
>
> In London we sealed our agreement with a handshake. Columbia pledged $10 million, but it reserved the right of refusal on the director and controlled several other territories aside from the United States—England, for example. All other territories were mine. I told Schneider to send me a telex as soon as he got home, setting out the terms of the contract. My job was to choose a director, inform the studio, and then travel to New York. Schneider sent me the telex, in which Columbia formally committed to the project, and meanwhile, I got the idea of tracking down John Huston.

At the time Dino didn't know the director of *The Treasure of the Sierra Madre*. He learned that Huston was near Puerto Vallarta, Mexico, shooting *The Night of the Iguana* with Ava Gardner. De Laurentiis placed a call to Huston.

"John, are you interested to direct *The Bible*?" I asked him.

"It's the dream of a lifetime," he immediately replied. I told him that I would join him in Mexico to discuss the project, and he asked me to come on the weekend, since he was working too hard during the week.

I showed up. I had him read the pages Fry had sent me, and he accepted on the spot. "Dino," he said, "I'm committing myself to this film right now. We'll work out the revisions together."

After we shook hands, I rushed to a phone to call Columbia, and I said exactly two words: "John Huston." They were happy. They promised to draw up the contract right away and said it would be signed within two weeks.

At once journalists began pestering Huston with telephone calls and interview requests. His response: "What interests me about the book is not so much its sacred character as its literary value. Because I'm not a believer in the strict sense of the word, I practice no religion, yet I'm not an atheist either. I believe in a kind of permanent creation." Questioned about how it felt to prepare for such a gigantic task, Huston replied, "I can only repeat what Leonardo Da Vinci said about his own approach to his art. He said that he always worked as if he found himself in the presence of God." Reading these statements, Dino was exultant. Huston already spoke like one of the patriarchs he was about to bring to life on the screen.

Just around that time I hired Luigi Luraschi, an Anglo-Italian who had been working at Paramount's public relations office in Los Angeles for twenty or thirty years. I got to know him there. And since my own English was deficient and he was a perfect quadrilinguist—he also spoke Spanish and German—I told him, "Luigi, you're the guy I've been looking for. Why don't you come and work for me?" Eventually he did, and he became a kind of right-hand man for all my dealings with foreigners.

Anyway, I told Luigi that we had to go to New York for the contract with Columbia. We showed up at the office. Abe Schneider, the vice chairman, Leo Jaffe, and Mike Frankovich, the head of international production, were all on their side of the table. On our side, there was just Luraschi and I, reading over the twenty-page contract.

At this point, if you were making a film of my life, you'd have a fantastic opening scene. When I finished reading, I turned to the three gentlemen and said, "You forgot only one thing."

"What?" they asked me. I stood up (word of honor, here), dropped my pants, and said, "*You forgot my ass!*" Because they had drawn up a contract in which every conceivable thing went to them, as if I didn't exist. It was an incredible scene, a classic moment: "I will never sign a contract like this, never, even if I'm already in preproduction." Then I tore up the telex they had sent me and went back to Rome.

How did they react? They began by saying that some things could be renegotiated, other things could not. But it was the spirit of the contract that was unacceptable to me. My attitude was "Yes, it's true, you're giving me $10 million"—an enormous sum at the time—"but I'm making a film that will cost me almost twice that much. The idea is mine, the creative, productive, and logistical aspects are all my responsibility. And you won't even be *paying* me the 10 million until I deliver a master print, which forces me to go into hock to the bank while you risk nothing. It's *unfair* for you to grab everything you want without even acknowledging the paternity of the project. 'Columbia Presents'? Forget it! It's 'Dino De Laurentiis Presents,' even in America!" I did conclude on a friendly note: "Don't worry about it, we'll make another picture together."

The Columbia contract stipulated that everything—and I mean everything—had to be subject to their approval. I couldn't go take a piss without their permission. The producer was considered half employee, half slave. On that occasion I realized that it was impossible for me to accept such a contract with a studio and that I should never surrender my creative and entrepreneurial freedom. In fact, I never did sign any contracts of that kind.

Eventually Huston showed up and I told him what had happened. "What will you do now?" he said.

"Don't worry," I replied, "something will occur to me."

Then he said, "We can always grab us a machine gun and rob a bank."

And I responded, "That won't be necessary. When you have a good idea, the money always materializes somehow."

All wisecracks aside, I now found myself deep in the preparations for a film that was slated to cost about $15 million, the equivalent of about $100 million in today's money. I did have a certain slice of the funding. I was moving forward partly by utilizing my own capital and partly by relying on the advance payments I had

> for the sale of the film in several territories, including Italy. But I was missing a good 70 percent of the total.
>
> To make a long story short, I went to Zurich, where I located a financier who was willing to give me the money. I brought him the outline of the Columbia contract, just so he could see that they had been taking the project seriously. I realize that I've always been a good salesman, in the sense that I'm very skilled at conveying the validity of a project. The important thing is to maintain an attitude of absolute honesty from the very beginning. Once you do that, it's not so difficult. In this case I told the Swiss bankers, "What I'm really running short of is time. Otherwise I could have hooked myself a contract for more than $10 million." Obviously they asked me for collateral. I offered them some of my property, they felt themselves sufficiently covered, and they gave me the money.

At this point, Dino found himself—alone—in charge of the riskiest project he'd ever undertaken. Pulling this off would require all of his ingenuity and all of his courage. He had covered the cost of the film but hadn't yet lined up an American distributor. Meanwhile, the actual production had begun, and the various episodes were already being shot in chronological order.

For Noah's Ark, the carpenters constructed an enormous vessel, sixty-six feet long and twenty-one feet high, even as the animals arrived from all over the world. Dinocittà was transformed into a zoo, which delighted Huston. Every morning the director made a tour of the cages and soon got to know all the occupants. He discovered that the elephant, Candy, liked to have her belly scratched. He also noticed that Beppo the hippopotamus would allow him to slip his hands between his yawning jaws, and that the two African giraffes, who were usually surly and rough, became much more malleable when they were supplied with sugar cubes. There was also an uncaged crow, who took flight and perched on John's shoulder at a simple summons.

Dino followed John's comings and goings amidst the animals with great pleasure, and an idea began to form in his head. For the role of Noah, there had been some discussions with Charlie Chaplin, who had at first seemed willing, then with Alec Guinness. But it soon became clear that most actors would find themselves ill-matched in that menagerie. Only a true friend of the animals would be capable of playing Noah—in other words, Huston himself. When Dino asked him, John agreed instantly, because the idea amused him and because as the director, he saw no other solution.

One aspect of the film that really intrigued Huston was the appearance of the world during the Creation. There had been some discussion of sending out a crew to shoot storm-tossed seas, rocks, ice, and other primordial sights, wherever they might be found. Huston suggested the great still photographer Ernst Haas, even though he had never made any movies. Haas crisscrossed the planet with a camera, and although his crew included only two or three assistants, his wanderings were expensive to underwrite. Still, in his autobiography, *An Open Book*, Huston stresses that Dino never grumbled about the money spent on this excursion into prehistory. Though he never let the director know, the ever-growing budget did worry Dino:

> I was in a more precarious position financially than I'd ever been in my life. But there was one thing I was sure of. As soon as the American studios heard that the contract with Columbia had been torn up, they would start jostling for the project. It was a matter of when, and how much. The first person to call me was Darryl Zanuck, who said that he was ready to come to Rome and sign an agreement.
>
> I told him, "Darryl, give me a moment here. Since the film costs a bundle, I'd prefer that you see something first—at least a little of the material we've already shot—so you'll have some idea of the quality. Then it will be easier for you to enter into an agreement of this size." If I had struck a deal with Zanuck before the Swiss guys gave me the money, I would have lost my shirt to him too. Now, however, I was autonomous and independent. Now the Americans could drop dead as far as I was concerned: instead of squeezing $10 million out of them, I could get even more.
>
> As I watched the dailies in the screening room, the results were so good that my conviction grew. "Why hurry to make a deal with somebody?" I asked myself. "So I can pay off the bank more quickly? I don't have a fixed due date. My only obligation is to repay the loan when I get financing from the Americans, or within thirty days of delivering the master print. What's the rush?"
>
> These things are hard to explain. I realized immediately just how good the film was: all it took was a few scenes. I knew *The Bible* was something extraordinary. And I knew something else: while I made the Americans wait, distributors from everywhere else in the

world would come courting. They were already offering me enormous sums for England, Latin America, France, and so forth. I knew that the moment I wanted to make those deals, I could make them.

In this fashion we approached the end of the shoot. We put together a rough cut of about three hours, which we then whittled down. Leaving the projection room, I said, "John, we've got a formidable film. When it's all mixed and the music is dubbed in, it's going to be extraordinary."

Huston said, "Do you think we'll be in the running for a Nobel Prize?"

I was dumbfounded for a moment. "I don't think so, John. The Nobel has never been given for a film, even if ours is a superlative piece of work." I went to my office and the secretary told me that Zanuck was on the phone from New York.

"How is it coming?" he said. "I have to go to London. Can I stop in Rome and see some of the material?"

"If you come to Rome next week," I replied, "I can show you the first cut."

He came, he saw the whole thing, and for the same territories that Columbia had offered $10 million, he offered $17 million. My gamble had paid off. If I had made a deal with Zanuck on the heels of the defunct contract with Columbia, I never would have gotten more than $10 million out of him. Having seen *The Bible* and grasped its potential, Zanuck grabbed the film. Then I settled things with the Swiss bankers and pocketed an excellent bit of profit for myself.

Huston's love of classical art clearly influenced *The Bible*. Huston also involved numerous contemporary Italian painters and sculptors in the production. Dino says that because of a lack of time, he never became an art collector like his former partner Carlo Ponti. Always, the cinema absorbed him completely. Still, *The Bible* allowed him to form relationships with such great artists as Giacomo Manzù (who sculpted the figure of Adam), Corrado Cagli (who created the Dawn of Consciousness and the Tower of Babel), Mirko Basaldella (who sketched out the panorama of Sodom on the slopes of Mount Etna), and many others. Silvana, whose curiosity and cultural ambitions were seldom at rest, was particularly enamored of these relationships. Indeed, Manzù eventually carved a beautiful bust of her.

For his part, Huston recalls that the sculptor wanted no compensation for his work on the film. When the producer insisted on paying Manzù something, he replied, "Fine, Dino, give me a hundred lire." De Laurentiis fished around in his pocket for the sum—less than a dollar—but all he had were bigger bills, and the scene ended in laughter.

In addition to the fiscal balancing act, the whims of the animals, and the thousand other problems that cropped up on a daily basis, the shoot was roiled by the tempestuous affair between George C. Scott and Ava Gardner. The two stars, playing Abraham and Sarah, shared a behind-the-scenes roller coaster of kisses, slaps, and black eyes, fueled by lots of alcohol. As the tensions and delays mounted, the papers were eager to chronicle every trashed hotel room, physical scuffle, and angry threat.

> Luckily Huston had a firm hand. True, George and Ava got smashed every night, but the next morning on the set they behaved the way they were supposed to. We shot the film in Sicily, Sardinia, and Egypt. Alessandro Blasetti did all the Egyptian battle scenes for me, and the sequence involving the miniature version of Noah's Ark was shot by another illustrious Italian filmmaker, Renato Castellani.
>
> I'm often asked how I managed to convince directors who were quite famous in Italy to oversee second-unit work, often without even having their names in the credits. Soldati did the job on *War and Peace*, for example, and Antonioni worked on *The Tempest*, Blasetti on *The Great War*, and Germi on *Five Branded Women*. The answer is that in my professional relationships, I've always put a great stress on the human and personal aspects. When I ask these friends for a favor, they recall the productive employment that I've steered their way, and since they feel a sense of solidarity with me, they're happy to oblige.
>
> *The Bible*, in any case, was such a great success that many years later, when I was in America, I thought of remaking it for television, with various directors. When I asked Jonathan Demme to direct Adam and Eve, he told me, "Of course I'll make it, but Adam has to be black!"
>
> "You want to get me in trouble with the Vatican?"
>
> He said, "Look, that's my only condition for making the film."
>
> I found out who was the appropriate authority in the Vatican, and I went over there for a chat. The prelate heard me out. Then he said, "Not to worry. You can meet your director's demand, because we too think Adam was black."

I screwed up my courage and answered, "You'll have to put it in writing for me. Because if I go to CBS and tell them Adam was black, they won't believe me—not unless I have an official declaration from the Vatican."

And in fact when I passed the news on to CBS, they said I was crazy: "A black Adam? You'll get us in hot water with everybody!"

De Laurentiis made no biblical epic for CBS. He did, however, produce a pair of less problematic episodes: *Solomon and Sheba* and *Slave of Dreams* were both shot in Morocco in 1994 and broadcast on television the following year.

CHAPTER 20

VILLA CATENA AND BEYOND

BUILDING THE IMMENSE STUDIO AT DINOCITTÀ MIGHT HAVE SATISFIED another man's appetite for real estate. But in 1964 Dino took the plunge again, buying a house that made the Cap Martin property look downright puny by comparison.

> I bought Villa Catena out of love for Silvana. She had seen the villa and she said, "This is the house where I would like to live." Actually, the architect Renzo Mongiardino had showed her a photo of the property, and one day they took the car without telling me and went to see it. She fell in love with the place, and it was, in fact, very beautiful. So I decided to make her happy, even if business wasn't so great at the time.
>
> I don't remember the price: about a billion lire, I think. But by now I had an excellent relationship with the banks. At the time, the general director of the Banca Nazionale del Lavoro was a Signor Longo, whom I knew quite well. I told him that if they would grant me a deferment on repaying the loan, I would buy the villa.
>
> "Of course I'll sell it to you," he replied. "I'll be happy to get it off my plate." Because when the banks foreclose on an immovable asset, they prefer to unload it.
>
> They turned it over to me, but I had to spend an arm and a leg to get it back into shape. It was enormous, with 205 acres of land, outbuildings, the whole deal. I really regretted leaving the place when I departed Rome for good. But I had to sell it, because the upkeep on a house like that costs a fortune.

The purchase of Villa Catena, and the relocation of the De Laurentiis clan from Via Appia to this monumental residence nearly twenty-five miles from Rome, became a kind of comedy of errors. Dino is now convinced that by making the purchase, he actually went *against* the wishes of his consort—who, behind her mask of complete indifference, had never given any sign of dissatisfaction with their previous home. In reality, perhaps, Silvana would have paid an arm and a leg to have been left in peace on Via Appia, where she had lived for more than ten years. But she in turn had no intention of opposing a move that seemed so pure an expression of her husband's grandiose tendencies. Besides, being able to receive his Hollywood partners in such a royal roost might make Dino a more prestigious figure overseas, which would certainly be good for business.

The historic Villa Catena extends over an ample stretch of land near the Faustiniano Hill, enclosed by the slopes of Monte Santa Maria, more than twelve hundred feet above sea level. It's entirely surrounded by fields, pastures, trees, olive groves, and vines, and a long boundary wall, with a natural layer of rock as its foundation, marks the border of the property. Four arched gateways guard the entrances to the villa off Via Prenestina, which runs back to Rome in one direction and toward Gallicano and Poli in the other.

Catena means "chain," and the name, which dates back to the sixteenth century, may derive from the villa's location amidst a chain of hills. (Another theory traces the name back to a chain that was used to prevent carriages from entering the premises.) In any case, the villa had been the traditional residence of the lords of Poli since the twelfth century. Annibal Caro, a man of letters and celebrated translator of the *Aeneid*, who was charged with making improvements to the place during the 1500s, found its beauty overwhelming. "It is a chain with which I would happily be bound," he wrote. "At every moment I keep picturing new delights, new enchantments." Over the centuries, the occupants have built various other buildings around the palace; the entire complex has been commemorated in numerous documents and images, most notably in a 1723 painting entitled *The Arrival of Pope Innocent III at the Villa Catena*.

Along with the enormous expense of buying the property, the producer was also obliged to pay for a thorough renovation, which he entrusted to Renzo Mongiardino. The porte cochere was transformed into an enormous, glass-enclosed living room. The frescoes on the upper floors were restored to their antique splendor. Workers installed central heating and elevators. The bathrooms were modernized, the villa was equipped with ten bedrooms, and Dino saw to the construction of a high-tech screening room downstairs. The outlying buildings were restored and remodeled as guest houses, servants' quarters, and so forth.

All this magnificence made Dino's friends slightly uneasy. They had the distinct impression that something had been lost when the De Laurentiis family changed residences. In his book *The Cinema According to Sonego*, the screenwriter Rodolfo Sonego confesses, "When Dino and *la Mangano* left the villa on Via Appia Antica (which was still a house of very human dimensions) for Villa Catena, my wife, Allegra, and I were quite disappointed. The new place seemed much less warm and welcoming, too dark and grandiose. . . . Mangano, an enigmatic sphinx, would sit in a corner of Villa Catena while she embroidered a pillow. She would make these immense tapestries with tiny little stitches. Dino was always very affectionate and devoted to her: 'Silvana, can I fetch you an aperitif? Silvana, would you like some strawberries? Do you want them with sugar or without?' And she was always very distant: 'De Laurentiis, you know I can't eat strawberries.' She didn't always call him by his last name, but often she did. Cigarettes and a pillow case provided more than enough company for the truly mysterious being that was Silvana."

This enigmatic woman featured prominently in Sonego's memoir, partly because he wrote many screenplays for her: "She was very timid, not much of a leading lady, a shrinking violet. She was full of anxieties that she kept completely inside herself, which you had to understand and respect. There weren't many people she liked. She kept her feelings and her tenderness in check. She never hugged you. . . . Once she left Via Appia, she was too tired to emerge from her room at Villa Catena." He adds, "The mystery of the relationship between Dino and Silvana is the mystery of all the relationships in the world. We're talking about Mysteries of the Bedroom: there's just no way to slip inside there. Dino was all extroversion and enthusiasm: contests, challenges, victories, spoils. He liked to do everything on a big scale, and she preferred a small one."

On Via Appia, the atmosphere had been relaxed, and friends could drop by. They were still eager to visit, but Villa Catena was far enough from Rome that each visit required a special trip, planning and scheduling. The relocation of the De Laurentiis clan also coincided with a significant change in their milieu.

The world of the Italian cinema—which had functioned like an enormous family, convening spontaneously, chattering away, exchanging and stealing ideas, quarreling and making peace—began to disintegrate. One by one their historic haunts, like Trattoria Menghi or Caffè Rosati on Via Veneto, closed their doors or moved away.

Perhaps those who had started families began to stay at home rather than go out. Perhaps it was a matter of generational change. It's also true that the postwar ferment, which had transformed an entire society, was ending: Italy had ceased to be a bubbling cauldron of energies and aspirations. The boom was making everybody lazier, more middle-class, and less available to other people.

No doubt all of these factors contributed to the shifting demographics of the world of the Italian cinema. When he shut down his house on Via Appia, Dino might have been marking the end of an era. Since 1950, when Italian filmmakers began to be household names around the world, that villa had been a fundamental point of reference: a setting for huge parties, with crowds of entertainment luminaries on hand, or for Sunday gatherings with close friends, along with the occasional Hollywood star passing through town. Back then, Dino would enjoy himself by showing off his skills as a cook, serving up delicious dishes. In the summertime he wore shorts and resembled a little boy, beaming and relaxed. The De Laurentiis children called all the visitors *Uncle* or *Aunt* and played with their offspring. Even Silvana, impeccably dressed in order to lounge around the edge of the pool, was capable of shedding her melancholic reserve and bursting into displays of girlish delight.

Though nobody realized it at the time, the curtain was about to fall forever on this scene, and even as the world of Italian film entered a state of flux, Dino had begun to drift away from it. The intricacies of financing his productions, which had grown ever more burdensome, now pushed him into the world of politicians and bankers, rather than cinematic cronies. As one Italian government succeeded another and he was forced to jump through an increasing number of bureaucratic hoops, De Laurentiis focused more and more on the international market. So in a sense, the relocation to Villa Catena signaled the end of one business cycle and the beginning of another.

The move also coincided with the start of a period of profound frustration—particularly on the personal level. Their squabbles aside, Dino and Silvana had retained their reputation as the model couple of the Roman cinema: the most powerful producer and the most inaccessible diva. But now, during the fateful year of 1964, all of their difficulties suddenly came to the surface, in a manner that affected both parents and children.

True, there were some positive aspects to the new house for the De Laurentiis offspring. Here they were free to take long walks, ride on horseback, and play with their dogs. (Everybody in the family had at least one dog.) The children were delighted to see Silvana fooling around in the kitchen from time to time. And then there were the sumptuous parties that Dino continued to throw: crouching at the top of the stairs, the kids leaned over the railings to gaze curiously at the guests, and Veronica and Raffaella, like the heroine of Billy Wilder's *Sabrina*, dreamed of the day when they would participate in events like these.

On the negative side, however, life at Villa Catena made for a great sense of isolation. This was the height of the 1960s, after all, and youth rebellion was raging, from the Beatles to Swinging London, from sexual liberation to student riots. None of these influences quite managed to scale the walls of the De Laurentiis residence, yet the times still had an effect on Veronica and Raffaella, who would have preferred to wear miniskirts instead of the longish skirts and knee socks selected by their mother. In addition, there was almost nobody for them to hang around with. They weren't even allowed to attend the little parties organized by their cousin Aurelio, who never failed to issue them affectionate invitations.

Silvana wanted her daughters to look impeccable at all times. While the independent Raffaella just barely got away with doing things her own way, Veronica didn't dare oppose her mother. When Silvana was in a cheerful mood, her daughters playfully begged for the outfits she no longer wore, and she enjoyed the process of assigning each garment to this or that daughter. But the moment to try on those gorgeous, sophisticated outfits never seemed to arrive.

On her sixteenth birthday, Veronica was finally allowed to give a party. She was thrilled and could hardly wait to wear one of the beautiful garments her mother had *essentially* given her: a pajama suit by Pucci. Silvana, however, didn't approve and substituted a pink, high-necked, schoolgirl's outfit made by Chanel. The whole scene was replayed when Veronica turned eighteen. This time Silvana brought the girl to Lancetti's salon. Slipping into one design after another, Veronica said, "That one is marvelous! This one too!" But in the end her mother made the decision ("I know what's right for you"), choosing a beige, high-necked, rather matronly dress.

The whole family, in fact, appeared to be on the verge of some kind of upheaval. Dino's career required increasing commitments and tensions. Silvana, who had grown more and more elusive, more and more anxious, was often gripped by depression. Federico remained the most pampered child, and being a boy, he was granted more freedom than his sisters. The youngest child, Francesca, was growing up in a solitary fashion, forming her closest emotional bond with the omnipresent butler, Ascanio Istanti. The relationship made perfect sense. After all, her siblings were too old to play with her, her father was seldom around, and when her mother wasn't away on the set, she tended to barricade herself in her room.

With little enthusiasm, Silvana continued to accept certain film roles, mostly to satisfy her husband or an old friend like Sordi. For some years, however, she had nursed an ambition to make her own career decisions. Dino himself finally offered her the opportunity, though not by design. On the set of *The Witches*, yet another De Laurentiis production, Silvana met Luchino Visconti and Pier Paolo Pasolini. And from that point on, it was almost as if a baton had been passed: without ever addressing the issue head on, the actress steadily loosened her husband's grip on her career; she began working almost exclusively with Visconti and Pasolini.

The Witches, which came out in 1967, called for a tour de force from Silvana: five different characters in as many episodes. The directors included her beloved De Sica, whose segment, "A Night like Any Other," chronicled an unmemorable slice of conjugal life. It did, however, involve the participation of Clint Eastwood, who had become a star thanks to the spaghetti Westerns he had made with Sergio Leone. In *Clint Eastwood: A Biography*, Richard Schickel recounts that in order to convince the actor to accept the role, Dino flew Eastwood from

Los Angeles to New York, put him up in a luxurious hotel suite, and tucked him into one limousine after another. As the biographer sees it, De Laurentiis knew exactly whom he was dealing with: he offered Clint "a flat fee of $25,000 for a month's work or $20,000 and a Ferrari. Thinking to himself he would never buy a new Ferrari, he [Clint] told his agents to accept the second alternative, realizing 'that there's no ten percent on that Ferrari!'"

Pasolini paired Mangano with Totò in "Earth as Seen from the Moon," casting her as a deaf-mute with a pallid face and platinum-blond hair. Visconti, meanwhile, shot the episode entitled "The Witch Burned Alive." The protagonist, Gloria, is a movie star married to a famous producer. Staying with a friend in the mountains, she feels restless and unable to sleep. Gloria telephones her spouse in New York, in the middle of the night, and announces that she's pregnant—news that he greets with some irritation, pondering the newly signed contracts that will now be nullified by the pregnancy. Such an attitude certainly couldn't be attributed to Dino, who had greeted the birth of each child with great joy. Still, whether by chance or out of malice, a photograph of De Laurentiis popped up among the furnishings in Gloria's house.

The Witches won Silvana the David di Donatello Prize, and it gave her the confidence to take on more and more sophisticated roles. For Pasolini, she would play Jocasta in *Oedipus Rex*, the mother in *Theorem*, and the Madonna in *The Decameron*. In an analogous manner, Visconti would summon her to incarnate his own mother, the beautiful and elegant Carla Erba, in *Death in Venice*—a role that earned Mangano another Silver Ribbon.

The diva's relationship with Visconti had a complicated emotional undertow. Visconti was gay, so there was nothing sexual about their relationship; indeed, at such an extreme level of identification, the bond joining two people is stronger than any amorous impulse. The director, almost literally bewitched by Silvana, insisted that she participate in his next two films, *Ludwig* and *Conversation Piece*, shot back-to-back after a stroke left him in a state of semiparalysis. In the latter work, directing from a wheelchair, he amused himself by concocting a tormented, nasty character for his friend. True to form, the actress accepted his challenge with only a slight trace of self-destructiveness.

Faced with this dramatic change in his wife's career, Dino was gripped by contrasting emotions. On one hand, he took pleasure in her accomplishments. His pride is evident in an anecdote recounted by Dan Rissner, the producer, in *Messages of Love*: "I was with Warner Bros. and we were making *Death in Venice*. . . . I had lunch with Dino and he asked me how Silvana was doing. I said she was the most beautiful woman I have ever met and she was great in the film. He immediately jumped up, got about twenty dollars in change, and called Silvana from the telephone booth and told me to repeat to her what I had told him. Since he felt he had to shout over the telephone, everybody in Girarrosto Toscano heard the conversation and congratulated him on his way back to the table."

As a producer, however, he was less than delighted by the fact that his cranky consort, who had shaken off his artistic control, was now sought out by a circle of sophisticated intellectuals. From time to time, in a not entirely playful manner, he warned her, "You've become the queen of the faggots." Pasolini, whom Dino had known since *Nights of Cabiria* (when the young writer had given an assist to the film's lowlife ambience and Roman dialect), wasn't his type. Nor had he ever established a warm relationship with Visconti, despite a strong feeling of mutual respect.

In fact, after "The Witch Burned Alive," Dino came across a rather nasty statement of Visconti's in a newspaper: "It was a nice little piece of work, but De Laurentiis completely ruined it. After endless battles between the two of us, I gave in, and the film lost whatever meaning it had. Dino understood nothing about the episode; his only concern was that it was too long in comparison with the others. At one point he suggested that I make it into an independent feature. I told him no: I had conceived it as an episode, structured like a novella rather than a novel. But he couldn't stand to leave the piece as it had been shot. And as a result, it lost most of the original flavor."

> The problem is that *The Witches* was an episodic film, and when you make such a film there has to be a certain balance between the episodes. There can be a difference of five minutes or so, but one segment can't be twice as long as the others. The public just won't accept such a lack of proportion—let alone the other directors!
>
> But Visconti went overboard, just as he had when I commissioned the "Joseph and His Brothers" segment for *The Bible*. He

> was supposed to make a thirty-minute episode, and instead he knocked out a four-hour script.
>
> I kept telling him, "When somebody asks you to shoot an episode in a comedic context, conceived in a certain manner, you have to think of yourself as a professional, whose primary obligation is to the public. If you give me an hour, then I'm going to suggest we shoot an additional half-hour. Then we can stitch together a complete film, put the name *Visconti* on it, and be done with it." In the end, he would have killed the episode, just like he said. But *The Witches* did quite well commercially, not only in Europe but in America, where it was distributed by United Artists.

There's no clue as to which position Silvana took during these discussions of the ill-fated episode. It's easy to imagine her siding with the director rather than the producer, then ducking behind her habitual reserve. Although the diva could be hard on her own spouse, however, she wouldn't tolerate criticism of Dino from anyone else.

Visconti, however, was hardly Dino's biggest problem. In the spring of 1967, while he was also coping with an attack of appendicitis and the whole mess with Fellini, De Laurentiis was struck by one of those sad events that mark every human life. On April 24, having just turned eighty-six, Rosario Aurelio De Laurentiis died in his Roman apartment. Throughout a long period of illness, the old man had always taken pains to appear good-humored and crisply turned out in front of his children and acquaintances. Now he was gone. Dino and his siblings buried their father; it would be the last time that De Laurentiis was willing to face the spectacle of death and its public rituals. He would never again attend a funeral.

Silvana, who cared for her husband in spite of their differences, was a source of comfort for him. For several weeks she visited her mother-in-law, Donna Giuseppina, now in her eighties, almost every morning, comforting the widow as best she could. For a time Dino and Silvana seemed to recover a certain sense of solidarity. Yet the familial situation was just now reaching a critical stage.

Taking into account *The Witches*, *Capriccio all'italiana*, *Oedipus Rex*, and *Theorem*, Silvana had made four films within the last two years, and she was exhausted by the constant shuttling between Poli and Rome. She rented a pied-à-terre that would let her avoid the long nightly commute and the bumper-to-bumper traffic on Via Prenestina. But more than that, she was attempting to reclaim some personal space, some new perspective, after having submerged herself for so many years in her role as wife and mother.

After all, Mangano married Dino when she was nineteen: she felt as though she had simply skipped her youth, since her marriage carried with it such a freight of responsibility. At the same time, by coddling her to the extent he did, Dino had protected her. He had allowed her to mature like a hothouse flower, with little sense of the struggle that life entailed. Being treated like a queen, however, failed to shield her from existential angst, and as she approached her forties, Silvana began to ask herself whether what she had was truly what she wanted.

She had her circle of friends, all of them intellectuals and homosexuals: Pasolini, Visconti, Bolognini. She would have liked to converse with them as an equal, and the fact that she lacked a sufficient cultural background was a source of pain to her. Still, the attention and admiration of these celebrated filmmakers gave her a great deal more confidence in her abilities as an actress.

When she told me she wanted to take an apartment on Piazza di Spagna, I was enraged. How could this be? I had bought Villa Catena out of love for her, I had installed her in a palace, and now she wanted to go off and live by herself! I told her that I was against the idea—completely against it. But she insisted, and I gave in, and something snapped inside me. I returned to Villa Catena with the intention of packing my bags and leaving. That's what I did with Bianca. But I didn't have any children with my first wife, and immediately I thought of my four kids at home. What was I going to do, abandon them? I couldn't! Nor did I want to leave them alone with her.

So for a long time, I sacrificed my own needs. Silvana and I continued to stay together in what we might call a friendly relationship—or no, let's call it a state of mutual tolerance. We did this for the sake of the children.

Now, this whole mess had nothing to do with jealousy, with other people on the scene. Our love didn't end due to external circumstances: it withered away all by itself. She may have had something going on after she moved to Piazza di Spagna, I couldn't say, and anything is possible. But at that point I didn't care anymore. As

As a student at the Convitto nazionale in Naples

As a salesman at Pastifico Moderno (1937)

Acting in *Pantaloni lunghi* (1938), directed by Pietro Germi

Acting in *Troppo tardi t'ho conosciuta* (1939)

On the set of *Il brigante Musolino* with Aldo Tonti (left) and Mario Camerini (1950)

With Assia Noris on the set of *Margherita fra i tre*

With Mario Soldati
on the set of *Malombra* (1942)

With Giuseppe De Santis (1948)

With Carlo Ponti (1949)

With Silvana and Carlo Ponti on the Lido in Venice (1954)

With Kirk Douglas on the set of *Ulysses* (1953)

With wife Silvana Mangano and daughters Veronica and Raffaella

With Silvana

With Ingrid Bergman and Federico Fellini

In Hollywood with William Wyler (1954)

With King Vidor at Mel Ferrer and Audrey Hepburn's arrival in Rome (1955)

With King Vidor, Audrey Hepburn and Mario Soldati during the filming of *War and Peace* (1955)

With Audrey Hepburn and Vittorio Gassman on the set of *War and Peace*

With King Vidor and Anita Ekberg

With King Vidor and Henry Fonda

With Henry Gris and Silvana celebrating *War and Peace* at the Hollywood Foreign Press Association (1956)

With King Vidor in Hollywood

With Silvana and the Golden Globe for *War and Peace* and the Oscar for *La strada* (1957)

With mother Giuseppina and daughters Veronica and Raffaella

With Federico Fellini

With Jerry Lewis and Federico Fellini

With Anthony Perkins during the filming of *La diga sul Pacifico*

With Vittorio Gassman and Alberto Sordi on the set of *La grande guerra* (1959)

In Rome with Silvana, little Federico and a crew from the BBC (1960)

In Hollywood with Luigi Luraschi, Alan Ladd and Ernest Borgnine

With Anthony Quinn on the set of *Barabbas* (1961)

On the steps of the Arena in Verona for *Barabbas*

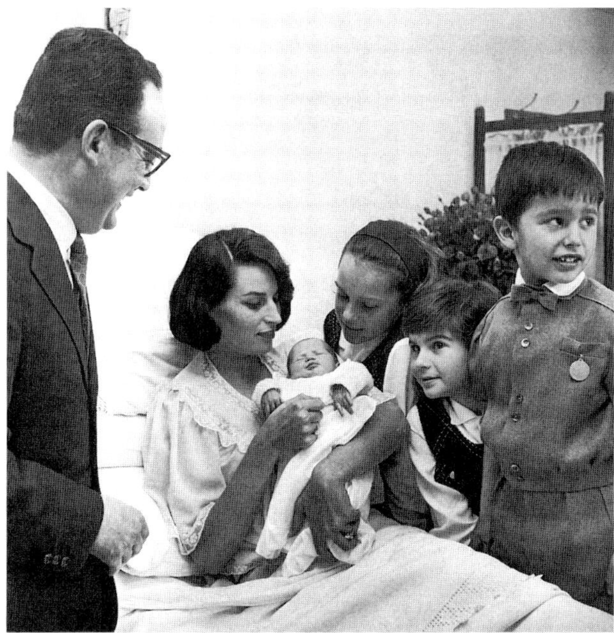

The family reunites around the newborn Francesca (1961)

With Alberto Sordi and Dino Risi on the set of *Una vita difficile* (1961)

With Alberto Sordi and Vittorio De Sica on the set of *Il boom* (1963)

Eric Johnston, president of the MPAA, visiting the construction site of Dinocittà

With Giulio Andreotti and Luigi De Laurentiis at Dinocittà (1964)

In the garden at the villa on Appia, the family celebrates the golden wedding anniversary of Rosario Aurelio and Giuseppina (1964)

An audience with Pope Paul VI

With Soraya during the rehearsals for *I tre volti* (1964)

With John Huston, director of *The Bible* (1964)

With Yul Brynner

With Luchino Visconti during the filming of *Le Streghe* (1966)

In Russia for *Waterloo* with Mario Garbuglia and Rod Steiger (1970)

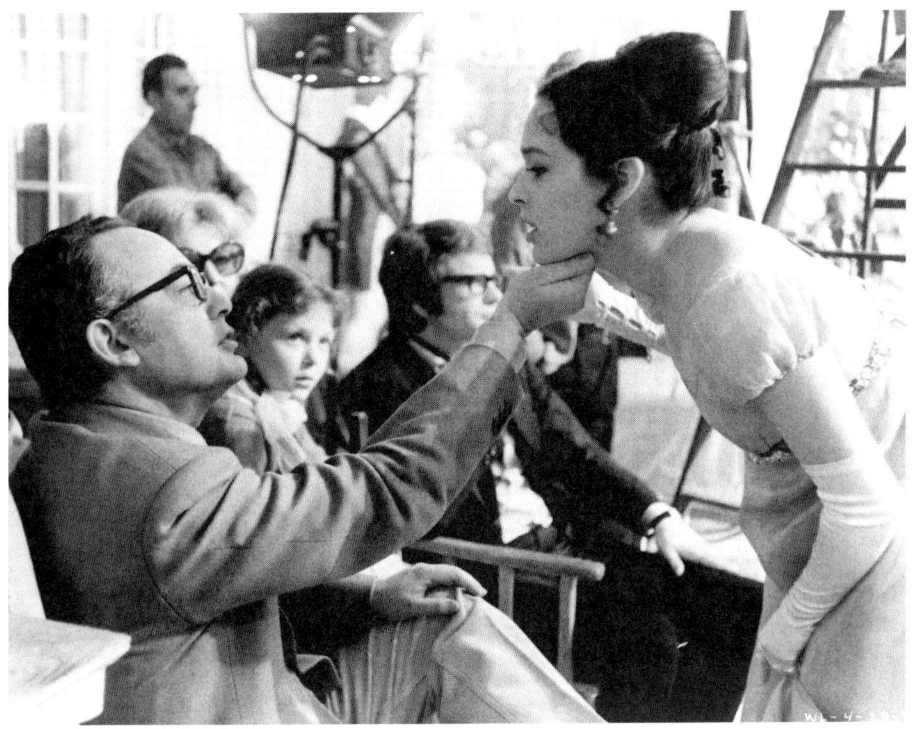

With daughter Veronica on the set of *Waterloo*

The grand ball scene in *Waterloo* at the Naval Palace

In New York with Charles Bluhdorn and Franco Zeffirelli

With Sydney Pollack during rehearsals for *Three Days of the Condor* (1975)

Dino in the United States 1976

With King Kong

Federico De Laurentiis with Jessica Lange on the set of *King Kong* (1976)

With Charles Bronson and his wife Jill Ireland

With Milos Forman on the set of *Ragtime* (1981)

With Arnold Schwarzenegger at DDL Foodshow (1984)

With David Lynch at DDL Foodshow

With Raffaella, producer of *Dune* (1984)

With Jonathan Mostow, Kurt Russell and Martha De Laurentiis on the set of *Breakdown* (1996)

With Brett Ratner

With five daughters. From left: Raffaella, Dina, Francesca, Veronica, and Carolyna (1997)

With Martha, Carolyna, and Dina at the house in Beverly Hills

Martha, Carolyna and Dina

With Martha during the production of *U-571* (1999)

With Martha, Dina, and Carolyna in Capri

With Martha at the Capri festival (1999)

An embrace with Hannibal,
Anthony Hopkins (2000)

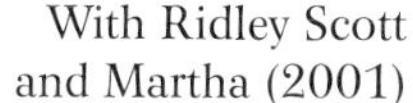

With Ridley Scott
and Martha (2001)

With Martha and director
Baz Luhrmann

Receiving the Irving G. Thalberg Memorial Award at the Oscars 2000

At the Venice Film Festival receiving the Golden Lion Award for Lifetime Achievement 2003

> for me, I had always been a faithful husband, but now I began to have a few romantic adventures. Nothing long-term, just ephemeral little affairs, and always conducted with discretion, in order to avoid problems.
>
> From time to time Silvana saw the children. Sometimes they went to see her at Piazza di Spagna, or she came out to the house. But it was during that first period that I stopped loving her. And now I'm not sure whether I should consider myself a coward, who didn't have the courage to make an unpleasant decision, or a responsible father, who wanted to stay with his kids until they became sufficiently independent.

Villa Catena's moment of glory ended when Dino moved to the United States. It would have required another De Laurentiis to bear the costs and sustain the splendors of such a residence, and no figure of equal stature appears in the subsequent history of the property. The villa has passed from hand to hand. Boarded up and practically abandoned, it was listed for sale once again in 2002, and one of the selling points was the "movie theater" Dino had installed in the palace of the princes.

CHAPTER 21

HIS WATERLOO

THE NAME *DINO DE LAURENTIIS* CAN BE FOUND IN HUNDREDS OF BOOKS and thousands of press clippings. It's impossible to assemble even a partial list of the contents of this monumental scrapbook: there are mentions of every kind, at every level of seriousness, and they range from hagiography to libel. Among the most vivid accounts, however, is that of director and producer Richard Fleischer in his autobiography *Just Tell Me When to Cry*. There is, from time to time, a hint of resentment in his account, which we can chalk up to the fact that during the director's fourth year in Rome, a contractual wrangle he had with Dino ended up in the courts. To be honest, though, this contention caused little irritation to either party. Fleischer went on to shoot several other films for De Laurentiis, including such hits as *Mandingo* and such flops as *Conan 2*. In any case, his recollections of Dino are vivid:

> There aren't many people in the world who are immediately recognizable by their first names alone, but Dino is one of them. Even in the Fifties, all you had to say was "Dino" and everybody knew whom you meant. He seems, somehow, to have been born a legend. An impeccably tailored bundle of raw energy and volatile emotions, he is not only a legend, but also a character. The impact of meeting him for the first time is something akin to sticking your finger in an electrical light socket. Short, dark, and with a high forehead, he has steely black eyes with bushy eyebrows that sweep up satanically at the ends. The word "gravelly" was invented to describe his voice, which he uses to bark out short, staccato, exclam-

> atory sentences. His personality is the same as his speech: curt, abrupt, brusque. And then there is his smile. It can be open and winning, even disarming. But it can be something else, too. He can give you a smile with his lips only, the rest of his face immobile. It is like looking into the face of icy Death. I know.

So did innumerable others who rubbed Dino the wrong way, even on a temporary basis.

Fleischer describes Dino's impossible English, comprehensible only when he spoke slowly, which created numerous challenges for his omnipresent interpreter. The producer would react to comments by shouting, banging his fists on the table, jumping to his feet, waving his index finger; then, after giving the impression of being irritated beyond all limits, he would drop back into his chair. The interpreter would say, "Doctor De Laurentiis said that he's perfectly satisfied with your statement."

Fleischer notes that Dino's English improved over time, though his pronunciation did not. And he confirms the rather widely held opinion that our hero understands at once what he wishes to understand—particularly when the discussion revolves around money—and when he finds it useful, he hides behind a selective inability to comprehend. Equally effective and entertaining to Fleischer was his recourse to primitive verbal structures: "I like! I not like! We do!" Finally, Fleischer recognizes that Dino, with all his faults, is a brilliant salesman and an unbeatable showman. No one else has his genius for making you an offer that you can't refuse, and giving himself a slightly better offer should the opportunity arise.

Even an unbeatable showman, however, has his moments of defeat. Such a moment arrives when all of his personal qualities, all his inventiveness and argumentation, are no longer enough to keep an enterprise afloat. It's a curious coincidence that Dino was producing *Waterloo* when he faced a Waterloo of his own.

> The idea for *Waterloo* came to me while I was casting about for a spectacular subject. Out of habit I read a great deal, flipping through the encyclopedia, and at a certain point my eyes happened to fall on the pages devoted to the battle of Waterloo. I thought it over: epic scenes, Napoleon, Wellington . . . Yes, there was a film to be made.

> But before spending any money on a screenplay, I decided to sound out Mosfilm, the Russian movie bureau, and find out what they thought about such a project. I could tell that we would need thousands of soldiers, thousands of horses. Those battle scenes go on forever! So I told myself, "I'm going to propose this idea to the Soviets. They can give me everything."
>
> The Soviets signed on, and they immediately suggested some possible locations for the shoot, but with one condition: I had to hire a Russian director. I told them I was happy to use Sergei Bondarchuk, a filmmaker I actually admired. And so the government granted me ten thousand soldiers and shipped them from Moscow to Uzgorod, which is like a trip from New York to Los Angeles.

The production called for the biggest set in the history of the world, extending over nearly four square miles and with meticulous attention to detail. To do the job, Dino called in Mario Garbuglio, a veteran of *War and Peace* and *The Great War*. The art director recalls, "Uzgorod is at the bottom of that little triangle of the Ukraine, which shares a border with Poland to the north, with Czechoslovakia to the west, and with Hungary to the south. And when the Soviet tanks converged on Prague in August 1968, they rolled right through there. We were already on the scene: we watched them pass from our hotel window."

Around the area set aside for the battle, about a half-hour drive from Uzgorod, a squad of Mosfilm officials and four hundred soldiers from the Soviet engineering corps were already hard at work. "The terrain was designed, staked out, and ploughed," Garbuglio explains. "We laid out roads and began construction on the enormous farms and castles and other structures that we would need for the battle. We planted trees and landscaping of every kind, because everything had to be ready when the shoot began. Meanwhile, the generals committed ten thousand infantrymen to the film, along with fifteen hundred mounted soldiers."

Dino remembers the shoot:

> When the horses arrived, they created a real logistical problem. Where should we put them, what do we feed them, where are they going to shit? Thousands of horses: sheer madness. Thanks to them, however, we were able to realize scenes without any precedent in the history of the cinema. And I personally shot the most beautiful cavalry charge.

The film was conceived as a vehicle for Richard Burton (as Napoleon) and Peter O'Toole (as Wellington). But in order to deploy the ten thousand soldiers, the Russians needed to get under way before the dead of winter, and Burton and O'Toole had theatrical commitments in London. Instead I hired Rod Steiger and Christopher Plummer—tremendous actors, both of them, but without the star power of the other two.

Unfortunately, Bondarchuk cut many of Steiger's best bits, because he thought he was overacting. On the other hand, Bondarchuk didn't speak a word of English and wasn't capable of reading the screenplay. To keep the situation under control, I went to work on the script with an American screenwriter, but in order to simplify things, we were forced to chop out all sorts of great stuff.

According to Garbuglio, the production also availed itself of a factory to produce fake soldiers for both armies, dead plastic horses, and other puppets—approximately five thousand items in all. "The whole idea was to scatter corpses across the terrain," Garbuglio recalls, "and to integrate the fake soldiers into the units on the battlefield. Each unit was composed of two real soldiers and another eight plastic ones. The fakes were in perfect formation, of course, and held in place by a single wooden plank."

An incredible encampment of soldiers and filmmakers came into being at Uzgorod. The inhabitants hailed from numerous countries and spoke numerous languages, which led to various predictable difficulties. But there were moments of merriment as well. "When Dino arrived at our Waterloo with Silvana and the kids," Garbuglio continues, "work usually ground to a halt for a week. In the evenings, the generals threw enormous banquets. Silvana, who was queen of these affairs, would perform Russian dances against a backdrop of songs, choruses, and all the vodka you could drink. To greet the dawn they set up baccarat tables, at which Dino and Silvana, victorious as always, would cheerfully win back whatever we were being paid to make the film."

Waterloo was an adventure that gave me great satisfaction. There was no way I could lose money on the production, because I had passed on the gross costs to the Russians, who had taken their own territory in return. In the USSR the film was a success: Bondarchuk was a mythical figure in that part of the world. And

> I'm sure that with Burton and O'Toole we would have cleaned up everywhere, even in the places where we didn't do as well.
>
> But a strange thing happened. We set up two previews, and I remember the outcome as if it were yesterday: the one in London was a great success, and the one in Paris, three days later, was a fiasco. Ultimately *Waterloo* did excellent business in all the English-speaking territories, since they were the ones who won the battle (at least that's how I see it). And since Napoleon lost, the film did horribly in all the French-speaking territories. All of which demonstrates once again that the public likes to side with a winner.

At the moment, however, Dino's biggest problem wasn't the fate of *Waterloo* but the troubled state of Dinocittà. Even Garbuglio became aware of the crisis toward the end of the shoot: "By now it was October and we were almost done, when Dino confided to me on the battlefield that he had decided to close the studio and look for new prospects. He was going to study the situation in Japan and in the United States and get some idea of what he could put together elsewhere. Within just a few years, he would regretfully shut down the whole business on Via Pontina."

What happened? What shattered Dino's dream of creating the biggest and most modern studio complex in the world? As it turns out, Italy's political situation was the biggest factor undermining Dinocittà.

When the country's first center-left government came into power on December 5, 1963, its ranks included Achille Corona, one of the founders of the clandestine Socialist Party during the Fascist era. Corona headed the newly created Ministry of Tourism and Entertainment, which he would continue to run during two subsequent administrations. Of all the ministers appointed to oversee the entertainment industry, he served the longest and made the biggest impact—mostly thanks to a new, cinema-related law, Number 1213. Enacted on November 4, 1965, this novel regulation might as well have been conceived and drafted in direct opposition to a producer like De Laurentiis.

Dino, of course, steered clear of any political affiliation. Yet his ascent took place during the heyday of the Christian Democrats, with whom he generally maintained good relations. It's no wonder, then, that the Socialists—who now exercised some real muscle in the coalition government—viewed him with little sympathy. They considered him the beneficiary of a defunct political structure and saw his empire as a stronghold to be dismantled.

And dismantle it they did. The new law was aimed at international productions, which were denounced as alien to the traditions of the Italian cinema. The state now intended to protect the national character of the film industry, on both the cultural and occupational fronts. Until that moment, if a filmmaker wanted to obtain "national" status for his creation—which would make the film eligible for subsidies, loan guarantees, and so forth—he had only to respect the provisions of the so-called Andreotti law, enacted in 1949. The law specified that a feature film must be "in Italian, or include an Italian-language version," and that it must be made from a story written by or adapted by an Italian author. In addition, the majority of the crew and cast had to be Italian. That meant that a film shot in English (or in any other foreign language) could qualify for "national" status, as long as slightly more than half of the crew and cast were Italians. What's more, according to the Andreotti formula, the director counted as just one more member of the crew and cast. The question of his nationality carried no extra weight, which gave the producer a great deal of room to adjust the proportions.

The Corona law, however, specified that the film must be made in Italian. The director too had to be Italian, along with a majority of the screenwriters, 66 percent of the principal actors, 75 percent of the secondary actors, and 75 percent of the crew and technical personnel. It was a law designed to safeguard nationalist values in a way that Dino considered shortsighted and controlling. According to this standard, many De Laurentiis films—including *War and Peace* (King Vidor), *The Sea Wall* (René Clément), *Five Branded Women* (Martin Ritt), *Barabbas* (Richard Fleischer), and *The Best of Enemies* (Guy Hamilton)—because they were directed by foreigners, could never be considered Italian. John Huston's *The Bible* won "national" status by a hair, having been completed right before the new law went into effect. But Bondarchuk's *Waterloo*, a spectacular conceived and created by Italians, would not be eligible.

> When the Corona law was passed, the export of Italian films to foreign markets collapsed overnight: go ahead, check the statistics. This was a serious blow to the image of our nation, whose best am-

bassador had been the postwar cinema. Film production was relegated to a provincial level, and with a few exceptions, it's never recovered. Our filmmakers are paying the price for this misguided law to this very day.

Meanwhile, the attacks on Dinocittà became more widespread. From every quarter, De Laurentiis was accused of entrepreneurial sleaziness and megalomania. The press launched a campaign to block any transfer of the obsolete Cinecittà to Dinocittà or even the creation of a joint enterprise—a commingling of public and private spheres then considered beyond the pale. (Within a few decades, arrangements like this would be considered completely normal.) Dino was accused of tampering with the official boundaries of the Cassa del Mezzogiorno, of using the state's money to construct an impractical white elephant. According to some of his critics, he was now conspiring to sell his creation back to the state itself!

They attacked me for spending the state's money. What money were they talking about? I built Dinocittà with my own cash. Yes, I got financing from the Cassa del Mezzogiorno, at a very reasonable interest rate: three percent, I think. But isn't that what the Cassa del Mezzogiorno was created for?

Now, at a certain point there was some thought of moving Cinecittà into my studio complex, which would have been a perfectly rational decision. It was an old facility, while mine was the most modern in the world. In short, after many negotiations with the appropriate ministry (which was headed by Flaminio Piccoli), we agreed that Cinecittà would officially acquire Dinocittà. The project involved bringing both studios under a single management. You would no longer have two competitors, but two facilities that worked together, side by side. Piccoli gave me an official letter to pass on to the president of Cinecittà, who wanted no part of the merger. And I ended up washing my hands of the whole mess. Whatever else you hear about the deal is nonsense, just like the assertion that I tweaked the boundaries of the Cassa del Mezzogiorno.

What crap! When I went to look at real estate, I obviously looked for properties that fell within the jurisdiction of the Cassa. Why would I need to fool around with the borders? Just take a look at the registry maps. The boundaries of the Cassa's territory were

> defined by Law Number 105, enacted on March 10, 1955. I made my first purchase of land for Dinocittà on June 30, 1959.
>
> I'm taking these dates from a petition I wrote on the occasion of a parliamentary inquiry. An honorable deputy from the Socialist Party had demanded "the truth about the De Laurentiis case." My response was, "Since the government requires certain information from me in order to answer these questions, I might as well give a truthful account directly to the committee and to the nation, assuming that the nation is eager to hear it."
>
> People attacked me on the basis of these lies, these false and unsubstantiated news items. I told them to see for themselves, to do a little research. And look: I certainly didn't fool around with the boundaries of the Cassa. But let's say I had. What would have been my motive for doing so? To build something that would bring jobs and prestige to Italy, and to do it with my own money, not with the state's money, as so many of my detractors kept insisting. The funds for Dinocittà came partly out of my own pocket, partly from the Cassa del Mezzogiorno, and partly from the Banca Nazionale del Lavoro, and I repaid the two lenders down to the last *centesimo*.
>
> You heard all these complaints: De Laurentiis got the state to pay for his studio, and now he wants to sell it back to the very same state. It's not true. The negotiations regarding Cinecittà got under way only after I had paid back all the loans. What's more, at a certain point it was Cinecittà that expressed some interest in acquiring Dinocittà, and so did RAI. But it was too hard to hammer out an agreement, and the whole business vanished into thin air.

It was a moment of enormous managerial and financial difficulty. Some of Dino's clients took their business elsewhere, and the workers at the studio, sensing the crisis, went on strike. The poisoned atmosphere was encapsulated in a single ugly episode: the lawsuit that De Laurentiis was forced to file against two journalists, the brothers Giorgio and Paolo Pisanò.

In early 1971 the minister of transportation, Italo Viglianesi, informed Dino that the weekly *Candido* was about to publish an attack on him. Anticipating a deal between Cinecittà and Dinocittà, the article accused the board of directors of artificially inflating the price of the transaction. In reality the attack was aimed at certain political personalities: the authors meant to contrast the ascendant Socialists with the decrepit public agencies. But Dino, worried about the effects of a smear campaign at such a delicate juncture, telephoned the editor of the magazine, Giorgio Pisanò.

He was then surprised to hear himself being shaken down for money: "It's your turn to make a gesture. . . . What you do is sign up for a certain number of subscriptions . . ." In a series of subsequent phone conversations, the editor (and neo-Fascist senator) upped the price again and again, until he was asking for 10 million lire.

Always a reckless gambler, Dino lulled Pisanò into compromising himself and recorded all the phone calls on tape. This pathetic dialogue would eventually be published in full by *L'Espresso*, under the headline, "Hello, Who's Paying?" De Laurentiis made an appointment to meet the editor's brother, Paolo, and handed over a briefcase of banknotes, all of them dutifully registered by serial number. Then he sat back as the *carabinieri* captured Paolo red-handed, even as Giorgio was being handcuffed in Milan.

The brothers were acquitted because of insufficient evidence (under a watered-down judicial formula that would soon be struck from the Italian legal code). On November 23, 1973, however, the Court of Appeals overturned the earlier verdict. On the basis of a new accusation of aggravated extortion, the Pisanò brothers were remanded into the custody of the criminal courts.

Here, at last, was some satisfaction. But for Dino, the generally negative trend had spread far beyond his professional travails. There was a corresponding pall over his family life, which had, astonishingly enough, become more difficult than ever.

CHAPTER 22

LIFE BEGINS AGAIN AT FIFTY

AMONG THE CROWD IN *WATERLOO*'S GREAT BALLROOM SCENE IS VERONICA De Laurentiis, who looks delightful in her period costume. The story of how Dino's daughter snagged her single role as an actress is, naturally, controversial. According to Raffaella, somebody had offered Veronica a role in another film, and in order to fend off the blow, Dino assigned her the small part of Madeleine Hall in *Waterloo*. According to Veronica, it was her father who took the initiative. In either case, this role could have been the beginning of a career for her—albeit one under Dino's iron supervision—if only her mother hadn't opposed the idea with all *her* will.

Veronica had other things on her plate. In the summer of 1969, when her dream of acting was nipped in the bud, she was a sensitive, somewhat innocent nineteen-year-old. She was vulnerable in her relationships with men, thanks to a horrible experience of the previous year, which she lacked the courage to discuss even with Raffaella. She was also impatient with her family situation, which grew tenser by the day, and with her rigid, old-fashioned education. In short, she was ideally positioned to fall into the arms of the first man who seemed to offer some escape from her gilded prison. Alas, the man in question wasn't the right one; in fact, he turned out to be precisely the wrong one.

It was during the annual vacation at Cap Martin that Veronica met Alex De Benedetti, a boy from a good family. Both Dino and Silvana disliked the young man from the very first. Still, the relationship developed quickly. In September Alex, who lived in Turin, came to visit

Veronica in Rome, and in December he spent Christmas with the De Laurentiis family. On New Year's Day, Veronica discovered that she was pregnant, and although she was terrified at the prospect, she knew she had to tell her parents.

To her astonishment, Dino and Silvana were quite understanding, but they insisted that she think matters over very carefully before rushing into marriage. Dino tried to change his daughter's mind right up to the eve of the ceremony, but the wedding took place in the Basilica di San Sebastiano on February 14, 1970, followed by an opulent reception at Villa Catena.

> The difficult relationship between my daughters and Silvana had repercussions in their emotional lives. Important repercussions: just look at their marriages. Let's begin with the first one, Veronica's marriage to Alex De Benedetti. I never liked him at all; I didn't trust him. But Veronica wanted to marry him at all costs, and when she sets her mind to something, she's stubborn as a mule, so I had to give in. She had four children with this guy before she figured out who he was: a playboy with a small pile of family money, which he promptly flushed down the toilet, meaning that I had to support him. That marriage ended in a dramatic manner, even a melodramatic manner: I'd rather not discuss it. Veronica can give you the whole story, if she wants to. And thank God, she's doing very well now. She got married again, to Ivan Kavalsky, a South African who had worked in America for some time. An excellent man.
>
> Let's move on to Raffaella. One day while we still lived at Villa Catena, she came to me and said, "I need to talk to you." I don't know why, but my daughters always proceed from the assumption that their parents don't understand a damn thing.
>
> "Tell me, daughter, what is it?"
>
> "I'd like to get married."
>
> "Aha!" I already knew whom she wanted to marry, I knew the whole story. "But is this a question?" I said. "Are you asking me if you can get married? Or is it a statement?"
>
> "It's a question, papa."
>
> "In that case, the answer is no. When you're no longer a minor, you'll be free to marry whether I give my permission or not. For now, though, the answer is no."
>
> Raffaella was then seventeen. She was in love with Gippi Viale, the son of the owner of Le Pirate. I had no objections in terms of

race, wealth, social standing, or anything else. I only wanted to be sure it was the right man. Time passed, and Raffaella once again appeared before me. "I need to talk to you."

"I already understand," I said. "You want to get married. I can no longer deny your request, but you're making a big mistake. He's not the man for you: in fact, if there were a single man in the world who was unsuitable for you, it would be him. Go to bed with him if you like, but don't marry him."

It was useless. Her mother carefully avoided siding with me: she detached herself from the debate without offering a word. On July 3, 1973, within days of her twenty-first birthday, Raffaella got married at Monte Carlo, and I organized a lovely reception at Cap Martin. This marriage also ended pretty fast. Then Raffaella met Buzz Feitshans, the co-producer of *Conan*, and since then they've had a very happy life together.

A few years later we went through the same thing with Francesca: the identical story, for the third time. She was going to college in Los Angeles. Raffaella asked if she could bring her sister along as a production assistant on the set of *Conan*. There Francesca fell in love with a guy named Escriva. I assumed it was the kind of thing that would end the moment she returned to Los Angeles. Instead, not long after, I was told that we were all going to Madrid, because Francesca wanted to get married.

"To Escriva?" I said. "Why does Francesca need to marry somebody named Escriva?" To me the name already sounded bad. My wife took the opposite tack: "We must go, we must go." Silvana had a weakness for Francesca, since she was the youngest. They convinced me to jet off to Madrid, and when I met the fiancé, I felt worse than ever. In front of everybody I said, "Why do you have to rush into this? My suggestion would be that you get engaged, take a little time to think things over, and meanwhile return to America."

Good heavens, everybody took me to task, starting with Silvana, Raffaella, and Veronica. The fact remains that in 1982 they got married, and after having two children together, they stopped getting along. They came to America. I tried to help them by bringing him into my business. Then they returned to Madrid, where the situation just got worse until they reached the breaking point.

Francesca called and said, "What should I do?" Since she always hated it when I disagreed with her, she hadn't spoken to me in a long time. But now her husband wouldn't give her permission to take the kids to America. He had gone to the courts, and the judge had sided with him, because the children were still very young and the move could be a traumatic one. I told her, "Pretend you're taking the kids for a stroll. Don't even say a word to the maid. Then go to the airport and get on a flight to Los Angeles. Once you're all here, we'll figure out how to handle it." After she arrived in America, I convinced the husband to grant her a divorce. Meanwhile Francesca returned to her studies in Los Angeles and got a degree in psychology.

Back in the *Waterloo* era, as De Laurentiis continued to fight his rear-guard actions on behalf of Dinocittà, Villa Catena was becoming ever more depopulated. Veronica had gone, Raffaella too was impatient to get married and depart, and by now Silvana spent most of her time at the apartment in Rome. Once this situation became widely known, the press had a field day with it, assuming that a legal separation had already taken place. In October 1972 a women's magazine issued an explicit pronouncement: "After 23 years of marriage, they have parted ways." A banner headline conveyed the same message: "*La Signora* Has Left: She Went to Live by Herself." The article took the split for granted, reporting that by now "the actress earns her own living, at a price of 30 million lire per film, and she hopes to make at least two each year." In fact Silvana wasn't really supporting herself: Dino continued to provide for most of the needs of the entire family. It was true, however, that by now a de facto separation was in place.

The magazine extracted a brief interview from Silvana, but she insisted on guarding her privacy: "It's no use asking questions about my personal life. People who know about it won't talk, and those who talk know nothing. For twenty years I haven't said a word about it, and I don't think that was a mistake." Turning to her professional life, the writer then asked her to rate her co-stars on the film she was then working on, *D'amore si muore*. She dryly responded, "Who am I to judge them? I've never done anything worthwhile myself." Her partner in the film, the young actor Lino Capolicchio, spoke enthusiastically about her work: "She's an extremely sensitive, smart, and refined woman. . . . I call her Madame de Guermantes, since her attitude is quite ironic and Proustian." Capolicchio also mentioned her embarrassment at shooting a love scene with him: "She kept repeating, 'But I'm a grandmother. You don't shoot love scenes with a grandmother.'"

Finally Dino abandoned Dinocittà and set up shop in the Roman EUR neighborhood and at Vasca Navale. One big-budget film was still under way at the Dinocittà complex—*Man of La Mancha*, starring Sophia Loren—and even after the official closure on June 18, 1972, an occasional quickie production was shot there. But these were the last gasps. For several weeks the shuttered studio presented a peculiar sight to drivers on Via Pontina: the laid-off workers had occupied the place and were waving banners and signs at the passing traffic ("Here's Where They Shot the Bible—But Now the Workers Are Lost in the Flood"). Then the protests died out until, finally, there was no one left. All that remained were the sets for *Mastorna*, the crumbling, spectral evidence of an interrupted dream: the cathedral at Cologne, the airplane, a row of building facades.

The director David Cronenberg later recalled a visit to the dilapidated facility: "There was moss on the walls of the office. And lizards. They had artifacts left over from *Waterloo*, the last film Dino had shot there." But the producer wasn't waiting around for the moss and the lizards. He didn't feel like witnessing the progressive collapse of his empire, and in any case, crying over spilt milk wasn't his style. Instead he came up with the equivalent of a surprise cavalry charge. Defeated at his own personal Waterloo, the Napoleon of the cinema refused to be confined to Saint Helena. Instead he came up with a radical solution. He would go to America.

One of his productions, *The Valachi Papers*, pointed the way. The film was adapted from a best-selling book by Peter Maas, in which the author had assembled the confessions of the first informer in Mafia history. Joe Valachi, who was serving a twenty-year sentence for drug trafficking, had killed another prisoner in 1962, after mistaking him for a hired assassin. Two years later, to save his own neck, he decided to cooperate with the justice system. He offered up reams of freewheeling testimony about the Mafia's structure and top brass. Some insisted that Valachi himself was small change and that his revelations were dubious stuff. But in any case, the gangster agreed to have Maas collaborate on his memoirs before he was transferred to a prison in El Paso, where he died in 1971.

Thrilled by the book, Dino immediately acquired the rights and put together a production. First he enlisted Charles Bronson, with a contract for three films at the then-astronomical rate of a million dollars a pop, plus a percentage of the box office and other profits. This new star of the tough guy school was then turned over to the English director Terence Young.

Dino planned to shoot most of the project in New York, but all it took was the mere mention of the hated Valachi's name to provoke threatening reactions from the local lowlifes. Bronson, familiar with the milieu, got the message immediately. He told the producer, "These people are out to sink the entire ship." The signals were unmistakable and the demands were nonnegotiable: change the title, remove the names of the bosses, and omit any reference to the Cosa Nostra or the Mafia.

For a little while, the work continued, with the shooting schedule circulated in sealed envelopes to deflect attacks, but ultimately it seemed wisest to transfer the entire production to Rome. The film was completed there. Still, when an advance screening was arranged in New York, the trouble started again: an anonymous caller claimed to have hidden a bomb on the premises, and the theater was evacuated.

Many would have found this slice of American life more than sufficient. But in the course of production, a paradoxical fact emerged: Dino was in love with New York, with the American system, and above all with the freedom it gave him to practice his trade. Returning to his homeland, he realized that he *liked* the risky business of shooting *The Valachi Papers*. Now he missed America. He longed for that atmosphere he had first learned to love as a young man watching the mythical films of the 1930s, an atmosphere he had taken for granted during his trips abroad.

Whoever said that life begins again at forty calculated on the low side: life can begin again at fifty too. Dino was ready to make a big leap and become an immigrant, albeit one with all the creature comforts. He would start over at square one, taking his challenge to the heart of the American empire.

One morning after Silvana had spent the night at Villa Catena, he presented himself in her room and announced that he was leaving for New York. Still half asleep, his wife asked him, "When will you be back?" His answer was clear and without equivocation: "I'm not coming back. I'm going to New York for good. I want to work there." A long pause ensued. Then Silvana, in keeping with her baffling temperament, came out with a reply that unexpectedly renewed their pact of matrimonial solidarity: "I'm coming with you. We're all coming with you."

CHAPTER 23

THE AMERICAN CHALLENGE

AMERICA'S RESPONSE TO DINO CAN BE GLIMPSED IN A *NEW YORK TIMES* article from July 25, 1973, describing Dino's visit to the enormous atrium of the Chamber of Commerce Building, where he was shooting a scene for *Serpico*. The producer popped out of a chocolate-colored Rolls-Royce, clad in a dazzling yellow suit, an open-collared shirt, and sunglasses. He greeted people dramatically, shook hands enthusiastically, embraced his colleagues left and right, and smiled at everybody. He proclaimed himself in love with the United States in general, which he called a fantastic country, and with New York City in particular.

He spoke nonstop, starting off in English and dissolving back into Italian: "Here I feel the same way I did when I started working in the cinema as an eighteen-year-old." Asked about his future plans, Dino declared that along with making films in New York, he would continue to ply his trade all over the world. That included Italy, naturally. At the moment, the producer added, he intended to shoot two films in his old Vasca Navale facility: Ingmar Bergman's *The Merry Widow*, which would star Barbra Streisand, and Fellini's *Casanova*.

Neither of these productions ever got off the ground, because in the cinema, as Dino had long since learned, you do what is possible, not what is desirable. Still, even if he had already known that these projects would come to nothing, he would have dismissed such setbacks with a shrug. For De Laurentiis truly felt himself at the beginning of a new chapter, and he was ready for anything. The article in the *Times* even suggested optimism about his family life. After all, Silvana was just then arriving in New York, along with Federico and Francesca. It was too bad that Veronica and Raffaella, both married by now, remained in Europe, but who knew what the future held? Perhaps Dino actually deluded himself into believing that everything could be the way it used to be, back when they lived on Via Appia.

Meanwhile, the day after the article appeared, an official letter from Mayor John Lindsay was delivered to Dino's new office on the fifteenth floor of the Gulf + Western Building. The mayor passed along his best wishes. He also declared himself happy and proud that the world's most famous independent filmmaker had chosen the Big Apple for his base of operations.

> I decided to move to the United States when I finished work on *The Valachi Papers*. I had filmed the interiors in Rome and the exteriors in America, and after that, I decided to give it a shot. At the time I was considered the number one producer in Europe, but I've always been aware of my limitations. "All I want to do is give it a try," I told myself. "If I fail, I'll come back to Italy."
>
> I parked myself in a beautiful apartment on the thirtieth floor of a skyscraper at 200 Central Park South, which I had bought back when I first started doing lots of international business. Owning the apartment meant that I could avoid staying in a hotel when I came to New York. Now that we needed to enlarge it, I simply bought an adjacent apartment.
>
> It seemed as if I had returned to my beginnings—as if I were back in the era when I founded Real Cine, but in New York rather than Turin. Surrounded by so many points of view, operating in a country with a different language and culture, I felt extremely uncertain. I had no way of knowing what sorts of cinematic narrative would work in the American market. I decided to start out with one film and see how things went, fully prepared either to stay in the United States or go back to Rome.
>
> I began calling a few friends: I knew plenty of people who had worked with me during the *War and Peace* era. And then I spoke to Peter Maas, the author of *The Valachi Papers*. We were friends; he had been my guest at Villa Catena. I said to him, "I've moved here; I want to make films in America. Are you writing something new that I can buy?"
>
> "I'm working on a book," he told me, "but I just started it."
>
> "What's it called?"
>
> "*Serpico*," he said, and explained the book to me.

Frank Serpico, the real-life protagonist, was a former detective in the New York City Police Department. This thirty-five-year-old son of a Neapolitan cobbler had been an unusual police officer: he lived in a Greenwich Village loft, wore hippie-style clothing, and loved lyric opera, slow-moving books, and fast-moving love affairs. Between 1967 and 1970, Serpico gathered unequivocal proof of corruption in his department. He then became the key witness for the Knapp Commission, which investigated New York's finest for almost two years. The commission concluded that fully half the members of the police force were guilty of corruption, ranging from such venial sins as overlooking fines to protecting drug dealers.

Maas contacted Serpico in 1971, after the ex-detective had miraculously survived an assassination attempt, and he agreed to collaborate. The author planned to complete his book for publication in 1973. When Dino telephoned him, however, he had just begun to write it.

> "Can I read it?" I asked.
>
> "All I have are the first few pages," he said, "just a sketch of the main character."
>
> I pressed on: "Let me read it just the same." He was reluctant, I insisted, and in the end he handed over twenty typewritten pages.
>
> I read them and dialed his number: "Congratulations! You've created an extraordinary character. I don't need to wait for you to finish the book. I'd like to buy the rights immediately."
>
> He responded, "You're crazy. I'm going to ask for $500,000 for the completed book, and if I take my time with the offers, I might get even more than that."
>
> "Fine, Peter. Let's not discuss it. I'll buy the book in its present form for $450,000." Given these conditions, he accepted.
>
> Here's an example of those famous intuitions, apparently devoid of logic, that I insist a producer must have. Why else would somebody pay almost half a million dollars for a book based solely on the first twenty pages? I've always trusted my intuitions. In this particular case I told myself (and I believe it to this day) that the key to every film is the character. If I discovered that Mass's story didn't work when he was finished, I could have him do a rewrite. I could ask him to change the narrative completely. But in the meantime, I had an extraordinary character, which is to say, I had everything I needed.

In an October 1974 article in *New York* magazine, the journalist Marie Brenner asked Maas whether Dino liked the book once it was finished. The writer responded, "I asked him if he'd read it once it was in galleys, and Dino said, 'You know, Peter, I start the book last night after supper—ask Silvana—and I stay up all night in bed reading the book. Finally as the sun is coming up, I finish, and I walk over to the window, and I look down at the park and I say, 'Bravo, Dino, bravo.'"

"The minute I announced that I had acquired *Serpico*," Dino recalls, "Paramount was all over me. My friend Charlie Bludhorn, the president of Gulf + Western, promised me, 'We're going to make this one.'" An Austrian emigrant and the veteran of numerous commercial enterprises, Bludhorn resuscitated Paramount from its moribund state in the mid-1960s. Since he and Dino both lived on Central Park South and worked in the Gulf + Western Building, they got into the habit of walking to the office together.

> We developed a little ritual: we met at my place for breakfast. It was a way of exchanging ideas and potential projects in private, before we were both sucked into the quotidian whirlwind at work. I knew that Charles really liked what he called a "spaghetti breakfast"—that is, spaghetti tossed in the skillet—and I always made sure there was some on hand. I personally cooked the pasta the night before, so it would be ready the next morning. In reality the spaghetti breakfast was invented by Neapolitan paupers, as a way of recycling leftovers.

In his anthology *Messages of Love*, the editor Dino Fabbri commented on the close understanding between Dino and Bludhorn: "The quality of Dino that has always impressed me so much is that instead of being a ladykiller, he is a 'mankiller'! I say this because I have been witness to Dino seducing men—even men very difficult to seduce, like the famous owner of Gulf + Western/Paramount, the late, great Charles Bludhorn. When Dino came to New York to set up his new film company during the 1970s, he started to invite Charlie over on a regular basis. . . . Before you know it, Dino was convincing Charlie on everything he decided Charlie had to do. This was no easy task, mind you, as Charlie was one of the most difficult men I've ever met. Charlie owned Paramount, but the motor behind Paramount was Dino."

"Who do you want for *Serpico*?" Charlie asked me.

"I don't want to make it with a star," I replied. By then my conversations with Maas had given me a better idea of the hero's personality, and I had also met Serpico himself. "I want an actor who physically resembles Serpico, even if that means we have to find somebody in the theater."

I made a tour of theaters and got lucky. I found Al Pacino. He had the right face, the same Italian background: they could have been brothers. And although I don't remember the play, it was clear from seeing him in the theater that we had discovered a force, a physical presence! I immediately invited him over for dinner. My house hadn't been furnished yet, and I remember that he sat on the floor to eat.

It's hard to imagine the conversations that transpired between these *paesani*: Al didn't know the language of his Sicilian ancestors, while Dino spoke a Neapolitan immigrant's English. In addition, this duet soon came to include a third voice, that of Serpico himself. The former police officer and the actor hit it off immediately and spent time together at Pacino's summer rental on Long Island. As for Dino, some witnesses insist that they heard him chat with Serpico in pure Neapolitan.

Meanwhile, Marty Bregman appeared on the scene. He was the head of Artists Entertainment Complex, the agency that represented Pacino. Dino was obliged to work with him, even though the introduction of yet another rooster into the henhouse would produce endless problems.

The first director I thought of for *Serpico* was Sidney Lumet. He was a dyed-in-the-wool New Yorker and filmmaking phenomenon, despite the fact that he had suffered a string of recent flops. But even though I had shelled out half a million dollars for the rights, I knew that Frank Yablans, the president of Paramount, would have problems with Lumet. My relationship with Yablans, incidentally, was excellent.

In walked Sam Cohn, a superagent at ICM. He represented not only Maas but Bregman, with whom I was pledged to make the film. And Bregman was pushing for John Avildsen, who was just then riding very high on the critical success of *Joe*. Since I'm open to alternative solutions and always willing to be the matchmaker, I got Avildsen and Pacino together.

The outcome was a complete disaster: they didn't get along at all. To add insult to injury, Avildsen read the script, which was being written by two top screenwriters, Norman Wexler and Waldo Salt, and found it laughable. We're talking about a classic case of what the Americans call "creative differences." Avildsen brought the situation to a head when he slapped an arrogant ultimatum on the table: "Either Pacino goes or I do."

This is precisely the kind of tune I hate to hear, and my answer was equally definitive. "Avildsen," I told him, "take a walk. You're fired." With him off the project, Lumet returned to the top of my list to direct *Serpico*.

Still, the problems weren't over yet. Yablans didn't want to work with Lumet and was prepared to annul the contract for the co-production and American distribution of *Serpico*. He tried the same line on me as Avildsen had: "Either Lumet goes or I do." Which was another way of saying, "Either Lumet goes or Paramount does."

At this point Bludhorn intervened directly. It would be fair to say that "the rest is history." Charles ordered Yablans to greenlight the project, with Pacino as the star and Lumet as the director, and *Serpico* was a huge success. Is there a moral to this story? I believe there is. It's my old conviction that creative freedom *must* be accorded to the producer, who's the only one with both an artistic and financial vision of the film.

There's a second moral, supplied by Sidney Lumet: "Dino was completely honorable about the way things occurred. Usually when a producer wants to replace the director, he goes to the new director first and asks him to read the script. Once he signs on, the producer fires the other guy. But this was all done on the up and up."

A slightly different version of events, evidently inspired by Dino's nemesis Marty Bregman, appears in Andrew Yule's biography of Pacino, *Life on the Wire*. In this account, Bregman insists that *he* first conceived the film as a vehicle for Pacino. He admits that he alone couldn't have nudged it over the hurdles at Paramount and that it was Dino—who was then "financially on his ass"—who wangled such a "terrific deal" for the project. Bregman also gives De Laurentiis credit for showing Avildsen the door and confirms the general satisfaction with Lumet: the director was such an old New York hand that he finished the shoot (much of it done on location) in a mere fifty-one days.

Serpico was both a critical and a popular hit. It also represented the unmistakable arrival of Al Pacino, whose image appeared on a giant Paramount billboard in Times Square. De Laurentiis couldn't have been luckier in his first outing as an American producer.

> The fact that this experience was so positive made me decide to stay in America. For various reasons it cost me an enormous effort to work here—much more than in Italy. Still, the satisfaction of seeing a film open worldwide and earn millions of dollars just wasn't possible in Italy, where the films live and die in the domestic market. In addition, a producer can operate with so much more freedom in America. For *Serpico*, an antipolice movie, the New York City Police Department gave me complete cooperation. And for *Crazy Joe*, I was actually allowed to shoot inside a prison!

In every interview from this period—and there were plenty, since Dino's move to the United States had aroused much curiosity—the producer expressed his enthusiasm. Speaking with James Brady of *New York* magazine, he reiterated, "Of course, there's a certain amount of bureaucratic nonsense to deal with here, but it's nothing in comparison with Rome. Here you can do what you like. You choose a script, sign up a star, and begin filming. . . . Obviously there are problems to deal with: Watergate, inflation. But these types of problems exist in every country. Only in America, people can have an open discussion about a mess like Watergate."

Dino spoke proudly about the fact that eighteen-year-old Federico was already working alongside him as vice president of the television division. He also marveled about the short trips he had been taking with his family on the weekends. "I'm just discovering how beautiful America is. I came here for the first time twenty-five years ago, but all I knew was Los Angeles and New York. Now I'm getting to know Vermont, New Hampshire, Connecticut, and it's all beautiful."

In her *New York* article from October 1974, Marie Brenner noted that the closure of Dinocittà had left the entrepreneur in debt to the tune of several million dollars. She then calculated that in his first eighteen months of residence in the United States, Dino's films had taken in the astronomical sum of $85 million at the box office. Clearly his American earnings allowed him to plug that notorious hole in the fiscal dike, even as they revealed his capacity to go from "gold dust to ashes and back again." He told Brenner, "Building Dinocittà was the only mistake I've made in my life. If I had built it in New York, it would have been fantastic: Rome is no longer the right city for these things. But that's where I built it."

Serpico was followed by more successes. The first was *Death Wish* with Charles Bronson, which came out in July 1974, followed by *Mandingo* in March 1975. Like their predecessor, both films involved their share of risky ideological implications. *Death Wish* prompted much internal discussion about its main character, an ordinary man who decides to exact his own brand of justice from a gang of marauding thugs.

Bronson's agent counseled him against appearing in such a "fascist film." But after a serious discussion with the producer, the actor—who had just made *The Stone Killer* with Dino—signed on. All he requested were a few modifications to the script. For example, he suggested that the protagonist should be an intellectual rather than an ordinary working man: this change would give an extra dimension to his single-handed clash with the underworld.

As usual, Dino paid little attention to the controversies. When *Death Wish* was released, he even joked about the whole debate in an interview: "The Italian title could be *Two Can Play at That Game*. Certainly *Death Wish* represents the very opposite of the evangelical mandate to turn the other cheek."

> My attitude has always been to ignore the ideological overtones. When I read Brian Garfield's novel *Death Wish* and decided to obtain the rights, I was told that United Artists had already bought the project and shelved it. For them it was too "politically incorrect," and the same thing would be true today. They ceded the book to me, but it was perfectly clear that no other studio would make such a film. Except, that is, for Paramount, where Bludhorn took it at once.
>
> We had some problems with the title. The fact that it included the word *death* made me a little uneasy, a little perplexed. Then I realized it might bring in an additional audience—the horror flick fans—so I left it the way it was.

Now, what was my intuition concerning this film? I thought: "When the protagonist begins killing the thugs after they've murdered his wife and raped his daughter, the audience will applaud." That's what I was betting on. I didn't ask myself whether it was a fascist film or any crap like that. I understood that it was a story the public could identify with. I knew that many of them would be saying, "In that situation, I would have done the same thing."

July 24, 1974, was a rainy day in New York: the climate seemed attuned to the depressing atmosphere of Nixon's impeachment. In a meeting with Dino and Frank Yablans, the director Michael Winner urged the producers to keep their expectations low for the opening day of *Death Wish*. But when the trio decided to drop by the theater where the film was being screened, they heard wild applause issuing from within. Over the weekend *Death Wish* broke every box office record, and Bronson's popularity went through the roof.

Here was one more demonstration of Dino's gift for divining the wishes of his audience. For him the experience confirmed the truth of Adolph Zucker's famous axiom: "The public is never wrong." A gifted producer has no need for a crystal ball (let alone a marketing survey): he relies upon his ability to discern what the people want at any given moment. Dino's intuition was somewhat understandable while he was living in Italy, a country he knew thoroughly. But even after he moved to the United States, his nose for popular success seldom failed him.

Italy or the United States, it's the same thing! Let's take *Serpico*, for example. What was it about? A reality that no American producer would have had the courage to portray on the screen: *Serpico* was a denunciation of what we Italians call *tangentopoli*, official corruption. When I said that I wanted to make a film from Maas's book, everybody protested. "Come on, Dino," they said, "enough cop movies, they've already made too many of them." But when Bludhorn understood what we were dealing with, he said okay.

The same thing happened with *Three Days of the Condor*, which was released immediately afterward. At the time it seemed like pure political fantasy, and now it turns out to have anticipated a great many hidden truths. Besides, hadn't I already made the first film about a Mafia turncoat in *The Valachi Papers*? As I see it, I continued to work in the United States just as I had in Italy, using the same principles I always did.

Returning to *Death Wish*, well, I was unprepared for such a big success: who would have expected it? And to think that I recently saw it referred to as one of my flops in a magazine! It was in fact an enormous hit. Just like *Mandingo*, which was a critical disaster but a huge success at the box office. And not only in America: throughout the world.

Adapted from a novel by Kyle Onstoff (which itself sold 15 million copies) and directed by the reliable Richard Fleischer, *Mandingo* was an interracial psychodrama set on a Louisiana plantation in 1840. The master of this particular manor happens to have a weakness for adultery. His outraged wife avenges her husband's betrayals by taking a black slave as her lover; she then allows their offspring to be killed. Dino faced the ideological pitfalls of the project with his usual brusque indifference. And when such high-profile personalities as Sidney Poitier, Harry Belafonte, and Muhammad Ali declined any role in the film, he refused to be disheartened. Instead he hired an unknown to play the protagonist: the fighter Ken Norton.

The incendiary racial politics of the film prompted several incidents during the shoot in Mississippi. Dino downplayed them with a wisecrack: "All it means is that we won't be showing the film in Harlem." When *Mandingo* finally hit the screen in May 1975, the critics slaughtered it. But none other than Andy Warhol sang its praises, and the public was enthusiastic.

It was such a big success that many people asked me to make a sequel. In general I'm opposed to number two, number three, and so forth. That's why I turned down the idea of continuing *Death Wish* and sold the rights to somebody else. I did the same thing with *Serpico*, when suddenly everybody wanted to make it into a TV movie or an entire miniseries. But with *Mandingo*, for some reason, I ended up making a sequel—a mistake I repeated much later with *King Kong Lives*.

The second installment of *Mandingo* was called *Drum*, and it's one more proof of my theory that if something goes wrong with a movie, it's the producer's fault. I screwed up everything on *Drum*: I signed up one director and fired him a week later, since I wanted to try out a young guy, Steve Carver. I always have a tendency to seek

> out new talent. But new talents are like watermelons: you never know if they're red until you open them up. Sometimes you win, sometimes not. With *Drum* I didn't win, and it was a mess.

At the last minute, in fact, Dino withdrew his name from the title credits on *Drum*. Although he had produced an enormous number of films, including his share of failures, he always made an effort to shield his good name. "The signature of Dino De Laurentiis," he insists, "is a guarantee for the consumer. If I squander it on second-rate projects, I'm in trouble. In this business, of course, some pratfalls are inevitable, and I don't duck my responsibility for them. But when it's appropriate, and possible, I also don't mind putting some distance between them and myself."

CHAPTER 24

FROM COAST TO COAST

DINO'S NEXT HIT, *THREE DAYS OF THE CONDOR*, BOASTED AN UNCOMPLICATED, irresistible plot. In an office that's actually a front for an intelligence operation, all the employees are murdered—except for one man. The survivor is forced to unmask a sinister conspiracy aimed at the high-ranking members of his own organization before the conspirators kill him. Robert Redford was the protagonist, Faye Dunaway the woman who helped him, and Max von Sydow the inexorable, ice-cold assassin.

> It was Stanley Schneider who alerted me to James Grady's novel *Six Days of the Condor*. (We cut it to three days for the movie.) Stanley was the son of Abe Schneider, the chairman of Columbia Pictures, and he wanted to break free of his father's orbit and produce something on his own. The novel had me hooked from the first few pages.
>
> Now, the book was fairly different from the film we ended up making. Still, there was a real winner of an idea in there. I passed Grady's novel on to my development office, where everybody voted against it, for all sorts of reasons. I wanted to move forward with it, though, and to write the screenplay I called in Lorenzo Semple, who's remained a great friend of mine.

Working with Dino, Semple learned to appreciate the absolute independence of his judgments: "In the course of our collaboration, I was never forced to sit through meetings with studio bigwigs or read their irritating memos. Dino shows the screenplay to his colleagues, of course, and listens to their suggestions. But these he filters through his own sensibility, implementing only the ones he finds persuasive. The screenwriter is always best off with just a single sounding board. What's more, I've never heard Dino whine about having followed the wrong advice: he doesn't have the bad habit of blaming his failures on other people."

During his work on *Condor*, Semple also discovered that the producer, still unsure about his English, was having everything translated into Italian. Much of the time, the translations themselves were fairly crude. Larry Gleason, who later became the head of distribution for DEG, the De Laurentiis Entertainment Group, observes that this reliance on translators may have kept Dino from ever improving his sometimes adversarial relationship with the English language.

"In the 1980s, when Dino was living in New York, he had a house in the Hamptons. He sent [screenwriter] Bob Towne there as his guest to revise a script. 'When you get there,' Dino said, 'my translator will also be staying, but don't worry, he'll be leaving the next day.'

"In the morning, Bob Towne came into the kitchen with his Great Dane and saw the translator at the table having coffee. The translator says, 'Oh, what a beautiful cat you have.' Maybe that explains why some of the American idiom was lost on Dino."

When Semple expressed a similar concern about the nuance of the *Condor* screenplay getting lost in translation, De Laurentiis was quick to reassure him: "I'm not interested in the literary value of the translations. In fact, I'm always worried that beautiful language will end up confusing me. All I want to know is that the story is moving forward—and how it's moving forward."

Lorenzo knocked out a first draft for me, and meanwhile I signed a contract with Peter Yates to direct. I also set up a deal with Paramount, since they really liked the script. As I recall, the contract with Yates was for $200,000 (which corresponds to about $2 million in today's money). For the protagonist, I was thinking of Warren Beatty, whom I knew quite well. I had been the one who sent Warren to Russia when I was considering a film about John Reed, the American journalist who participated in the October Revolution. The idea was that Bondarchuk would direct it. Beatty then withdrew because he didn't get along with Bondarchuk, and

I shelved the project. Still, Warren remained so enamored of the idea that he eventually made *Reds*, which won him three Oscars in 1981.

Anyway, I had Beatty read the script for *Condor*, and he said to me, "Maybe I can do it. Just give me a little time to think it over." It went on this way for three weeks, with me in New York and him in Los Angeles. Finally I flew to Hollywood. Once we were face to face in my bungalow at the Beverly Hills Hotel, eating supper, I said to him, "Warren, you have to make up your mind. If you step out the door this evening without making a decision, I'll look for a new actor tomorrow."

When it came time for him to leave—I remember this as though it were yesterday—Warren sat down on the ground at the entrance to my bungalow. He said, "Dino, you have to have a little more patience."

"No," I told him. "With all your hesitations, you're worse than Gillo Pontecorvo. This business is busting my balls."

The next day I called Freddie Fields. He subsequently became a producer, but back then he was head of one of the biggest talent agencies. I told him: "Freddie, I have a script for Bob Redford." I had already considered Redford, because when you put together a cast you always keep in mind a second or third choice for the big roles. In this case Redford was my second choice. I gave Freddie the script and I told him, "I have to go back to New York tomorrow. Could you please try to get me an answer within two days?"

The next day he called me and said that he liked the script: "I'm sending it to Redford immediately. I swear I'll get you an answer in two days at the most. All I ask is that you wait until then." Forty-eight hours later Freddie called. "Dino," he said, "Bob's in love with the script and wants to do it. He has only one condition: he wants Sidney Pollack to direct."

I told him, "We have two problems here. First, I already signed a contract with Peter Yates. And second, I don't know if Pollack wants to make this film." Freddie replied that the second problem was already taken care of: Redford had sent Pollack the script, and the director said to count him in. "It's a deal," I said. "Anyway, Pollack is better than Yates."

Dino still had a sizable problem to contend with: easing Yates off the production. He summoned the director and bluntly explained how things stood. Experience had taught him that in this sort of situation, there were two things you must do: speak frankly and honor your commitments.

> I said to Yates, "We're friends, and I'm talking to you frankly. We have a contract for *Condor*, which is supposed to pay you $200,000 for a year's work. I've found a star, Bob Redford, who for his own reasons prefers Pollack, and I'm sure you'll understand that I can't say no to a package like that one. So, listen to what I'm going to propose. I'll give you a check for $200,000, which fulfills our contract one hundred percent. That way, although you're cut loose from the film, you earn in twenty-four hours what you would have earned in a year."
>
> Yates embraced me, declaring that I was a gentleman and that he'd never before received such a generous offer. Then he wished me good luck and made his exit. If we had begun by negotiating, I would have offered him a quarter of the original sum, or half. Then the agents would have jumped into the fray, all hell would have broken loose, and I would have wasted a chunk of time. So I paid off the entire sum. Then I did the project with Redford and Pollack.
>
> For the female protagonist they wanted Faye Dunaway. Fine: all I needed to do was tweak the budget and slip in the extra $50,000 for her salary. Then everything went smoothly during the shoot in New York, and they made a magnificent film.

Pollack's recollections confirm just how serene the atmosphere was on the set: "It was more or less the first time I had made a film with an independent producer. I approached Dino with a certain amount of caution: he was financing the project by selling the rights in various overseas territories, and I was worried that this would lead to problems. But instead of finding myself attached to a risky enterprise, I became part of a family. I spent many hours eating spaghetti and drinking good red wine at Dino's house in California (or should I say his headquarters?) up on Schuyler Drive and then in his New York apartment. Dino wasn't merely our producer but a friend. Plus, his instincts about casting and his thoughts on the script always turned out to be solid and useful."

As did his thoughts on the finished film itself. "After looking at the first two days' dailies, Dino said, 'Is very good Syd-a-ney.' He would hold his fingers together, then put them to his nose. 'You can smell this. You can smell a good thing.' I thought, 'This guy's pulling my leg.' But he knew. He's got the eye. I kept waiting for there to be a problem. He once said to me, 'Sid-a-ney, I think you need to reshoot something, it's not good enough.' I said, 'Let me cut it first,' and I did. Then when he saw it cut, he said, 'You're right, you're right.' We never disagreed. I think it's because Dino knows that art is mostly accidental. You work at craft and occasionally you get lucky and art happens."

Dino's cockiness too appealed to Pollack.

"Before the premiere, Dino called and said, 'Sid-a-ney, you meet me Friday night. We go to look at the lines in the theater together.'

"I said, 'How do you know there'll be lines?'

"'I tell you, there be lines,' he said.

"So we had dinner in some restaurant and afterwards we went for a walk by the theater and sure enough, there were enormous lines. And he was never surprised."

Pollack's surprise at being enfolded into a family instead of ensnared in a risky, competitive enterprise is another demonstration of Dino's skill at shielding his writers, directors, and actors from anything that might interfere with their work. Dealing with problems and anxieties was the producer's job.

> To tell you the truth, we did have a real problem before the shoot even began. Not a creative problem, but a financial one: while we were waiting for the cash from foreign-rights sales, we needed a line of credit to cover that portion of the production costs.
>
> Let me explain. Generally speaking, the funds for a film come from two primary sources: the American distribution (which is financed by a big studio such as MGM or Universal) and the foreign distribution (meaning the advance sale of the rights to various territories overseas). I always sold the foreign rights myself. Now, in recent years, with the evolution of newer media, there are quite a few additional rights you can sell up front: TV, videocassette, cable, and so forth. But during the mid-1970s, when we were making *Condor*, those things didn't yet exist. Back then, even the sale of foreign rights was in its infancy.
>
> My problem, then, was to find a financial institution that would extend me a line of credit. It wasn't an easy task, because the intrinsic risks of the film industry terrified all the major American banks, and they were very reluctant to go out on a limb. My financial consultant of the time, a really sharp guy named Blake Lowe,

> suggested that I contact a bank that was still (cinematically speaking) a virgin: the Slavenburg Bank in Amsterdam.
>
> At Slavenburg I got in touch with Frans Afman, a banker of great intelligence and broad vision, who was destined to become a key figure in the evolving relationship between the cinema and international banking. He knew nothing about the financial mechanisms governing the sale of movie rights. But Frans was more than willing to hear me out. And as for *Condor* itself, he understood that with a great director at the helm and two superstars on the screen, the likelihood of taking a bath in the foreign markets was more or less zero. So Slavenburg promptly extended me the line of credit for the foreign contracts. This was their first move (and certainly not their last!) into the film sector. And from then on, both the American and European banks made themselves available for similar transactions. In this sense, Afman and I were pioneers.

When *Three Days of the Condor* came out in September 1975, it was recognized as an instant classic, consolidating Dino's image in the United States. True, he already enjoyed a certain fame as a European producer when he arrived in the New World. Success in America, however, was not guaranteed, but after hitting the trifecta with *Serpico*, *Death Wish*, and *Condor*, De Laurentiis won a new level of respect, and his habit of keeping so many irons in the fire aroused more curiosity than ever.

His private life too seemed to be improving. Assisted by her excellent command of English—quite literally her mother tongue, after all—Silvana soon made herself at home. She liked New York, the apartment was large and comfortable, and from the semicircular window in her corner room, she had an astonishing view of Central Park. Federico and Francesca still lived with their parents, and at regular intervals Veronica flew in from Rome with her children: Giada, Dino, and little Eloisa. Raffaella, living in Monte Carlo with her husband, also popped in for the occasional visit. To keep the household running smoothly, Dino brought Concetta the cook from Italy, as well as her husband, Vincenzo, who functioned as a barber and right-hand man.

Neither nostalgia nor homesickness was a problem for Dino. He explained in an interview several years later: "Nostalgia, I realized, is the fate of those emigrants who can't afford a return ticket. But if an emigrant has the option of going home—even for a weekend—and embracing his family members, then nostalgia is nonexistent. Plus there's the fact that I begin work at five in the morning and finish at eight in the evening: I don't even have *time* for nostalgia."

Silvana was probably more nostalgic than her hyperactive husband. During the initial period in New York, however, she spent many happy hours furnishing their house, visiting antique dealers, going to the movies, and taking long bicycle rides in the park with her daughter. A certain number of people on the street recognized her, paying her compliments or requesting an autograph. Even so, it was clear that to most Americans, Silvana was famous for being the wife of Dino De Laurentiis. And unlike his former partner Carlo Ponti, who had prodded Sophia Loren into an American career, Dino made no effort to enlist Silvana in his current productions. Delighted at seeing his wife in such an unusual state of relaxation, he was happy to give her a breather. Why create additional problems just when things seemed to be going so well?

But the cards were about to be reshuffled once again. It was becoming increasingly clear to Dino that in order to stay in close contact with the film world, he would have to move to Los Angeles. Without a doubt, this change of scene would entail a certain risk. There was a real danger that in Los Angeles, a much more elusive and unfocused city than New York, Silvana might be stricken once more with what Dino had come to think of as the Villa Catena syndrome. To avert such a depressive slide, De Laurentiis insisted that she join him in choosing a West Coast house. Price was no object, he declared, as long as she was happy.

CHAPTER 25

ON THE ROAD WITH KING KONG

"AT THE PRECISE MIDPOINT OF SUNSET BOULEVARD, DINO HAS BOUGHT A villa with eleven acres of land. Gazelles roam freely and happily across the fields, while an additional two acres are covered with orchids." Describing the new De Laurentiis residence in the September 1975 issue of *Il Giornale*, the journalist (and family friend) Carlo Mazzarella was hardly able restrain his enthusiasm: "The marvels of the villa are innumerable. The garage has room for thirty-five cars, a mechanic on call, and a gas pump hooked up to a 12,000-gallon reservoir. The boudoir includes a collection of sixteenth-century Venetian fans; the wine cellar, stocked with the most famous vintages, is on a par with that of the Hôtel de Paris in Monte Carlo. There are four bungalows for the servants: two gardeners, two drivers, plus four Filipino maids that Dino imported from Italy. . . . From their nearby villas in Beverly Hills, actors and directors can only gape in amazement, noting that it took an Italian producer to restore the splendors of the Twenties to Hollywood."

Our relocation to Los Angeles was a long and elaborate process. Quite early on we found a splendid villa in Bel Air. After agreeing to buy it and putting down the deposit, we decided to delay our move by a couple of weeks in order to do some structural renovations.

When we showed up, however, we had an unpleasant surprise waiting for us—a surprise by the name of Warren Beatty. He had quietly taken possession of the property to shoot the interiors for his film *Shampoo*. This irritated me beyond measure, for two very specific reasons. First: I've always refused to allow anybody to shoot a

> film in my house, and that includes me too. And second: Mr. Beatty hadn't even bothered to alert me, let alone obtain the necessary permission. This incident, if we can call it that, was more than sufficient reason for me to cancel the contract and get my deposit back.

And so the search began again. Dino and Silvana soon fell in love with a property on Doheny Hill, located at the very summit of Sunset Boulevard. "The Knoll," as it was called, had once belonged to one of the city's original founders, the oil baron Edward L. Doheny.

> The property had been on the market for some time, but nobody would buy it, perhaps due to the insane price the owner was asking. Cutting right to the chase, I offered him $2 million in cash, take it or leave it. It was a classic shot in the dark, but in this case it paid off—in every sense. The owner accepted the offer, because on a strictly financial basis it was a good deal for him: he got a giant tax break for selling the place so far below the market price. And many years later, it was my turn to get a good deal: I resold the villa for $15 million.

This change of scene marked a distinct shift in Dino's professional priorities. Thanks to his early successes in America, he'd been classified as a producer of socially conscious, thematically risky films, in keeping with his neorealist origins. What he wanted to do now, however, was both more traditional and potentially more lucrative: the production of family-oriented spectaculars. It was, he insisted, a matter of "anticipating the public's changing tastes and needs." More than ever, this was the moment to "think big." No wonder he had to move his base of operations to Los Angeles, where the studios were lavish enough to match his new ambitions.

His first effort along these lines was *King Kong*. As usual, there are plenty of people eager to take credit for the idea of remaking the 1933 classic. Dino insists that the inspiration came to him one day while he was studying an old movie poster in Francesca's room. There was the giant ape perched atop the summit of the Empire State Building, surrounded by a swirl of airplanes. Suddenly it occurred to him that this mythical image had endured for nearly half a century. Wasn't it time to create a *new* King Kong, one who would scale the Twin Towers of the World Trade Center? The idea dovetailed neatly with the recent success of *Jaws*. In the wake of Spielberg's film, in fact, Dino had already begun talking with Paramount about the possibility of making a monster movie.

Then history repeated itself. Just as De Laurentiis and Mike Todd had once locked horns over *War and Peace*, the producer now found himself battling with yet another charismatic, powerful rival. This time it was Lew Wasserman, the chairman of MCA Universal, who had his own designs on the project. However, Dino had launched something of a preemptive strike. Learning that the author of the original 1933 screenplay intended to assert his (possibly dubious) rights to the story, he solved this dilemma by following his self-imposed rule: pay the money. Experience had taught him that if there were even the slightest risk of a suit for copyright infringement—or, say, a shred of doubt about whether a text was in the public domain—it made the most sense to pay up front. Squandering a relatively small amount of cash at the beginning was much preferable to facing delays or injunctions later on.

Put on the defensive by Dino's move, Universal still seemed unwilling to renounce its right to remake *King Kong*. The dispute dragged on and on, generating ever-larger legal fees. Finally Sidney Korshak stepped in as mediator.

In Dennis McDougal's biography of Wasserman, *The Last Mogul*, Korshak emerges as an elusive oddball who just barely escaped the long arm of Senator Estes Kefauver's anticrime commission. As a lawyer, he was barred from practicing in California. Yet his many connections in show business, politics, and the underworld made him a figure to reckon with. After his brush with Kefauver, he had helped Bludhorn get Paramount back up to speed, then sponsored Robert Evans as head of production. And thanks to Korshak's finagling, the *King Kong* controversy was indeed resolved—not in the kitchen of the lawyer's house, as reported in McDougal's book, but at a supper in Bludhorn's office, attended by Wasserman, De Laurentiis, and Sidney Sheinberg, one of the directors of MCA. During this conclave, Wasserman promised not to produce *The Legend of King Kong*. In return, Dino conceded a percentage of his own film's receipts to Universal.

From the very beginning, before Dino made his deal with Wasserman, the idea had been to hurry the film along in order to beat the competition. To his collaborators, the producer issued a directive that summed up the entire project: "It will be the most expensive film in history, and the one made in the least amount of time."

He phoned Lorenzo Semple in Colorado and said, "What would you say to doing a rewrite of *King Kong*?" It sounded like an enticing idea to the screenwriter. "Great, let's do it," Dino replied. Working at a breakneck pace, Lorenzo knocked out the new script, updating it, as the producer requested, with a modern ecological theme: the explorers in search of the giant gorilla became unscrupulous oil prospectors.

Mario Chiari and the puppet master Carlo Rambaldi got to work on reinventing the protagonist, whom De Laurentiis envisioned as "the most human-looking ape possible." He had them produce version after version, because he wanted the simian hero to be absolutely charming. For the contemporary family audience, this monster was not supposed to excite fear, like his predecessor of the 1930s, but instead supposed to arouse sympathy. And the girl, of course, had to fall in love with him. Was this not an adaptation of one of his favorite fables, *The Beauty and the Beast*?

Expectations for the film were sky-high. If *Jaws* made $240 million, the logic went, then *King Kong* would make at least $241 million, because the audience would include all those kids who were excluded from watching Spielberg's shark opera. As Rambaldi labored at the exhausting task of constructing the thirty-six-foot puppet, he was joined by Glen Robinson, who handled special effects. Theirs was a precarious collaboration, since neither spoke a word of the other's language. Nonetheless, the two of them, along with Frank Van der Veer, supervisor of photographic effects, would go on to win the film's only Oscar, a Special Achievement Award.

The first director Dino approached was Roman Polanski, who promptly declined: he had little interest in making a monster movie. In his place the producer hired John Guillermin, an Englishman who'd already handled the pyrotechnics of *The Towering Inferno* with considerable bravura. Guillermin was a crisp, laconic type. He did, however, experience occasional bouts of anxiety and impatience when confronted by a producer who demanded everything—at once.

For the female protagonist, Dino chose a gorgeous model named Jessica Lange and dyed her hair blond. Lange had never appeared in a movie before, and there were those who suggested that her career would begin and end in the palm of the giant gorilla. Dino, however, believed in her, and time proved him correct: she would be one of the very few actresses ever to win two Oscars. Later, when Lange appeared in another De Laurentiis film, *Crimes of the Heart,* film insiders traded unconfirmed rumors about a supposed affair between the producer and the star. But when Larry Gleason accompanied Dino to the film's premiere, he noticed that Lange was very chilly.

"Dino, Jessica's very quiet," he said.

"I don't know what's the matter," Dino replied. "I think she forget she ever knew the monkey."

In his book *The Creation of Dino De Laurentiis's King Kong*, Bruce Bahrenburg chronicled an eventful, occasionally terrifying shoot, which took place in Los Angeles and on the island of Kauai, north of Hawaii. This time, Dino was the active line producer, a role he hadn't previously assumed on his American films. His son, Federico, acted as executive producer, proving himself a valuable presence on the set. Accidents and weather problems cropped up on an almost-daily basis. The biggest delay, however, occurred when the cast and crew returned from Kauai to Los Angeles: the ape puppet's arms and legs were broken in transit. Dino kept the entire production on hold (and on salary) while the technicians tinkered with the faulty hydraulics.

Dino also did something that was then unusual for producers. He organized trips to the set for exhibitors, the businessmen who ran the theaters in which the film would show. This innovation made them aware of the project long before it was completed, but it also served another purpose, according to Larry Gleason. "The exhibitor of the film is the guy with the four walls who deals with the nickels and dimes. He sees none of the glamour. But Dino would invite them to the set while the movie was shooting in order to seduce them. I was once on a back lot with six exhibitors during *King Kong*. Dino introduced us to talent, showed us how the monkey worked, and told us the whole story. He wrapped it up in typical dramatic fashion by saying, 'When the monkey die, everybody cry!' When it came time to release another Dino De Laurentiis film, those exhibitors always gave him the same special treatment he gave them."

Not only did Dino woo the businessmen, but he worked hard at seducing the press. One would have to go back to *Gone with the Wind* to find a film that enjoyed such massive journalistic coverage while it was being made. Among the innumerable articles, perhaps the most interesting one appeared in the December 1976 issue of *New West* magazine: Mary Murphy's "The Kong Papers: Ten Days in Dino's Palm." The story opened with a promising gambit: "Dino is a mystery man, and it is my perception that his secret, like Jay Gatsby's, can only be discovered in his past." Murphy's shrewdest observations, however, pertained to the present: the article recounted a journey the reporter took with her subject, departing from Los Angeles, stopping in New York, London (twice), Monaco, Amsterdam, Paris, Milan, and Rome. Why did the producer suggest that Murphy accompany him?

> At a certain point you began to read in the American press, "The only reason that De Laurentiis can finance such expensive films himself is that he's supported by the Mafia. He launders dirty money for the Cosa Nostra." These kinds of comments were inevitable, because the Americans still knew nothing about the financial formulas that I had more or less invented (and of which I'm still proud). As I already explained, I got 50 percent of the funding for my films from the American studios, in exchange for the domestic rights. I got the other 50 percent from the advance sale of rights to overseas territories.
>
> I was perfectly aware that every Italian in America was sooner or later accused of Mafia connections. Still, I was interested in stopping this nonsense—in eradicating it completely—before it got any uglier. So when Mary Murphy requested an interview on the topic, I said, "Not only will I give you an interview, but I'll do it on a grand scale. Next week I'm traveling to several different European cities on business. Come with me, follow me on a daily basis, and I'll introduce you to the secrets of the Mafia." She was completely enthusiastic. She consulted with the magazine, got their approval, and together we took off.
>
> At the time I was still getting my financing from the Slavenburg Bank, although they had been acquired by Crédit Lyonnais. Two days before arriving in Amsterdam, I called Frans Afman and said, "Frans, I'll be there the day after tomorrow. Do me a favor. Organize a little cocktail party in my honor, with all the general directors, because I'm bringing along a journalist who thinks that I'm funded by the Mafia. If I bring her to the bank she'll figure out the joke immediately. But if I bring her to a cocktail party, the first thing she's going to think is that you're a bunch of Mafiosi, and we can have a good laugh about the whole thing."
>
> Afman found the idea very amusing and organized the party

> for me. I said to Murphy, "When we get to Amsterdam, I'll introduce you to the guys who give me the money." She was thrilled at the idea of getting such a scoop. At the party I presented her to everybody and finally revealed that they were only bankers. Still, she was so enchanted by the trip that she wrote this long article: it was widely circulated and had a huge effect on my image.

In the article Murphy didn't dwell on the cocktail party. She did, however, recount a one-on-one breakfast she had with Afman. "*We* certainly aren't the Mafia," he assured her. Then the banker explained the whole system: unlike other producers, Dino raised only half the costs of each movie from American studios. The rest he obtained from advance sales abroad, which allowed him to play to his strengths. After all, he'd spent years putting a global network in place, tapping into his knowledge of respective markets, each with its own multiplicity of players. (In the producer's own phrase, he functions as a one-man "United Nations of film distribution.") Thanks to this modus operandi, he's able to hedge his risks and assure himself a more consistent margin on his earnings.

During his conversation with Murphy, Afman stressed that in recent years Slavenburg had had only a single occasion to worry about its business with De Laurentiis. "When the budget for *King Kong* jumped from $10 million to $24 million," the banker confessed, "we were afraid he wouldn't be able to finish the film." But ultimately, of course, he did. And as usual, he did it his own way.

Dino expanded on this self-reliant style elsewhere in the article. "Conglomerates want to buy me," he noted, "and all majors want my worldwide distribution. But I do it alone. I no want partners with money, I no want someone to tell me what to do. . . . I am no 25-year-old boy like so many think when I come here. I only adopt attitude of a 25-year-old since I am in new country. I build my distribution contacts worldwide for 40 years, I no cut off now just because I have a big-a hit everybody wants to distribute." There was no Mafia involvement in his financing, nor did he cut deals with oil sheiks, as another rumor suggested. No, it was simply (or not so simply) a matter of a daredevil balancing act, one founded on the faith of the Slavenburg Bank.

Still, the subject of Dino and the Mafia wasn't quite exhausted yet. There was a prologue too, going back to *The Valachi Papers*.

When I made the film about Valachi with Paramount, I hadn't yet moved to America, although I had begun to think about it. But I decided to shoot the exteriors for the film in America and the interiors in Italy. I struck a deal with Paramount for $2 million and made the film, which came out very well. The studio was delighted, as was my friend Bludhorn.

One morning, however, Charlie left me an urgent message to call him. When I got him on the phone, he said, "Dino, I can no longer distribute *Valachi*. We got a telephone call from the Mafia, and they told us in no uncertain terms that if we release this film, they'll put a bomb underneath Paramount headquarters."

We were talking about the Gulf + Western Building on Central Park South, so that was one hell of a prospect. Although I was still in shock over the news, I absorbed the blow like an old pro and replied, "Charlie, I see your point. You're the head of an enormous company, and you can't run the risk of tangling with the Mafia. But I don't think the solution is to sweep the film under the rug and write off the $2 million. Here's my proposal: I'll pay back the money you advanced me. Then you relinquish the film to me and I do with it as I please." Bludhorn couldn't have asked for a better deal. At once we signed a letter canceling our prior contract.

Then I showed the film to Steven Ross, who was then chairman of Warner Brothers, and he was very enthusiastic. We shook hands and signed a contract guaranteeing me $3 million—which is to say, a million dollars more than Paramount had been paying. It happens every time: if you ask for a certain sum before you shoot a film, you can ask for more once it's done, assuming it's done well. They told me that it would take a week, maybe ten days, to draw up the contract, and I said that was fine. "I'm going back to Italy. Give me a call when you're ready."

A week later, in Rome, I got a telex inviting me to come to New York. When I got there, I immediately became suspicious, because instead of setting up an appointment at his office, Ross said, "I'll come see you at your hotel." He showed up, and in so many words he told me, "We like the film very much. But we heard about the Mafia threat over at Paramount, and that's not something we can handle." A second washout! How were we going to solve this problem?

One of my assistants in New York was Ralph Serpe, an Italian-American who had some familiarity with the Mafia. He wasn't personally involved, I should say, but he knew people who were in the thick of it. I asked him which boss I should approach. He told me that the guy lived in Miami, that he was of Calabrese descent, and that they called him Jimmy Blue Eyes. I'll omit his actual last name.

Serpe wangled me a phone number and I made the call. "I'd like to speak with Jimmy Blue Eyes," I said. "He doesn't know me, but I'm Dino De Laurentiis, and at the moment I'm in New York."

They very courteously took down my number, and an hour later, the boss called: "What can I do for you?"

"There's something I need to discuss with you, preferably in person. We're both of Italian descent, you and me. You don't know who I am, but—"

"No, no, I know exactly who you are. Come see me in Miami. Meet me at Joe's Stone Crabs."

I took off with Serpe, who was acting as my interpreter, and headed for the restaurant. I got a warm welcome and quickly laid my cards on the table. I told my host that somebody in his circle (I never pronounced the word *Mafia*) had called Paramount and threatened them. Paramount withdrew, and now Warner had passed too, after hearing about the earlier threat.

"This film is important to me," I told him. "It's the first one I've produced in America. You have to help me out."

"What can I do?"

"Just leave me in peace. Let me strike a deal with another company and release the film."

"Don't worry about it," Blue Eyes told me. And with this reassurance we became friends. He was extremely pleasant, small in stature, and he reminded me of my old cameraman Aldo Tonti, although he was much more handsome, with those famous, eerily ice-blue eyes.

Once I got the word from him, I went to Columbia, showed them the footage, and asked for an advance of $4 million. They accepted, since the film was worth the price, and *The Valachi Papers* was ultimately an enormous success in the United States.

According to Dino, the threats were "real, very real." And Blue Eyes was undoubtedly a genuine player in the American Mafia: his name appears in many books on the subject. He had the power to make this decision on his own. But for every favor he did, there was an implied payback down the road. In this case, says Dino, it was a relatively small thing.

One fine day Blue Eyes asked for a favor in return. It concerned a friend of his, and in this case too I don't want to throw around any names. Let's call him Mister X. This guy was so close to Jimmy that when the boss went to prison for some fiscal irregularity, Mister X had himself arrested for a stupid trifle so he could stick close by. He stayed in jail for five years, not a day less, and with this gesture he earned enormous credit with Jimmy.

As it turned out, however, Mister X had a mania for the cinema, which he considered his true vocation. His dream was to leave the Mafia and move to Hollywood. So one day Jimmy called and said that he was coming to see me in New York. He arrived, we had dinner together, and he discussed Mister X with me. "I know you're about to move out to Los Angeles," he said. "Do me a favor. Give the guy a desk and teach him a little bit about filmmaking."

At the end of dinner Jimmy introduced me to Mister X, and I told him, "Not to worry. Give me some time to get settled in Los Angeles, and then I'll call you."

So Mister X finally came to Hollywood. From the very start I took him behind the scenes and showed him how things worked, and he grasped the whole business immediately.

The rumors about Dino and the Mafia entertained Fellini, who embroidered them with invented details and spread them around Rome. For several weeks he recounted one particular tall tale, in which De Laurentiis figured as a "target of the Jewish Mafia," and since nobody in Italy had even suspected the existence of a Jewish Mafia until that moment, this whopper may well have inspired Sergio Leone to get to work on *Once Upon a Time in America*.

The Jewish Mafia? No way. If anything, I was a target of one of those anticrime commissions the Americans are always setting up. Look, in 1978 I made *The Brink's Job* in Boston, with William Friedkin directing. Ralph Serpe was organizing the shoot, because at that point, I could no longer personally supervise every film. After putting together the story, screenplay, director, actors, and budget, I would limit myself to occasional visits to the set, and one of my trusted right-hand men would oversee the production on a daily basis.

Anyway, one day Friedkin asked to have a certain street blocked off so he could shoot a scene. Serpe (the poor guy, he's dead now) was anything but a mafioso, but sometimes he liked to give that im-

> pression. And thanks to this behavior, he succeeded in blocking off every window on the long, long street where Friedkin wanted to film.
>
> Some time later, in New York, an interviewer from NBC asked to talk with me. I granted him the interview, calmly and in good faith: I knew nothing about the incident and hadn't even been there when they shot the scene. But the journalist, in hopes of getting a scoop, insinuated that by making a deal with the Mafia, I had managed to close one of Boston's most important arteries for hours. And in February 1979, on the basis of this sort of gossip, I was summoned to testify in front of a federal grand jury that was convening in Boston to fight the Mafia.
>
> These commissions are extremely dangerous. If I didn't state things in precisely the right manner, I could be in for big trouble. I answered the first few questions tranquilly. Then they started playing hardball: "Do you know Jimmy Blue Eyes?"
>
> I certainly couldn't deny it: they were well aware that I had known him since I made *Valachi*. So I told them the truth. "Sure, I know him," I said, "but I know plenty of people. I know President Ronald Reagan, I know this person and that person, all important figures in their fields."
>
> The inquisitors asked, "And why do you hang around with people like that?"
>
> "I know people of every kind," I replied, "including Jimmy Blue Eyes, because of my profession. A film producer needs to know a little bit about everybody, he needs to have some acquaintance with the characters he's going to put in his movies." This explanation convinced them, and they dismissed me without any further questions.

Mary Murphy's *New West* article, which was illuminating on this topic, also provided a close-range portrait of the producer. Shadowing Dino for nearly two weeks, the reporter was able to observe him with his guard down. The piece included a delicious description of a family dinner at the Beverly Hills mansion. Murphy appreciated her host's tact in urging his wife and children to speak in English in order to spare their guest any discomfort. Murphy's portrait of Silvana was especially subtle and skillful. Seated at the end of the table, opposite her husband, she struck the journalist as "a fragile, pale woman with deep-set dark eyes and an ethereal manner. . . . She is quiet, intense, at times acerbic toward her husband as well as toward life." Fragile or not, Silvana quickly stiff-armed any questions from Murphy: "Ask me nothing about him, we have been together too long, I know him too well, I have nothing to say."

At the table they discussed *King Kong*, which would be released in less than a month. The studio was shipping 2,200 prints—the biggest debut in the history of the film industry—and the receipts too were expected to shatter all existing records. (Ultimately, of course, they didn't.) Five dubbed versions had already been prepared for Italy, France, Spain, Germany, and Japan. Meanwhile, Dino and Silvana still disagreed about some aspects of the production. For example, he thought that Jessica Lange would become a star; Silvana didn't.

In her article, Murphy described how the producer spent a typical day in Los Angeles. He awakened before dawn, even on Christmas Day. He took his coffee alone in the kitchenette, sometimes with half a grapefruit, then rushed to his Renaissance-style desk in the cream-colored study. Taking advantage of the time difference, he talked to his European contacts on the phone, read scripts, and stretched out in an armchair at precisely 7 A.M., at which point the faithful Enzo gave him a shave.

After spending five minutes on a stationary bicycle, Dino hurried to the office. Usually he covered the two miles on foot, and in a city devoted to the internal combustion engine, he was occasionally stopped by the police. At the office, he worked until lunchtime, but unlike the other executives, he went home for a light snack of salad and cheese, followed by a nap of at least forty-five minutes. He returned to the office and worked until 8 P.M., then attended dinners or receptions in connection with his work, always with the secret hope of getting to bed at a decent hour.

Accompanying Dino on his rounds, Murphy encountered quite a few famous personalities and managed to elicit comments from a few of them. Charles Bludhorn enthused, "Dino is one of the greatest showmen in the history of movies, an eighth wonder of the world, like Mike Todd." The director Bob Fosse was somewhat less complimentary: "Dino is brilliant, charming, and dangerous. I mean, how can you have come as far as he has without having many things to hide?"

Between these two extremes, there was the judgment of Robert Evans: "Like the great producers, Dino is a gambler. Unlike a lot of people in Hollywood, he's got balls. . . . He is a self-starter, a doer, not a talker. He gets things done when others can't. He thinks positively rather than negatively, and for this I admire him. But I do not agree with the way he operates. I think, in the long run, he is very destructive for all of us." This was the scolding that Hollywood types administered to the Italian intruder. He didn't play by the industry's rules. And even worse, he dangled enormous salaries in front of actors and directors, often without any real certainty that his projects would materialize in the end. But that was exactly what made him a great gambler.

Murphy's travels with Dino did include some less flashy, more personal encounters. The moment the pair arrived in Rome, for example, the producer went to visit his mother. The scene that the journalist sketched out was a touching one. By now Donna Giuseppina was ninety-three, a widow for the last decade, and according to her son, she remembered only what she wanted to. Murphy described her as "old and beautiful," with translucent skin and snow-white hair. Dino caressed her, murmured "*Bella, bella, bella, Mommy*," and kissed her while the puppy at the foot of her armchair growled jealously.

Dino's sister Titina (Celeste) had prepared a huge Neapolitan supper, in the course of which the journalist followed the conversational crossfire as best she could. As the topic shifted from politics to childhood memories, the discussion took on an explosive character, complete with animated, classically Italian gesticulations. It was November 25, 1976. The ancient matriarch had less than two months to live. Perhaps, then, this was the last time she saw her expatriate son, whom she had welcomed by whispering his real name, *Agostino*.

CHAPTER 26

KIDNAPPED BY THE CINEMA

While Raffaella was still living in France with her husband, Gippi Viale, I got a call from my criminal lawyer in Rome, Carletto D'Agostino. He told me, "I received a telephone call from somebody in the Mafia or the Camorra, I'm not sure which. They want $2 million or they're going to kidnap Raffaella."

At once I understood this was no joke but a real threat. So I asked D'Agostino to stall and I hired a bodyguard. I put him on a plane immediately and sent him to "kidnap" Raffaella and her husband for me. He went to Monte Carlo, picked up Raffaella and Gippi as ordered, spent the night with them in a room at the Hôtel de Paris, and the next day they were in Los Angeles. This was Raffaella's chance to make a definitive move to the United States. She understood that she could no longer return to France, and in reality, she didn't want to.

Raffaella's memory of this singular episode is quite different. Thinking back on it, she has sometimes suspected that the threatened abduction was simply a hoax on her father's part, designed to bring her to America. (It certainly *sounds* like some screenwriter's bright idea.) At other times, she has insisted that the threat came from the infamous bandit Musolino—the same one Dino had celebrated in his 1950 production *Il brigante Musolino*—despite the fact that he had died in a psychiatric prison many years before. In either case, the producer begs to differ.

No, that's completely wrong. I may not recall having hired Pabst for *Ulysses*, but these are personal matters, and I remember them very well. D'Agostino called me and said, "They want to kidnap your daughter Raffaella, and they're demanding $2 million."

That sum hardly seemed accidental. You have to remember that this was the early 1970s, the worst period for that kind of activity in Italy. So I had taken out an insurance policy against kidnappings, with a value of $2 million for any member of the family. However, I had canceled the policy before I left for America.

Worried sick, I said to D'Agostino, "But how will they get to her in Monte Carlo?" He said, "It appears that it's very easy to get there from San Remo." I knew that perfectly well, because I had often taken the motorboat from my villa at Cap Martin to San Remo to do the shopping, and nobody ever stopped me, nobody even said a word. I begged Carlo to stall them for another forty-eight hours. I don't remember whether I called Raffaella. I do know that I sent a confirmed expert in these matters to "kidnap" her on my account.

For her part, Raffaella insists that her father called and ordered her to depart for America immediately: in other words, no emissary was sent to guard her and Gippi. Upon her arrival in Los Angeles, she recalls, her father told her that she must never again return to France. "Then I asked if I could at least take the time to close up shop," she continues, "because we had a house in Paris too. He gave me a week and practically glued two bodyguards to my ribs."

Back and forth the story goes. The long-distance dialogue between father and daughter dissolves repeatedly into a chorus of amused and reciprocal protests. On March 5, 1999, while at Cinecittà for the filming of *U-571*, Dino decided to clear up the matter once and for all. Judging from his half of his phone conversation with his daughter, a partial meeting of the minds may have taken place:

Ciao, Raffaella! I was lucky you weren't in the shower at this hour. . . . What? Oh, I understand. . . . But you're doing fine, right? Okay. Listen: how can you not remember that I sent somebody to Monte Carlo to kidnap you? . . . Ah, you came here first and then I sent you back to Monte Carlo with a bodyguard? As I remembered it . . . I understand. I told you "I can't explain anything to you. No questions. Get on an airplane, don't ask me why, and come here immediately." And it was only *after* that, when you returned to Monte Carlo to close the house, that one of my people was there to protect you. Great, now we've clarified things.

> But this had nothing to do with Musolino! Too bad that D'Agostino died, he would have remembered everything. . . . Right, he's dead, I knew that. . . . Forget Musolino, the guy who wanted to kidnap you was a *Sardinian* bandit. . . . Have I ever made a film about a Sardinian bandit? The answer is yes, there was *Barbagia*, the story of Graziano Mesina. But no, I'm telling you, Musolino had nothing to do with this. So we have two different points of view. Will you do me a favor? Tell Francesca to give me a call. . . . Good. A big kiss.

This conversation posits yet a third version of events. According to one source, somebody telephoned Dino's lawyer, claiming to be a spokesman for Graziano Mesina. The bandit was supposed to be demanding $2 million for the use of his name and history in the film *Barbagia*. Without a doubt, this is the stuff of comedy, and it's surprising that De Laurentiis never thought of making it into a movie. But in the Italy of that era—which witnessed the abduction and assassination of Aldo Moro—kidnappings were a more or less daily reality, never to be taken lightly. The reaction attributed to Dino, on the other hand, is fairly characteristic. Faced with a threat from a kidnapper, he immediately proved himself a bolder, speedier kidnapper.

> Raffaella was the last one to arrive in Los Angeles: the rest of my family was already here. Inmediately I realized that she intended to stay. When we were still in Italy, she had loved the art of filmmaking, and her dream was to become a producer. Looking back on the experience I had with my father, who encouraged his children to realize their own dreams, I didn't stand in her way. But I did give her some advice: "Look, Raffaella, this work requires a great deal of humility. I'm telling this to you in particular, because you're starting out with the advantage of being my daughter."
>
> With this in mind, the first job I gave her was cleaning up the sets: between one shoot and another they got very dirty and needed to be scrubbed. She rolled up her sleeves without a murmur of protest. Then, after a certain amount of this scut work, I told her, "Very good. Now we'll move on to the next level." Since she was good at drawing, I promoted her to assistant set designer, then to assistant wardrobe designer, then to production assistant.
>
> Raffaella understood all of it right away; she had a feel for it. So when I returned to Los Angeles and was preparing to make *The*

Hurricane, I asked her to come with me to Bora Bora along with her husband. She accepted with great enthusiasm.

The making of *The Hurricane* added one more bizarre and exotic episode to Dino's colorful history. With disaster movies doing such big business at the box office, De Laurentiis decided to remake John Ford's 1937 classic of the same name. (Then as now, this obscure film was remembered mostly for the hallucinatory special effects in the title sequence.) To rewrite the creaky script, Dino turned again to Lorenzo Semple, thinking that he would update the plot and add some extra nuance to it. No longer would the protagonists be two native islanders pursued by racial hatred. Instead, a Western girl would flout convention by falling in love with an aboriginal.

To direct, Dino again approached Roman Polanski, who had declined his offer to do *King Kong*. Now the director accepted his proposal, which stipulated his biggest paycheck yet: $1 million. By this time, of course, Polanski had some problems of his own. He had been accused of statutory rape and was currently awaiting trial; the whole incident had generated enormous publicity. No wonder he welcomed a change of scenery. Climbing aboard the producer's private jet with Dino and Lorenzo, he took off to scout locations in French Polynesia. The moment the plane was in the air, he began to laugh and joke, recovering his famous high spirits.

After rejecting several South Seas locations, the filmmakers decided on Bora Bora. Meanwhile, Dino had another suggestion for Polanski. Since there was some thought of an international coproduction, why didn't he make a side trip to Bavaria in order to check out a number of German actors? The director agreed. Oktoberfest was in full swing just as he arrived and, unfortunately, Polanski was photographed at a table in a beer garden—surrounded by a crowd of nubile teenage girls. To make matters worse, several American journalists manipulated the image by erasing the other men at the table.

Of course, the photograph made its way back to the Superior Court of Los Angeles County in Santa Monica, where Polanski's trial was taking place. The presiding judge, Laurence Rittenband, already resented the supposed arrogance of Hollywood celebrities. He was even more outraged at the thought of the director and alleged sexual predator knocking back tankards of beer in such youthful company.

Dino's testimony, which confirmed the reason for the Bavarian jaunt, just managed to save Polanski from a conviction for violating the terms of his bail. However, because the court ordered a psychiatric evaluation, the director was obliged to spend forty-two days confined at the California Institute for Men. De Laurentiis visited him there toward the middle of January. At that point the producer had an embarrassing confession to make: because of the pressures of the project, he had replaced Polanski with Jan Troell, the acclaimed director of *The Emigrants*.

Eventually Polanski was released. Troell declared his willingness to step down, and the production looked like it was about to get back on track. The judge took a hard line, however, and rumors circulated that he was about to hand down a fifty-year prison sentence. On February 2, 1978, Polanski decided to flee—immediately. Roman hurried off to catch the first plane to London. From there he continued to Paris, where he would remain in voluntary exile for decades.

With Polanski gone, Dino handed the reins back to Troell. Then he set about hiring a female protagonist for *The Hurricane*. Ideally he preferred a novice, but after reviewing hundreds of candidates, he chose an experienced actress: "If they're the right age, they have the wrong face. If they have the right face, they can't act. But at thirty-three, Mia Farrow had the face of an eighteen-year-old." He told his people to sign her up.

Farrow would treat her sojourn in Polynesia as a vacation for her numerous children and as an opportunity to immerse herself in Dostoyevsky. "In Bora Bora," she later recalled, "you can read by the light of the stars." With her marriage to André Previn in crisis, she also enjoyed a dalliance with the great cinematographer Sven Nykvist, who initiated the affair with a romantic tryst beneath the Southern Cross.

Federico, meanwhile, insisted that *he* was the ideal candidate for the role of the irresistible native. Without batting an eyelash, Dino told him, "Fine. Get all the hair removed from your chest and we'll set up a screen test." His son reconsidered and dropped the whole matter; the part went to the Hawaiian surfer Dayton Ka'ne. Dino was relieved by the outcome: "God willing, none of my children will aspire to be an actor."

The shoot progressed in a relatively tranquil manner, more or less on schedule, putting aside the inevitable difficulties that arise when

150 people are confined to an isolated location, without even a telephone. Lorenzo Semple, whom Dino had dubbed executive producer mostly to keep him in close proximity, often seemed to be in a state of shock. But he always remembered something De Laurentiis told him during a particularly discouraging moment. "Son," he confided, "there's one thing you have to remember about moviemaking. Every film begins, and every film ends."

When it was released in April 1979, *The Hurricane* turned out to be a critical and popular fiasco. Nonetheless, by relying on his business instincts, Dino managed to carve out a profit from this semi-catastrophe. And it was at precisely this point that Raffaella returned to center stage:

> As we prepared for the shoot on Bora Bora, it came time to organize the set and reserve accommodations for the cast and crew. At that moment I discovered there was nothing on the island. Today there are plenty of resorts, but back then there was only the Hotel Bora Bora, which was already booked up with tourist groups for the next two or three years. For that reason I decided to buy a nice piece of land by the ocean and build a hotel myself—prefabricated, of course, given the amount of time we had. That way, I would have the sort of logistical headquarters that I needed, and when the film was over, I'd still own the property.
>
> Thanks to a stroke of luck, I didn't have any difficulties putting this plan into action. At the time, the government of Tahiti allowed only Polynesian or French citizens to make investments on the island. Due to her marriage, however, Raffaella had a passport from French Monaco, so it was a breeze for me to obtain permission and favorable financing.
>
> I called in a local architect and entrusted the operation to my daughter, promising her that if she pulled the whole thing together, I'd bump her up to producer on the next film. The work took seven or eight months to complete. The hotel was composed of several one-story bungalows on the beach, some outfitted with a terrace jutting out into the water, with a little staircase descending right into the sea. Naturally there was a central building with a reception desk, restaurants, and other amenities. Raffaella was so enthusiastic about the project that she asked to be cut in as a partner, using her own money. I allotted ten percent to her and ten percent to her husband, whose share I later bought out.
>
> When the film was done, we let Sofitel manage the hotel. Then

I ceded the place to Silvana when we separated, with the stipulation that upon her death, she leave it to her daughters, which she did. Eventually the girls sold it. They made an excellent profit, especially when you consider how little it cost in the first place.

Anyway, promises are made to be kept: it was time for Raffaella to produce her first film. I suggested that she shoot it right in Bora Bora, where we already knew everybody and had everything at our disposal. It occurred to me that she could do a remake of *Ti-Koyo e il suo pescecane* and call it *Beyond the Reef*. I also wanted to set her up with a friendly, capable director, a sensible person who could be helpful to her. So I hired Franco Rossi, who had made the RAI version of *The Odyssey* for me. His one request was that he be billed under an American pseudonym: Frank C. Clark.

As soon as the script and locations were approved, I said goodbye. I told Raffaella, "Attend to your responsibilities." At the time the film cost about $500,000, which wasn't a huge sum, and we did decent business with it. That was Raffaella's debut as a producer. After that I entrusted her with more important movies, such as *Conan the Barbarian* and *Dune*, until she went off on her own.

CHAPTER 27

THE AUTEUR'S ENEMY?

MUCH HAS BEEN SAID AND WRITTEN ABOUT DINO'S CONTROVERSIAL relationships with his directors. De Laurentiis has always divided directors into two categories: the extraordinary ones, the Auteurs with a capital *A*, and the others. This latter group runs the gamut from gifted to average to downright mediocre, and the producer tends to regard all of them as essentially hired guns. Still, he denies ever having made the statement attributed to him in the headline of a newspaper story: "The director? He's my employee."

After his initial flurry of films in the United States, Dino began to feel some nostalgia for a more intense relationship with his directors. He longed for the kind of rapport he shared with Fellini during their heyday—or even for the sort of intermittent bond he had with Germi and Rossellini, based more on friendship than professional solidarity. It was this impulse that led him, during the mid-1970s, to seek out relationships with Robert Altman and Ingmar Bergman.

Dino's initial statements about Altman were ecstatic: he proclaimed him a genius, in the same class with Fellini and Kurosawa, and an exalted cinematic artist. For his part, the director seemed no less fond of the producer and shared his hope that they could create something lasting as a team. They decided to commence with a truly all-American subject: *Buffalo Bill and the Indians, or Sitting Bull's History Lesson.*

This was the story of the famous Wild West Show, which had transformed the conquest of the American continent into a theatrical spectacle. It was also a pitiless analysis of how Colonel William Frederick "Buffalo Bill" Cody exploited the tragedy of the Native Americans for commercial gain. The director shot the film in Canada, at great expense and with a terrific group of actors, including Paul Newman, Burt Lancaster, and Geraldine Chaplin. On paper, it was a cast that should have sent out sparks. For some reason, however, the whole package never quite ignited.

> If things didn't go the way they were supposed to, there was a very simple reason. When Altman's agent proposed the film to me, I specified that I would be happy to make it as long as I found the script convincing. We had a series of meetings with Altman and made many revisions to the screenplay, at which point I approved the final version. But when I started watching the dailies, I realized that he was continually making changes to the script without consulting me. And those changes were what created all of the film's problems.
>
> After viewing the first cut, I wasn't at all happy with it. I organized a sneak preview to get a sense of how an audience would react, and it was immediately clear that everybody else felt the same way I did. I said to Bob, "Didn't it seem like the public was bored? Don't you think the film is too long?" He disagreed. He hardly glanced at the cards we got back with the audience's comments, most of them negative, and I asked him, "What's the use of a sneak preview if you're going to ignore the responses?"

Dino reluctantly played his trump card: he asserted control over the final cut. Over Altman's protests, he chopped several minutes out of the film. Unfortunately, another disagreement flared up at the same time, this one regarding the second project Altman was supposed to make for Dino: *Ragtime*. The producer was a great admirer of E. L. Doctorow's best-selling novel; he had raced through the page proofs in a single night, and he bought the rights before the book even arrived in the stores. Altman immediately prepared to write the screenplay. To celebrate his own burgeoning friendship with the author, in fact, he had already given Doctorow a bit part as Grover Cleveland's secretary in *Buffalo Bill*.

During his chats with the novelist, the director had a brainstorm: he would transform *Ragtime* into a two-part, six-hour spectacular. Dino, perhaps recalling his old skirmishes with Visconti, refused to hear a single word about this expansionist scheme. Instead he yanked Altman off the film and reassigned it to Milos Forman. Soon critics began clucking their tongues over this dual reprimand: first the producer had cut Altman's revisionist Western, then he had kicked him off a second project.

The director had his defenders. In July 1976, for example, *Buffalo Bill* was screened at the Berlin Film Festival and unexpectedly won the Golden Bear. The jury, chaired by the Polish director Jerzy Kawalerowicz, intended to slap Dino on the wrist for cutting the film. "This prize," they announced, "is awarded only to the original, uncut version presented in Berlin." In reality, both the long and short versions of the film remain among the great director's lesser accomplishments. From a financial point of view, the project was a disaster.

> I made mistakes on both fronts, artistic and commercial. Altman, who for me remains one of the great American filmmakers, doesn't listen to anybody. Now that I think of it, I never had any arguments of this kind with Fellini, nor with Rossellini, nor with Bergman. Invariably we exchanged our respective opinions and ended up finding some sort of middle ground. With Bob Altman things went very differently, and it wasn't my fault.
>
> Look, in this business we're ultimately showmen. We work for the customer, who forks over his cash in order to spend an enjoyable evening at the cinema. If we forget the audience, we're all dead, producers and directors. You're simply not allowed to say, I've made a masterpiece and I don't care about anything else. If you play it that way, it's all over.

Dino's friendship with Ingmar Bergman, on the other hand, was a much sunnier affair. It began when De Laurentiis acquired the exclusive rights to distribute *Face to Face* in the United States. A letter that Bergman wrote on July 20, 1975, testifies to their rapport: "Thanks for your kind messages and thoughts during and after my work on the film. I'm no less grateful for the money, which has always arrived punctually. . . . For the first time in my life, I feel secure and satisfied at entering into an agreement with a foreign producer. I truly hope that my film will make you feel the same way."

Face to Face comprised four episodes of fifty minutes apiece, designed to be broadcast on television, plus a feature version for commercial release. Liv Ullmann played the protagonist, who returns to her childhood home and is hurled into a cosmos of pain and fear. It was a harsh, even abrasive work, and certainly not the kind of film that usually appealed to Dino's tastes. He was, however, wildly enthusiastic, sending Bergman an ecstatic telegram the moment he finished watching the print: "I'm still in shock at the sheer beauty of the film. It's a masterpiece."

Intent on continuing his relationship with the Swedish director, De Laurentiis decided to produce *The Serpent's Egg*, a dark drama set during the rise of Nazism. Bergman, juggling several projects, completed the screenplay in early 1976. On January 30, however, the police interrupted his rehearsal of Strindberg's *Dance of Death* in Stockholm and dragged him down to the station, where he was charged with tax fraud. At once it became clear that the auditors had inflated some minor wrinkle in his accounting to generate publicity. But the accusations, and the threatening manner of the magistrate, had a terrible effect on Bergman. He suffered a nervous breakdown and spent three weeks in a psychiatric ward at the Karolinska Hospital. At the end of March, the embittered auteur decided to go abroad, abandoning his native land for the next nine years.

One of his first stops was Los Angeles, where Dino, who had been following the whole mess with fraternal trepidation, welcomed him with open arms. At once the producer organized a press conference, where he excoriated Bergman's tormentors and announced *The Serpent's Egg*. Originally he had hoped to shoot the English-language production in Berlin. But after a fruitless search for locations, it was made in Monaco and released in December 1977.

The Serpent's Egg was neither a critical nor a popular success. Yet Dino, captivated by the project, defended it to the bitter end. When the film came out in Italy and was panned by the critics, the producer persuaded Titanus, the distributor, to pull it from circulation. Then he followed up this unprecedented gesture by running an advertisement in the daily newspapers, in which he defended Bergman's work. He'd always maintained a hands-off relationship with the press, so this was perhaps a unique event in Dino's career: nobody expected such a visceral reaction from him. The director appreciated the effort. At Christmas he expressed his thanks in a holiday telegram: "I also want to tell you how grateful I was for your stimulating collaboration. I hope you're not too unhappy at the mixed reactions our controversial film has provoked." De Laurentiis replied, "I can assure you that I'm not worried about *The Serpent's Egg*. It's not the first time we've gotten mixed reviews for an important piece of work. I continue to feel that your film is a masterpiece."

By now Dino revered Bergman more than any other living filmmaker. And what did the director think of his admirer? According to Mary Murphy's *New West* article, Bergman was fascinated by the producer's bulletproof persona. "It is very interesting to find the man behind the mask," he told her, "because few people I have met in my life are as well masked as Dino. . . . His mask is almost perfect, so you almost have the feeling that it's real." The director then described a dinner party he had attended at the Beverly Hills mansion. The fifteen-year-old Francesca had joined the group at the last minute, and Bergman was struck by Dino's paternal tenderness. "Suddenly this man was vulnerable and warm and quiet," he recalled. "It was very strange and very beautiful, because he completely changed when he was sitting with this young woman."

The Swede added that Dino was "in charge 24 hours a day, and I have the feeling that he is sometimes in charge when he sleeps." He continued, "Not many producers have the talent to talk to artists in their language, but he talks the language and he understands the language." Bergman also loved De Laurentiis because he kept his word, which was "more than you can say about 99.99 percent of the producers in this business." Noting a "certain Italian brutality" in the producer, he pointed out that both of them were highly pressurized personalities: "He is like me in the sense that we both have such a terrible tension inside if we don't say or do what we think—I think we would both explode." Alas, no other films would emerge from this happy, if theoretically explosive, collaboration.

Nor would Dino feel such a fraternal bond with the other great directors he sought out during this period. For example, he fought bitterly with David Lean over *The Bounty*, a project that Lean had been discussing for some time with the screenwriter Robert Bolt.

The movie's subject, of course, was the famous shipboard mutiny of 1789, on the eve of the French Revolution, and the idea of a remake had been floating around Hollywood ever since 1935, when *Mutiny on the Bounty* was first released. That accident-prone production, featuring

Charles Laughton and Clark Gable, had earned a reputation for being cursed. Still, it won that year's Oscar for Best Film, along with seven additional nominations, and did tremendous business throughout the world. That was enough to reassure the creators of the 1962 remake, which starred Trevor Howard and Marlon Brando. Yet this second production of *Mutiny on the Bounty* did seem to be dogged by misfortune. There were difficulties and delays of every kind, the film failed to win a single Oscar, and it ultimately flopped at the box office.

And what of the latest remake? Dino stumbled into the initial planning stages quite by accident, when he crossed paths with Lean and Bolt in Tahiti. The director and screenwriter were brainstorming, but to the hyperactive producer, they seemed to be moving in slow motion. As one observer later recounted, "Since he was Dino, the wheels in his brain were always spinning. He couldn't understand how David could spend day after day seated on the balcony, just staring at the sky. 'What is he doing?' he kept asking."

To hustle things along, De Laurentiis offered to fly Lean's agent, Phil Kellogg, back to Los Angeles on his private plane. During the flight, Kellogg shared his anxieties about getting the film into production. Operating as he always did, Dino came up a proposal: "Let's do it together. I'll take it to Paramount."

These facts can be found in a scrupulous study, *David Lean: A Biography*, by the film historian Kevin Brownlow. Not surprisingly, the author presents the story entirely from his subject's point of view. Dino's recollections are different:

> When I signed the contract with David Lean, which featured an estimated budget of $20 million, he set out two conditions. The first was that he would write the screenplay with Bolt in Tahiti. The second was that we would immediately start constructing the ship. I discussed these stipulations with Bludhorn and he agreed.
>
> When he completed the screenplay, however, Lean had a surprise for us: he intended to make two movies, not one. He also asked me to attach Kellogg as a producer and announced that he would require complete freedom of movement during the shoot. None of these things was part of our contract.

In the meantime, De Laurentiis had approved the construction of the ship in a New Zealand shipyard. This undertaking alone would be the source of endless quarrels and delays, and at one point the vessel itself became subject to seizure. By now, all the budgetary problems had become impossibly complicated.

Bernie Williams, an expert manager who had left Stanley Kubrick's organization to join Dino's, and who was just then making preparations for *Flash Gordon* in London, witnessed these troubles. De Laurentiis brought him on to Lean's project in a temporary assignment, asking Williams to join the director's assistant on an exploratory trip to scout locations and evaluate logistical challenges. For eight weeks the two emissaries wandered Fiji, the Cook Islands, and New Zealand. Then, to report his findings, Williams joined Dino on a flight from Tahiti to Los Angeles.

High over the Pacific, they nibbled on a breakfast of cheese and fruit. Dino asked his companion how much he thought the film would cost. As Williams recalls, "I tell him that it would take me ten days to come up with an approximate figure, but he's the kind who wants an answer immediately. 'Grab that!' he says, pointing to my air-sickness bag. 'Write the estimated budget at the top. Then do some calculations: how many weeks, how much per week, how much for the costumes, the ship, the music, the cast, the screenplay, and everything else.' I obey: I take the bag and write down the numbers. 'Now, add it up,' Dino orders. The figures add up to $42 million. 'You see?' concludes the boss. 'Now you've given me what I need to bail out of this project.'"

At a meeting in Los Angeles in September 1978, the producer submitted a new financial plan to Lean. According to its provisions, the film would be feasible only if the price could be kept within $25 million. Otherwise, the whole operation would be impossible. In reality, De Laurentiis was reluctant to entrust such an important project to a neophyte like Kellogg. He was equally reluctant to hand over more than $40 million to a fledgling producer. Nor did he want to shoot two films instead of one. He urged the director to make a decision and then sent Bernie to meet with him.

"We were at the Beverly Hills Hotel," recalls Williams.

> Lean's girlfriend, Sandy, and his assistant were present. David strutted up and down, complaining that I had made him one of the world's most expensive directors. I replied that he was.

> The meeting became increasingly uncomfortable. At some stage I glanced around and out of the corner of my eye I noticed a man with a tape recorder reflected in a mirror in the bathroom. I froze. I then told Lean that I could not continue with the meeting and would have to leave. He screamed for the man inside the bathroom to come out. He was a famous Hollywood lawyer.
>
> When Dino heard what had happened, he called for an immediate meeting with Lean; his agent and producer, Phil Kellogg; Dino's financial executive, Fred Sidewater; and me.
>
> Dino, who had already spent $6 million of his own money on the film, turned to Sidewater. "Do me a favor," he said. "Write out a check for $20 million, and make it payable to David Lean." Fred drew up the check. Dino handed the check to Lean and said, "David, here's the money to make the film at the price we originally discussed. You've insisted that Bernie's estimate is completely inflated, and if that's the case, please, take the check and keep going with the film. But there's one important thing I should add, David. I have no intention of selling my house in order to finance a movie. If you spend more than this, you'll have to come up with the cash yourself." Kellogg jumped up and said that he couldn't allow his client to accept such a proposal. The meeting ended, Dino wished David luck, and at that moment the possibility of these two giants making *Bounty* went up in smoke.

During the next year, Lean and Kellogg approached many producers, including Joseph Levine and Lew Grade, but none of them felt like taking the risk. Eventually they were forced to give up. Their disappointment was so bitter that ten years later, after receiving a prize at Cannes, Lean let loose with a tirade aimed at producers in general and Dino in particular.

In the meantime, Dino managed to make *The Bounty* by himself, hiring Roger Donaldson to direct and entrusting the production duties to Williams. For a while he toyed with the possibility of a TV miniseries, but ultimately he returned to the idea of a feature film. It was released in 1984. The cast was an impressive one. Mel Gibson acquitted himself handsomely in the role of Mr. Christian, the chief mutineer, while Laurence Olivier presided over the court-martial that opens the film. For the role of Captain Bligh, which would always be associated with Laughton's charismatic performance, Dino hired an actor who had been in the midst of an irresistible ascent for some time: Anthony Hopkins.

Dino's relationship with another distinguished director, Milos Forman, was somewhat more successful, with alternating patches of harmony and argumentation. In *Turnaround: A Memoir*, the director concedes that on the whole, De Laurentiis was much preferable to his former partner Carlo Ponti (who supposedly attempted to resolve one professional dispute by having Forman thrown into a Czechoslovakian prison). Recalling his work on *Ragtime*, Milos paints a sympathetic portrait of Dino. He calls him a "dynamo," with a small man's abundance of energy. And what of the producer's English? The *Mitteleuropean* emigrant can only shake his head: "It's even worse than mine."

Regarding *Ragtime*, Dino had only a few ideas, but those were crystal clear. The novel was jammed with a throng of characters and a kaleidoscopic assortment of events, both historical and fictional. To De Laurentiis, this meant that major cuts would have to be made. (Altman's approach, of course, had been precisely the opposite.) Forman agreed with Dino and, after studying the multiplicity of plot lines, he decided to focus on the story of the pianist Coal House Walker, who had been transformed into a terrorist by the aggressive and obtuse racism of his contemporaries. By the end of the movie, he would barricade himself inside the Morgan Library, which he threatened to blow up—destroying not only himself but also a priceless Gutenberg Bible and any number of additional treasures.

Unable to find a star to play the protagonist, the director and producer launched a wide-ranging search, which was soon compared to the famous casting call for the role of Scarlett O'Hara. In the end they hired a relative unknown, Howard Rollins. Meanwhile the director recruited several other unknowns, sticking to some rigorously creative criteria of his own. Struck, for example, by a physical resemblance between Norman Mailer and one of the historical characters, the architect Stanford White, Forman offered the role to the novelist. In both the film and in real life, White was killed by a jealous husband while he watched a variety show on the roof of Madison Square Garden. (There would seem to be a certain slyly malicious twinkle to this bit of casting, since the author of *The Naked and the Dead* had years earlier stabbed his own [now former] wife during a drunken quarrel.)

The lack of star power was a concern for Dino. It complicated the sale of advance rights in Europe, where the distributors insisted on marquee names. On the other hand, James Cagney's return to the screen aroused plenty of interest. It was Forman who pulled off this coup, by dint of being Cagney's neighbor on Martha's Vineyard—and by approaching him through a mutual friend, Mikhail Baryshnikov. Away from the set for more than twenty years, the Little Giant suffered from sciatica, diabetes, and occasional apoplectic fits. He dragged his feet when he walked, had trouble remembering anything, and was moody to the point of lunacy. Invited to choose a character from the script, he surprised everybody: he asked to play the hateful cop, who orders the protagonist to be shot when he emerges from the library with his hands over his head. Here was a human type with almost no connection to Cagney's customary persona. The choice was a stark departure from the sort of characters that had made him the public's darling for decade upon decade.

The veteran's return met with great curiosity. The New York Yankees asked Cagney to throw out the first ball at the World Series, and when people recognized him during the shoot in Brooklyn's Park Slope, they burst into applause. A problem arose, however, when the production moved to Shepperton Studios in England, where the interiors were being filmed. Refusing even to consider boarding a plane, Jimmy threw a temper tantrum and threatened to return to Martha's Vineyard. Dino reassured the veteran star by booking a passage for him by ship, and to keep him happy, he enlisted another veteran, Pat O'Brien, as a traveling companion. This seemed to do the trick. Upon his arrival in London, Cagney proceeded to paint the town red: he went out to dinner, attended the theater, and when he was presented to the Queen Mother, this dyed-in-the-wool Yankee cut the conversation short by removing his hearing aid.

All things considered, the film did more for Cagney than he did for the film: his performance was rather blank and inexpressive. Still, this fresh immersion in the world of the cinema rejuvenated the actor, and he faced his remaining days with renewed serenity. At his funeral, five years later, Forman would be one of the pallbearers.

Ragtime was released in November 1981 to favorable reviews, and there was a general agreement that the director had done an exquisite job with the material. Yet the film didn't have the box-office success it deserved. Perhaps the public instinctively recoiled from such a disenchanted vision of American history, with its heavy freight of injustice and racism. Following his self-imposed rule, De Laurentiis blamed himself for the film's lack of success: he hadn't worked hard enough to shape the screenplay, he had given the director too much autonomy, and so forth. For his part, Forman also laid some of the blame at Dino's door. As he saw it, every film had its own internal rhythm, and cutting—which was supposed to tighten up the narrative—sometimes made the final product less comprehensible and more boring.

Ragtime was released at a hefty 156 minutes. Still, the director had opposed a good many of Dino's cuts. The one that pained him the most was the elimination of the plot's most politically aware character, Emma Goldman. This committed anarchist, who devoted her life to radical agitation, would hardly seem like a typical cinema heroine. But by a bizarre coincidence, she figured not only in Dino's movie but in another release of that same year, Warren Beatty's *Reds*. In fact, Maureen Stapleton's portrayal of Goldman won her an Oscar in 1982, even as *Ragtime* failed to win a single trophy.

A final footnote. In the midst of the Emma Goldman debate, Forman proposed that they let the author decide—assuming, of course, that Doctorow would fight to retain his character. Surprisingly, Dino agreed to the idea. Even more surprisingly, when Doctorow emerged from the screening room after seeing the shortened version, he claimed that he "didn't miss" Emma. The director caved. Not long after, however, he learned that Dino had just then been acquiring the rights to the author's new novel, *Loon Lake*. A suspicion flashed through his brain. . . . But we'll have to leave the final judgment on *that* one to the conspiracy theorists.

CHAPTER 28

IN THE KINGDOM OF FANTASY

IN 1979 DINO TOOK ON YET ANOTHER GRANDIOSE PROJECT: *FLASH Gordon*. This film, like *King Kong*, was inspired by one of the producer's pop-cultural infatuations of the 1930s. It was almost as if by settling in the real America, he was now obliged to revisit each of those imaginative territories that had so enchanted the European schoolboys of his generation. This mythic itinerary took him from Buffalo Bill to King Kong—and now, to the comic-book universe of Flash Gordon.

It's a good bet that in 1934, the boy Agostino De Laurentiis bought the first issue of *L'Avventuroso* at the newsstand in Torre Annunziata. On its cover, the magazine announced the first installment of the adventures of Flash Gordon. This "police officer," who had hurled himself from an airplane in the embrace of the beautiful Dale Arden, promptly collided with the nutty Doctor Zarro (a.k.a. Zharkov). He ended up on board the doctor's "celestial rocket," attempting to prevent a meteorite from destroying the Earth. Instead the trio made landfall on the planet Mongo, where the Emperor Ming ruled over a kind of medieval kingdom with high-tech trimmings. The realm was threatened by antediluvian monsters and inhabited by bizarre crossbreeds: Hawk Men, Lion Men, Lizard Men, and so forth.

For De Laurentiis, as for so many adolescents around the world, Alex Raymond's comic strips were a source of indelible memories. But how could these surrealistic images be transferred to the screen? In a sudden inspiration, Dino called the great Danilo Donati. And Fellini's brilliant art director, then at the height of his fame, didn't disappoint

De Laurentiis. Donati created an astonishing cinematic environment, and he, rather than the outrageously costumed protagonist, would prove to be the real hero of the project.

When it came time to hire a director, however, Dino's first choice turned out to be less inspired: Nicholas Roeg. As Bernie Williams recalls, "I went with Roeg to Dino's house to discuss *Flash Gordon*. Nick was thinking of an intellectual version of the famous comic strip, with a highly stylized vision of the planet Mongo. Dino, on the other hand, wanted to maintain the comic-book flavor of the original. These differences led to some sharp disagreements, and so did my estimated budgets, which everybody thought were unacceptably steep."

Here Williams adds an interesting gloss, which applies to Dino's working methods in general. "The problem with presenting a budget to De Laurentiis," he notes, "is that he always thinks they're too high. But that's because he's a complete realist, by necessity: he finances the films himself, using certain tactics available to an independent producer, and there's always a limit to the amount of money he can raise at any given moment. Still, for the guy putting together the budgets, it's not an easy row to hoe."

Sensing that he and the producer had very different visions of the film, Roeg withdrew. Dino replaced him with another Englishman, Mike Hodges, who had gotten his start directing television programs. Then he announced that the project would cost $30 million, and he at least considered the idea of returning to Rome for the shoot. Williams took the opposite tack. "Dino wanted to make the movie in his Roman studio," he recounts, "and he sent me over there to check it out. Since it hadn't been operating for a long time, Dinocittà was in ruins. I reported this to the producer, adding that it would make more sense to set up shop in England: having already made *Star Wars* and *Superman*, the British crews knew exactly how to pull off this kind of production. At first he argued with me. Then he went to study the situation in person and ended up accepting the English solution."

> It's true that I wanted to make the film in Italy and entrust it to Raffaella. However, we were still in the era of the kidnappings, which raised the problem of protecting her. We took a trip to Rome to study the situation, bringing along a kidnapping expert from the FBI. We considered the idea of Raffaella's staying in my

apartment at Dinocittà, but that also seemed too risky. Meanwhile we had begun discussions with the Italian labor unions and found ourselves nowhere near an agreement.

I finally let them know that the British solution had become an obligatory one. And not (as some have written) for technical reasons. After all, whether we shot in London or Rome, many of the special effects were going to be created in California. And the Italian technicians and artists were certainly as skilled as their British counterparts, if not more so. No, the problem was the unions. They wouldn't grant me any flexibility in regard to the schedule: it had to be eight hours a day, five days a week. When I asked about working Saturdays, and eventually prolonging the daily schedule and paying overtime, they wouldn't budge. In the end it wore me down and I said, "We're going to London."

Once they arrived, Dino wanted an apartment and office in the West End. Bernie Williams found him a beautiful building on Park Lane next to the Dorchester Hotel overlooking Hyde Park. His favorite colors at the time were red and gold, so the apartment was carpeted in red and furnished with antique furniture. For his office, Williams recalls, Dino issued additional requests:

Dino told me to buy four very comfortable and expensive chairs for the office and not to let the crew know how much they cost so they wouldn't get the wrong impression about expenditures. He reasoned that when he held meetings with bankers, they would be so comfortable listening to his sales pitch that he would eventually get what he wanted.

He also wanted a large sheet of Plexiglas on the floor behind his very large desk so he could roll his chair from one end to the other quickly, or swivel his legs up onto his desk when on the telephone. "That's a dangerous request," I replied. "You're on the second floor and there's a very large window behind you. I'd hate to see you go through it."

"Nonsense," said Dino, "I'm used to it. I have the same flooring in Beverly Hills and never had any problems."

"Okay," I relented, and got on with it.

A few weeks later Dino was rushing into his office, and on the way, he asked his secretary to call Nat Cohen of EMI. The telephone rang, Dino picked it up, swiveled his chair on the Plexiglas, spun around, and BAM! disappeared somewhere behind the desk.

> I started to laugh. Dino's financial executive was standing next to me. He was frozen and white-faced, which made me laugh even more. I thought, "This is it for me." I heard Dino struggling behind the desk and Nat's voice on the dangling telephone screaming "Dino, are you there?"
>
> Dino struggled to get the chair off him. Then he crawled up, peeked over the desktop, looked at me, and burst out laughing. Eventually he grabbed the phone giggling and continued speaking.

With his offices up and running, De Laurentiis made an abortive attempt to buy Pinewood Studios. Like Dinocittà, the vacant facility was falling to pieces. Nonetheless, the management refused even to rent the complex to *Flash Gordon*. They were afraid that problems would arise between their permanent staff, who were badly paid, and the workers on the film, who were getting higher, freelance wages. Faced with these obstacles, the producer ended up leasing twelve soundstages at Shepperton and EMI.

The Flash Gordon cast included the lovely Melody Anderson, who was never heard from again, and the shining presence of two Italian beauties, Ornella Muti and Mariangela Melato. Chaim Topol added a comic Borscht Belt spin to his role as Zharkov. And the Bergman veteran Max Von Sydow put in the film's best performance as the Emperor Ming. For the most part, these were seasoned professionals, and they behaved as such. But Sam Jones, the newcomer Dino hired to play the hero, turned out to be a real problem.

"He was an unknown," Williams recalls. "Before that, I think he had a job hanging wallpaper. A week before the shoot began, Dino summoned him and gave him some wise counsel. 'Sam,' he said, 'you're about to become the protagonist of a film costing many millions of dollars. If everything goes well, you'll become a star overnight. So my advice would be to keep a low profile in London for the next twenty weeks. Get plenty of sleep, work hard, and keep in mind that you can enjoy yourself afterwards. Take care of yourself, especially once people in the street start identifying you as Flash Gordon: believe me, some of them will be tempted to pick fights with you. Stay on your toes, be careful, and good luck.'"

This lecture fell on deaf ears. That very same night Sam was involved in an early-hours brawl at Covent Garden and was rushed to the hospital with a gash on his face, which required two stitches. "Dino swept into the operating room in a fury," Williams recalls. "He proclaimed to the doctors and nurses, 'Don't touch him, he's my star. If you ruin his face you'll destroy my film!' 'With all due respect, mister,' the surgeon calmly replied, 'you'll have to get out of here. This is a hospital, not a film studio.'"

The producer withdrew. But according to Williams, his salvo did cause the surgeons to treat the actor with particular care. "Looking back on it, if Dino hadn't made his unconventional entrance into the operating room, Sam probably would have ended up with a visible gash. That would have created a disastrous situation. We would have been forced to find another Flash, which wouldn't have been easy. He was a blond, buff American boy, in great shape and even capable of acting."

Having learned exactly nothing from his nasty experience, the young man got into scrapes throughout the shoot. He also kept requesting pay increases. Then, at Christmas, he took off for Los Angeles and never came back. There were still eight weeks of work left on the visual effects, but Dino refused to be rattled. "We'll keep going," he ordered, "with the very best stand-in you can find." It was perhaps the first time in cinematic history that a $30 million production was completed after the star had gone AWOL. (Jones, who never got another starring role, later filed suit against the production, arguing that his options for two additional *Flash Gordon* films should be honored. The sequels, of course, were never made.)

Dino remembers:

> The film presented other problems, especially technical ones, because it was crammed with special effects from start to finish. These days computer-generated images have revolutionized the entire field. But back then, the only valid technique for shooting those effects was the blue screen. This was an enormous screen, lit a uniform blue, in front of which the actors or stunt doubles performed the scene. Practically speaking, they were acting in front of a nonexistent backdrop. But once you were in postproduction, you could superimpose landscapes, assorted monsters, spaceships, or whatever the screenplay called for.
>
> When we were making *Flash Gordon*, the continuous use of the blue screen created a problem. The high-voltage arc lamps shining on the backdrop poured an enormous amount of heat on the actors.

> I went to Lee Brothers, a technical laboratory, and asked them to design a different kind of lighting. They found a solution: a low-intensity grid three square yards in size, made up of sixty-four bulbs in adjustable rows. This revolutionary light source was attached to the base of the blue screen, illuminating it in a perfectly uniform manner. They called the new units Dino Lamps, which made me proud. It's always nice to leave your mark on something.

Flash Gordon had a worldwide release of two thousand prints, and in interviews he gave on the occasion of the London premiere, the excessively optimistic De Laurentiis predicted that it would garner at least four Oscar nominations: set design, costumes, special effects, and editing. Not a single one materialized. Still, the public seemed to enjoy the film.

Dino, in any case, was already moving forward with his next project, a vehicle for Arnold Schwarzenegger. The two had met during the initial preparations for *Flash Gordon*, when somebody had proposed the gigantic Austrian for the title role. According to Schwarzenegger, the initial meeting didn't go quite as well as he had expected.

"Our first meeting lasted exactly one minute, forty seconds. I walked into his office with my agent, who had spent two months setting this up, and I made some stupid remark about his height. I think I said, 'Why does a little guy like you need such a huge desk?' He said quickly, 'Ah, you have an accent.' I said, 'Look who's talking,' and he said, 'You're not a-right for the part. I talk to you later.' That was the end of the meeting."

But clearly Arnold's monumental physique had made a big impression on Dino, who gave Schwarzenegger a call the moment he began preparations for *Conan the Barbarian*. Conan was the creation of Robert Howard, a fanatical bodybuilder who cranked out volume after volume of fantasy before committing suicide in 1936. His pulpish protagonist might well have vanished into history, but when the series was adapted for a popular comic book, the Barbarian got a second wind. Conan was a prehistoric soldier of fortune, living in the kingdom of Hyboria ten centuries before the birth of Christ. He's been called a mixture of Tarzan, Superman, and the Thief of Baghdad.

> In 1980 a young producer in Los Angeles, Ed Pressman, got me to read a screenplay adapted from *Conan the Barbarian*. It was

the work of an up-and-coming screenwriter, Oliver Stone, who was destined to become a celebrated director. Anyway, the initial script was full of exaggerated violence, and it was too costly to make, but what fascinated me was the way it conveyed the feeling of a primitive and brutal epoch. It seemed like a great project to offer to a talented director.

My first choice was Ridley Scott, who was already in the midst of a great career: he had progressed from making commercials to the worldwide success of *Alien*. I had been in contact with him since 1977, when I saw and admired his first film, *The Duelists*, but we hadn't yet done anything together.

Well, I went to see Ridley in London and gave him Stone's screenplay, which he liked very much. Immediately he asked which actor I intended to use for the film, and I told him, "Arnold Schwarzenegger. I know what you're going to say: he has no experience as an actor. But he's got the ideal physique for Conan." Ridley didn't agree. He assured me that he would sign on right away if I changed my mind about the protagonist. For me, though, Arnold was fundamental, so I began looking for another director.

I eventually signed up John Milius. Along with being a successful director, Milius was an excellent screenwriter. He revised the script, cutting back the prohibitive costs, and enthusiastically prepared to shoot the film. I entrusted the project to Raffaella: it was her first international production.

Work on *Conan the Barbarian* began in Spain in January 1981. A physically demanding production, it inflicted a seemingly endless series of injuries on poor Arnold. But the director comforted him with his patented tough-guy mantra: "Pain passes. The films remain." He also let Arnold know, in his own particular way, that any past contretemps had been forgotten.

"Dino came to the set after four days of shooting. He had seen the dailies and he came up to me on the steps of a big battle scene. 'Eh, Schwartzanegre, come here,' he said. 'You're Conan!' He didn't say, 'You're great!' or 'You look fantastic!' Instead he gave me the biggest compliment by letting me know that I *was* the character. 'Ah!' I thought, 'I think we have just solved our differences.'"

Not only were any differences resolved but the two worked together again on *Conan the Destroyer* and *Raw Deal*. On the latter film, one incident in particular stands out in Schwarzenegger's memory. "We were meeting about the script, and Rafaella said, 'Dino, this is fantastic, but it's going to cost $13 million to make and our budget is only $11 million.' Dino said, 'That's easy. Arnold, watch this.' And he opened the script and grabbed ten pages and ripped them out. 'Now it's worth $11 million.' And that was it. When the film came out, no one ever knew those scenes were missing."

Upon its release in 1982, *Conan the Barbarian* did generate a certain amount of flack for its excessive brutality. Still, it was a huge popular success, raking in $100 million worldwide and propelling the star directly into the upper tier of the action-movie pantheon.

In an affectionate letter published in the anthology *Messages of Love*, Arnold reaffirms that the producer's English is still completely incomprehensible to his ears: "I think you are turning 80, but I never could understand you, so you may have said 40. Either way, happy birthday! Seriously, though, I can never express in words how grateful I am to you for believing in me when no one else did and for trusting my work. . . . As a matter of fact, it was your *Conan* movies that launched my international career. . . . You are a genius in this industry and a wonderful example of how one should live his life. You are demanding and perfectionist in business, but you are kind and loving as a human being. Dino, you have always been like a father-figure to me, and for this alone, I am grateful to know you."

The two years encompassing both *Flash Gordon* and *Conan the Barbarian* had amounted to a heavy dose of fantasy for the producer. At the same time he was facing a more forbidding reality at home: Silvana's deteriorating psychological condition. His wife had never felt comfortable in Los Angeles. She never knew how to adjust to the place, didn't particularly want to, and failed to make any close friends there. All the move had accomplished for her was to add a tremendous sense of isolation to her already formidable quota of anxieties. Paradoxically, the career she once despised might have now lifted her spirits. But her major champions were gone—Pasolini had been beaten to death by a young male prostitute in 1975, and Visconti died the following year—so there were few opportunities for her to appear in front of the cameras.

Dino, suffering, watched her spend day after day, month after month, shut up in her room. Finally he was convinced that, to salvage their relationship, there was no other choice: they needed to move back to New York. There his wife could immerse herself in a more European, more congenial atmosphere. As quick as ever when it came to making decisions, he closed the villa and organized the move. He did, however, leave his Los Angeles office open—with the hope, perhaps, of returning before too long to the capital of the cinema and the epicenter of his frenetic trade.

CHAPTER 29

SOMETHING ENDS

JULY 15, 1981, WAS THE BLACKEST DAY IN DINO'S LIFE. THAT MORNING, Federico De Laurentiis, at age twenty-six, died in an airplane crash not far from Anchorage, Alaska. Dino's beloved son had spent the last three weeks making a documentary about salmon fishing on Bristol Bay. His plane, a Cessna 185 with a camera mounted on one wing, was flying at low altitude over the bay in order to film the fishing fleet at work. The other plane, a Cessna 206 piloted by a fish supplier, had just lifted off the beach and was clearing a rise, maneuvering in such a way that the pilot's line of sight was probably blocked. Despite wild efforts at evasive action, the collision was inevitable.

Federico's Cessna was nearly split in two, and along with the other plane, it plummeted into a mud flat. A witness stated that both pilots were already dead by the time the medics arrived and that the young filmmaker, the only passenger, died a few minutes later without ever regaining consciousness.

The younger De Laurentiis had often clashed with his father. Several years before, an Italian weekly had distorted the boy's words and maliciously entitled an interview with him, "*Mama Is Fabulous, Papa Is Not.*" Federico explained that he had a strong psychological affinity with Silvana. From her he had learned "how to feel, how to think about life." His father, on the other hand, displayed the intransigent toughness of a self-made man, which scared Federico. Yet he never had any doubt that Dino was fundamentally a "decent person."

Given his youth, it's not surprising that Federico's cinematic aspirations remained somewhat uncertain. Still, he brought both curiosity and eagerness to his work. Bruce Bahrenburg describes him in his book on *King Kong*: "Federico is friendly and well-educated, with the manner of somebody who's attended the best foreign schools. He learned English in Europe, and speaks the language clearly and slowly—it's certainly much better than it was when he came to the United States for the first time in the summer of 1974, to work as a lowly production assistant on *Mandingo*. What he learned then he now applies to *King Kong*. He throws himself into getting the sets built, the lights arranged, the costumes sewn, and the cables plugged in." At one point, a storm began to blow in while the shoot was going on, and the young man joined the frantic rush to get things under wraps: "Many members of the crew, who haven't yet gotten to know Federico De Laurentiis, are pleasantly surprised to see the producer's son throwing himself into the toil of physical labor."

Now all that youthful energy had been thwarted by a horrible accident. At six o'clock in the morning, the producer's secretary, Liliana Avincola, called Dino and Silvana at the Beverly Hills Hotel and conveyed the tragic news. The reactions of the two parents were diametrically opposed: he burst into uncontrollable weeping, while she didn't shed a single tear.

At once Raffaella's husband, Gippi, flew to Alaska to recover Federico's body. Then Silvana and Gippi transported the corpse by car from the West Coast to Pawling, New York. The De Laurentiis clan had recently bought a large property in this upstate community, and Dino wanted to bury Federico on the grounds. The rest of the family, however, convinced him to stick with a consecrated plot in the tiny local cemetery.

The young man was laid to rest in a clearing, in the shade of cypress trees, and Silvana would later have two small statues of dogs affixed to the grave. His shattered parents were too devastated to attend the funeral. As Raffaella recalls, "My father went to Federico's grave only once, the day after the funeral. My mother may have gone there too often." Luciano Vincenzoni later wrote, "Quite a few times I accompanied Silvana to that lovely place where they buried him. We would go there with Federico's dogs, whom he loved so much. She would remain seated there for two or three hours at a time, afflicted with unbearable pain. I would wander off, keeping one eye on her and smoking an entire pack of cigarettes."

To escape the siege of reporters, Dino and Silvana took refuge at Casa Luna, their summer house in Santo Domingo. The house was Silvana's favorite. She went there often and treated the place as a special sanctuary, until the property was sold, several years later. In the weeks following the tragedy, Laura Eberspacher, a close school friend of Veronica's, came to Santo Domingo for a visit. "I was a guest at Casa Luna during that sad period," she recalls.

> And I must say that I've never sensed the sort of profound disquiet in the air that I did at the De Laurentiis place. Silvana took long walks alone on the beach, while Dino seemed to be petrified: they were two beings enclosed in the same desperation but completely unable to communicate. I remember the day of Dino's birthday, August 8. Raffaella made him an unusual gift: she had a star, one of the many identified only by numbers and letters, named after Federico De Laurentiis. We were at the table, and for fifteen minutes Dino kept his eyes fixed on his plate, struggling with tears, but it was much worse than if he had cried. We didn't know where to look after a while. For Dino, Federico had been everything: he was his father's projection into the future.

Some newspapers reported that De Laurentiis had decided to abandon the cinema. In Italy, his friend Alberto Sordi told one interviewer, "He had planned for everything, aside from certain kinds of pain. . . . He did everything for the boy; it's a terrible wound." Then, as the weeks went by, a strange dynamic developed. While Dino tried somehow to revive himself, reluctantly making a handful of business calls, Silvana became more and more withdrawn. It was she who was unable to escape her silent desperation. A visiting friend heard Silvana imploring Dino, "Leave me alone with my grief!"

> I've never spoken about these events: this is the first time. But perhaps I need to talk about them. Federico's tragedy was a terrible blow for us. It was a cruel death, the death of an extraordinary, intelligent, handsome boy.
>
> He wanted to be a director, and I kept telling him, "In that case you need to go back to school, to the university. Because a director needs to have a certain background: you've never studied very hard, so you're missing the cultural fundamentals." I tried to explain all of this to him, and bit by bit I was making some headway. But then he

wanted to surprise me—to prove that he was capable of directing this documentary in Alaska. If he had told me what he was going to do, I would have advised him differently. And he lost his life because in order to film the salmon swimming upstream, his airplane made a risky maneuver very close to the water and smashed into pieces on the ground.

He lost his life and wrecked ours too. What I mean is, the relationship between Silvana and me, which had grown more and more difficult despite our return to New York, now became impossible. In theory, these tragedies are supposed to bring about a rapprochement between the father and mother. In our case, it made us more distant, as if I blamed her and she blamed me. We went back to Santo Domingo, we tried to cheer her up, but . . .

Anyway, after two, three, or four months, a producer friend came to visit and tried to convince me to get back to work. I told myself: the only thing I can do is make films again. I had come to understand that the pain from the loss of a child doesn't kill you. Instead it remains forever inside you, in your mind, your heart, your soul.

I don't talk about Federico, I don't want to talk about him, but he's the child who has the biggest presence inside me. Veronica, Raffaella, Francesca: I see them, they're alive, they do things, they're *out there*. He's no longer out there, and he was only a boy. . . .

I was saying that I started working again. That distracted me a little from those unrelenting thoughts. Yet my relationship with Silvana continued to deteriorate. When we returned to our New York apartment, she lived in one room and I lived in another. We almost never spoke. We no longer slept together. And every day I told myself, "I can't keep living this way. The kids are grown up by now, and it's time to make a decision."

During this torment, another piece of agonizing news arrived from Italy: Dino's brother Alfredo had disappeared. On the morning of November 17 he had left his villa at the wheel of his brown Fiat 124, and he hadn't been heard of since. There was some speculation about a kidnapping, and for the next twenty-four hours Dino sat by the phone, waiting to hear if a ransom note had been delivered. Then a municipal worker in charge of highway maintenance spied a wreck in a ditch on Via Cristoforo Colombo. The windshield was shattered, and the car's nose was smashed into the muddy earth. In the driver's seat there was a corpse, which the highway police identified as Alfredo's. There was no abduction. Instead, Alfredo had suffered a heart attack and was perhaps already dead when he careened off the road. Whatever the cause, the death of his younger brother was yet another unexpected blow for Dino and another source of grief.

For De Laurentiis, something changed forever. With the death of his son, Dino was forced to recognize certain inevitable truths. Some roads could no longer be traveled, some obstacles could no longer be surmounted, not even by a will as determined and imperious as his own. He had endured difficult periods, sometimes extremely difficult ones, and had always been willing to dig in and fight back. But there was no way to fight the verdict of fate. There was no way to fight the absolute fact of death, which he had traditionally exorcised by means of ceaseless activity.

Dino tried to make sense of it all. Over and over he told himself that the tragedy of losing a child was the same for everybody. Accustomed as he was to considering himself a special case—to going his own way—he now tried to console himself with the thought that there was an ideal community of parents who had been struck by the same cruel fate. Meanwhile, friends and relatives spurred him on, affectionately urging him to resume his old rhythms. In the end, his exuberant vitality won out over his self-destructive impulses. Dino decided: he would not be consumed by grief; he would attempt to live with it, to grapple with life once more. But throwing himself into his work would not itself be sufficient to draw him up out of the abyss. That would require a kind of miracle—or more specifically, what he now calls "an encounter with an angel."

CHAPTER 30

MARTHA

THE YEAR WAS 1980, AND AT THE DE LAURENTIIS OFFICE IN NEW YORK, preparations are under way for *Ragtime*.

> I always keep my office door open, because one of the basic premises of the cinema is that there are no secrets. It's no use shutting the door. Even if you want to keep something to yourself, two minutes later the whole place knows about it. Anyway, on this particular day, my door was open, and I saw an angel pass by. I was stunned. "Who's that?" After checking around, I discovered that her name was Martha Schumacher and that she worked in the administrative department. I told myself, "I'd better get right on the case with her!" And that was how my relationship with Martha came about.

As usual, Dino gets the essentials but leaves out a great many details. The fact is that a fair amount of time passed between that first apparition outside his office and the eventual blossoming of their romance. But what he means to suggest is something else: that his vision of the willowy Martha dazzled him, that he immediately understood this to be a fateful encounter. It's interesting to compare Dino's version of events with Martha's. According to her, it was he who passed by her office door, not the other way around. In any case, the producer's distinct memory of that wide-open door suggests that he was lowering his guard, making himself available in a new way, which would prove to be unconditional.

Martha was born on July 10, 1954, in Lancaster, Pennsylvania, to a family of Dutch extraction. Her father, Walter, was an agricultural engineer; her mother, Mary, a housewife with a master's degree. When the little girl was five, her father's job took the family to Piqua, Ohio, a town of twenty thousand inhabitants. In that sleepy village in the American heartland, Martha and her two brothers grew up and attended school.

During her senior year of high school, she participated in a beauty pageant in nearby East Liverpool. Like many such pageants, this one was meant to encompass more than physical appearance: the judges also evaluated each candidate's education, behavior, attitudes, and capacity for self-expression. After running this gauntlet, Martha won the local competition, then both the county and state contests, until she reached the nationals in Alabama. At that point she was eliminated. "It was better that way," she says.

> Still, the experience made me realize that there were other realities, more stimulating ones, and that I wanted to know more about them. I had grown up in a small town, with only a single movie theater, which never showed a foreign film. I knew next to nothing. Yet I was confident that one day I would get involved in something worthwhile, and now I had the opportunity: when I won the pageant, the prizes included some modeling classes in a big city. Thanks to that, I ended up signing a contract with an agency in New York. Since my parents wanted me to complete my education, I enrolled in a small college in Indiana, Ball State University, and got a degree in business administration. But every summer, when I was on vacation, I went to New York and worked as a model.
>
> New York is a place that offers you infinite possibilities, so when I finished at Ball State, I moved there. It was 1976; by day I worked as a model, and at night I waited tables in restaurants or nightclubs. I had plenty of work, I made money, had my own apartment, a car, I was independent. But meanwhile one of my fellow waitresses had a day job in the casting department of a TV miniseries, something starring Albert Finney. In November she told me that they were looking for somebody to do bookkeeping. How right my mother had been when she insisted that I learn a trade, something where you had to use your brain!

Martha applied for the job at NBC, got it, and enjoyed it. She had lost interest in modeling: unless one reached the very highest level, it soon became boring. From then on, she worked continuously in the administrative end of the movie business, and in 1980 she joined the *Ragtime* team at the De Laurentiis office.

The production had two bases of operation: one in England, where all the period interiors were being built in a studio, and the other in New York, for the exteriors on the Lower East Side and in New Jersey. The boss trotted back and forth between the two sets, and when he made his intermittent appearances in the New York office, terror spread among the staff.

"Every time Dino arrived," Martha recalls, "panic set in."

> You were in big trouble if you were wearing violet, a color he had forbidden because it brought bad luck. Anyway, I remember the first time I saw him. My office looked out onto the corridor through a glass wall. He passed in front of it, glanced in at me and smiled, passed by once again, glanced in at me and smiled, passed and smiled one last time, then shot into the executive producer's office.
>
> After a little while, the executive producer gave me a call. The chief wanted to see me, which was kind of thrilling. When I stepped in there, he opened his briefcase, took out a packet of instant coffee, and waved it under my nose, saying, "Would you make me a coffee?" He added more precise instructions: "Get a coffee cup, fill it this high with hot water, shake the envelope like this, and pour it in."
>
> "Okay, I'll give it a try." I went back to my office, at which point everybody ran inside to ask me what he wanted. I told them he wanted a cup of coffee: incredible, huh?
>
> Anyway, I made the cup of coffee and brought it to him. He repaid me with a smile and asked, "What's your name?" (Actually, his English made it sound like, "What your name?")
>
> "Martha," I said.
>
> "*Thank you*, Martha."
>
> To this day, when people ask me who Dino is, I tell them, "He's the man who asked me to make him a cup of coffee."
>
> During the production we had very few chances to run into each other. But during the postproduction phase, our offices were quite close together. He came to work early in the morning, and so did I, since it was more peaceful and easier to concentrate then. He

would call me in to check the weekly costs, totals, advance payments, and so forth. First he asked me to prepare a cup of coffee for him (still!): then he asked me to sit down next to him at his enormous desk, and he began to look at the books. "What's this? And what's that?" I would explain what this was and what that was. Maybe he just wanted to keep me close by. In any case, it was no problem for me: I was always so good with numbers.

For some time it went on this way. Then there was the tragedy with his son, and Dino disappeared for several months. When he turned up again in the office, he was always very sad: it was terrible to see somebody so sad. . . . I tried to smile. I fixed him his coffee and made myself as useful as I could. Meanwhile, my project had ended, and he offered me the job of office manager, which I accepted.

One day he summoned me to his beautiful office overlooking Central Park. He had me sit on a little chair in front of him, while he took a seat behind his immense desk. I remember it was sunny, because what he basically said to me was "I'm here because I need you. You're the sunshine of my life." He talked to me about Federico and told me that I was his sole reason for living. I was completely astonished. He had always been *charming*, but he had never flirted with me, not once. I'm talking about a professional sort of charm, an attitude of sympathy, and that's it. Anyway, as thrilled as I may have been, I was then living with another man, so I found myself in a bind.

In fact, Dino also had a dilemma on his hands. In his heart he knew that this was more than a tawdry extramarital adventure. Martha was different: she was intelligent, perceptive, and capable of discussing anything with him, including his work. But for precisely this reason—because the relationship struck him as truly important—Dino held off on making any impulsive decisions. He needed to give Martha as much time as she needed, and certainly he couldn't just leave Silvana on the spot. The deep wound left by Federico's death made this situation particularly delicate. For the first time, our hero was obliged to admit the word *patience* into his vocabulary.

The relationship progressed in secret for nearly two years. Throughout this period, the producer threw himself into a frenzied round of activities and gradually reacquired his appetite for life. At the same time, Martha's presence became indispensable: beside her he felt like a new man, young again, and "different on both the physical and moral plane."

On the professional plane, meanwhile, he just kept rolling forward. When *Ragtime* turned in a disappointing performance at the box office, he just shrugged and kept going. In March 1982 he prepared for the release of *Conan* and put five additional titles into production, including David Cronenberg's *Dead Zone* and an adaptation of Stephen King's *Firestarter*. He also decided to make the latter project into a proving ground for Martha's career as a producer.

> Since I always wanted her beside me, I realized she could no longer work in the administrative department. At the time I had acquired the rights for Stephen King's *Firestarter*, which we were making with Drew Barrymore. The director, Mark Lester, was a newcomer, which meant that I controlled the film one hundred percent. I said to Martha, "I'm going to have you make this film as associate producer."
>
> The fact is that I already had an additional producer on the project, Frank Capra, Jr. So I got Martha together with Frank, and she did fine, learning everything very rapidly. She proved that she had natural gifts. In theory these things can be taught, but if you don't have a certain something inside, you're out of luck.
>
> Let me put it this way: in the cinema, two plus two may equal fifteen, or thirty-six, or zero—anything but four. Certain problems in this business don't follow any normal logic. Instead they have a distinctive logic of their own. When people ask me why I did something a certain way, my most frequent answer is "I don't have any explanation, it just felt right to me." And in ninety percent of the cases, my intuition is correct. It's as if you asked, "Excuse me, Picasso, why did you put that red there?" Picasso couldn't explain his motivation. He simply felt that a strip of red right there would be the best thing for his painting.

Dino wanted to make sure that Martha mastered the entire production process. He resolved to pass along everything he knew and to demonstrate that the cinema required an abundant dose of creativity, even from those in apparently marginal roles. As this tutorial progressed, the two spent long periods of time together at various isolated locations, including one that was to play a large role in their future.

> In *Firestarter* there's a farm where the FBI agents hide out, and we were searching for a real location. One day I was with Martha at a newsstand, and on the cover of a magazine, I saw a cottage identical to the one I had imagined. "This is just what we need for the film!" I said. "Where is it?" It turned out to be in Wilmington, North Carolina, near the Cape Fear River. The next day we went down there, and I was right, the place was perfect. However, we needed a studio to construct the other sets. And there wasn't one: there was nothing, it was just a tiny coastal town. So I leased a big warehouse, and we built the additional sets in there.

Along with being the right environment for shooting *Firestarter*, Wilmington, with a long white beach on the Atlantic, turned out to be the ideal spot for an anticipatory honeymoon. Dino, who had been born a stone's throw from the sea, got an extra jolt of energy from the place, and Martha was equally attached to nature and the open air. The two spent as much time as possible in their rented house overlooking the water. "For us Wilmington remained a special place. That's why I built a cottage right next to the water, on that extraordinary white beach. We spent some wonderful vacations there, along with the children. I still own the property, but unfortunately we don't get down there very often."

In that tranquil setting, as their own relationship deepened, Dino discovered a side of himself that he had hardly known. Thanks to Martha's presence, he was rejuvenated. He felt ready to begin again, and at the same time he acquired a certain calm, a serenity never granted to him by his problematic marriage with Silvana. As Martha recalls, "He would tell me stories about his experiences, which I had heard him do many times, but with these stories he won my heart. He said to me, 'Not even my children know me this well.' He made it clear that he had never had a relationship in which he felt so at ease. It should be pointed out, of course, that the circumstances of our relationship were very different: earlier in his life, he had been absorbed in building his empire, and Silvana was a movie star. But by the time I came onto the scene, the situation had changed. He was much more available and much more relaxed with me."

A relaxed Dino, however, was hardly a sluggish Dino:

> In 1983, right after I finished shooting *Firestarter*, I had a visit from James Hunt, the governor of North Carolina. He thanked me for having brought new jobs and new economic activities to his state and asked if I had any intention of making other films in Wilmington. "I was just thinking about that," I told him. "If you give me a little hand, I just might buy this warehouse we've been renting and transform it into a movie studio." With the governor's encouragement, I acquired the warehouse complex and some adjacent land. I built the studio bit by bit, and gradually we began to shoot other films there.

By March 1984 the North Carolina Film Corporation (NCFC), a subsidiary company with Martha Schumacher as its president, was already in operation, with three studios ranging from 1,400 to 2,500 square meters. Over the course of the year the producer purchased adjacent land, doubling the area of the property from sixteen to thirty-two acres. With an anticipated investment of $10 million he pushed the work forward, constructing new buildings. When he was done, the imposing complex included five studios of various sizes, along with three wings devoted to production offices, dressing rooms, makeup, design shops, warehouses for costumes, carpentry, scenery, editing rooms, projection rooms for the dailies, postproduction facilities, and special effects.

Dino didn't receive a single dollar from North Carolina to build the facility. He was, however, supported with fiscal incentives and low-interest loans, courtesy of the governor, and indeed, the rise of NCFC had a real impact on the state's economy. As for De Laurentiis, he clearly hoped to lure as many filmmakers as possible down to his cinematic Promised Land. According to a brochure published by the studio, the inhabitants of Wilmington were more than ready to meet the needs of any production that set up shop in the community. The airport, five minutes away by car, offered easy connections with daily flights to New York, along with biweekly nonstop flights to Los Angeles. Finally, there was an exquisite variety of landscapes available for exteriors, from the picturesque beaches to the nearby mountains clad in forests of red spruce.

To Dino it seemed that he had returned to the old days in Rome, when he founded one studio after another, in an escalating series that took him from the Teatri della Farnesina to Vasca Navale and ultimately to Dinocittà. Now, ten years after having crossed the ocean to America—and in the euphoria of a new love—he sensed that he was leaving a black period behind him.

CHAPTER 31

DDL FOODSHOW

BETWEEN THE DISCOVERY OF WILMINGTON AND THE FOUNDING OF HIS North Carolina studio, Dino had plenty to occupy his time. Yet in 1982 the producer decided to launch yet another grandiose initiative: the DDL Foodshow. Inspired by such models as Peck in Milan and Fauchon in Paris, De Laurentiis planned to bring high-end gastronomy to the United States. Why was an Italian mogul investing so much cash in order to satisfy his culinary passions? In interview after interview, he explained that he wanted to prompt a reevaluation of Italian cooking, particularly given the onslaught of the French nouvelle cuisine, which he considered infinitely less tasty and less healthy. In his opinion, Americans were "a great people, but they eat garbage." It was time for things to change.

Conceived as a takeout place, the Foodshow would sell delicious cooked dishes and high-priced groceries, mostly but not exclusively Italian. Dino announced his goal to journalists: "Whatever I do, I want it to be something special. This will be a unique place. . . . I've been thinking about this project since 1975 and had hoped that my son-in-law [Alex, Veronica's husband] would dedicate himself to it. Seeing that he didn't want to get involved, I'm doing it myself."

After the events of the past year, he seemed his old self again: efficient, crisp, with one eye on his watch as he pushed and prodded the conversation. It was noted, though, that he spoke extraordinarily fast in his accented English, that his hands never stayed still, and that he smoked continuously.

For the first DDL Foodshow, Dino chose a location on Manhattan's Upper West Side: the entire ground floor of the former Endicott Hotel, an art nouveau building just recently converted to condominiums. The location was a canny choice. After a long period of decay the neighborhood was beginning to revive, thanks to the appearance of new restaurants, bars, and watering holes for the younger set, and the Foodshow seemed destined to become the biggest draw of them all. On November 24, 1982, the inaugural store opened for business. An excited crowd gathered at the corner of Columbus Avenue and Eighty-first Street before a barrage of television cameras and microphones. Impeccable in a tailored pinstriped suit, Dino received his guests and introduced them to his kingdom of delights: an immense alimentary emporium of almost four thousand square meters.

The design of the place had been entrusted to Adam Tihany, an Israeli architect trained in Milan, who knew how to evoke an Italian atmosphere with classy restraint. He installed a floor of blue and russet terracotta tiles, display cases framed in resplendent oak, brilliant brass finishes, and Roman-style colonnades that were lit in a cinematic style by hundreds of spotlights. Where the hotel's Palm Court used to stand, Tihany created a vaulted ceiling out of glass. Yet the overall atmosphere remained warm, thanks to a profusion of green plants in terracotta vases and the colorful arrays of food.

The labyrinthine interior was divided into sectors. There was a cheese department with 150 varieties, a lavishly stocked *salumeria*, and racks of jarred or boxed delicacies from every corner of Europe: caviar to peppers *sott'olio*, mustard to *passato di pomodoro* to pasta with the DDL label on it. There were counters loaded with extra-virgin olive oil, chocolate, and various teas and coffees. In the prepared foods area, customers had their choice of 70 types of pasta, 150 different salads, and a rich assortment of hot and cold dishes: *involtini di melanzane*, smoked capon, lasagna *al pesto*, lobster thermidor, marinated zucchini, cannelloni with chicken and radicchio, duck à l'orange, and many, many more.

In one corner there was a bakery with twenty-five types of bread, and in another there was an inviting pastry shop: both were outfitted with an oven and a squad of six cooks. The kitchens, staffed by more than twenty chefs, were visible to the customers through an enormous glass wall, which made them something of a tourist attraction. As Dino put it, "In this enterprise too, I'm following my calling as a showman. The Americans love a spectacle, so I'm giving them one." Asked how an epicure like himself was able to retain so perfect a physique, he replied, "I'm going to reveal a secret to you. All truly talented cooks eat very little, and I'm an excellent cook. I make food for the joy it brings my friends."

In advance of the opening, Dino had fielded many offers from aspiring partners and declined them all. "When this initiative is successful," he told the press, "as I hope it will be, I'll list the DDL Foodshow on the stock exchange. Then I'll hang on to 30 percent of the shares and offer the remaining 70 percent to the public." Along with the Foodshow he set up two additional companies, DDL Food Imports and DDL Wine Imports. Taking into account the entire conglomerate, Dino estimated that the annual revenues would reach around $15 million. And if things went well, the idea was to keep expanding. Eventually De Laurentiis hoped to create a chain of locations scattered all across America, with a total turnover of $200 million each year. To that end, he explored the idea of a joint venture with Veggetti and Forni Polin, two of Italy's foremost suppliers of bread and pastries. However, these projects would never get off the drawing board.

Customers made their pilgrimages to the New York Foodshow as if they were visiting a house of marvels. To those astounded by the level of luxury, Dino replied, "Why shouldn't food be presented in the most advantageous manner, in beautiful settings like those at Cartier or Bulgari? The people buying the food should realize that it's made with love, tenderness, and creativity." De Laurentiis insisted that his establishment catered to every budget, from the ambassador's to the taxi driver's. But that opinion was not widely shared: perhaps America's fast-food culture was simply too entrenched.

> I lost nearly $20 million on the Foodshow, because it was too far ahead of its time. People came inside, gazed at the delicacies in their display cases as though they were looking at jewelry, and fled in terror at the idea of spending so much money. It was a question of price—along with the fact that even in the 1980s, when I opened these stores, Italian cooking hadn't yet become so popular.
>
> There was another, even bigger problem: we launched the business without a capable manager. We had enormous general expenses, and our receipts weren't even covering our costs. Originally I was supposed to get some help from Alfredo Beltrame, owner of

the Tulà chain. He was a very dear friend of mine, who had done a superb job organizing the hotel restaurant in Bora Bora. He was going to manage these stores too, but we had slightly different ideas about how to do it, and then, sadly enough, he died. That meant I was left without any kind of operations department. I turned to Peck, and the people there promised me a capable manager, but instead they sent one who couldn't even speak English.

Oh yes, there was a shortage of management. I had nobody who was capable of taking the situation in hand. There was a person overseeing the administrative department, but he wasn't the type to say, "The duck *a l'orange* isn't going to work, because it's too expensive to prepare and we're not selling enough of it." We needed somebody to produce an analysis of every single dish, figuring out costs and proceeds.

Let's face it: in this kind of establishment, you have to keep an eye on business from the moment you open to the moment you close. Why? Because in the food business, the margins are three or four percent, no more. The only way to realize a solid profit is to hang in there and build a franchise: that is, you create a brand name, and then take a percentage from many, many different locations.

I did what I could. I got there at 6 A.M. and theoretically opened the store. But then I had to run, because I was still a producer: the films were expensive and I couldn't just ignore them. At a certain point, I was forced to decide: "What am I doing? Am I leaving the film business?" And the answer, obviously, was no.

Despite the difficulties that immediately appeared on the horizon, the second DDL Foodshow opened as planned in the spring of 1983. This one was installed on the garden level of the Trump Tower on Fifth Avenue, surrounded by other stores catering to the rich and famous. In this "fantastic land of cut crystal, emeralds, and cashmere," Tihany's luxurious space, which echoed the design of the Columbus Avenue branch, should have found its ideal clientele. Dino also fiddled with his formula by including a bona fide restaurant and bar on the premises, both of which got off to an excellent start. Still, they weren't enough to push the operation into the black, so the Los Angeles Foodshow, which opened on January 2, 1984, was destined to be the last.

Located on North Beverly Drive, this third DDL was also designed by Tihany. Like its predecessors, it featured an immense gourmet food department full of delicacies, which faced out onto a veranda restaurant and bar. The exposed red brick of the walls and the wooden roof conferred a slightly folkloric feeling on the place.

As usual, the opening aroused plenty of interest from the media: Rolls-Royces and Mercedes sedans jammed the parking lot, while the city police struggled to control the enormous influx of traffic out front. Flanked by Raffaella and Veronica, Dino stood at the door to receive his guests, who made up the entire beau monde of Hollywood. The manager, Jim Leahy, explained to the assembled masses that some of the dishes had been modified to suit the Californian palate: for example, the salads were much lighter than the ones served in New York. Meanwhile one patron assured the proud proprietor, "Finally you are civilizing Los Angeles." And when ten chefs entered the room carrying a baking sheet with fifteen square meters of pizza margherita, the crowd roared.

Dino spoke optimistically about his latest venture. But for the moment, he added, he would not be opening any further branches, because he needed expert staff and couldn't seem to find them. One newspaper commented, "Admission to the store is free, but to take home any of De Laurentiis's gastronomical offerings requires an enormous sum." Another critic predicted a limited engagement: "The high production values of this extravaganza will assure an excellent first week of receipts, but they won't be sufficient to assure a good box-office over the long run." Nonplussed, Dino continued to make a weekly appearance at the L.A. branch. He may well have been the only person to taste everything on display in his "hyperbolic Italian grocery store."

In January 1985 the Beverly Foodshow announced that it would be "remodeling" and closed its doors for three weeks. When the branch reopened, everything was much more compact and manageable: Dino compared it to "a three-and-a-half-hour film edited down to ninety minutes." The restaurant and bar were now the focal points. The shelves loaded with gourmet merchandise were largely gone, although the loss made the atmosphere less cheerful, and the prices were lower, but at the expense of quality.

> In Los Angeles, and especially in New York, there are double-decker buses that take the tourists all over town. And one of the

> places where they took them was my stores: they thronged inside by the hundreds, admired everything, and bought nothing. It was a tourist attraction! Each time we opened a new branch, the television news shows went crazy all across America.
>
> My other major mistake was not taking on any partners at the start. If I had done that—20 percent here, 10 percent there—we would still be open and would be a big success. But I was alone. And by the time I decided to seek partners, we were already in the red, and nobody wants to join a business in the red.
>
> A final, unfortunate problem: I don't have much patience. If I see that something isn't working, I prefer to cut my losses and move on. It's not like me to hang in there, hang in there, until everything is used up. No. I tell myself, "Something is wrong." I try to understand what the problem is. And in this case, it was the lack of management. It was like making a film without a director. Just try to imagine a place like Harrod's without a brilliant manager. It would go out of business in twenty-four hours, there's no doubt about it.

Within the span of two or three years, Dino closed all the Foodshow locations. Certainly the debacle stung him, not least financially. But throwing himself headlong into the business had helped him to forget the tragedies of the recent past. At the same time, it satisfied his ineffable nostalgia for Italy, which had grown more powerful in the wake of the tragedy, taking him by surprise. It's as if the trauma had created a kind of fracture, through which his most distant memories emerged.

In truth, De Laurentiis had never severed his connections to his native country. He had remained in close contact with his sisters, brothers, and nephews, and there was a constant stream of relatives and acquaintances visiting his house. In addition, he still had a secretary in Rome—the indispensable Elvira La Mastra—who kept him up to speed on developments in Italy.

On the other hand, he never forgot a comment made by his old colleague Aldo Tonti. When the cameraman first learned of Dino's move to America, he predicted that this departure would signify the end of their friendship. Of course Dino protested at the time. But Tonti was right, and the producer knew it. Given the freewheeling and frenetic quality of his life, he would always choose his friends from among his current collaborators. His older friendships were bound to suffer, and was that truly a surprise? After all, he hadn't even managed to spend much time with his children while they were growing up: now he wished that he had. Perhaps something similar could be said of his relationship with Silvana. Perhaps they would have been able to understand each other better if . . .

But these were thoughts to be suppressed at any cost: under the present circumstances, they were intolerable. He couldn't return to the past. All he could do was go forward, as he had always done.

At the same time, the failed Foodshow represented something different: a regenerative attempt at immersion in his past. With his mother, Giuseppina, in mind, Dino opened an alimentary emporium, a deluxe version of the family business that she had so expertly overseen in the sun-drenched Torre Annunziata of his childhood. With his father Aurelio in mind, he stamped the name *De Laurentiis* on a pasta package for the first time in nearly half a century. His ovens resurrected the ancient aromas of the bread his grandmother bought at Pallonetto. And many of the savory dishes on display at the Foodshow were based on recipes handed down from his mother, an exquisite cook who had taught him how to appreciate food—and in a sense, how to live.

His excursion into the culinary business allowed Dino one additional recuperation of his past. Through the Foodshow he met a young chef, born about seven miles from Torre Annunziata. Luigi Ferraioli was the same age his son would have been, and he cooked "almost" like Dino's mother. When the Foodshow closed, the producer welcomed Gigi into his new household: here was at least one little piece of Italy that De Laurentiis was determined to hang on to!

CHAPTER 32

LOST IN THE STARS

WHEN DE LAURENTIIS ASKED DAVID LYNCH TO DIRECT *DUNE* IN 1983, HE was sixty-four years old, and his new employee was thirty-seven; the two were separated by more than a quarter-century. In addition, Lynch was a distinctly avant-garde artist, the creator of such eccentric films as *Eraserhead* (which Dino hated) and *The Elephant Man* (which Dino loved). The director embodied a conception of the cinema that would seem to be completely alien to the man who had produced *The Bible*. Yet none of this prevented the two from establishing an excellent collaborative relationship.

In a collection of interviews entitled *Lynch on Lynch*, the director recalls that Dino telephoned him and proposed that he make *Dune*. Not being much of a science-fiction fan, Lynch had never read the original novel. What made him curious, however, was the fact that Dino wanted to create a science-fiction film based on character rather than ray guns and spaceships. Lynch adds, "Dino was very different from how I expected—charming, warm, and very persuasive. We discussed the concept, and I was convinced the novel could be adapted to film."

> I got in touch with Lynch after my failed attempt to get Ridley Scott to direct *Dune*. It wasn't easy acquiring the rights to the novel—there were both legal and copyright problems to surmount—and it seemed like an obvious choice for the guy who had just made *Blade Runner*. I met with him in London, and he was quite interested. However, he insisted that I bring on board a co-producer whom (rightly or wrongly) I didn't trust, so that was the end of that idea.

> On the other hand, I trusted David Lynch immediately, thanks to that wholesome face of his. He looks like a clean-cut American boy, with more than a touch of Jimmy Stewart.

He sounds the part as well. "There is no mind darker than the mind of David Lynch, but it's deceptive because his speech is punctuated with 'Gosh,' 'Gee whiz!' 'Whoopie!' 'Neat!'" says Larry Gleason, DEG's head of domestic distribution. "He sounds like this innocent midwestern guy, but inside his head is darkness amplified. He's an excellent artist. He dissects animals and people in pen and ink, then lays them out on an autopsy table. And he collects really weird things. Raffaella once had a hysterectomy; David has her uterus in a jar on a shelf."

Originally published in 1965, *Dune* is Frank Herbert's best-known novel. Herbert followed it up with several more books on the same theme: the destruction of the environment in a world lost in the stars. The story is set in the twelfth millennium, on the desert planet of Arakis, where a decaying empire and a courageous tribe of nomads mount a bitter struggle for supremacy. The hallucinatory inhabitants of the planet include a race of giant worms, who also happen to be the bearers of a priceless, mind-expanding drug.

> Given the complexity of the interlaced narratives and the cultural implications, I realized that even a pared-down version of the novel was going to be a tremendous enterprise. Lynch soon delivered a vast screenplay. It gave an excellent sense of the book's political and psychological twists and turns, not to mention its intermittently freakish quality. But perhaps it conveyed all that stuff too well. It was a fascinating script, I mean, but it was also full of deformities and unpleasant details.

"Dino was my editor," the director recounts in *Lynch on Lynch*. "He helped to shape the script." After much labor, the two managed to shave the screenplay down to 135 pages. Then the producer gave Lynch a small lesson in visual style: "At one point Dino and I went for a trip into Venice. He took me into Saint Mark's Square, but by a certain route and at a particular point. . . . I got the idea then that Venice would be a big influence for *Dune*. I talked to our designer, Tony Masters, and things developed from there."

During this period, the costs of shooting a movie in Hollywood were skyrocketing. No wonder Mexico seemed destined to become a cinematic mecca: the Churubusco studios in Mexico City offered excellent facilities and qualified workers at affordable prices. Along with Raffaella, to whom he'd entrusted the complete responsibility for *Dune*, Dino decided to move the production south. Not only were the prices right, but there were excellent desert locations available within just a few miles of the capital.

Although he had never shot any films on such a large scale, Lynch did an expert job directing the actors and managing the ubiquitous special effects. He would later speak of the entire sojourn with real enthusiasm: "We had a great time in Mexico City, and there were so many people coming in all the time, new people from all over the world, flying in and being part of this thing." According to Raffaella, her relationship with Lynch was "like a marriage of three or four years, with a quarrel every three or four months." Meanwhile, the fact that Richard Fleischer's *Conan* sequel was being shot at the same time as *Dune* led to fits of jealousy from both directors. As Raffaella puts it, "If I told David that I was going to be busy with Fleischer for a little while, he turned purple."

As Dino recalls,

> The first rough cut of *Dune*, without special effects or transitional passages, was about three and a half hours. The management at Universal got worried about distributing a science-fiction film that ran as long as *The Ten Commandments*. If a film is long, that means fewer showings per day at each theater, which means a reduction in the box office.
>
> In short, they asked me to eliminate one hour of footage. As usual, I had full control of the final cut, and I could have refused. But given the amount of money Universal had pumped into the project—$30 million, which was no joke at the time—I felt morally obliged to snip away. It was a big mistake, because everybody could sense that the film was missing something.

Not surprisingly, Lynch was unhappy about the cuts. "If you don't have final cut, not a day goes by that you're not into it with Dino. It was a nightmare for me. I died a death on *Dune*."

Yet he understood the situation: "I've got to say another thing: I love Dino and I love Raffaella and I loved working with them. We were like a family. I just know the way they are, and they know the way I am. We loved each other in spite of everything that happened."

Dune, which was eagerly awaited as *the* media event of Christmas 1984, flamed out at the box office. This was an inexplicable outcome, especially given the lavish press coverage. *Life* magazine, for example, devoted a splashy feature entirely to Raffaella. Some critics had even predicted that *Dune* was about to change the face of the cinema—that instead of serving up the usual celluloid pap, it would offer a worldwide audience a myth of great intellectual and cognitive depth. Everybody assumed that the movie would break all box-office records. Certainly the producer thought so: despite his customary aversion to sequels, he planned to make two more chapters at a rapid clip, optioning the actors and asking Lynch to write the new screenplays.

> Despite what everybody says, it's not completely true that the film was a flop. It wasn't a triumph, there's no doubt about that. But the original investment was largely recouped due to excellent worldwide distribution. And for David, anyway, *Dune* represented a launching pad for the next phase of his career, which began with another of our collaborations: *Blue Velvet*.

Lynch recalls, "After *Dune* Dino asked me if I had any ideas or anything I wanted to do. I said I wanted to do *Blue Velvet*. And he asked me if I owned it and I said yes. I didn't know it at the time, but I didn't own it. When Dino found out, he grabbed the phone, called the head of Warner Bros. and in about three minutes bought back *Blue Velvet* from the studio. And that's how it started. Then he said if I halved my salary and the budget, I'd get final cut. It was a beautiful experience."

Released in 1986 under the De Laurentiis Entertainment Group, or DEG banner, *Blue Velvet* found the director toying with all the morbid seductions of American noir but in a more explicit key. Creating his own distinct universe of alarming images and flattened emotions, Lynch assembled the movie with sneaky brilliance. Dino, working side by side with an avant-garde director, appeared to be enjoying a new lease on life. Some claimed to recognize the producer's thumbprints on the happy ending, a suspicion Larry Gleason confirms. "The first two cuts were a little too extreme for the audience. I was at a test screening sitting in the audience with a French distributor, and he turned to me and said, 'You have to stop Dino from making movies like this with crazy filmmakers.'"

Dino went into the editing room and made a few changes with David, and in the end the film won critical raves, though it was a box-office disappointment. It cemented Lynch's reputation as one of America's most promising young directors, and while Dino and Lynch continued to talk about other collaborations, they could never find the right one. Larry Gleason recalls one failed effort:

"After *Blue Velvet* David wanted to make this movie about a three-foot-tall musician who lives in a dark Liverpudlian city and who turns out to be the world's greatest rock guitarist. He runs on electricity. It was amazingly, spectacularly weird. Lynch is arguing with Dino about making it and Dino says, 'You just had success, David. It's time to make a big movie. I know you have a $100 million movie inside you. I just hope I'm not broke before I can get it out of your head.'"

In the meantime, Dino was about to become an American citizen at last. In light of his crowded schedule, he received VIP treatment from the Immigration and Naturalization Service. He would not be obliged to join the party at the Universal Amphitheater on September 16, when six thousand foreign-born citizens would be sworn in at once. Instead, a brief private ceremony took place two days later at the Federal Courthouse.

After taking the oath, Dino was congratulated by District Court Judge Mariana Pfaelzer. Outside, on the steps of the building, the new American citizen posed for the photographers, waving a small version of the Stars and Stripes in one hand and smiling. Visibly moved, he declared, "Getting a passport was purely a formality. I felt like an American from the day I arrived here."

CHAPTER 33

GOOD-BYE, SILVANA

In the wake of Federico's death, Dino slowly got back on his feet, and with the aid of love and work, he managed to right himself again. Silvana did not. Although at first she seemed the stronger of the two, she soon sank into a bottomless abyss of grief. She had never been happy, but this was different. Now she lost interest in everything: walled up inside herself, she let life slip away. When she wasn't making a pilgrimage to the cemetery in Pawling, she holed up at home in New York, smoking and embroidering. At other times she took refuge in the tranquility of Casa Luna: when a beautiful, vivid butterfly once entered the room and perched beside her, she was sure that Federico had come to pay a visit.

Gravely concerned, Dino observed Silvana becoming ever more pale and gaunt and felt her withdrawing further and further. As often happens, the tragedy was now finishing off a relationship that had been in a state of crisis for a long time. According to numerous witnesses, Dino had remained deeply in love with his wife through one trial after another. Yet he had never quite understood Silvana's feelings toward him.

> Although Silvana's attitude toward me was sometimes scornful, I sensed that deep inside, she did feel esteem and respect for me. But not love. At least not love as I understand it, not the sort of love I felt for her. She was never interested in my problems; she never showed me any affection or gratitude. As far as I recall, I heard her say "I love you" only once. That was when her mother died in Monte Carlo.

> We were already living in America at the time. Silvana and her sisters were too devastated to go, so that left me. I flew there immediately and took care of the funeral and everything else. Me of all people: I avoid those sorts of ritual like the plague! Anyway, Silvana had begged me to find a beautiful, sunny spot for her mother's grave. I called her from Monte Carlo to let her know that everything was arranged. And it was then—for the first and only time in thirty-five years of marriage—that Silvana, weeping, said to me, "Dino, I love you."

In the end it's impossible for an outsider to truly understand the delicate equilibrium of a relationship. Yet the question remains: over the years, what caused the destructive elements in the De Laurentiis marriage to prevail at last over the positive ones? Perhaps the actress took on the duties of wife and mother too young, before she really understood what she wanted from life. Perhaps she aspired to a kind of freedom that the gilded cage of matrimony prevented her from attaining. Or perhaps she wanted precisely what Dino offered her—love, admiration, protection, children, affluence—but without knowing it. In any case, a barrier gradually came to separate the spouses. And with their son's death, it became an insurmountable wall.

Silvana no longer communicated with Dino. It was as if she held him responsible for her grief, or on the contrary, as if she were afraid of resuscitating his own grief by her very presence. For his part, Dino was no longer able to tolerate his wife's hostile behavior, especially now that he had gotten involved with Martha.

This new relationship kept progressing. In October 1983, while they were in Rome, Dino gave the younger woman an engagement ring and arranged a kind of private wedding ceremony in their room at the Grand Hotel. Martha recalls, "He wanted to let me know that he was very secure in his feelings, that he intended to spend the rest of his life with me. Personally, I consider *that* the real date of our marriage. That's what I've told our children too, since they're very curious about the whole story."

Dino realized that the time had come to make a decision: his relationship with Martha was essential. Without her, his life would be empty. Federico was gone, Veronica, Raffaella, and Francesca were grown up, and his relationship with Silvana was over. Still, he wasn't sure how to make a definitive break after so many years.

> When Raffaella was producing *Dune*, she thought of offering a part to her mother, in order to distract her, to pull her out of her depression. "You talk to her," I said. "If I ask her, the answer will be no. Maybe she'll do it for you." And in fact Raffaella managed to convince her. And since Silvana always did a very professional job when she was working, she made the best of the opportunity: she was precise, punctual, never threw any tantrums, and never behaved like a diva.

Absent from the set since 1974, when she had made *Conversation Piece* with Visconti, Mangano had long since thought of her career as over. If she accepted the relatively marginal role of the Reverend Mother in *Dune*, it was only to avoid disappointing Raffaella. As always, though, she accepted without complaint the physical discomforts associated with the role—which included getting her head shaved, just as she had earlier for *Five Branded Women*.

Dino remembers how he reached a crisis:

> The film was shot in Mexico, and since it was a very costly, difficult production, I went down there twice a week to look at the dailies. Raffaella had rented a large villa for the duration. Silvana had her room, and I had mine. I would show up, she would stay in her part of the house, and I would stay in mine: she ignored me completely. This happened once, twice, then three or five or seven times, and finally I decided that I was through. I had been chained to her, and profoundly in love with her, for thirty years. In Mexico the whole thing finally fell apart. I said to myself, "I can't go on this way. But I can't leave her while she's still working on the set."
>
> Once the shoot was over, Silvana wanted to fly back to New York on a private plane, and I sent one for her. She returned home and greeted me like a complete stranger. That very evening I told her in no uncertain terms, "Silvana, we can't keep ignoring the situation. I'm leaving."
>
> She had no reaction. I threw a few things in a bag, went to a nearby hotel, and never came back. Knowing her as I did, though, I was aware that she would fall into a dangerous depression. So the next day I took a plane to Los Angeles: that's where Raffaella and Veronica were living, and I didn't want to give them this kind of news over the telephone.
>
> I explained the whole thing to them: "Girls, I'm in love with another woman." They told me, "Papa, we're happy for you." They

also realized that things couldn't go on the way they had been. I continued, "I've never asked you for anything. But this time, if you love me, you'll do me a favor. Call up your mother, leave this very day, and spend some time with her in New York. There's no doubt she's going to have a breakdown."

I was certain of this, because during our life together I had seen her fall into more than one severe depression and overdose on pills. We were living at Villa Catena then, and it became my duty to load her into the car and drive as fast as I could to the hospital.

Raffaella and Veronica had long since guessed that their father was in love with Martha, and they reassured him: she was an extraordinary woman, he couldn't have chosen better. The sisters departed at once for New York, and their shattered mother greeted them with a surprising confession: "I've loved that man my entire life."

After Silvana and I broke up, I continued to stay in regular touch via the telephone. I asked her if she needed anything, I tried to help her, I tried to remain her friend, but at a certain point she asked me not to call anymore, and our break became definitive. During one of our last conversations, I said, "What can I do for you?" And she replied, "You can't do a thing anymore, you're in love with somebody else. . . . It was bound to happen, I made so many mistakes, I never really understood you."

Dino wanted an immediate divorce, but once Silvana grasped the depth of his relationship with Martha, she was hurt and decided to complicate things. This resistance in turn stirred up ancient resentments on the producer's part. As he dug in his heels, the negotiations dragged out, and the girls were caught in the middle, with the thankless task of mediating. Martha, meanwhile, was coping with some challenges of her own. As she points out,

It can be tough to join a family with such a different language and culture, and on top of that, I had a sense of inferiority, because I felt that I was being tagged in that clichéd fashion as the young, dependent woman who marries the powerful older man. I needed to prove myself somehow, to be deserving. . . . Still, the girls were extraordinary. Even though their mother, for understandable reasons, had insisted that they not associate with me, they came to see me out of love for their father. It must have been a very challenging period for them.

Soon word of the separation reached Italy. Luigi De Laurentiis had always enjoyed excellent relations with his sister-in-law and loved her very much. Now his wife, Maria, pressured him to intervene with his brother. But he declined, knowing it would be useless: if Dino had made this decision, he must have had good reasons, and he would not change his mind.

Silvana, meanwhile, discovered that she was gravely ill. Many of her friends believed that in some sense she chose to die at the very moment she learned of her son's death. Silvia d'Amico, who often accompanied her to the radiologist, remembers Mangano knitting intently in the waiting room, cloaked in a singular serenity. In any case, the effects of her illness soon became visible, and the Italian cinema's most reserved star became even more withdrawn, spending the long, solitary hours with her books and her stitching.

At the urging of her friend Suso Cecchi d'Amico, the diva left America for Madrid, where Francesca was then living. Suso and her daughter Silvia took Silvana under their wing, and Silvana made frequent trips to Paris and especially to Rome. There she visited her oldest and most beloved friends: Monicelli, Sordi, and her in-laws Luigi and Lina De Laurentiis. The latter, by a terrible stroke of fate, had experienced an identical tragedy—the death of her son, who was a cousin and friend of Federico's—and the two women found great comfort in their time together.

Ever more emaciated, Silvana still possessed a charismatic and ethereal beauty. It's visible in her very last appearance on the screen, in Nikita Michalkov's *Dark Eyes*. At this point, of course, she was hardly looking for work. But her young friend Silvia was producing the film, and at her insistence, Silvana agreed to one last role, which finally paired her with Marcello Mastroianni.

At first her old flame seemed a bit hostile. Perhaps he still harbored some resentment toward Silvana for abruptly breaking off their youthful romance. But then Silvia, ignoring Silvana's protests, dragged her along to the opening night of the play *Tchin-Tchin*, which featured Mastroianni in a French-speaking role. In his dressing room after the play, the actor saw how fragile and exhausted Silvana looked.

Moved, he slipped his arm around her shoulders and began talking to her as if the conversation had never stopped, all those decades ago.

During these last, painful years, Dino and Silvana were occasionally in touch over details of the divorce. However, their paths almost never crossed.

> When Silvana was already ravaged by cancer and was living with Raffaella in Los Angeles, I went to see her every now and then. But at a certain point I stopped: to see her in that state was too difficult for me. Then she moved to Spain, to a beautiful house I lined up for her. I thought of everything, I did whatever I could right up until the end. But I didn't go to Silvana's funeral.
>
> We all have our peculiarities. Every human being has his own nature, his own limits. When my father died, I was at his side during the last week of his life. Then, while I was at the funeral, I told myself, "This is the last time. I can't go to the funerals of the people I love, because otherwise I'll have a heart attack and I'll die as well." In fact I didn't even go to Federico's funeral—and you could never say that I didn't love my son. I didn't go to the funeral of the woman I loved most in the world, who was my mother. To tell you the truth, perhaps I would have gone to Silvana's. But I didn't want to create embarrassment for our children, who knew that our relationship had been finished for a long, long time.

The divorce became final in August 1989. On December 16 of that same year, in Madrid, Silvana died following an operation. Her corpse was cremated in the presence of her daughters. Then her ashes were transported to Pawling, where she was buried beside her son.

De Laurentiis spent that holiday season with Martha on the Côte d'Azur. The loss of the woman he had loved so passionately had a deep impact on him, yet that relationship—which had been nerve-wracking and terrible for years before collapsing entirely—was now behind him. It was a completed chapter of his life, the memory of which he scrupulously kept to himself. He was wise not to revisit it too often: why stir things up? Dino, after all, had been reborn in the warmth of a new love. Martha reciprocated his feelings in a way that Silvana had never been able to, and that's what mattered now.

As for the diva's ambiguous and incomprehensible attitude toward her husband, there are two last bits of testimony. After the separation,

Suso d'Amico would often hear Mangano talk about Dino with great admiration. Finally, she couldn't restrain her curiosity: "But why did you behave with him the way you did?" Silvana replied, "But that was all a joke." Silvia d'Amico reports another discovery. In the purse that Mangano always brought to her radiation therapy, the younger woman found, carefully conserved in a jewel box where the actress used to keep her needle and thread, several of the ancient and amorous notes with which Dino had accompanied his gifts to her.

CHAPTER 34

WILMINGTON, NORTH CAROLINA

By early 1985 the Wilmington complex, which started out as a modest prefabricated warehouse, had become a fully functional studio. Once again Dino was taking a big risk: he was competing with Hollywood, and doing so from the most unlikely state in the union. What's more, his strategy seemed to be working.

For the Wilmington studio, *The Year of the Dragon* was a trial by fire. For a long time I had wanted to make a gangster movie about the infamous Chinese Mafia. Then this novel by Robert Daley crossed my desk. It was nothing special, the book, but it contained a valid idea: the clash between a policeman and an emerging heroin dealer who had moved from Hong Kong to the USA. There had already been several attempts to extract a screenplay from the novel. However, even a seasoned professional like Richard Brooks came up with nothing, as had another excellent writer, Stanley Mann.

Then I had one of my crazy brainstorms: why not bring in Michael Cimino? He had already created one brilliant movie, *The Deer Hunter*. Yet he was now considered an absolute risk within the studio system after turning *Heaven's Gate* into a financial sinkhole. In that case the management at United Artists was largely to blame: they had made the mistake of giving the director control over the final cut. What's more, not a single UA executive had the time or patience to oversee a production in the remote state of Montana. They gave Cimino free rein, and in return they got a film that was too long and impossible to digest.

I called Cimino and told him, "Michael, let's be absolutely clear. The studios have made you into a whipping boy. You insist on the final cut and the last word on everything. That's a little much, don't you think? I'm ready to have you make a film—a project that will clean up your image and put you back on your feet. But if you want to come and discuss it with me, forget the final cut, because I'll never give you control over that."

He didn't allow me to say it twice. He came immediately, read Daley's book, looked over the existing screenplays, and said he was interested. He had only one condition: he wanted the script to be written by Oliver Stone, who by then had won an Oscar for *Midnight Express*. But Oliver too had his own condition. "I'll write *Dragon*," he said, "if you let me direct a film about my military experiences in Vietnam." That was the first time I heard a word about *Platoon*.

Making *The Year of the Dragon* was an adventure. From a strictly dramatic point of view, Cimino and Stone managed to overcome the narrative incongruities of the project. Dino was able to keep a tight cap on the budget, because the greedy theatrical unions that existed in New York hadn't yet gained a toehold in North Carolina: Wilmington furnished all the necessary labor on the cheap. And the designer Wolf Kroeger did a tremendous job of reconstructing Chinatown's Mott Street in the new studio, giving an ironic spin to the concept of "local color."

Some of the adventures, however, were not confined to Wilmington. Stone's screenplay called for a location shoot in the jungles of Thailand. The feasibility of this Asian sequence, budgeted at $3 million, provoked some lively discussions. Dino wanted to find some way to eliminate the scene, while Cimino insisted that it was essential. De Laurentiis clinched the argument by naming the director as associate producer on that single piece of film: now he would be personally responsible if the costs rose above $500,000. This tactic took the nervous Cimino by surprise. Yet he managed to get the job done for even less money and brought back the most beautiful episode in the film.

As Dino recalls, the shoot in Wilmington suffered a setback:

Regarding *Dragon*, I have one unforgettable memory. North Carolina, like most of the states on the southeastern coast of the U.S., is often directly in the path of subtropical hurricanes. There's a very specific season for these storms, and due to coastal flooding and the damage caused by rain and wind, some of them are real catastrophes. Often the authorities declare a state of emergency, with orders to evacuate.

Anyway, one day we heard some bad news: a cyclone, among the most violent ever seen in the region, was heading toward Wilmington. At the studio, many of the employees scampered off and fled to safety. Others decide to remain. In the end Cimino, Michael Mann, Stephen King, and I, plus a handful of technicians, all ended up taking shelter in the sturdiest of the soundstages. To keep up our courage, I improvised a phenomenal spaghetti dinner while the tempest was raging outside. The next morning, however, we had a problem on our hands: the Chinatown street we had constructed for the film was basically destroyed. More than a million dollars in damage! That was the most expensive spaghetti dinner in history.

Now came an early, abortive attempt to make *Platoon*. In return for getting the *Dragon* screenplay at well below market price, Dino had promised Stone that he would be able to film his Vietnam project sometime soon.

The film, of course, is a work of the imagination. But the platoon was real: it's the one Oliver served in during the Vietnam War. He volunteered shortly after his eighteenth birthday and was posted to an area along the Cambodian border.

Oliver came up with a screenplay of rare narrative power. It was not only a gripping story but a dark reflection on the folly of America's involvement in the "dirty war." Now, until then there had been just a few notable films on Vietnam: Francis Ford Coppola's *Apocalypse Now*, Hal Ashby's *Coming Home*, and *Go Tell the Spartans*, with Burt Lancaster. For Hollywood in general, the whole subject remained something of a taboo, even though ten years had passed since the American military machine suffered its first real defeat. So I found myself at a crossroads. On one hand, I had a screenplay that was likely to become an important film, directed by an emerging talent. On the other hand, there was no ignoring the fact that Vietnam remained off-limits for almost the entire movie industry.

Platoon was not a costly film: all of the action takes place in the jungle. Still, one big studio after another passed the project back to me. At a certain point, after many efforts, I convinced Frank Yablans (who had moved from Paramount to MGM) to cover the co-production and distribution costs in the States. In fact, *Platoon* was supposed to inaugurate a series of six collaborations with MGM. It seemed like a done deal. When I returned to New York, I authorized Stone to begin the preproduction and casting. Alas, I discovered almost immediately that my victory had been an ephemeral one. Yablans was forced to go back on his decision, because all the executives had lined up against it.

This put me in a difficult position vis-à-vis the director. He asked me to return the rights to the screenplay, and without any form of restitution, even though it was worth between $200,000 and $300,000. Back then (and even now!) that was a sizable sum. But out of the high regard that I had for him, I consented.

A few years later Stone and his producer Arnold Kopelson managed to obtain a distribution agreement for *Platoon*. Ironically enough, it was with Orion Pictures, one of the many companies that had refused the project when I was trotting it around. And in 1986 the film became an enormous popular and critical success, earning eight Oscar nominations and four Academy Awards. It also initiated a new vein of movies about the Vietnam War, many of them not so great.

Putting aside my regret that such a stupendous project slipped through my hands—along with the money I invested—I have only one explanation: embracing the cause of *Platoon* put me ahead of the times, and as far as the reality of film production goes, that's often a mistake.

During the mid-1980s, meanwhile, an entire platoon of famous or soon-to-be-famous directors came to work in Wilmington. Michael Mann, who was riding high on the success of his television series *Miami Vice*, shot the ill-fated *Manhunter*. Commercially at least, the film was a complete flop. Yet it had the distinction of introducing that memorable psychotic, Hannibal Lecter. Nearly two decades later, Dino would produce a second version of the same story, *Red Dragon*, which performed much better than the original, thanks largely to a mesmerizing star turn by Anthony Hopkins.

Then there was Roger Donaldson. Having already won his spurs on *The Bounty*, he set up shop in Wilmington to make *Maria: A True Story*. Based on yet another book by Peter Maas, the film starred Sissy Spacek as a Tennessee government employee turned whistle-blower.

Next came Bruce Beresford, an Australian who'd transplanted himself to America. With some reservations, he urged Dino to read a script by Beth Henley, *Crimes of the Heart*. "I was afraid of subjecting De Laurentiis to a tale of three sisters in the Deep South," Beresford recalls. "The whole affair depends very much on the nuances of regional character, and since he was Italian, I thought they would elude him. But at our very first meeting, after sending out for coffee, Dino launched into an enthusiastic analysis of *Crimes of the Heart*. Although he had received the script only a few days before, he had already procured an Italian translation and seemed to have a perfect grasp of the characters and the plot. He remembered even the minor details.

"The thing that continues to astound me about Dino," Beresford continues, "is the fact that he personally reads every script and immediately picks out, in an extremely precise manner, the strong points and the weak ones. This is not the case with most producers. He's also capable of confounding everybody with sudden decisions, which involve enormous sums of money and the hiring (or firing) of famous actors and directors."

Over the course of a long friendship, Beresford spent a great deal of time observing the producer at work. "Dino isn't an intellectual in the usual sense of the term," he notes. "I can't imagine him passing the time by reading novels or poetry, not unless there's some possibility of adapting them for a film. And I've never heard him talk about painting or music. But he has a solid, innate sense of quality, and he's a shrewd judge of directors, designers, cameramen, composers, and actors. For *Crimes of the Heart* he made a strong pitch on behalf of an unknown Italian cameraman, Dante Spinotti, because he had seen a low-budget short that Dante had shot and thought he had talent. And he was right. Spinotti came to America, and after my film, he made many others, always of high quality. I'm not saying that Dino is infallible. But much of the time, he hits the nail right on the head."

Dino also gave a boost to Sam Raimi at a time when the maverick filmmaker needed it most. In 1985 Raimi had released a bomb called the *The XYZ Murders*, which had been butchered by Embassy Pictures. The studio removed Bruce Campbell from the lead, fired Raimi's musician, and then recut the film without the director's involvement. It a was low time for Raimi and his partners, who were trying to arrange financing for a sequel to his previous cult hit, *Evil Dead*. Raimi remembers:

> Dino called us into his office and asked, "How much you need to make *Evil Dead 2*?"
>
> We said, "$3.25 million."
>
> He clapped his hands as if he was washing them. "I'll give you the money, now go make the picture.' It wasn't much of a negotiation. He gave us a chance to make the movie, which was great, and we took it. And I had never had a yes like that without any hesitation and then without any backpedaling. We figured he had done some research, figured out that the movie was worth a lot overseas and that we could make the picture fairly well.
>
> There was only one stipulation. Dino said, "Boys I've got a studio in North Carolina and I want you to shoot the movie there because we have favorable tax advantages."
>
> We didn't want to spend that much money in the studio, so we said, "No, we're going to shoot in the mountains." He okayed that but asked us to stay nearby so he could drive by and check up on us.
>
> "The place we found was about four hours away. Dino called one day when we were in preproduction and asked us to a meeting at his studio at 8 A.M. the following morning. This meant we had to leave at 4 A.M. When we arrived, he asked, "How long did it take you guys to get here?"
>
> We looked at our watches. "Four hours, fifteen mintues."
>
> He clapped his hands together again and said, "Great. Good luck with the shoot."
>
> That was the meeting. We got in the car and drove back. In our morning fog it slowly dawned on us that we didn't like driving four hours and fifteen minutes to have a meeting and he wouldn't like it either. He showed us just how far away it was.

The Wilmington era also encompassed most of Dino's collaborative efforts with Stephen King. The producer adapted five of King's creations for the screen, beginning with *The Dead Zone* in 1983. The other titles included *Firestarter*, *Cat's Eye*, *Silver Bullet*, and *Maximum Overdrive*.

This last film, released in 1986, had an ingenious premise: in the wake of a comet's collision with Earth, various motor vehicles and machines spring malevolently to life. *Maximum Overdrive* also marked King's debut as a director. In *The Stephen King Story*, George Beahm summed up his subject's workaholic lifestyle during the shoot: "King's work routine, six days a week, included getting up at six, riding to work on his Honda motorcycle, stopping at McDonald's for a quick $2.38 breakfast, shooting all day in the North Carolina summer heat and humidity with a small army of people waiting for him to make things happen, and reviewing the dailies after that day's shoot."

Dino recalls:

> Although it was basically limited to a single location not far from Wilmington, the film required a considerable knowledge of directorial technique and a more-than-casual dose of special effects. In an attempt to give King the maximum support for his first effort behind the cameras, I brought in Martha as a producer, along with my old friend Armando Nannuzzi, one of the greatest directors of photography. Unfortunately, Nannuzzi was the victim of an absurd accident: he was struck by a power lawnmower that he was shooting at ground level, and suffered some real damage in one eye. For a cameraman—whose very life revolves around light and images—there couldn't have been a worse mishap. Yet the marvelously unselfish Armando saw the film through to completion.

Despite the brilliant conceit at the heart of *Maximum Overdrive*, the film got off to a slow start. "The first two or three days were terrible," recalls Larry Gleason. "Watching the dailies was like watching a play. King would just set up the camera and watch the actors move across from stage right to left. Finally, Dino said, 'Stephen, you've got to move the camera.'"

Not surprisingly, *Overdrive* turned out to be a dud.

Adding up the figures, King concluded that if he had spent the four months writing a novel rather than working himself into a state of exhaustion on the set, he would have earned $5 million instead of $70,000 (which he referred to as "disaster pay"). The film's disappointing performance may well have soured his relationship with De Laurentiis. It should be noted, though, that King wasn't exactly famous for his breezy temperament. Accustomed to success, he had difficulty accepting failure, which explains why he began squabbling with the director Mark Lester after *Firestarter* bombed at the box office. In the end he cut all ties to De Laurentiis:

> The breakdown of my relationship with Stephen remains one of my biggest disappointments. We were very friendly. He was always

at my house, and I took care of him when he got sick in North Carolina. We had something of a father-and-son relationship.

Now, King is an extroverted guy, extremely intelligent, very rich. All over the world, people are lining up to make films from his books, and you can understand why: the moment you mention his name, the public shows up in droves. He's earned a fortune and lives in Maine, where he sets most of what he writes. He's never had anybody work for him, no ghostwriters or anything like that: he does it all himself. He's a kind of Dickens.

Along with his wife and three children, he holes up in his houses—a summer place on a lake, a winter house in town—and as far as I can see, the only thing that makes him passionate is writing. He has no other real interests in life, although he loves baseball and rock and roll. Each of his books contains something astonishing: he has an incredible ability to reinvent himself. He never does the same thing twice.

I don't know (and never will know) exactly when the machinery of our friendship ground to a halt. I've been told that Stephen never intends to see me or speak to me again: it seems that he read an interview in which I handed down some extremely negative judgments on him and his work. I've never laid an eye on this interview, and what's more, I never gave it! I must say that I'm still amazed and pained by the fact that a man of King's sensibility could fall into such a silly trap, destroying a bond of affection and esteem. The whole thing has never been clarified for me. Stephen obstinately refuses to have the slightest contact with me, even by telephone. To say the least, it's a depressing conclusion to such an intense relationship. Naturally I continue to read his books: I could do no less.

CHAPTER 35

DEG

IN THE MID-1980S A NEW EPOCH BEGAN FOR THE HOLLYWOOD STUDIOS, as most of them were absorbed by vast international conglomerates. As part of this process, the gargantuan Coca-Cola Company snapped up both Columbia and Embassy Pictures. Coca-Cola had acquired Embassy in its entirety, but as far as management was concerned, the real prize was the studio's television library. And since the new proprietors already owned Columbia, they had no use for a second film studio—and were therefore determined to get rid of it.

At the time my main offices were in New York, and my studio in Wilmington was working at full capacity, churning out one film after another. One day one of my closest financial collaborators (an individual whose name I won't mention) paid me a visit and proposed that I acquire the entire distribution arm of Embassy, including the film library.

Both in theory and in practice, this would be a colossal undertaking. Between the DDL offices, the Wilmington complex, and Embassy's own facilities, my company would be transformed into a real, Hollywood-style studio, with all the consequent advantages and potential pitfalls. My first instinct was to reject the proposal. Being the president of a studio is very different from being an independent producer. I would be accountable to a board of directors, and if we took the company public, there would be shareholders to reckon with as well. My freedom as a producer, which counts more than anything for me, would be seriously compromised.

Absorbed as I was by my current projects, I didn't pay much attention to the proposal. In fact, I assumed that the whole thing

> was a dead issue. I was wrong. Encouraged by the backing of a second financial expert (whose name I'll also keep to myself), my longtime collaborator tried again. He insisted that we could make an extremely advantageous deal with Coca-Cola. Mostly to end the conversation, I asked the two of them to examine the initiative in very concrete terms.
>
> Within a few weeks, they reappeared and presented me with a scenario that was (to put it mildly) astounding. To get rid of Embassy Films, the owners were ready to give it away for almost nothing. In fact, they were even willing to enter into a partnership by purchasing a small piece of the new company I would be heading. On paper the proposal looked truly enticing. For close to zero cost, we would get an entire distribution apparatus and a library of dozens of titles. It seemed like too good an opportunity to miss, so I decided to go ahead with it.

In October 1985 Dino and Coca-Cola wrapped up the deal. The producer announced that he would transform Embassy into a major studio with a complete production and distribution cycle. At the press conference, he also discussed his potential expansion into television and the home video sector, which was already generating as much revenue as the movie theaters and would eventually surpass them.

DEG was slated to make a dozen movies each year. With the vast resources of his new company, Dino hoped to streamline the entire process. "When you produce a film," he explained at the time, "even if you're financing it all by yourself, you have to make a deal with a distributor. You're obliged to tell them where you're shooting it, how much it will cost, what the script is like, and so on. . . . It's not always easy to explain what you have in mind, especially if you're putting six or seven films into production each year. In the end you lose more time trying to find a distribution deal than you spend making the movie. I've been thinking about distributing my own films for a several years. Now the moment has arrived."

The moment had also arrived for De Laurentiis to return to Los Angeles. He and Martha found a home in Beverly Hills and leased new office space. In February 1986, just a few weeks after the formation of DEG, Dino announced that the company would release twenty-two titles over the next fifteen months. The program was an ambitious one and clearly would require an enormous infusion of capital. To raise the funds, De Laurentiis—who was now DEG's majority stockholder—took a step that he would have sooner avoided.

In the spring of 1986 my financial advisors convinced me to take the company public. I knew nothing about the process, and it transformed the DEG adventure into a nightmare. According to the business plan, we needed to raise $500 million—a gigantic sum during the mid-1980s. The idea was to bring in $300 million by listing the company on Wall Street, then generate the remaining $200 million by setting up various tax shelters, which were completely legal at the time. It seemed like a safe, smooth operation, so in the end I agreed to give it a shot.

As it turned out, things were much more difficult and complicated. Because of my lack of knowledge about American stock exchanges, I hadn't realized that all public companies were subject to the scrutiny of a powerful federal agency called the Securities and Exchange Commission. The SEC checks the regularity of every single transaction, much like the Italian CONSOB. But the American agency is much more rigorous, much more efficient.

In April, banking on the prestige of my name, we organized what they call a road show. This was a long trip across the United States, during which we spoke to all possible investors: big and small, individual and institutional. The results were extremely positive. [Larry Gleason recalls Dino's pitch in Hartford, Connecticut, after which one of the bond salesmen told him, "If you ever need another job, come to work for me. You'd be the best salesman ever."] In fact, we sold enough stock to raise the projected $300 million. In the meantime, however, the laws regarding tax shelters had changed, and we found ourselves with a $200 million shortfall.

I told myself, "Let's hope we can recuperate the money from the films." So in the face of a discouraging financial picture, I was now under enormous pressure to produce movies—plenty of them, and quickly. Between the spring of 1986 and the summer of 1987, we searched for new projects and put them into production at an insane clip. The hurried pace led to some questionable choices and to some mistakes. In our hunger for material to distribute—which we needed in order to justify the scale of the IPO—we ended up repossessing four films that were supposed to be distributed by other companies: *Maximum Overdrive*, *Raw Deal*, *Crimes of the Heart*, and *Tai-Pan*. Inauspiciously, not a single one of those films was a success, which triggered an additional, dangerous spiral of losses.

As a matter of fact, all the films DEG released in 1986 did lousy domestic business. Even the critical success of *Blue Velvet* didn't prevent it from being a box-office disappointment.

The situation was anything but rosy, and meanwhile, Dino kept exploring other options for expansion. In August he traveled to Sydney, Australia, where he announced the formation of a new company to produce, distribute, and acquire local films. The producer also promised to construct the first major Australian studio. The idea was a prescient one, because although the Australian cinema had begun to make a big splash internationally, the country still lacked any large-scale production facilities.

Bruce Beresford recalls the birth of this particular project:

> A few months after *Crimes of the Heart*, Dino asked me to step into his office because he had a couple of questions. Without any preamble, he unfolded a map of Australia on his desk and asked me where the films were made. I pointed out Sydney and Melbourne. Then he asked me where people went on vacation. Hesitantly, I pointed to the Gold Coast, about 440 miles north of Sydney, with its beautiful beaches and horrible tourist developments. "Great!" Dino responded. "That's where we'll build the film studio."
>
> I objected, "But there's nothing there. There are no technicians living there, no actors. You'll have to import everybody and everything."
>
> "That's no problem," Dino replied. "You said it's a holiday spot. They'll be delighted to go there." The whole idea seemed unlikely to me. It would require that hundreds of people abandon their lives in the cities for a remote area of the country. I called up a few Australian producers to get their opinions, and they all agreed that the construction of a studio on the Gold Coast would be a fiasco. Dino went ahead just the same, with various Byzantine financial arrangements that I think only he understood. And now, at the dawn of the third millennium, the Gold Coast studios are a huge success. Producers from all over the world are shooting films and TV shows in New South Wales.

Dino was also ahead of the curve in Europe, where he contemplated a venture similar to his Australian one. In a meeting with Wall Street analysts, he explained, "Now is the time to sew up the European market, which rivals the American market in terms of audience size."

Given the growing importance of overseas revenues for Hollywood during the 1990s, this too was a prescient impulse. Unfortunately, the project never got off the ground.

In the meantime, the situation at DEG grew worse by the day. Dino proposed various solutions but always felt as if he were speaking into a void. He began to understand that he had made a serious mistake.

> Faced with a bleeding balance sheet, I kept making strategic suggestions about how to restructure our finances. At a certain point, however, I had a terrible realization: I was surrounded by people who knew how to run a business but not how to make films. Unfortunately, by the time I figured this out, the public company was busting my balls. Everywhere I looked there were obstacles and restrictions.
>
> I had thought that I could run DEG the way I always ran my companies. Instead there was always somebody blocking my path, insisting that this or that project couldn't be done. I proposed that we acquire such films as *Good Morning, Vietnam* and *Crocodile Dundee*—both of which went on to become big hits—and was rebuffed by bureaucrats who had never shot an inch of film in their lives. If we had picked up those projects, DEG would probably still be around.
>
> There was another problem with running a publicly held studio. To avoid a slump in the stock price, you had to come up with good quarterly numbers, which forced you to schedule your releases around the quarterly balance sheet. All the big studios do it, of course: Paramount, MGM, Columbia, Warner Brothers, and so on. But that meant we had to accelerate the postproduction process, which is actually quite delicate and decisive in regard to the quality of the finished product.
>
> This was not how I intended to make films. I finally admitted to myself, "I made a mistake." I could have managed Embassy well enough, but I should never have fallen into the trap of a public company.

In November 1987 the *Los Angeles Times* reported that De Laurentiis would probably resign from DEG and resume his career as an independent producer. At this point the announcement was hardly a surprise. According to the paper, the company would require at least $120 million to get back on its feet, and although negotiations with several possible investors were currently under way, no agreement was in sight.

A *Wall Street Journal* analyst gave his own interpretation of events: Dino would step down for the good of the company and because he was eager "to retreat from the pressures and negative publicity that have accrued from being the head of such a troubled enterprise." There was also some speculation that the producer had been seriously wounded by the failure of his recent films. For some time, the article noted, "the ink on the balance sheets has mostly been red."

To the very end, De Laurentiis struggled to save DEG. Yet his plans for recovery kept getting scrapped, and he began to suspect that he was being set up as a scapegoat for a lost cause. To placate his critics, he relinquished his duties as managing director of the company. In February 1988, tormented and under great pressure, the producer threw in the towel and stepped down as president. He hoped that this gesture would restore at least a modicum of stability to the tottering DEG empire.

> I was told that my departure was the only way to save the company. With the interests of DEG at heart, I submitted my resignation, under two conditions. First: seeing that I was obliged to keep my mouth shut in regard to corporate issues, I asked that my name be removed immediately from the company. And second: I didn't want to be involved in any bankruptcy proceedings.
>
> The company kept neither of these promises. The person who took my place was no improvement, and the problems just got worse. To make a long story short, in August 1988, six months after my resignation, the company (which had never changed its name!) went into receivership. Then I was dragged into a series of lawsuits. Nobody even bothered to warn me in advance: only by reading the newspaper did I learn that a financially troubled corporation bearing my name was about to file for bankruptcy.

In September, during a press conference at his Beverly Hills office, the producer stated that he was forbidden to discuss DEG, since the case was currently in litigation. In meetings with stockholders, however, he was rumored to strike a more apologetic note. He made it clear that his biggest mistakes were forming a public company and hiring "the wrong people." Yet he recognized his own responsibility for the disaster. Confronting his investors, Dino may well have felt as if he had let down all of his previous benefactors: the shopkeeper who sold him the black shoes on credit, the banker who loaned him the money for *I pompieri di Viggiù* on the strength of his honest face. But he too had paid a big price for the collapse of DEG.

I surrendered my North Carolina facility and my own film library to DEG, at a loss of about $200 million. The Wilmington studio still exists: a New York firm took it over to shoot publicity spots. And the complex I built in Australia, which is still going great guns, now belongs to Warner Roadshow.

Yet my intuitions were all correct. I'll say it again: despite the setbacks, despite the difficulties, despite everything, if I hadn't been forced to step down as president, things wouldn't have gone as badly as they did. I would have ended up finding backers, banks, a partner, something. And assuming that I did, the Embassy film library would never have been sold, and DEG would still be around. I was wrong to get into that company, but I was also wrong to walk away from it.

Of course Dino had already survived several professional catastrophes, and he knew how to face up to them: Don't crumple to your knees. Instead, think things through calmly, roll up your sleeves, and start over. In April 1988 our hero threw his hat in the ring once again. He founded a new production company, the Film & Television Company, with Martha as president. This time he was determined to stick to his time-tested intuition: what the cinema needed most was fresh ideas, and if you had those, the money would materialize.

He also intended to revive his original modus operandi. That is, he would cede the American rights to a major studio in exchange for fifty percent of the costs, then raise the remaining fifty percent by the advance sale of overseas rights. As Dino explained at the press conference, he was already negotiating deals with Paramount, Universal, and Tristar. His own share of the expenses would be underwritten by the Crédit Lyonnais Bank Nederland, his financial ally for the previous twenty years. Nothing in the world, he stressed, would ever tempt him to form another public company. "In order to feel comfortable," he insisted, "I must remain a free man. For me, the movie business is a one-man operation. From now on, I will be the only one to make decisions regarding my work."

Dino seemed to have bounced back yet again. Still, he wasn't quite intact: the DEG disaster had caused some damage to the producer's previously shatterproof psyche and left him vulnerable to yet another unhappy adventure.

During the period when DEG was being sold off, the people at Crédit Lyonnais called to announce the arrival of a certain Gi-

> ancarlo Parretti, who was interested in buying the company. He showed up and presented himself as the king of cash. "My dream," he kept saying, "is to buy Metro-Goldwyn-Mayer." So the whole delusionary process began again: there were dinners, meetings, phone calls, and a few suggestions of my own, which were sometimes welcomed and more often not. At that point I would have been happy to slink away. But Parretti made me a written offer of $40 million over two years, simply to act as his consultant. Needless to say, I never saw any of that money.

Who was this brash financier? Giancarlo Parretti was in fact a former waiter from Orvieto, who had gone to work at London's Savoy Hotel in 1963, then found employment in Zurich and on the *Queen Elizabeth*. For a short period he cooled his heels in Australia. Then he returned to Italy, where he assumed the management of a large hotel in Syracuse and became president of the local soccer team.

These activities led to charges of fiscal fraud, which landed Parretti in jail for the first time. He served a reduced sentence, then ended up behind bars once again, this time for passing bad checks. At this point, clearly, he decided that there was no point in being a petty criminal and moved into the major leagues. Finding a toehold in the publishing industry, he promoted a chain of daily newspapers called *Diari* and set up shop in the Veneto, where his political contacts kept him out of the courts—most of the time. Meanwhile the wily ex-waiter established a holding company in Luxembourg, which allowed him to found a whole string of shell companies. Fairly soon he had operations in Spain, Liberia, and elsewhere: banks, petroleum, newspapers, and TV stations.

Then Parretti, like Dino's old associate Mister X, was bitten by the cinematic bug. To get started in the business, he ingratiated himself with the Vatican by coproducing Jean Delannoy's 1987 adaptation of *Bernadette*. He followed up with a second, larger project: the purchase of the historic French studio Pathé. After that, he felt prepared for the conquest of Hollywood, and at this point he crossed paths with De Laurentiis. Parretti's attraction to the charismatic producer wasn't hard to figure out: with his experience and contacts, Dino was able to pick up the phone and call anybody in Hollywood. As for De Laurentiis, after an initial moment of curiosity about this modern-day incarnation of Balzac's speculator Mercadet, he began to feel deep reservations.

In November 1988 *Variety* reported that Dino would play an important role in Parretti's group. Next came the announcement that Dino had formed a new company called Dino De Laurentiis Communications. Its mission would be to mobilize high-level talent for important films, such as an impending adaptation of André Malraux's novel *La Condition Humaine* (which would never be made). Parretti promised that he would be a "silent partner" and refrain from meddling in artistic matters. Dino meanwhile stressed his wish to remain independent—to make his own decisions about every aspect of his work—even though his partner was about to assume ownership of MGM.

> It's important to remember what a mess DEG had created for me, and that Parretti had promised to pay me $40 million. Not $4 million, but $40 million. For a moment, at least, that gave me the illusion of being able to solve many weighty problems. Soon enough, however, I realized that the financier from Orvieto wasn't a very trustworthy partner. With infinite contractual acrobatics he succeeded in buying MGM. Then he was unable to listen to advice or manage his acquisition, until finally Crédit Lyonnais sued him, at which point they kicked him out and repossessed the company. This business with Parretti is perhaps the only chapter I'd like to erase from my biography. I wasted two years on it, accomplished nothing, and didn't make a single dollar.

For a long time Parretti continued to make regular appearances in the papers. Article after article documented his reckless acquisitions, bankrupt enterprises, and flying visits to prison. After a certain point, though, Dino's name no longer appeared in these reports. Evidently the two worked out some sort of consensual separation, after which De Laurentiis happily parted ways with the so-called king of cash.

The impact on De Laurentiis from the DEG debacle was crushing. Box office failures, creative suffocation, a forced regulation coupled with having no control over his own name, losing millions, and eventually personally paying out to class action shareholders are only part of the story. De Laurentiis's former private company, already stripped of assets by DEG, was now being sued by DEG. But, De Laurentiis prevailed.

Roberta Shintani, president and CFO of De Laurentiis's private companies, watched DEG's metamorphosis from glory to demise at a distance. "It was one of the most difficult times, both emotionally and financially, through which I saw Dino struggle," says Shintani. "There were lawsuits, negative publicity and rejection from those who once supported him, but Dino persevered. Then, of course, Giancarlo Parretti and the MGM fiasco arrived on the heels of DEG. One began to ask, 'How much can one guy take?'"

But Shintani, with De Laurentiis for more than twenty years, sees that, "Dino is a man of strong character: he keeps true to his word, stands up for what he feels is right and never loses sight of the ultimate goal no matter what the particular distractions of the moment. He seeks his own counsel and lives but one life—he doesn't pretend to be someone he's not. He thinks very innovatively, in both a creative and business sense; to Dino there is *always* a way to get something done. And much of what he has conceived has since become industry standard. For example, Dino created the model of 'pre-sales,' selling a film before it is made, which remains a worldwide industry practice to this day. Not only was this a revolutionary concept at the time, but the fact that the industry has become comfortable with this practice over the years—largely through Dino's lead—has enabled the production of countless films that otherwise would not have access to advance production capital. Dino had literally changed the industry for the better—for filmmakers, distributors and, most importantly, for the film-loving public."

So it comes as no surprise that while the DEG and Parretti years would have been the death of many, for Dino they were but another chapter in his past—never to be repeated. After all, it was time to look forward: there were projects in development and Dino was anxious to get back to producing!

CHAPTER 36

A NEW FAMILY

IN 1985, WHEN DINO AND MARTHA WERE LOOKING FOR A HOME IN LOS Angeles, they came across a two-storied white Mediterranean structure set in the greenery of Beverly Hills North. The luminous elegance of the place enchanted them, and they bought it at once. He pulled a few beautiful antiques out of storage. She supplied some pieces inherited from her grandmother. The rest of the furniture they purchased together, installing it in the beloved house where they live to this day.

The period between 1985 and 1990 was extremely taxing for De Laurentiis, for it encompassed both the rise and fall of DEG and the monkey business with Parretti. Yet it was during these very years that Dino discovered a novel serenity in his domestic environment. Perhaps the accumulation of years and sorrows had had a mellowing effect on him. Perhaps Martha had, with her adaptable temperament: she worked alongside him, stayed with him, understood his problems, and didn't create any additional ones. What vanished, in any case, was the atmosphere of tension that Dino had come to consider a fact of married life.

Being older, and with a larger fund of experience and resources, the producer fell into the role of Pygmalion. And as he helped Martha to discover a thousand new things, he enjoyed himself by rediscovering them through her eyes. From the very beginning of their relationship, they had made frequent trips to Europe, especially to Italy. Dino never severed his connection to his native land, and now there was an additional reason to go back there: the desire to introduce Martha to the people and places that had remained close to his heart. For her part, Martha demonstrated to Dino just how spontaneous and relaxed daily life could be. At first he insisted on a certain amount of privacy; then he began to appreciate the pleasures of a tranquil intimacy.

Over and over, Dino would be struck by Martha's beauty, and she would remain fascinated by his unflinching personality. Yet these attributes hardly explain the cement of the relationship: that combination of complicity, esteem, and mutual faith without which no passion is destined to last. It seems paradoxical that De Laurentiis, a Southern Italian to his fingertips, would ultimately find the right woman in the guise of an American of Dutch descent—and much younger to boot. Yet they shared a common small-town background and had both been raised by hardworking and affectionate pragmatists.

"Martha was raised in a tiny town in Ohio," Dino explains, "and her parents brought her up the way all provincial parents do: they skimped on everything in order to provide for her. Martha's mother and father weren't rich. They were normal people who supported themselves by working, who had a house and three children to raise. People of solid principles, with a sense of responsibility. Martha is like that too."

As his work situation grew more and more stressful during the late 1980s, Dino got unstinting support from his companion. Martha was confident that Dino would get through the whole mess, and that confidence never wavered, not even during the height of the DEG crisis in 1987, when she discovered she was pregnant. The couple hadn't planned on having children, and Dino felt more than a touch of anxiety about his age and professional situation. But in the end he decided, Why not? On February 26, 1988, just around the time he resigned as president of DEG, the frazzled producer rushed to the hospital. Cutting the umbilical cord himself, he became a father for the fifth time, to Carolyna.

Dino was a bit concerned that his rapport with Martha would be disturbed by the arrival of this third wheel. Instead, the presence of the little girl gave him an additional lift. In a certain sense, her birth completed the process of rejuvenation that Martha had started.

Nor was this the final alteration in his family life. Complicated by legal problems and by the progressive deterioration of Silvana's health, his divorce had taken much longer than expected. Soon after the divorce, in 1989, Martha was pregnant once again, and at this point, the two insisted on formalizing their union. Dino and Martha were legally married on April 7, 1990. Then came the second member of Dino's second brood. At dawn on September 21, 1990, Dina was born. This time the proud father was more tranquil, and his grown daughters joined him in the delivery room for an on-the-spot celebration.

By then Raffaella had won her independence, which was no small accomplishment: it's not easy to liberate oneself from the affectionate tutelage of an autocratic father. She had a "first look" production deal with Universal, where she was highly regarded, and had found real peace in her relationship with fellow producer Buzz Feitshans.

On the other hand, Veronica and her four children were living through a domestic catastrophe, one that had first erupted while Silvana was still alive and was now leaving a wake of psychological and emotional trauma. Dino, having some idea of the nightmare Veronica's marriage had become, supported her wholeheartedly when she cooperated in a criminal suit against her husband, Alex De Benedetti.

Francesca, in the meantime, had fled from Madrid under Dino's supervision. In Los Angeles with her two children, she filed for a long-distance divorce and returned to school to study psychology. The three sisters lived within five minutes of each other. They were very attached to one another and to their father, with whom they shared the memory of their difficult, beloved mother and of Federico.

Enmeshed in a network of relationships that mingled the past and present, Dino had established a new family, just as he had long ago on Via Appia. Back then, however, he had been a young man. Was it possible to start over at age seventy? It was. Indeed, Dino's familial narrative of the 1990s could well be entitled *The Calm after the Storm*. He seemed to be shooting a remake, with a script that was both old and new.

As always, he rose every day at 5:30 A.M., had his coffee, put in thirty minutes on the exercise mat or stationary bicycle, and arrived at the office by 7:30 A.M. Martha worked at his side, even as she took pains to stick close by the children. As Carolyna recalls, "When I was little, my mother brought me to the office with her before school. Once I got to be two or three, she was forced to leave me with the babysitter, since I was too much of a live wire. But even then, she constantly stopped by the house and came home for lunch. She was always there."

Here, then, was one great contrast with the past. The routine of *this*

De Laurentiis family was simple: there were no despised nannies to create barriers between parent and child, and everything was more direct. During the weekend, the couple might have dinner with a few intimate friends. And unlike the sybaritic Dino of old, they threw parties only on special occasions: to celebrate a birthday or the completion of a film.

Dino—who tastes everything but eats quite moderately—continued his custom of manning the stove in an apron. Often he was assisted by the children, to whom he issued careful commands. In this manner he prepared such tasty dishes as Neapolitan spaghetti, pizza, and eggplant *alla parmigiana*. Martha too enjoyed cooking. She was intimidated, though, by the fact that her husband was such a connoisseur. And then there was the brilliant, incomparable Gigi. Aside from his culinary gifts, the young chef functioned as a kind of secondary dad for the young children, even as he maintained affectionate relationships with Dino's older daughters. He would spend hours on the telephone, especially with Francesca, and De Laurentiis, who was vexed by things beyond his control, wouldn't be able to contain his curiosity: "What the devil are you talking about?"

Dino was starting over in other ways too. His love of the sea had never waned: whether he was in Wilmington, Santo Domingo, or Bora Bora, he always felt a powerful attachment to the water. For many years, however, he had given Capri a wide berth. Perhaps the memory of his wartime confinement kept him away. In any case, the producer did eventually rediscover the island, thanks to his nephew Aurelio. "In August 1995," Aurelio recounts,

> Dino called me on the phone: "I'm in Paris with Martha, and I'll be in Europe for a few more days. Where can I take a short vacation?"
>
> "Come see me in Capri," I told him. At the time I was living in Villa Monte San Michele, an extraordinary place: there's a lemon grove and an Italian-style garden, yet this paradise of calm is just a few steps from the hustle and bustle of the Piazzetta. They came. And Dino realized that he had always kept a little bit of Capri inside him, ever since he had disembarked there as a spaghetti salesman and wartime refugee.
>
> Instead of feeling at odds with the rhythm of the place, he abandoned himself for once to the art of *dolce far niente*. He allowed himself to be won over by the beauty of the island, by the

> familiar speech, by the kindness of the people, and by the food, which reminded him of Nonna Giuseppina. I took him for a dip along the Galli, four miles off the coast, and he swam for more than an hour. We stopped at the mythical Antonietta dello Scoglio di Nerano, one of the finest kitchens in the world, to have lunch at five in the afternoon. We also swam in the Blue Grotto (and in the Green and White ones), never eating dinner before midnight, and ended the evening with some Neapolitan *canzoni* at a local tavern. One night an unexpected downpour took us by surprise, and my uncle, who's always ready for the unforeseen, quickly threw together some raincoats made out of plastic garbage bags.

On the day of his departure, as Aurelio took him for one last boat ride, Dino was heard to exclaim, "But where was I all these years?"

From that point on, whenever it was possible, the producer would return to the sea of his childhood for a period of repose. Torre Annunziata was just a few miles away on the opposite coast, and despite the influx of tourists and consequent decay, the colors and aromas remained the same. In fact, Dino began to like the idea of returning to his native land.

Over the years he also enjoyed sending some of his favorite associates there, each one of whom was treated to his own inimitable generosity. "A few years ago I went on a long-delayed honeymoon with my husband to Capri," recalls Stacey Snider, chair of Universal Pictures. "Dino hooked me up. The minute we arrived, we were met at the boat by his nephew Aurelio. When you're in Italy with a De Laurentiis, it's insane. You're so taken care of you feel like you need to hide. There's always a De Laurentiis waiting for you, or a concierge calling, or a boat idling in the harbor for you. It gets to the point that if you want to lounge at the pool reading a magazine, you feel like you are letting someone down."

Dino is well aware that Carolyna and Dina, who enjoy their vacations in Italy, consider Los Angeles their home. It's too bad, because Martha—content "under any skies"—would be more than amenable to a move.

> I must say that of my three wives, it's Martha who has truly made me happy. She has many incredible qualities, apart from her beauty and intelligence: in all the years we've been together, we've

never quarreled. Through the good and the bad, we've always been in agreement. She understands my problems, and I understand hers.

What's more, we work together, which usually makes the situation worse. But . . . Martha loves the cinema as much as I do. And on the job, she makes people love her, just as Raffaella does. The fact is that I involve her in every phase of production, and except for the most delicate matters, I dump everything in her lap: "Talk about it with Martha!"

I'm always repeating that my work is a matter of humility. After so many years, I figured out a fundamental fact: the cinema is about connection. If you have a solid project, the money will materialize, but you've got to have respectful relationships with everybody. I'm appreciated even by my enemies, by my rivals in Los Angeles and around the world. Why? Because of what I've done, because of the way I behave, and because I love my work. You must love your work to the very end if you want it to go well. That's the message I've passed on to my children and to my wife.

Which reminds me of another great quality of Martha's: she's a marvelous mother. She's crazy about the kids and they're crazy about her. I have no worries about her future or about the future of our children.

In 1998 the producer ordered two rings from Bulgari. Then he and Martha summoned Carolyna and Dina, and he made the following speech: "These rings are for both of you, when you turn eighteen. I gave similar gifts to your big sisters when they grew up, and I want you to have them as well, even if I'm no longer here." The little ceremony was a touching one. Luckily it was downplayed by the girls, who, pondering the long wait before those beautiful jewels would come into their possession, had only one request. Since their eighteenth birthdays were so far off, couldn't they get the rings when they turned sixteen?

CHAPTER 37

THREE SISTERS

RAFFAELLA: WHAT WAS OUR DAILY LIFE LIKE WHEN WE WERE LITTLE? MY father certainly remembers nothing about that. Now things are very different, but during the time we're talking about, quite a few years ago, no Italian man spent much time worrying about his children. It was our mother who took care of our education and all that stuff.

Dino was a typical working father, whom we loved very much, and whom we basically saw on Sundays. Back then, he was quite severe. As children, we were afraid of him. I remember that he used to say, "If you don't do what I tell you, I'm going to count to three and . . ." We never let him get to three: at the most we let him get to two and three quarters before we obeyed. If he tried that now with Carolyna and Dina, they would start laughing. In this sense Dino really has changed, and it's something that gives me a great deal of pleasure. When I see him with the children, of course, I recognize a side of him that brings back my own childhood, because he does and says the same things. "Eat this, don't do that, you'll catch a cold, be careful"—you know, the sweet, typical urgings of a despotic Neapolitan pain in the ass. On the other hand, he's a completely transformed man, and this is the great gift that life has given him. Most people grind to a halt as they get older and become dull-witted. But not Dino. He's changed profoundly, and almost (I said almost!) become a modern father.

Yes, we had a producer for a father and an actress for a mother, but for me, that was a normal life. On this subject it will be interesting to hear what my sisters have to say. For example, Francesca, the youngest one, was born much later and never shared what was the happiest period of our childhood. She arrived at the end of it, and grew up as if she were an only child, in what was already a dicey marital situation. For me, on the contrary, our childhood was a marvelous thing. I should add, however, that my sister Veronica tells me, "You're crazy. We had a terrible childhood." My memory of it is different. We had those tutors, sure, but at the time, they were a typical feature of the Italian bourgeois, not some wild extravagance. We always went to private schools: first a convent school on Via Nomentana, then another on Piazza di Spagna. Not that we were particularly observant at home. "You must go to mass on Sundays": that was the extent of my papa's religious philosophy. As we grew up, we quit going.

When we were very little, our mother was *the* phenomenon. I must have been four when people took to stopping us in the street and asking if we were the daughters of *la Mangano*. It was only much later that Papa became equally famous.

I knew that I had special parents. But although they both worked in the cinema, they kept telling us that it was a horrible business and that we should avoid it at all costs. This is a common type of behavior: everybody who works in the film industry tells their children the same thing. Still, when I think about it, it makes me laugh. It seems absurd, no?

Our family life was very structured, because my mother was good at that. She was of English origin and quite severe: if anything, the problem was that life was *too* structured, not spontaneous enough. Personally I never had any clashes with her; we worked things out. Mamma was tall, beautiful, elegant (she took great care with her appearance), and formal—all things I couldn't care less about. So I rebelled. And from that rebellion came a kind of alliance or pact: she knew certain things would never work with me, so she didn't even try them. I'm the exact opposite of my mother, even if now I occasionally make a gesture and tell myself, "*Oddio*, I look like Mamma." For example, she found it absurd that a woman would voluntarily go to work. While my sisters tried to adapt themselves to this maternal model, I did the opposite. In a certain sense, though, the two of us were ultimately more similar than we were different. At least that's what I think.

The relations among us sisters have always been excellent: we're very close. Federico, alas, is no longer here, but we were very attached to him too. He wanted to be a director, and this didn't go down well with Papa. He would have liked Federico to be like his nephew Aurelio, somebody who could pick up the reins of the family business. But Federico wasn't Aurelio, he couldn't be: he didn't have that kind of personality, that kind of character. My brother had an artistic temperament, and I believe this contrast with his father caused him a great deal of suffering. He never really discussed it with me, since I seemed to be the sort of person Papa wanted *him* to be. So there were some moments of tension between us. But Francesca has a better idea of what Federico went through: they were pretty close.

I know that Papa finds it difficult to talk about Federico. It's just part of his character, and it's the reason he's managed to make it to eighty with his strength intact. He refuses to go where he knows there will be too much suffering. It's a form of self-defense: in the face of death—in the face of those things that really scare him—he holds back. Some people understand this idea, and some don't. Most of the latter group are hobbled with an illness of one kind or another. Big surprise!

We changed houses several times: there was the villa on Via Appia, Villa Catena, and so forth. In addition, my mother went to live on Piazza di Spagna. She left, she came back, she left again, and those were terrible years, really terrible. Their marriage was a wreck. Veronica had already gotten married, and Federico was in college, so Francesca and I were alone at Villa Catena, in that gigantic house. It was a situation that really brought us together. I was a kind of mother to her during that era.

The first major squabble I had with my father involved my education. I wanted to attend the artistic high school, and he didn't want to hear a word about it. He wanted me to go to a school specializing in modern languages. With my mother's help, I managed to win that battle.

Then, during my summer vacation, I started to work on one of my father's productions, a crappy film called *Boccaccio*. I must have been fourteen or fifteen, and I did a little bit of everything, working alongside an excellent production designer, Luigi Scaccianoce. I had a really great time. And when I got my first paycheck—I recall the sum exactly, it was fifteen thousand lire—my life changed. Suddenly I understood what people meant by *economic independence*. It was as if a switch had been flipped inside me, and I told myself, "I will never give up this kind of independence again." At first I thought I would become a set designer. Then I realized I had solid organizational gifts and was best suited to production work.

I discovered only two years ago that Veronica had wanted to be an actress. I knew that, as a girl, she had been offered a part in a film: she was very beautiful, Veronica. Papa wouldn't give his permission. He told her, "If you really want to act in a film, I'll put you in one of mine." Typical, no? And he gave her a tiny role in *Waterloo*. Then she got married and had two kids, and I never thought of the whole issue again: I assumed she had wanted to be an actress when she was eighteen and then lost interest. I never would have imagined that one day, while we were up in the mountains having a chat, she would confess that her inability to pursue an acting career had caused her great pain. "Why didn't you ever pursue it?" I asked. It was hard for me to understand how she could have harbored such a strong passion without expressing it. Anyway, I found a school for her, and now she's been studying acting for two years.

In the end, Mamma was also glad that I was working. She kept telling me that I didn't dress well, that I didn't know how to comb my hair. For her I was something of an extraterrestrial, but she understood me. Perhaps there was even a moment when she was a little jealous of me, because I enjoyed the kind of independence she never had. (That's what my sisters say, anyway. I don't believe it.) It was my good fortune, I think, to have been the second girl. That way, I didn't have the privilege of being the oldest or the youngest, nor was I a boy, like my brother. I had to learn to take care of myself, to defend myself.

Still, it was my father who taught me my profession. Papa remains one of the few producers—virtually the only one I know—who truly *produces* a film. I don't know how it is in Italy, but these days the only thing American producers do is make deals: they're businessmen. They may commission the script or package it, but they couldn't care less how the film comes out. They move right on to the next project, because they make more money that way. My father, on the other hand, really educated me about production: how to make a film, how to monitor the process, how to edit, and so forth. What I've learned is that very few people have this skill. And look, the thing that makes me happiest is that I know how to practice my trade, and that Papa taught me how.

I should also note that he was sometimes an intrusive presence, bossy and autocratic. He gave me many opportunities, for heaven's sake, and taught me an immense number of things, but while he gives to you with one hand, he takes away with the other, because he always wants to remain in control. He's not the type to say, "I'm giving you this opportunity, go, run with it, do as you like." This need to control led to frictions and disagreements, and in 1987 I decided it was time for me to go off on my own. It was a risky move for me when I left: I was thirty-five years old. He didn't like it, and it wasn't easy. But now we have an excellent relationship—better than it was before.

Why? Obviously because we're not in each other's hair. But there's also the fact that he has a little more patience than he used to. You can almost have a discussion with him! Papa still has a minimal attention span, of course: while he's putting the first forkful of spaghetti in his mouth at lunch, he's already asking what's for dinner. (At Christmas he always used to ask what we were doing for Easter.) Now he actually relaxes. He's beginning to enjoy the things in life that he had no opportunity to enjoy before.

Anyway, the final break between Papa and Mamma came when he told her, "I'm leaving you, I'm in love with another woman." The truth is that my mother never made life easy for my father. As in all relationships, the fault is always divided between both parties, but I have a theory. I'm convinced that if my brother, Federico, hadn't died, my parents would still be together, for better or worse. They would have been squabbling, and perhaps even cheating on each other, but they would have stuck it out. True, after his death they kept going for a while. But instead of consoling each other in turn, it was as if they were intent on keeping their grief alive: it's like a page out of a psychoanalytic handbook. My father couldn't endure the pain, though, so he left her. Otherwise, and despite having his relationship with Martha, he wouldn't have taken such a definitive step. At least that's what I think. But I should add that I'm glad things turned out this way. My father has had a much more peaceful life since the day he found the courage to pack his bag. I can see that he's much happier.

To some extent I consider myself the family's memory. My sisters are just like my father, who can't recall a single date or anything else. Or to put it another way: he remembers certain anecdotes, like the Tale of the Shoes, or his amorous adventures, but he has absolutely no memory of the things he doesn't want to remember. Dino erases the ugly things. Let me put it another way. If a film of his comes out on

Friday and flops, on Saturday he says, "I'll just have to digest the pill." What he means to say is "I'll just have to take my medicine," and we always laugh at the way he mangles the expression. Anyway, he digests the bad things in life too. Then he deposits them someplace where he has no intention of revisiting them. That's what has allowed him to go on.

I know it's difficult to get him to say anything negative: when he talks about actors, directors, or other producers, he absolves them all. You'll have to try and ambush him, though, because otherwise the book will become extremely boring: after all, he already has plenty of enemies. At the same time, this attitude of his can be chalked up to the extra patience, and the extra wisdom, he's attained over the last few years. He's much calmer, which causes him to look at the past in a new way. Now that he's in Italy making *U-571*, he seems so content to me! I asked him if he wanted to go back and live in Italy: if I were he, I'd go back.

Veronica: For me, our childhood was completely different from that of a normal family. I have no memory of when I was very little. I do remember a few things beginning when I was eight or nine, and what strikes me the most is that Mamma and Papa were never at home. And since there was a shortage of affection, I felt this frustrated desire to have my parents nearby, so I could feel secure and protected. Little kids really need this, and I missed it.

It was never their fault: it was because of their jobs. I know that they tried to be present for our birthday parties, for important occasions, but that didn't always work out. For example, I performed at a lot of school recitals over the years: my mother came once, and my father, never. Not that I took it so badly at that age, not that I was thinking, "How come you're never there?" It just made me sad. On the other hand, my family—like all Italian families back then—believed that children should keep to themselves and not bother the adults. You were supposed to obey the adults and never talk back.

Anyway, when I finished high school, I decided that I didn't want to attend the university. I wanted to work with my Papa. I asked him if I could, and he told me, "Sure!" I began to do some chores alongside his assistant, Liliana Avincola: I translated things, helped out with organizing, and basically tried to win my spurs. After three or four months, Papa began work on *Waterloo*, and he said to me, "Veronica, I'd like to assign you a small part. Okay?"

I was astonished. I had never thought of being an actress. And on top of that, I had a mother who was incredibly famous when we were little: just taking a walk with her meant that we would be stopped over and over. Anyway, I had already concluded that production work wasn't for me and that I needed to channel my energies into something else. My father made his proposal at the very moment I was mulling over these issues, and I was delighted to appear in *Waterloo*. The problem came afterwards, when other producers began calling Papa and asking if I could appear in their films. Don't forget, I was the daughter of Silvana Mangano, the daughter of Dino De Laurentiis. I received many, many offers, and major ones too. Zeffirelli, for example, wanted me in *Romeo and Juliet*. (I did a screen test, but at the time my English wasn't quite good enough.)

Given all these proposals, I decided that I wanted to try being an actress. I told Papa, who laid down only a single condition: "I'll find a drama school for you. But you'll have to take only the parts I tell you to. I don't want them using you in trashy, semipornographic films or junk like that." In short, he backed me up one hundred percent. When he told my mother that I wanted to be an actress, though, an insane quarrel broke out right in front of me. Mamma began saying that she was absolutely opposed to my entering the world of the cinema. Papa argued with her, and I wasn't strong enough to oppose my mother: I was too afraid. At eighteen or nineteen, I was terrified of my mother. If she told me something, I felt obligated to do as she said. So when Papa failed to convince her, I gave up. Soon after, I got married, I had children. . . . And that's how it went.

Aside from being the classic Italian father who you saw only on Sunday, Papa was a very authoritative type, and sometimes he scared me a little. To talk to us, he called us into his office, and there we found him waiting behind that enormous desk of his. . . . He's also a tender, sweet man, but he keeps his emotions under control. If by chance you tell him, "I love you," his reaction is: "Aaaah." He fends you off, that is.

As for my mother, well, Mamma was always depressed; she never loved herself. And if you don't love yourself—if you don't know how to face the troubling things inside you—then you're not capable of loving another person, not in any recognizable way. I remember all those evenings that Papa came home and sat down next to my mother, hugging and caressing her. If only just once she had returned his embrace, his kiss! I never heard her say, "How are you, my love?" Nothing. The only thing she would say was "What do you want, De Laurentiis?" And the only times she displayed any sweetness or affection were when other people were around, for a party or something like that. Then it was as if she were shooting a scene in a film, I think: she would pretend that we were fine, that we were happy. The fact is, if you speak to her friends, they'll tell you that she was a woman of incredible sweetness. And she was! Yet she never managed to show it to the very people who loved her: to us, that is.

In the summer we went to Monte Carlo. Papa would join us for the weekends, and in August he took off two weeks solid. Now, Papa adores the sea. At Monte Carlo he had a fishing boat and a motor launch, and every morning he woke us at seven thirty to go fishing. When I was little, he *really* fished: he would have somebody set out the nets or trawls the previous evening, and in the morning we went and pulled them in, which he loved doing. Later on—when I was, say, thirteen—we climbed into the boat at seven thirty each morning, but we went off to find the fishing smacks, went aboard, and Papa bought entire crates of fish. Then we returned home and he said to Mamma, "Here's the catch!"

For us, our parents' closest friends were our aunts and uncles: that's what we called them. But we had no friends of our own age. We were fairly secluded as children. They never let us go out: instead we hung around at home, and even as we grew up, things didn't really change. When I was eighteen, the rule was that you had to be home by midnight. And since we were living at Villa Catena, which was an hour from Rome by car, that meant the evening was over at eleven. Even during our vacations in Monte Carlo, our parents made us rush home like Cinderella. We returned by midnight, went to say hello to our mother, and gave her a kiss good night.

Of course that wasn't the whole story. Her bedroom was at one end of a long corridor, while our bedrooms were at the other end. We would sit in the corridor, waiting, and as soon as Mamma turned out her light, usually around one, we went out again. Our friends would wait for us outside, and since the house was so enormous, nobody could hear us leaving. We climbed over the gate and went dancing or stopped at a nightclub, returning home around five. Ascanio, my father's manservant, would be waiting for us. After serving coffee, he always told us, "Go to bed now, girls. I need to wake your Papa at six thirty." We went to bed, and an hour later our father would be shouting at us that it was time to go fishing: "Wake up, sleepyhead!"

By now I'm sure my father knows all about this stuff. At one point I told my mother about it, and she said, "But of course, I knew the whole time!" "In that case, why didn't you just let us go out?" We did it for years. Later on, after I got married, they once caught Raffaella sneaking out and punished her. She was with Federico. He was much less supervised, because he was male. If you were a boy, you could do anything, and if you were a girl, you could do nothing.

That's the way it was then, anyway. The problem is that in order to learn anything, you need to have at least a few experiences. We never had them; they didn't let us go out; we never had the time or the opportunity to fortify ourselves—or to understand what it meant to have a relationship between a man and a woman. Another crazy idea of my mother's: when we moved to Villa Catena, she decided that Wednesday was the only day we could talk on the telephone. Maybe it was because there were three of us and we were always on the phone, but I'm not sure about that. The fact remains that all of our friends made fun of us, because whoever picked up the phone would say, "No, I'm sorry, Veronica can't come to the telephone. Call back Wednesday, please." Ridiculous! I have no idea if Papa would remember this. He may not even have known about it at the time: he was never there; he was always at the office.

In regard to our men, well, when a father sees his daughters starting to become women, with their own romantic lives, it must be a difficult phase to accept. But since Papa has a problem dealing with his emotions, he quickly substituted a different reaction: he grew jealous of our suitors. All the more so because he saw that we were choosing the wrong men! Now I know that he was right. Back then, however, I was a girl with certain problems, which I tried to resolve through romantic relationships. I got married early, because after I gave up acting, I had a terrible experience, which I never discussed with anybody until fifteen years ago, when I overcame a block.

Here's what happened. At Monte Carlo, I was invited out by a guy much older than me. (I think he's dead.) I had met him at a photographer's house, where I had gone for a photo spread in a magazine. It was right after *Waterloo*: I was eighteen, and he was a charming forty-year-old. Only later did I discover that he was a real snake. At first, though, he was kind to me, and I fell for him immediately (just imagine that!), the way a bee is drawn to honey. . . . I had such a need for compliments, for reassurance, since my mother was always putting me down. The moral of the story? A month later, while I was in Monte Carlo, the guy called and invited me to a party in Saint-Tropez, given by a friend who was opening a club. I said, "Sure, why not?" and told my father. He said to me, "He's too old for you, and he's not the right kind of man." I insisted, Papa gave in, I went out to the party, and a terrible thing happened. I was raped by this man. For twenty years I didn't discuss it with anybody. I don't know if Papa is aware of it, by now, I would guess that he is.

Anyway, a month later I became severely depressed: the fallout from an experience of that kind is awful. In short order I met and married Alex De Benedetti. I chose him because he seemed like a man in need of help, and it seemed to me that by helping him, I would feel better about myself. It was the same thing I had done with my mother, whom I had always tried to protect. I replicated my familial situation with my husband. And he was the wrong man! The day before my wedding, my father said, "Veronica, I accept Alex like a son. But you're making a big mistake." How right he was!

We had four children: Giada, Dino, Eloisa, and Igor. It seemed to me that I had to make the relationship work at any cost, if only for the kids. I also fooled myself into thinking he could change. Yet there's an additional fact to keep in mind: since I had experienced an unhappy family life myself, I didn't think there were any other alternatives. Until I got out of the relationship, it struck me as a normal one.

When I married him, Alex was doing nothing. His grandfather had left him a small fortune, and he hadn't yet decided on a trade. First he tried his hand as a coffee importer, but that didn't pan out. Then he began working with Papa in the movie business. And the second tragedy of my life took place: my husband turned out to have a violent streak. There was a trial. My husband ended up in jail, I never spoke to him again, nor did I allow him to see the children. In fact I changed their last name: they're all called De Laurentiis.

Mamma and Papa always fought; they never got along. When Federico died, they became closer, but every time my mother saw my father, she thought of her son. In reality, the moment that my brother died, she decided that she would die too. Federico resembled her in many ways, but that wasn't the reason. For her, the fact that her son had died meant that she needed to join him. We told her that the rest of us were still here, but she didn't want to hear it. She just kept repeating, "I want to die."

I got married again four years ago, to a marvelous man born in Cape Town, South Africa. My kids adore him, although only the youngest one, who's seventeen, still lives with us. And now I'm doing what I always wanted to do in life. I've just finished my second year at acting school, I'm writing a book, and I'm helping my husband with his new company. He works in the fashion business, making sweaters for women. It's a market I'm familiar with: I worked in it for ten years, designing women's clothing under the Veronica De Laurentiis label. My specialty was body suits and sexy tops. Still, even though things were going well, I closed the business because I wanted to take a shot at realizing my old dream of being an actress.

I'm studying with an excellent teacher in Los Angeles, Joanne Baron. Since I'm not twenty anymore, I can't hope for much besides character parts. I know that it's extremely difficult at my age to begin this type of career—my friends tell me I'm nuts—but I have to try, even if the deck is stacked against me. Acting is the only thing that makes me feel complete. And every time I do a scene at school, I sense my mother's presence. When I go home late at night and have a challenging scene to read through, I slip on one of her sweaters. And I know she's *there*: it makes me shiver just to say it. And I know that if she's no longer in this life, she will be there in the next one. I've managed to resurrect this aspiration of mine, and whatever happens, happens. It's very beautiful, it's very sad, but now I'm at peace with myself. The truth is that in this life, things happen to you when you're ready, not before. It took me a long time, but now I feel complete.

Francesca: When I was born my family still lived on Via Appia, but I don't have any memories of that place: we moved to Villa Catena when I was little. It was a lovely house but extremely isolated. Raffaella and Veronica, who were already adolescents and wanted to throw little parties, always had a hard time living there. As for me, I was a solitary child.

Mamma and Papa were seldom around, and I never knew what was going on, yet I could sense a powerful tension in the air. Only as an adult did I realize that my mother was suffering from depression. Sometimes she shut herself in her room, got in bed, and refused to come out. Papa would then enlist my help in trying to coax her out of this depressive cycle, but it was very difficult. And I always felt myself caught in the middle: it was a kind of triangle.

Things went slightly better during our holidays at the beach, in France. At least we were all together then. But there too I recall a strong sense of loneliness, because in the end I was the only kid. At the time, Federico was an adolescent and wanted nothing to do with a little girl like me. Later, however, when we moved to New York, I became very close to him.

I believe I was a typical daughter conceived to save a marriage, except that the marriage was beyond salvation. As an adult I can understand this dynamic, but as a child I found it very confusing. . . . I felt a kind of resistance. I don't want to say that my mother didn't love me, but I understood that there was something getting in the way of a true mother-daughter relationship. Evidently Mamma didn't want to have any more children, and instead she got this little girl who kept her marriage from crumbling.

At Villa Catena, my only friends were the children of the people who ran the household. There was Angelina, there was Adele, there was Anna. Above all there was Ascanio, one of the butlers. When I was a child, he was my real emotional support: he's the person who saved me; he was always there, the stable presence in my life.

Since I was so alone, it wasn't traumatizing for me to leave Rome. No, what traumatized me was arriving in New York. In Italy, we basically lived in the country, while in Manhattan we lived in a skyscraper, and it was hard to adapt to a culture so different from the one I had been raised in. Why? Other young people had a great deal of freedom, but in New York too I was forbidden to go out much or attend parties. The rules, in short, were as rigid as ever. Only in America, I suffered from them more keenly.

Initially the only person who seemed to be faring better was Mamma. She was less isolated; she went out more. I don't know exactly how things were going for Papa during that period. I continued to sense an atmosphere of conflict. The real trouble began, however, when we moved to Los Angeles. Mamma hated Los Angeles. We lived in a huge house in Beverly Hills, and she began to shut herself in her room again, to sink into a depression. At this point it was Federico and I who tried to pull her out of it. Mamma would lock herself in, and to reassure ourselves, we would scramble up the wall to peek in her window. We were afraid that she had taken an overdose of pills: it was always possible.

I've never liked the ambience of the cinema. It never interested me because—how can I explain this?—the life that film people led seemed like a dream to me, and because I lacked any real stability at home, the last thing I needed was more fantasy. In that sense, even my parents struck me as out of this world. Still, Papa thought I should give it a chance. "How can you say you don't like the cinema if you've never worked in it?" he asked. "Try it!" So I did. When I was eighteen, I went to Spain with Raffaella to work on the *Conan* set. There I met a man and told myself, "You know what I'll do? I'll get married. That way I won't have to go home." But all I really did was jump from the frying pan into the fire.

My ex-husband was named José Antonio Escriva, and he's now a television producer, but back then he was trying to be a film producer. We lived in Madrid and had two children: Luca, who's fourteen, and Claudio, who will turn eleven in October. We were married for almost ten years. Then I returned to America, where my third son, Jack, was born. I filed for my divorce from here.

As soon as I arrived in Los Angeles, I went back to school. I got my degree in English and psychology and am now working on a master's in psychology—or more specifically, in counseling. I'm not a psychiatrist, but I do therapy with patients, which is a long, long way from the cinema.

I've never understood why my mother even became an actress, given that she had such a contemptuous attitude toward the film world. In New York, at least, my parents saw a fair number of people, but in Los Angeles, my mother's depression ushered in another cycle of isolation. Mamma never really adapted to Los Angeles, and when she got divorced from Papa, she came to live with me in Spain. On one hand this gave me great pleasure, but it was also very hard. Right away she began to deteriorate: she had never truly recovered from Federico's death.

I don't think I have much physical resemblance to my mother. Papa, however, has always insisted that I had the same character as she did, and that's created some friction between us. He considers me similar to Mamma because I was a silent little girl and spent my time reading. When there were family reunions, I would always keep my nose in a book. I held myself apart, in somewhat the same way my mother did, and my reserve risked creating a barrier between Papa and me.

What I've inherited from *him* is his tenacity, his ability to get back on his feet. Each time he takes a tumble, Papa bounces back up, demonstrating incredible energy and recuperative power. In my case, that trait allowed me to return to school after so many years away and to enter a professional field completely different from my family's. Paradoxically, my struggle to be Francesca and not De Laurentiis is something that brings me closer to my father.

When I was little, Raffaella seemed to me like my mother and father united in a single person. During my adolescence she took me under her wing, because Veronica had already gotten married. All of us daughters married young, in fact, in order to escape from the house as soon as possible. In each case Papa opposed our marriages, and with good reason, because it's not as if we married marvelous men. The facts proved him right. Still, I believe he would have protested even if we had presented him with Prince Rainier. . . . Anyway, Raffaella was always strong, like our father, from the time she was very young. She always had a sense of responsibility and courage. For me she was a support and a model: I was timid, introverted, and insecure, and when I looked at her, I realized that it was possible to be different.

Papa now strikes me as much more relaxed with children, more willing to let them freely express their own personalities. He wasn't always like that with me. To tell the truth, both my father and mother wanted me to live up to their expectations, and their expectations were quite different. For this reason I grew up with a very low level of self-esteem, and it took me many years to find some kind of equilibrium.

Federico was like me: he didn't believe in himself. He adored America because it offered so many, many possibilities, and he was curious about all of them, impassioned about a thousand things, from building model airplanes to making documentary films. But he would start one project and then drop it halfway through. I was just rereading his notebooks: he had good intentions, excellent ideas, but he never carried any of them out.

He felt misunderstood: I think that's the right word. Mamma adored Federico—I adored him too, he was the greatest love of my life—yet she didn't know how to give him a sense of security. He felt that he was obliged to do what Papa wanted, but he had an artistic temperament, a different sort of creativity. And my father isn't good at understanding people who think in a different way, especially if they happen to be his children. To him it seems impossible that they might have their own particular sensibilities, fears, doubts. And since he always turns his back on his own fears and doubts, he's never liked seeing them reflected in us.

CHAPTER 38

IN STEP WITH A CHANGING CINEMA

BY THE EARLY 1990S, SOME OBSERVERS FELT THAT DINO'S STAR WAS BEGINning to dim. The producer had endured a bad patch: first there was the bitterness over the collapse of his public company, then his nebulous, frustrating relationship with Parretti. Even the films he produced during this period, such as Michael Cimino's *Desperate Hours*, did only fair-to-middling business.

To be honest, Dino could have easily quit. He was hardly without personal resources, and in addition, he was surrounded by an extended family that would have been more than sufficient to fill up his time. Hadn't the moment finally come for him to stop and enjoy his emotional life, his affluence, and his serenity? No. His philosophy remained the same: as long as there was some passion left in the game, he refused to leave. And despite all his problems, he still enjoyed producing as much as he did when he was twenty.

He had, however, clarified his strategy. He would no longer keep up the frantic pace of production he'd maintained for decades. Instead, he would resume his role as a great craftsman who personally followed every stage of each project. In this way he built up a business devoted to low-profile genre films, meanwhile demonstrating that he still had an undeniable feeling for the contemporary cinema.

It was in this spirit that De Laurentiis hooked up with Madonna. In 1991 he accompanied her to Cannes as the distributor of her kiss-and-tell documentary *Truth or Dare*. At this point the Material Girl had just appeared in *Dick Tracy*, and Dino was convinced that the singer had real potential as a dramatic actress. The next year he offered her the lead role in a neo-noir feature called *Body of Evidence*. Madonna played a woman who was suspected of having killed her lover during a sex-and-drugs binge—and who also seduced her own lawyer, played by Willem Dafoe, in a series of pulse-pounding encounters. The footage was steamy enough that Dino prepared two versions for the American market, one uncut and the other tastefully expurgated.

> I entrusted *Body of Evidence* to Uli Edel, who's a good director. However, the project ran up against a problem: contrary to my advice, Madonna wanted to publish her famous album of scandalous photos, *Sex*, right before *Body of Evidence* hit the theaters. Because of that overlap, the public assumed that the film was an attempt to build a character around the actress herself, even though it was nothing of the kind. In any case, I had made plenty of advance foreign sales, so *Body of Evidence* did reasonably well.

As an incubator of talent, Dino had better luck with directors than actors. In 1991 an unknown named Jonathan Mostow showed up in the producer's office, with a very simple, very bold request. He asked for $400,000 to finish his first film, a thriller called *Black Angel*, made on a budget whose sum total would just about buy lunch for the extras in a Spielberg movie. Dino took a look at the material and found it impressive, particularly in the light of Mostow's shoestring finances. So he gave the young man the cash he had requested, in exchange for a minor concession: the right to distribute the finished film in several foreign territories.

> This was the happy beginning of a long collaboration with Mostow. I would have hired him right away to make *Unforgettable*, which I had set up at MGM. By then, however, the continuous changes in ownership and management were driving everybody at the studio crazy. The head of production was Michael Marcus, who had formerly been with the all-powerful Creative Artists Agency. I should mention that during this period, the recycling of high-profile agents into even higher-profile executives was a widespread phenomenon, but it didn't last for long. The reason was simple. As good as these superagents had been at selling their clients' talents, they were incapable of understanding anybody else's talents.

Dino knows what he's talking about. The art of producing films demands a rare intuition and the sort of experience that can't be faked. It certainly requires more than a corporate fiat, although this was a common idea in fin-de-siècle Hollywood. So Marcus refused to give Mostow a shot, and John Dahl was hired to direct the utterly forgotten *Unforgettable*.

Mostow, however, formed a special connection with Dino, who was at that point at a sort of career interregnum. Mostow remembers:

> There were several years when he had a hard time getting anything off the ground. People thought he was at the end of his career; I was at the beginning of mine and somehow it wound up being a great pairing.
>
> Even in Dino's most difficult times, he was in that office 7:30 sharp every morning, reading scripts, looking for material. He was relentless in his pursuit of getting a movie together. I know because I lived five blocks from his office and I started getting calls three or four times a week. The phone would ring at 7:30 A.M. and there was this voice on the other end. "Mos-toooow. How soon can you be here? Come right away." He always had a script he was offering me to direct. This went on for a couple years. I kept passing. For the first year I was flattered that Dino was offering me movies before anyone else. Then I realized I was the director who lived closest to the office. He didn't have to wait around to call some agent who would call a client and set up a meeting next week. I had to read it instantly and respond by 9:30 A.M. That suited Dino. He's constantly in a hurry. No moss grows underneath his feet. This is why he's had a successful producing career. He doesn't wait. He doesn't even wait for other people's money. He's too impatient.

Dino recalls how he and Mostow finally got together on a new project:

> After some time Mostow turned up with a script of his own, *Breakdown*, the story of a motorist whose car dies in a desert area of the Southwest. He sends his wife to call for help, and when she doesn't return, he sets out in search of her, at which point he's *really* put through the wringer.
>
> It's an invented story that could be true: for me, that's the biggest strength of *Breakdown*. We were supposed to make the film

for $3 million. But as soon as I read the screenplay I became very enthusiastic, and I told Jon that we should pitch it to an important actor. I managed to convince Kurt Russell, and thanks to his name the budget jumped from $3 million to $40 million.

However, when I began looking for an American distributor, I ran into the Michael Marcus phenomenon again. All the studios wanted the film, all the studios wanted Russell, and none of them wanted Mostow. This time I decided to stick with my director. I would fund the production using only the cash I raised from advance foreign sales. And from now on, if a studio insisted I change directors, I would change studios.

But there's a well-known saying: if the mountain won't come to Mohammed, then Mohammed must come to the mountain. Toward the end of the shoot, I got a call from Sherry Lansing, head of production at Paramount. She asked if she could see a sample of the film she had heard so much talk about. I stopped by with forty minutes of edited footage, we watched it together, and when she turned the lights back on, the contract was practically signed. The success of the film put Mostow on the map of new Hollywood directors.

The moral of the story? Too often the studios have neither the time, the interest, nor the ability to listen to young directors. They prefer the famous names, even at the risk of amassing famous flops.

Dino went through a similar experience with Andy and Larry Wachowsky. The producer had bought a screenplay of theirs called *Assassins,* an action movie about a duel between two professional killers, one old and the other young. Nobody would even consider the idea of the film's being made by the Wachowsky siblings. It was the old pro Richard Donner who shot the script in 1995, and the production, which starred Sylvester Stallone and Antonio Banderas, did decently enough, especially overseas. Still, Dino was curious to know more about these eccentric screenwriters, who had earned their living as carpenters.

They came to visit me and pitched another idea for a thriller—a *very* politically incorrect thriller—called *Bound.* It featured an explicit lesbian relationship between a tough working-class woman, who had just gotten out of jail, and a typical gangster's moll. The story really intrigued me. I asked for a couple of changes, which they agreed to, and they told me they needed $1.5 million to make

> the film. That was no problem. With such a modest investment, it's basically impossible to end up in the red.
>
> A month later the Wachowsky brothers gave me their final draft, and I found myself in a situation analogous to the one with Mostow. Here was a well-written, original, and highly corrosive screenplay. To hell with the minuscule budget! I decided to boost my investment to $5 million, we signed up Jennifer Tilly and Gina Gershon as the two protagonists, and with these extra resources, the brothers made what became a cult thriller, acclaimed at the Sundance Festival and applauded by the public. Immediately afterward, this time with a budget of $70 million, the two carpenters filmed *The Matrix*, a special-effects extravaganza and worldwide sensation. True, they didn't make it with me. But nobody can take away my satisfaction at having opened the door for these two young talents.

After the release of *Breakdown* in May 1997, Dino had a chat with Martha and decided to cut his general expenses. By now he didn't need such a large staff to sell the films overseas. All it took was three or four telephone calls, as long as they were the right ones.

> Let's say you spend $8 million on general expenses and $4 million on project development annually. At that rate you have to amortize $12 million each year, which means that you're forced to make five or six films in order to balance the books. I didn't want to do that anymore. I wanted to take things at a calmer pace, to produce one film at a time, maybe two.
>
> Now I have only five regular employees in the office, and I keep costs down. The fact is that cinematic mass production is no longer effective. The studios are so big that they're still forced to release twenty to twenty-five films each year, but most of them are junk and result in dead losses.

After paring his operation down to a more human, more congenial scale, Dino dedicated himself to Mostow's next film, which was very close to his heart. *U-571* recounted a famous episode from World War II: the Allied capture of the Enigma secret code, which the Germans protected by stashing it in a submarine. The production also brought De Laurentiis back to Italy, where he hadn't shot a film since 1973.

According to Dino, the decision was strictly practical. He had examined numerous other possibilities and finally settled on Cinecittà, motivated by cost comparisons and the proximity to Malta, where he planned to film the exteriors.

"Once we realized we needed a submarine," Mostow recalls, "the first thing we did was find out which World War II subs around the world were available. There are about a dozen on display in museums; a few are at piers. These vessels are fifty years old and not particularly seaworthy. Even the most well-cared-for sub could be towed at a slow speed at best. You couldn't take them out; they wouldn't dive. So we had to build a full-size sub. It took about a year. Then when it came time to find engines, Dino calls his pal Agnelli, the head of Fiat. He loves that: the bigger the problem you can throw in his lap, the more energized he becomes."

To stay on top of the production, Dino spent the winter and part of the spring in Rome, renting a house on Via Appia, not far from the villa where he had lived for so many years. Since he and Martha refused to tolerate such a lengthy separation from the children, Carolyna and Dina came along as well. To keep the girls from falling behind in their education, their grandparents Wally and Mary joined the party as private tutors.

At Cinecittà the work proceeded efficiently and in an atmosphere of eager collaboration. Two full-size, six-hundred-ton submarines were reconstructed in Theater 5, and the actors spent most of their time imprisoned within those steel coffins. For this project, Dino had deliberately hired a lesser-known cast, and the shortage of star power gave *U-571* an extra dose of plausibility. Some would later suggest that the producer, who had been nurtured by Italy's wartime cinema, intended to bring Francesco De Robertis's 1941 submarine masterpiece *Uomini sul fondo* into the modern age of special effects. He may have been equally inspired by the setting itself: between the fake sea at Cinecittà and the real sea at Malta, De Laurentiis was once again breathing the air of the Mediterranean.

The finished product ignited at least one controversy. The original military operation had been conducted by the British. In the film, however, the heroes became Americans, which scandalized English veterans and led to a parliamentary inquiry when the film was released. *U-571* was hardly the first screen spectacular to tinker with historical truth. Dino calmly dismissed the patriotic clamor, repeating his old axiom: in the cinema, all is permitted in the name of showmanship. Generally speaking, though, the film got a warm reception throughout the world. Dino and Martha studied the box-office reports with great satisfaction.

Mostow wasn't the only promising young director to get a career boost from Dino. Brett Ratner, director of the rollicking *Rush Hour*, also built a productive relationship with the producer. Stacey Snider at Universal Pictures recommended Brett to Dino to direct *Red Dragon*. It was an unconventional pairing of relatively low-profile talent and very high-profile project, but Ratner managed to convince Dino that he was right for the job.

"I walked into his house with the lions outside the doors and saw this elegant, well-dressed man," recalls Ratner.

> The first thing he says to me is, "Who are you? What is *Rush Hour?* I don't understand why Stacey Snider sent you to me."
>
> Some people would be intimidated, but I loved that he challenged me. I jumped right in. I said, "Because I know how to make this movie." But the words didn't matter. The fact that I sat there showed him that I could make the movie.
>
> Afterwards, people would ask "Why Brett?" And he'd say, "Because Brett has youth, which makes him hungry. He has fire in his eyes. Brett wants to win." His philosophy was to hire younger directors because he knew the younger guy was hungrier, more desperate to win. He didn't say, "Brett's the next Fellini or Brett's so talented." He said, "Brett wants to win." And that's what Dino wants and his methods are fascinating.
>
> Dino has the studio put their money where their mouth is. He hires a guy who costs $2 million to write a script because it's rare that the studio will pay that kind of money for something, then throw it away. Dino knows the most important thing is the script. His philosophy is "With a great script and a good director you get a great film. With a great script and a bad director you still get a good film."
>
> But there are two sides to his strategy. When we first spoke he said, "Who do you want to shoot the movie?" I said, "Dante Spinotti. He's the greatest." He also makes $20,000 a week. So Dino says, "I discovered him. I call him now for you."
>
> He picks up the phone and makes him an offer of $10,000 a week. Of course, no one can say no to Dino.
>
> I got so scared that Dante would be insulted that I called him up later myself. He says, "Brett, this is an Italian producer. He can't help it. Don't worry about it, we'll make a deal."

> Later, when we were shooting, if our call time would be 7 A.M., Dino would be standing outside the door with his arms crossed across his chest at 6:30 waiting for me. I felt like he was my father waiting for me to get home after a late night. Then I figured out a plan. I'd sneak in the back and start working. He'd come in twenty minutes later and I'd say, "Good morning! Where've you been? I've been here the whole time."

Of course, sometimes the collaboration between seasoned professional and youthful willfulness hit a few rough patches.

"Brett likes to do a lot of takes, an endless number of takes, and it would drive Dino mad," recalls Anthony Hopkins, the star of the film. "You can read Dino's face; he comes over looking like Attila the Hun, glowering. One day, on the fifteenth take, he said, 'This is crazy. Too much coverage. Too much film wasted.'

"Brett said, 'It's not even your money.'

"Dino responded, 'If it was my money, I'd strangle you.' He doesn't waste words."

Ratner recounts how at other times, however, the two found harmony in their differences.

> After the first week of shooting I was falling behind. Dino said, "If you go on like this you'll be millions of dollars behind." Then he goes into the studio and tells them I'm going to run $6 million over budget.
>
> The execs freak out and call my agent, and I get very concerned. Dino says, "Brett, you don't understand, we're only going to be $2 million over budget. If I say we're $6 million over, we're good. We save $4 million!"
>
> At times there was frustration on both parts, but I learned that the screaming and yelling was more about passion than about ideas. Almost one hundred percent of the time, he'd relent to my way of seeing things. No matter how furious he was, he'd say "Fine!"

Edward Norton, Hopkins's co-star in *Red Dragon*, recalls that once the film was complete, Dino applied the same single-focus intensity to marketing it:

> When we finished making the film, I was getting ready to do a play in New York, *Burn This*. Dino was starting a European promo-

tional tour for the movie and I told him I'd be unavailable. It was a typical Broadway schedule, eight shows a week and matinees on weekends.

Dino called me at some point and said, "Ed, is very important you come to Europe. Ralph Fiennes, Anthony Hopkins, and Brett Ratner are all going."

I apologized, "I'd love to go, Dino, but I'm committed to this play."

He said, "You do the play another time."

I said, "But I'm doing it right now."

"We have a private plane. We send it for you. You come for the weekend."

"But Dino, I do it twice a day on weekends."

I was impressed by his total noncomprehension as to how or what you could possibly be doing that could be more important than promoting a Dino De Laurentiis production in Europe. Later, when he and Ralph and Brett and Tony came to see the play, Dino was still shaking his head. "I no know why you couldn't come to Europe to promote the film . . ."

CHAPTER 39

HANNIBAL: THE RETURN

The *U-571* shoot wrapped in May 1999, and that summer the producer allowed himself a well-earned vacation. He settled down in a villa in Capri, with a splendid terrace overlooking the Faraglioni. And it was there, on August 18, that Dino threw a big party to celebrate his eightieth birthday, amidst toasts, tarantellas, and fireworks.

His face lined but his posture impressively upright, dressed with sober elegance, De Laurentiis was an exquisitely convivial host, mellowed by Martha's presence and surrounded by all five daughters. There were the little ones, Carolyna and Dina, whose lively energy made them resemble two imps who had escaped from a book of fables. And there were Veronica, Raffaella, and Francesca, who had arrived from Los Angeles with their children and spouses. Naturally Dino's beloved sisters were on hand: Lina, Rosa, and Anna. (Sadly, Tina had passed away a month before.) Then there was Aurelio and his wife, Jacqueline, who lived in Capri. But along with inviting this inner circle, Martha had hatched the idea of bringing together the entire De Laurentiis clan, which accounted for about a third of the 180 guests.

Heading up a battalion of cooks, Gigi prepared a feast that mingled sophisticated cuisine with the island's more rustic delicacies. And in the middle of the crowds that circulated among the groaning tables, there was one guest—tall, bulky, bearded, and sly-looking—who, between one cocktail and the next, seemed to particularly relish the gastronomical treats. This was the writer Thomas Harris, a fifty-nine-year-old Mississippi native whom Dino had invited for a visit.

Harris had never been to Capri before, and he was having a great time. Accompanied by his wife, Pace, who snapped nonstop photos, and wearing conspicuous suspenders, Tom prowled the alleyways of the white Mediterranean village. He was most enthralled, however, by the famous grottos, which he encountered during a motorboat trip with Dino and several other guests. While the boat rocked on the waves, most of the passengers took a swim or relaxed on deck. Tom found another diversion. Wearing long khaki pants and a small beret (his only concession to the maritime theme), he lingered in the White Grotto to contemplate its harsh and hallucinatory caverns. Truly these were infernal images. And Tom was perhaps their ideal spectator, having created the most diabolical criminal of our era.

The author's most recent book, *Hannibal*, had come out just a few weeks before. This sequel to *The Silence of the Lambs* was at the top of the best-seller list, having sold more than a million books within fifteen days of publication. Copies of *Hannibal* were displayed prominently in every bookstore. And nobody was more pleased by this success than Dino, who had paid about $10 million for the movie rights to the novel.

Eight years earlier, during the 1991 Oscar ceremonies, De Laurentiis had watched the triumph of *The Silence of the Lambs*. It received seven nominations and five Academy Awards: Best Film, Best Screenplay, Best Director, Best Actor, and Best Actress. Having been excluded from such a landslide, Dino felt exactly as he had when he had fumbled *La Dolce Vita* or when he had been forced to let his option on *Platoon* lapse. He was irritated with himself, that is, for discovering a vein of gold and then failing to exploit it.

> Tom Harris's *Red Dragon* had been brought to me by Michael Mann, who wanted to make it, but Warner Brothers owned the rights. I liked the book very much and forked over $2 million for it. But our agreement included a clause granting me the option on any sequel written by the author that featured the character of Hannibal Lecter. So when Harris published *The Silence of the Lambs*, I had the right of first refusal.
>
> Alas, I was totally absorbed at the time by the miserable situation at DEG. And since it would have been a big chore for me to read the book in English, I sent it along to my development office for an evaluation. They told me to skip it. To explain this error—which seems quite glaring in retrospect—I should at least note that

> *Manhunter* hadn't gone over very well with the public. In addition, we already had two projects based on serial killers in the pipeline. Still, I made a big mistake by not reading the book and deciding for myself, as I usually do.
>
> I passed. Then Orion picked up the novel for Jonathan Demme. Tom Harris called and asked me if they could use the name Hannibal, and I agreed without asking for a single dollar in return. I figured that if the movie came out well, it would boost the value of the rights I already owned. And I wasn't wrong about that.

Dino was convinced that the Cannibal had plenty of life left in him and that his character could be developed in new and surprising directions. So he kept nudging Harris, who was just starting to write a third Hannibal Lecter novel.

Harris was a very different author from Stephen King: he was slow, meditative, full of doubts about whatever he was writing. Over the years, however, he and Dino developed a mutual sympathy that went beyond their professional relationship. And so the film producer became a kind of literary midwife. As the author recalls, "When you're in the middle of a book, you always reach that discouraging moment. Writing is a solitary task, after all, with little in the way of confirmation. So Dino's affectionate interest has been a great help to me."

"Martha and I got into the habit of visiting Tom and Pace at their house in Miami," Dino recalls. "Sometimes I brought Gigi along with me, and Harris really appreciated his gifts. Anyway, each time I went to see him, Tom kept repeating, 'I promise you the book will be finished within six months.' Fine, but I had to wait eight years to get my hands on it."

The first draft of *Hannibal*, whose creation Dino had so consistently encouraged, showed up in Malta while the producer was finishing the *U-571* shoot. He read it in a single sitting, fell in love with it, and wanted to put the film into production as soon as possible.

> I had an option to sell Universal the domestic rights to *Hannibal*, but they asked for worldwide rights. I told them it wouldn't be worth my while. "This film will cost about $80 million," I explained. "I'll be able to sell at least $70 million in advance rights overseas, and the option you have calls for fifty percent of the budget, which means I get $40 million from you for the American rights alone. At

> that point I'll have already earned $30 million on paper. How are you going to beat that for me?" Still, they kept insisting, so I said, "Make me an offer I can't refuse."
>
> "Can you give us a couple of days?"
>
> "Take four days," I told them. Four days later they made me an offer I couldn't refuse, and I gave them the entire world.

Given the large sums involved, MGM joined Universal in a kind of financial consortium. And with the money in place, Dino moved into his full operational mode. Upon reading the book, he had immediately suggested that Harris send Demme a copy.

> When I reached him on the phone, Demme assured me that he also liked *Hannibal* very much. I flew to New York to meet with him and sketch out our initial plans, then returned to my submarines off the coast of Malta. A month went by. Then I got a call from Demme's agent, telling me that Jonathan was dropping the project. He didn't say why.
>
> My suspicion was that Jonathan doubted he could make something as good as *The Silence of the Lambs*. I've always considered this a mistaken attitude on the part of a director. Every film has its own tale to tell. So I told his agent, "I'm sorry, but in Italy we have a saying. *Morto un papa, se ne fa un altro*: If a Pope dies, we get us another one." Throughout my entire life, I've forced myself to see the positive side of any negative situation I encounter. In this case, I decided that a director with a fresh approach might actually be better for the project.

By a happy coincidence, Ridley Scott was shooting *Gladiator* in Malta at that very moment. Dino went to see him on the set and asked, "What would you say to making *Hannibal*?" The alarmed director replied, "Forget it, Dino! For heaven's sake, I've been working on this movie about ancient Rome for the last year. The last thing I want is to start filming a herd of elephants crossing the Alps." De Laurentiis clarified: the Hannibal in question was *not* the Carthaginian general. Scott then took the novel back to his hotel, read it, and immediately called the producer. "This book is a symphony!" he exclaimed. "I absolutely want to make the film." Now it was time to choose a screenwriter.

You could say that David Mamet appointed himself as the screenwriter. I had put his name at the very top of my shortlist, along with Steve Zaillian. But I was slightly hesitant, because Mamet lives in Boston and spends long stretches on Martha's Vineyard. (The Americans love this island, but it's not half as nice as Ischia, and let's not even mention Capri.) The idea of having to trot over there from Los Angeles every time we wanted to discuss the screenplay was already busting my balls. So I contacted Zaillian instead, who was enthusiastic about the project.

Unfortunately, he was also booked for the next three months. One morning Ridley and I were sitting around wringing our hands in confusion when I got a phone call from Mamet. "Dino," he told me, "I just finished reading *Hannibal*. It's the only novel that's truly impressed me for the last few years. If you don't have a writer to do the screenplay, you should know that I'm available." I accepted his proposal on the spot, because he knows exactly how to pin the characters down. He's a real dramatist, with a great eye for structure: first act, second act, third act.

With the script in place, the next task was to sign up the protagonists from the first film: Anthony Hopkins and Jodie Foster. In Capri, Dino stayed glued to the telephone, whether he was swimming, sunbathing, or taking the boat for a spin. The laborious negotiations moved along at a crawl, and the newspapers followed the whole business with growing curiosity.

Tony Hopkins had received the book directly from Harris: he liked it and let me know that he was eager to read the screenplay. I've always had an excellent relationship with him. We made *The Bounty* and *Desperate Hours* together, and in fact, I had modified the shooting schedule of the latter project so he could accept *The Silence of the Lambs*. After reading the first draft of the script, Hopkins told his agent to work out the contract. I was relieved, because I knew that the film couldn't be made without him.

The conversations regarding Jodie Foster, however, were very different. I confess that from the start I had some doubts about her: she didn't seem right for the part. In *The Silence of the Lambs*, Clarice Starling is a young, inexperienced agent. In the new book, Clarice is much more mature—both as an FBI agent and as a woman—and her relationship with Hannibal is different. Along with Harris and Scott, I became more and more convinced that the part wasn't suit-

> able for Jodie. At Universal, though, they wanted her at any cost. So I had to have a chat with her agent, Joe Funicello, who informed me that his client wouldn't even read the screenplay unless I were willing to give her $20 million plus 15 percent of the gross receipts. I answered, "Many thanks, Joe, and send Jodie my warm regards."
>
> For me the Foster issue would have ended right there, but Universal kept pressuring me to hire her. They begged her to read the script and finally she agreed. But all they got was a firm refusal. Her official reason: the dates of the shooting schedule clashed with a film she was about to direct. However, I think she pulled out because she's an intelligent person and an excellent actress, and she herself realized that the changes in Clarice Starling's character made her the wrong choice for the part.

Jodie Foster's refusal made headlines around the world. Inevitably the articles included her declaration of principle: "The original film worked because people believed in the heroism of Clarice Starling. I don't want to play her with negative attributes that have nothing to do with her."

Once Foster took herself out of the running, other candidates began to surface, including Cate Blanchett, Helen Hunt, Gwyneth Paltrow, Angelina Jolie, Gillian Anderson, and Ashley Judd. As it turned out, many, many major actresses wanted to play Agent Starling. Certainly she was a charismatic character: after the first film, the FBI supposedly received an avalanche of applications from young women, all of them eager to pursue a career in law enforcement. But as Dino and his team reviewed their options, the correct choice soon became obvious. The part belonged to Julianne Moore, a thirty-nine-year-old actress with two Oscar nominations to her credit. Hopkins agreed at once, and the decision proved to be an ideal one.

Meanwhile, the screenplay had once more become a thorny issue:

> The collaboration with Mamet hit some snags. He had given me a first draft two months after we hired him. Ridley and I agreed that it needed some changes, and we hooked up some video conferencing equipment so we could discuss it with David in Boston. The author accepted most of our arguments. But he also said that he was about to direct a film and that it would take several months to get the rewritten scenes from him. My response was that we couldn't wait that long, and I went back to Zaillian, who had be-

come available in the meantime. Steve, Ridley, Martha, Tom Harris, and I spent entire days holed up in a suite at the Beverly Hills Hilton, discussing the development of the plot. Steve compiled all our ideas, picked out the ones that worked for him, and rewrote the screenplay.

When the *Hannibal* shoot began in Florence on May 8, 2000, Dino was very calm. He was also delighted at the prospect of another extended stay in Italy. Installed in a beautiful villa in the hills, Dino and Martha regretted only one thing: the absence of their children, who had remained in Los Angeles with their grandparents to avoid any interruption of the school year.

Perhaps the most gratifying part of the shoot was observing Ridley Scott at work. At certain moments his endless ingenuity, his attention to detail, and his perfectionism reminded Dino of Fellini. Confronted with talent of this caliber, some producers panic, knowing that demanding directors tend to forget that the clock is ticking. De Laurentiis, however, never got rattled. As always, he believed that it was more important to do good work than to do it quickly. In an apparent paradox, this belief also caused the production to move along more smoothly. Negotiating the film's complex Florentine setting with great ease, and functioning in tandem with Martha as the director's guardian angel, Dino finished the Italian portion of the shoot three days ahead of schedule.

The American portion was much less pleasurable. It was the hottest part of the summer, and as the production shifted from Washington, D.C., to Virginia, and then to North Carolina, the humidity made the climate even more unbearable. Meanwhile, they still had to figure out the right finale to the drama.

None of us thought that Harris had concluded the novel very effectively. It needed something more powerful. Then Ridley developed a great idea: after Hannibal has been handcuffed by Clarice, he raises the axe as if to cut off her hand and delivers the blow. But in the next scene, after the protagonist has fled, we see that she still has both hands, and we realize that Hannibal, on an airplane bound for Japan, is missing one of his. To save the woman, in other words, he mutilates himself.

When we presented the idea to Harris—who understood that the book and the film were two different things—he declared him-

> self absolutely opposed to it. I told him, "Listen, Tom, if you don't like it, I promise you we'll change it." To cover ourselves, we shot two separate versions of the finale: one with the blow from the axe, and one without it. When Harris saw the film in Los Angeles, he jumped up from his seat and said, "Dino, Ridley, don't change a thing, for God's sake. Your intuition was fantastic. The film has a better ending than my book."

Dino declared himself satisfied with the finished product. Ridley's vision of Florence was intriguing; Hopkins infused the role with exactly the right dose of ironic, ominous charm, and a secret love story emerged from the depths of this horrific thriller. Launching the film was yet another major chore, of course. In February 2001, Hopkins, Scott, Martha, and Dino hit the road for an exhausting promotional tour, with stops in London, Rome, Paris, Berlin, Madrid, Mexico City, and Tokyo. These efforts yielded an astonishing payoff. Indeed, the worldwide success of *Hannibal* went far beyond the producer's expectations. Breaking all sorts of box-office records, the film quickly surpassed the $250 million raked in by *The Silence of the Lambs*. The Cannibal had made a triumphal return, and so had Dino De Laurentiis.

CHAPTER 40

FOR THE MOMENT . . .

AND SO WE RETURN TO THE EVENING OF MARCH 25, 2001. OSCAR NIGHT.

Checking for his glasses, Dino, who's already wearing his shirt and vest, asks Gigi to bring him his tailor-made tuxedo: it's superbly elegant, the lapel adorned with the emblem of the Cavaliere del Lavoro della Repubblica Italiana, awarded by the Italian government in 1966. On a sunny afternoon in Los Angeles, the crew of the BBC documentary *The Last Movie Mogul* preserves for posterity the spectacle of the entire De Laurentiis family departing for the Academy Awards. Martha, Carolyna, and Dina have taken their places with the producer in the limousine. Dino pretends to be slightly overwhelmed: he speculates that when it's time to give his speech, his memory will start playing tricks on him, but this is pure coquetry. When he holds his hands out in front of him to see if he can keep them still, he ends up shaking them ironically in a vaudevillian tremor.

As he climbs out of the automobile in front of the Shrine Auditorium, he's recognized by the large crowd of bystanders, who start cheering, "Dino De Laurentiis! Dino!" And during the first part of the ceremony, while the producer sits in the audience and awaits his moment in the limelight, Uncle Oscar has an additional little surprise for him: Jon Johnson wins a statuette for his sound editing on *U-571*. Dino squeezes Martha's arm and exchanges a smile with her. Clearly this recognition of their *other* recent collaboration leaves them anything but indifferent.

Finally Anthony Hopkins, Thalberg trophy in hand, introduces "my dear good friend, the great Dino De Laurentiis." As the actor moves toward the middle of the stage to greet him, Dino realizes that, paradoxically enough, Hopkins is more overwhelmed than he is. The standing ovation that follows might have justified at least a moment of emotional display. But no: not a single tear trembles on the producer's eyelash. That wouldn't be his style. In the end De Laurentiis is not the type of man who requires much in the way of praise from others. Although he's visibly gratified, he's determined to remain lucid, and in his brief speech he avoids the usual Hollywood pieties. In fact, during the mere forty-five seconds granted to him by the academy, he even manages to introduce a couple of novel perspectives on the future of the seventh art.

First, Dino thanks Hopkins, adding an affectionate, impromptu salute to this colleague of twenty years, declaring him not only a superlative actor but a great human being. Next, he dutifully expresses appreciation to the Board of Governors "for this great honor." And as the camera picks out Martha, Carolyna, and Dina in the audience, he continues, "My gratitude is also due to the six beautiful women who love me and who keep me young: my wife, Martha, and my daughters, Veronica, Raffaella, Francesca, Carolyna, and little Dina." Ad-libbing again, he tosses in an ironic allusion to his multitude of daughters and to the surprisingly tender age of the youngest, "for the moment . . ."

Then he moves on to the prize: "I must say that I've been very lucky in my life—in my long life. On three continents, in diverse cultures, through happy moments, not-so-happy moments, and moments as marvelous as this one, I've had the privilege of working with the cinema's greatest masters." He sends greetings to his homeland: "I would like to dedicate this happy occasion to the Italian film industry, in the hope that it will return with new talents and fresh ideas." And finally, admonishing the Hollywood powers that be, he underlines one of his own strengths: "I'm very proud of having offered a first chance to so many young talents. And let me say to the big studios: don't be afraid of new talents. New minds, young minds, are the future of this industry. Don't forget that Irving Thalberg himself was only twenty-three when he began running MGM."

In his final words Dino extends his appreciation once again: "Let me conclude by saying that I share this prize with all the talented people—young and old—who have worked behind the scenes to make my films. I thank them and I thank everybody who has ever bought a ticket to a film—above all to one of *my* films. Thank you very much! Good-bye!" As he utters this ringing farewell, Dino raises the trophy above his head, igniting a thunderous round of applause. The atmosphere of apotheosis is shared with a television audience estimated at 1 billion people. A showman couldn't ask for more.

After the ceremony the elder statesman (as he's now dubbed by *Variety*) leaves the auditorium with Martha and the kids, plus Aurelio and Jacqueline, who have come to Los Angeles for the occasion. They proceed to the Governor's Ball, which is this year's key event, with about two thousand guests cramming the Exposition Hall. Throughout the entire evening, among so many celebrities, Dino keeps smiling, shaking hands, and repeating "thank you" until it's time to go home.

Slipping away from the clamor, the producer finally manages to stretch out on his bed and sleep for a few hours—just a few, as always. Then he rises early, has his coffee, and seated at his desk, he begins to mull over ideas and projects, taking notes for some calls he has to make. Everything is as it always is, except for the tiny bronze head of Thalberg, who regards his epigone with a statue's blank and indecipherable gaze.

In the tranquility of the silent house, where Martha and the kids are still asleep, Dino asks himself how he managed to remain so calm the previous night. And now, perhaps, the answer comes to him in a flash: he had felt calm because the occasion hadn't arrived out of nowhere, because it was the crowning achievement of an entire, intense existence, one lived with imagination, courage, and tenacity. A man who has fallen and risen a thousand times, who has loved and suffered so deeply and has never stopped struggling, may find it hard to get worked up over a prize—even a prestigious one. Dino studies Thalberg's bronze face: surely his famous predecessor must have had similar thoughts. Meanwhile, the driver is waiting out front with the Rolls, to take the producer to his office at Universal. This evening he's leaving for Bora Bora, for a few days of rest. When he returns, he'll get going with a new, packed agenda, fresh projects and new adventures.

CHAPTER 41

THE FOURTH ACT

Within a few weeks of returning from his respite in Bora Bora, Dino embarked on a truly major project. Almost fifty years before, he'd produced *War and Peace*, one of the most ambitious projects ever brought to the screen. At the age of eighty-two, Dino took on another epic: *Alexander the Great*, the story of the twenty-year-old warrior who led his armies to victory over the great powers of the fourth century B.C. Legend has it that Alexander wept when he realized there were no more worlds to conquer.

Dino had dreamed of making *Alexander* for over twelve years, but most of the histories and other source material focus on Alexander's great battles, not his character, the man himself. Then one day he received a hefty package—three books, over a thousand pages in all. Valerio M. Manfredi, Dino's friend and a best-selling Italian author, had sent De Laurentiis his recently published trilogy, *Alexander*. The producer had finally found the story he'd been looking for. "I bought the book right away. I said, 'Martha, I need one week with no telephone, no business, nobody. Let's go to Bora Bora. I need to work through these three books to make an outline of what I want to do.'"

First, Dino booked Ted Tally, screenwriter of *The Silence of the Lambs, Red Dragon,* and *All the Pretty Horses*, to do the adaptation. Then the fun began.

Dino first brought the project to Stacey Snider at Universal, who set the bar high. She told Dino that the studio would consider the project only if he used a director from a short list she provided. It was a very short list: only five names. Dino first approached Ridley Scott. He was interested until a similar script came across his desk and prompted him to pass. Dino went next to Sam Mendes, but he was on his way to London to film another project. The very short list was quickly becoming extremely short.

Now Dino was after Baz Luhrmann, the Australian visionary behind *Moulin Rouge.* The initial enquiry did not get past the gate because it was made clear that he had an exclusive deal with 20th Century Fox, and he never worked with outside producers. What nobody knew was that Luhrmann had been quietly plotting a trilogy of epics, one of which was his ten-year interest in the character of Alexander the Great.

Luhrmann became deeply aware of Dino after watching a BBC documentary on his life, but it was Dino's acceptance speech at the Academy Awards that really caught his attention.

"The fact that he took the time to make the point about being open to young talent struck me. I couldn't believe that this was the spirit of an eighty-year-old man. He seemed like Sam Spiegel, a man who gets a thrill out of making it happen, and for whom filmmaking is not like a nine-to-five job, but a life experience where art and life are not separate but one, like a circus life. I thought, if I'm going to make an epic, he's who I'd like to work with; and I rarely do that."

But Luhrmann and De Laurentiis weren't the only filmmakers interested in the visionary-conqueror. Martin Scorsese was developing an Alexander project with Leonardo DiCaprio, Oliver Stone also had one in the works; Mel Gibson was creating an HBO movie based on Mary Renault's Alexander Trilogy. Baz was therefore thinking about moving on to other projects. When Scorsese decided to make *Aviator* instead, Baz thought that this was his moment. Having wanted to collaborate with Leonardo Di Caprio on another film, he realized that *Alexander* was going to be the perfect project. He asked his agent to call De Laurentiis to ask if he was interested. "Almost immediately, the phone rang and there was the voice: 'Bahhhhz. This was written in the stars. We were wondering if you'd ever pick up the phone.'"

And so the courtship began. Hollywood insiders know that before Luhrmann enters a collaboration, he likes to see how his partners live. So Dino invited Baz to talk about the particulars of the deal over dinner at his home in Beverly Hills. After a low-key supper and discussion, Dino agreed to send Baz the first-draft script when it arrived.

When Dino mentioned the meeting to Universal, the response was ecstatic: "He's the one we want."

Dino sent Baz Ted Tally's script and Baz was incredibly impressed by the way Ted had managed to compress and capture the spirit of the three Manfredi novels. However, he already had a very specific point of view and way in which he wanted to tell the story in which he would hugely invest in the character's childhood as well as his adult life.

Luhrmann's tight schedule meant that he could not engage in the telling of the story until spring 2003, a full year away. Ted's further writing commitments would not allow him to wait that long; so Baz would be rewriting on his own. This schedule was not ideal for Dino, but he agreed.

20th Century Fox and Universal agreed to come together in a partnership and support the union of Dino and Baz. An announcement went to *Variety*. Baz signed on as a director and coproducer with Dino and Martha De Laurentiis on what was to be one of the biggest movies ever made.

Then Dino and Martha invited Baz and Catherine on a trip. Ostensibly it was to scout locations, but Dino knew it would also serve to see how they all got along. Dino did everything possible to make sure the trip was a pleasure for everyone.

"Dino's attention to detail turns life into a heightened experience," recalls Luhrmann. "Dino comes on the plane with a giant round locatelli, a white Italian round cheese. He wakes us up, unpeels the cheese, brings out the tomatoes from Naples, and then pours the coffee. That night we flew from Naples to Jordan where we had dinner with the King. Two Black Hawk helicopters landed in Petra. The young king spoke about supplying us with the army—four thousand soldiers, one thousand horses, for six months for free. It was an offer you can't refuse. And what was so amazing was that the King of Jordan replied to Dino as 'Your Excellency.' I realized that kings are made in many different ways. Dino's life and his accomplishments have given him a wisdom that can only be called majestic.

"I remember when Dino and I were in Morocco at a banquet party with his Moroccan business partner and the mayor of Ouarzazate. At the end of the night a huge traditional dance of maybe one hundred and fifty tribal female dancers started to surround us. We were all incredibly jetlagged and tired but as we were leaving, all of a sudden Dino lurched forward, pushed himself to the middle of the crowd and after inviting Martha and myself, started taking the female dancers by their hands, dancing with them, spinning them around. Everyone joined in and then Dino's business partner turned to me and said, 'Look at that: He is a big man, a huge man; this is the man I want to be working with.' I felt that this story really captured the spirit of Dino. He was able to make a moment more than it actually was; fearlessly making everybody feel that anything is possible."

The war in Iraq was looming and since Jordan is perched between Iraq and Israel, Dino decided that they should fly to Morocco and meet with that country's king as well. Dino knew it would be cheaper to do the location and studio shoots in one country. "If we started to split the locations between Morocco and a studio in London or Rome, the budget goes up," says Dino. "It's more economical to build a studio than move thousands of horses, actors, and costumes." So for the token price, the Moroccans offered horses, army—and land to build a studio, just to sweeten the deal.

The deal went forward, and shooting was set for Morocco—until the spring of 2003, when terrorist attacks spread to North Africa.

Now the project was moving along and they had true volition but suddenly there was a crisis. Realizing the budget was rising around the $150 million mark, 20th Century Fox called for a meeting. The cochairmen Jim Gianopulos and Tom Rothman questioned Dino as to whether the budget could be brought down to $100 million. "One of the reasons for working with Dino is that he tells the truth when it comes to money," Luhrmann states.

Dino replied that he could tell a lie, but the truth was it was going to be $150 million. It was too much for Fox; they dropped out but agreed that Luhrmann could continue without them.

This caused a temporary shake-up, as there were competing projects in town.

Having heard of the possibility of Fox being shaky, Steven Spielberg was waiting in the wings to take over their share. Now Dreamworks and Universal were shepherding *Alexander* forward with Martin Scorsese attached as an associate. "There are a lot of generals," Luhrmann notes, "but as generals go, I've got the best of them.

"People implied that Dino was a pirate of sorts," says Luhrmann.

"I'm not naïve, but I also know what people say about me. Whatever the current perception, it's always based on a few observations and it's never the full version. My philosophy is: I'd rather be with a pirate who's captain of a ship on the high seas with his own beliefs, than with a pirate who is hiding behind some expensive suit and who doesn't really care about movies. The bottom line is he's made Fellini, he's made *The Bible*. As Dino says, 'I've made genius and I've made shit.' He's built studios, careers, he's made movies but above all he's lived his life to the fullest. Dino and Martha, who is such a vital element of his life and work, have managed to incorporate their family into their work and their work into their family in a way that one feeds the other. It is this ability to engage the entire family in the creative process, it is this circus life that I so much admire and can personally relate to.

"Out there on the high seas, there aren't any rules to play by. It's just: Can I get this ship across the ocean and not get anyone killed, and that requires you to write your own rules. That's the kind of person I want to be working with. He's a one-off, extraordinary character and no matter how *Alexander* turns out the experience of being part of Dino and his family has already made the journey a success."

As this book goes to press, Dino is in the midst of preproduction, juggling countless meetings and phone calls and crises, confronting all the decisions and disputes and discrepancies that must be dealt with before the film can move forward.

And while the legendary producer continues his crusade to bring one of history's greatest figures on the screen, De Laurentiis himself continues to make history. During the Sixtieth Venice International Film Festival in September 2003, Dino was awarded the prestigious Golden Lion for his expansive and prolific career—the first time that a producer has been lionized by the festival. During the awards presentation, festival director Moritz de Hadeln noted, "He is still a very active young man. Along with him, we intend to pay homage to a category that has made Italian cinema great and that luckily is finding young and dynamic successors."

And halfway around the globe, the Producers Guild of America named Dino as the recipient of their 2004 David O. Selznick Award for his "historic contributions to motion pictures as the champion of many of our industry's greatest talents and as a true visionary of international cinema." He joins a very exclusive club comprised of other industry giants similarly lauded by the Guild, including Billy Wilder, Saul Zaentz, Brian Grazer, and Robert Evans.

Yet such awards are icing on the cake for a man who lives and breathes to make movies. And, if all goes well, by the time the book reaches the shelves, shooting will have begun on his latest project and Dino will be his usual relaxed, genial self back on the set.

"By then," as the cinema prodigy said more than sixty years ago in an interview with the Italian magazine *Film*, "I've already done everything that was necessary. My task, aside from a few minor details, is done the day the filming begins. . . . The producer's job is organizational. It only makes sense, then, that his job ends the moment the film is actually being realized. If that's not the case, everybody is in trouble. . . . And if a film is deficient for any reason, ninety times out of a hundred the fault is that of the producer, who didn't select the right collaborators, who didn't organize the production, who doesn't (to be blunt) know how to practice his trade. And if, on the contrary, a film is released and becomes a big hit, the credit should go to—well, I'll say no more."

Will *Alexander* be Dino's last project, his last chance to practice his trade? After all, the man celebrated his eighty-four years in August 2003; how long can he sustain his pace? Still, no one who knows Dino would count him out. Baz Luhrmann is the latest young director to benefit from Dino's decades of experience, but he probably won't be the last.